Beautiful Data

Edited by Toby Segaran and Jeff Hammerbacher

O'REILLY®

Beijing • Cambridge • Farnham • Köln • Sebastopol • Taipei • Tokyo

Beautiful Data
Edited by Toby Segaran and Jeff Hammerbacher

Published by O'Reilly Media, Inc. 1005 Gravenstein Highway North, Sebastopol, CA 95472

O'Reilly books may be purchased for educational, business, or sales promotional use. Online editions are also available for most titles (*http://my.safaribooksonline.com*). For more information, contact our corporate/institutional sales department: (800) 998-9938 or *corporate@oreilly.com*.

Editor: Julie Steele	**Proofreader:** Rachel Monaghan
Production Editor: Rachel Monaghan	**Cover Designer:** Mark Paglietti
Copyeditor: Genevieve d'Entremont	**Interior Designer:** Marcia Friedman
Indexer: Angela Howard	**Illustrator:** Robert Romano

Printing History:

July 2009:   First Edition.

ISBN: 978-0-596-15711-1
[F]   [5/10]

All royalties from this book will be donated to Creative Commons and the Sunlight Foundation.

CONTENTS

Preface

When we were first approached with the idea of a follow-up to *Beautiful Code*, this time about data, we found the idea exciting and very ambitious. Collecting, visualizing, and processing data now touches every professional field and so many aspects of daily life that a great collection would have to be almost unreasonably broad in scope. So we contacted a highly diverse group of people whose work we admired, and were thrilled that so many agreed to contribute.

This book is the result, and we hope it captures just how wide-ranging (and beautiful) working with data can be. In it you'll learn about everything from fighting with governments to working with the Mars lander; you'll learn how to use statistics programs, make visualizations, and remix a Radiohead video; you'll see maps, DNA, and something we can only really call "data philosophy."

The royalties for this book are being donated to Creative Commons and the Sunlight Foundation, two organizations dedicated to making the world better by freeing data. We hope you'll consider how your own encounters with data shape the world.

How This Book Is Organized

The chapters in this book follow a loose arc from data collection through data storage, organization, retrieval, visualization, and finally, analysis.

Chapter 1, *Seeing Your Life in Data*, by Nathan Yau, looks at the motivations and challenges behind two projects in the emerging field of personal data collection.

Chapter 2, *The Beautiful People: Keeping Users in Mind When Designing Data Collection Methods*, by Jonathan Follett and Matthew Holm, discusses the importance of trust, persuasion, and testing when collecting data from humans over the Web.

Chapter 3, *Embedded Image Data Processing on Mars*, by J. M. Hughes, discusses the challenges of designing a data processing system that has to work within the constraints of space travel.

Chapter 4, *Cloud Storage Design in a PNUTShell*, by Brian F. Cooper, Raghu Ramakrishnan, and Utkarsh Srivastava, describes the software Yahoo! has designed to turn its globally distributed data centers into a universal storage platform for powering modern web applications.

Chapter 5, *Information Platforms and the Rise of the Data Scientist*, by Jeff Hammerbacher, traces the evolution of tools for information processing and the humans who power them, using specific examples from the history of Facebook's data team.

Chapter 6, *The Geographic Beauty of a Photographic Archive*, by Jason Dykes and Jo Wood, draws attention to the ubiquity and power of colorfully visualized spatial data collected by a volunteer community.

Chapter 7, *Data Finds Data*, by Jeff Jonas and Lisa Sokol, explains a new approach to thinking about data that many may need to adopt in order to manage it all.

Chapter 8, *Portable Data in Real Time*, by Jud Valeski, dives into the current limitations of distributing social and location data in real time across the Web, and discusses one potential solution to the problem.

Chapter 9, *Surfacing the Deep Web*, by Alon Halevy and Jayant Madhavan, describes the tools developed by Google to make searchable the data currently trapped behind forms on the Web.

Chapter 10, *Building Radiohead's House of Cards*, by Aaron Koblin with Valdean Klump, is an adventure story about lasers, programming, and riding on the back of a bus, and ending with an award-winning music video.

Chapter 11, *Visualizing Urban Data*, by Michal Migurski, details the process of freeing and beautifying some of the most important data about the world around us.

Chapter 12, *The Design of Sense.us*, by Jeffrey Heer, recasts data visualizations as social spaces and uses this new perspective to explore 150 years of U.S. census data.

Chapter 13, *What Data Doesn't Do*, by Coco Krumme, looks at experimental work that demonstrates the many ways people misunderstand and misuse data.

Chapter 14, *Natural Language Corpus Data*, by Peter Norvig, takes the reader through some evocative exercises with a trillion-word corpus of natural language data pulled down from across the Web.

Chapter 15, *Life in Data: The Story of DNA*, by Matt Wood and Ben Blackburne, describes the beauty of the data that is DNA and the massive infrastructure required to create, capture, and process that data.

Chapter 16, *Beautifying Data in the Real World*, by Jean-Claude Bradley, Rajarshi Guha, Andrew Lang, Pierre Lindenbaum, Cameron Neylon, Antony Williams, and Egon Willighagen, shows how crowdsourcing and extreme transparency have combined to advance the state of drug discovery research.

Chapter 17, *Superficial Data Analysis: Exploring Millions of Social Stereotypes*, by Brendan O'Connor and Lukas Biewald, shows the correlations and patterns that emerge when people are asked to anonymously rate one another's pictures.

Chapter 18, *Bay Area Blues: The Effect of the Housing Crisis*, by Hadley Wickham, Deborah F. Swayne, and David Poole, guides the reader through a detailed examination of the recent housing crisis in the Bay Area using open source software and publicly available data.

Chapter 19, *Beautiful Political Data*, by Andrew Gelman, Jonathan P. Kastellec, and Yair Ghitza, shows how the tools of statistics and data visualization can help us gain insight into the political process used to organize society.

Chapter 20, *Connecting Data*, by Toby Segaran, explores the difficulty and possibilities of joining together the vast number of data sets the Web has made available.

Conventions Used in This Book

The following typographical conventions are used in this book:

Italic

> Indicates new terms, URLs, email addresses, filenames, and file extensions.

`Constant width`

> Used for program listings, as well as within paragraphs to refer to program elements such as variable or function names, databases, data types, environment variables, statements, and keywords.

`Constant width bold`

> Shows commands or other text that should be typed literally by the user.

`Constant width italic`

> Shows text that should be replaced with user-supplied values or by values determined by context.

Using Code Examples

This book is here to help you get your job done. In general, you may use the code in this book in your programs and documentation. You do not need to contact us for permission unless you're reproducing a significant portion of the code. For example, writing a program that uses several chunks of code from this book does not require permission. Selling or distributing a CD-ROM of examples from O'Reilly books does require permission. Answering a question by citing this book and quoting example code does not require permission. Incorporating a significant amount of example code from this book into your product's documentation does require permission.

We appreciate, but do not require, attribution. An attribution usually includes the title, author, publisher, and ISBN. For example: "*Beautiful Data,* edited by Toby Segaran and Jeff Hammerbacher. Copyright 2009 O'Reilly Media, Inc., 978-0-596-15711-1."

If you feel your use of code examples falls outside fair use or the permission given here, feel free to contact us at *permissions@oreilly.com.*

How to Contact Us

Please address comments and questions concerning this book to the publisher:

O'Reilly Media, Inc.
1005 Gravenstein Highway North
Sebastopol, CA 95472
800-998-9938 (in the United States or Canada)
707-829-0515 (international or local)
707-829-0104 (fax)

We have a web page for this book, where we list errata, examples, and any additional information. You can access this page at:

http://oreilly.com/catalog/9780596157111

To comment or ask technical questions about this book, send email to:

bookquestions@oreilly.com

For more information about our books, conferences, Resource Centers, and the O'Reilly Network, see our website at:

http://oreilly.com

Safari® Books Online

 When you see a Safari® Books Online icon on the cover of your favorite technology book, that means the book is available online through the O'Reilly Network Safari Bookshelf.

Safari offers a solution that's better than e-books. It's a virtual library that lets you easily search thousands of top tech books, cut and paste code samples, download chapters, and find quick answers when you need the most accurate, current information. Try it for free at *http://my.safaribooksonline.com*.

CHAPTER ONE

Seeing Your Life in Data

Nathan Yau

IN THE NOT-TOO-DISTANT PAST, THE WEB WAS ABOUT SHARING, BROADCASTING, AND DISTRIBUTION. But the tide is turning: the Web is moving toward the individual. Applications spring up every month that let people track, monitor, and analyze their habits and behaviors in hopes of gaining a better understanding about themselves and their surroundings. People can track eating habits, exercise, time spent online, sexual activity, monthly cycles, sleep, mood, and finances online. If you are interested in a certain aspect of your life, chances are that an application exists to track it.

Personal data collection is of course nothing new. In the 1930s, Mass Observation, a social research group in Britain, collected data on various aspects of everyday life—such as beards and eyebrows, shouts and gestures of motorists, and behavior of people at war memorials—to gain a better understanding about the country. However, data collection methods have improved since 1930. It is no longer only a pencil and paper notepad or a manual counter. Data can be collected automatically with mobile phones and handheld computers such that constant flows of data and information upload to servers, databases, and so-called data warehouses at all times of the day.

With these advances in data collection technologies, the data streams have also developed into something much heftier than the tally counts reported by Mass Observation participants. Data can update in real-time, and as a result, people want up-to-date information.

It is not enough to simply supply people with gigabytes of data, though. Not everyone is a statistician or computer scientist, and not everyone wants to sift through large data sets. This is a challenge that we face frequently with personal data collection.

While the types of data collection and data returned might have changed over the years, individuals' needs have not. That is to say that individuals who collect data about themselves and their surroundings still do so to gain a better understanding of the information that lies within the flowing data. Most of the time we are not after the numbers themselves; we are interested in what the numbers mean. It is a subtle difference but an important one. This need calls for systems that can handle personal data streams, process them efficiently and accurately, and dispense information to nonprofessionals in a way that is understandable and useful. We want something that is more than a spreadsheet of numbers. We want the story in the data.

To construct such a system requires careful design considerations in both analysis and aesthetics. This was important when we implemented the Personal Environmental Impact Report (PEIR), a tool that allows people to see how they affect the environment and how the environment affects them on a micro-level; and your.flowingdata (YFD), an in-development project that enables users to collect data about themselves via Twitter, a microblogging service.

For PEIR, I am the frontend developer, and I mostly work on the user interface and data visualization. As for YFD, I am the only person who works on it, so my responsibilities are a bit different, but my focus is still on the visualization side of things. Although PEIR and YFD are fairly different in data type, collection, and processing, their goals are similar. PEIR and YFD are built to provide information to the individual. Neither is meant as an endpoint. Rather, they are meant to spur curiosity in how everyday decisions play a big role in how we live and to start conversations on personal data. After a brief background on PEIR and YFD, I discuss personal data collection, storage, and analysis with this idea in mind. I then go into depth on the design process behind PEIR and YFD data visualizations, which can be generalized to personal data visualization as a whole. Ultimately, we want to show individuals the beauty in their personal data.

Personal Environmental Impact Report (PEIR)

PEIR is developed by the Center for Embedded Networked Sensing at the University of California at Los Angeles, or more specifically, the Urban Sensing group. We focus on using everyday mobile technologies (e.g., cell phones) to collect data about our surroundings and ourselves so that people can gain a better understanding of how they interact with what is around them. For example, DietSense is an online service that allows people to self-monitor their food choices and further request comments from dietary specialists; Family Dynamics helps families and life coaches document key features of a family's daily interactions, such as colocation and family meals; and Walkability helps residents and pedestrian advocates make observations and voice their concerns about neighborhood

walkability and connections to public transit.* All of these projects let people get involved in their communities with just their mobile phones. We use a phone's built-in sensors, such as its camera, GPS, and accelerometer, to collect data, which we use to provide information.

PEIR applies similar principles. A person downloads a small piece of software called Campaignr onto his phone, and it runs in the background. As he goes about his daily activities—jogging around the track, driving to and from work, or making a trip to the grocery store, for example—the phone uploads GPS data to PEIR's central servers every two minutes. This includes latitude, longitude, altitude, velocity, and time. We use this data to estimate an individual's impact on and exposure to the environment. Environmental pollution sensors are not required. Instead, we use what is already available on many mobile phones—GPS—and then pass this data with context, such as weather, into established environmental models. Finally, we visualize the environmental impact and exposure data. The challenge at this stage is to communicate meaning in data that is unfamiliar to most. What does it mean to emit 1,000 kilograms of carbon in a week? Is that a lot or is that a little? We have to keep the user and purpose in mind, as they drive the system design from the visualization down to the data collection and storage.

your.flowingdata (YFD)

While PEIR uses a piece of custom software that runs in the background, YFD requires that users actively enter data via Twitter. Twitter is a microblogging service that asks a very simple question: *what are you doing right now?* People can post, or more appropriately, *tweet*, what they are doing via desktop applications, email, instant messaging, and most importantly (as far as YFD is concerned), SMS, which means people can tweet with their mobile phones.

YFD uses Twitter's ubiquity so that people can tweet personal data from anywhere they can send SMS messages. Users can currently track eating habits, weight, sleep, mood, and when they go to the bathroom by simply posting tweets in a specific format. Like PEIR, YFD shows users that it is the little things that can have a profound effect on our way of life. During the design process, again, we keep the user in mind. What will keep users motivated to manually enter data on a regular basis? How can we make data collection as painless as possible? What should we communicate to the user once the data has been logged? To this end, I start at the beginning with data collection.

Personal Data Collection

Personal data collection is somewhat different from scientific data gathering. Personal data collection is usually less formal and does not happen in a laboratory under controlled conditions. People collect data in the real world where there can be interruptions, bad network connectivity, or limited access to a computer. Users are not necessarily data experts, so when something goes wrong (as it inevitably will), they might not know how to adjust.

---

* CENS Urban Sensing, *http://urban.cens.ucla.edu/*

Therefore, we have to make data collection as simple as possible for the user. It should be unobtrusive, intuitive, and easy to access so that it is more likely that data collection becomes a part of the daily routine.

Working Data Collection into Routine

This is one of the main reasons I chose Twitter as YFD's data proxy from phone or computer to the database. Twitter allows users to post tweets via several outlets. The ability to post tweets via mobile phone lets users log data from anywhere their phones can send SMS messages, which means they can document something as it happens and do not have to wait until they have access to a computer. A person will most likely forget if she has to wait. Accessibility is key.

One could accomplish something similar with email instead of Twitter since most mobile phones let people send SMS to an email address, and this was in fact the original implementation of YFD. However, we go back to data collection as a natural part of daily routine. Millions of people already use Twitter regularly, so part of the challenge is already relieved. People do use email frequently as well, and it is possible they are more comfortable with it than Twitter, but the nature of the two is quite different. On Twitter, people update several times a day to post what they are doing. Twitter was created for this single purpose. Maybe a person is eating a sandwich, going out for a walk, or watching a movie. Hundreds of thousands tweet this type of information every day. Email, on the other hand, lends itself to messages that are more substantial. Most people would not email a friend to tell them they are watching a television program—especially not every day or every hour.

By using Twitter, we get this posting regularity that hopefully transfers to data collection. I tried to make data logging on YFD feel the same as using Twitter. For instance, if someone eats a salami sandwich, he sends a message: "ate salami sandwich." Data collection becomes conversational in this way. Users do not have to learn a new language like SQL. Instead, they only have to remember keywords followed by the value. In the previous example, the keyword is *ate* and the value is *salami sandwich*. To track sleep, a user simply sends a keyword: *goodnight* when going to sleep and *gmorning* when waking.

In some ways, posting regularity with PEIR was less challenging than with YFD. Because PEIR collects data automatically in the background, the user just has to start the software on his phone with a few presses of a button. Development of that software came with its own difficulties, but that story is really for a different article.

Asynchronous data collection

For both PEIR and YFD, we found that asynchronous data collection was actually necessary. People wanted to enter and upload data after the event(s) of interest had occurred. On YFD, people wanted to be able to add a timestamp to their tweets, and PEIR users wanted to upload GPS data manually.

As said before, the original concept of YFD was that people would enter data only when something occurred. That was the benefit and purpose of using Twitter. However, many people did not use Twitter via their mobile phone, so they would have to wait until a computer was available. Even those who did send SMS messages to Twitter often forgot to log data; some people just wanted to enter all of their data at the end of the day.

Needless to say, YFD now supports timestamps. It was still important that data entry syntax was as close to conversational as possible. To accommodate this, users can append the time to any of their tweets. For example, "ate roast chicken and potatoes at 6:00pm" or "goodnight at 23:00." The timestamp syntax is to simply append "at hh:mm" to the end of a tweet. I also found it useful to support both standard and military time formats. Finally, when a user enters a timestamp, YFD will record the most recent occurrence of the time, so in the previous "goodnight" example, YFD would enter the data point for the previous night.

PEIR was also originally designed only for "in the moment" data collection. As mentioned before, Campaignr runs on a user's mobile phone and uploads GPS data periodically (up to every 20 seconds) to our central server. This adds up to hundreds of thousands of data points for a single user who runs PEIR every day with very little effort from the user's side. Once the PEIR application is installed on a phone, a user simply starts the application with a couple of button presses. However, almost right from the beginning, we found we could not rely on having a network connection 100% of the time, since there are almost always areas where there is no signal from the service carrier. The simplest, albeit naive, approach would be to collect and upload data only when the phone has a connection, but we might lose large chunks of data. Instead, we use a cache to store data on a phone's local memory until connectivity resumes. We also provide a second option to collect data without any synchronous uploading at all.

The takeaway point is that it is unreasonable to expect people to collect data for events at the time they happen. People forget or it is inconvenient at the time. In any case, it is important that users are able to enter data later on, which in turn affects the design of the next steps in the data flow.

Data Storage

For both YFD and PEIR, it was important to keep in mind what we were going to do with the data once it was stored. Oftentimes, database mechanisms and schemas are decided on a whim, and the researchers regret it further down the road, either because their choice makes it hard to process the data or because the database is not extensible. The choice for YFD was not particularly difficult. We use MySQL for other projects, and YFD involves mostly uncomplicated insert and select statements, so it was easy to set up. Also, data is manually entered—not continuously uploaded like PEIR—so the size of database tables is not an issue in these early stages of development. The main concern was that I wanted to be able to extend the schema when I added new trackers, so I created the schema with that in mind.

PEIR, on the other hand, required more careful database development. We perform thousands of geography-based computations every few minutes, so we used PostGIS to add support for geographic objects to a PostgreSQL database. Although MySQL offers GIS and spatial extensions, we decided that PostGIS with PostgreSQL was more robust for PEIR's needs.

This is perhaps oversimplifying our database design process, however. I should back up a bit. We are a group of 10 or so graduate students with our own research interests, and as expected, work on individual components of PEIR. This affected how we work a great deal. PEIR data was very scattered to begin with. We did not use a unified database schema; we created multiple databases as we needed them, and did not follow any specific design patterns. If anyone joined PEIR during this mid-early stage, he would have been confused by where and what all the data was and who to contact to find out. I say this because I joined the PEIR project midway. To alleviate this scattered problem, we eventually froze all development, and one person who had his hand in all parts of PEIR skillfully pieced everyone's code and database tables together. It became quite clear that this consolidation of code and schemas was necessary once user experience development began. In retrospect, it would have been worth the extra effort to take a more calculated approach to data storage in the early goings, but such is the nature of graduate studies.

Coordination and code consolidation are not an issue with YFD, since there is only one developer. I can change the database schema, user interface, and data collection mechanism with little fuss. I also use Django, a Python web framework, which uses a model-view-control approach and allows for rapid and efficient development. I do, however, have to do everything myself. Because of the group's diversity in statistics, computer science, engineering, GIS, and environmental science, PEIR is able to accomplish more—most notably in the area of data processing, as discussed in the next section. So there are certainly advantages and disadvantages to developing with a large group.

Data Processing

Data processing is the important underpinning of the personal data collection system that users almost never see and usually are not interested in. They tend to be more interested in the results of the processing. This is the case for YFD. PEIR users, on the other hand, benefit from seeing how their data is processed, and it in turn affects the way they interpret impact and exposure.

The analytical component of PEIR consists of a series of server-side processing steps that start with GPS data to estimate impact and exposure. To be precise, we can divide the processing into four separate phases:*

---

* PEIR, *http://peir.cens.ucla.edu*

1. **Trace correction and annotation:** Where possible, the error-prone, undersampled location traces are corrected and annotated using estimation techniques such as map matching with road network and building parcel data. Because these corrections and annotations are estimates, they do carry along uncertainties.

2. **Activity and location classification:** The corrected and annotated data is automatically classified as *traveling* or *stationary* using web services to provide a first level of refinement to the model output for a given person on a given day. The data is also split into *trips* based on dwell time.

3. **Context estimation:** The corrected and classified location data is used as input to web-based information sources on weather, road conditions, and aggregated driver behaviors.

4. **Exposure and impact calculation:** Finally, the fine-grained, classified data and derived data is used as input to geospatial data sets and microenvironment models that are in turn used to provide an individual's personalized estimates.

While PEIR's focus is still on the results of this four-step process, we eventually found that users wanted to know more about how impact and exposure were estimated. So for each chunk of data we provide details of the process, such as what percentage of time was spent on a freeway and what the weather was like around where the user was traveling. We also include a detailed explanation for every provided metric. In this case, transparency in the estimation process allows users to see how their actions have an effect on impact and exposure rather than just knowing how much or how little they are polluting their neighborhood. There is, of course, such a thing as information overload, so we are careful in how much (and how little) we show. We address much of these issues in the next section.

Data Visualization

Once data is collected, uploaded, and processed, users need to be able to access, evaluate, and explore their data. The main design goal behind YFD and PEIR was to make personal data understandable to nonprofessionals. Data has to be presented in a way that is relatable; it has to be humanized. Oftentimes we get caught up in statistical charts and graphs, which are extremely useful, but at the same time we want to engage users so that they stay interested, continue collecting data, and keep coming back to the site to gauge their progress in whatever they are tracking. Users should understand that the data is about them and reflect the choices they make in their daily lives.

I like to think of data visualization as a story. The main character is the user, and we can go two ways. A story of charts and graphs might read a lot like a textbook; however, a story with context, relationships, interactions, patterns, and explanations reads like a novel. This is not to say that one or the other is better. There are plenty of interesting textbooks, and probably just as many—if not more—boring novels. We want something in between the textbook and novel when we visualize personal data. We want to present the facts, but we also want to provide context, like the who, what, when, where, and why of the numbers. We are after emotion. Data often can be sterile, but only if we present it that way.

PEIR

In the case of PEIR, we were met with the challenge of presenting scientific data—carbon impact, exposure to high levels of particulate matter, and impact to sensitive sites such as hospitals and schools. Impact and exposure are not a part of everyday conversation. Most people do not know whether 1,000 kilograms of carbon emissions in a day is a lot or a little. Is one hour of exposure to high levels of particulate matter normal? These types of questions factor into PEIR's visualization design. It is important to remember, however, that even though the resulting data is not immediately understandable, it is all derived from location data, which is extremely intuitive. There are perhaps few types of data that are so immediately understandable as one's place in physical space. Therefore, we use maps as the visualization anchor point and work from there.

Mapping location-based data

Location-based data drives the PEIR system, so an interactive map is the core of the user interface. We initially used the Google Maps API, but quickly nixed it in the interest of flexibility. Instead, we use Modest Maps. It is a display and interaction library for tile-based maps in Flash and implemented in ActionScript 3.0. Modest Maps provides a core set of features, such as panning and zooming, but allows designers and developers to easily customize displays. Modest Maps implementations can easily switch map tiles, whether the choice is to use Microsoft's map tiles, Google's, custom-built ones, or all of the above. We are free to adjust color, layout, and overall style, which lend themselves to good design practice and useful visualization, and the flexibility allows us to incorporate our own visualizations on the map or as a supplement. In the end, we do not want to limit ourselves to just maps, and Modest Maps provides the flexibility we need to do this.

Experimenting with visual cues

We experimented with a number of different ways to represent PEIR data before deciding on the final mapping scheme. During the design process, we considered several parameters:

- How can users interact with a lot of traces at once without cluttering the map?
- How can we represent both stationary (user is idle) and traveling (user is moving) data chunks at the same time?
- How do we display values from all four microenvironment models?
- What colors should we use to represent GPS trace, impact, and exposure?
- How do we shift focus toward the actual data and away from the underlying map tiles?

Mapping multivariate location traces

In the early stages of the design process, we mapped GPS traces the way that users typically see location tracks: simply a line that goes from point to point. This was before taking values from the microenvironment models into account, so the map was a basic implementation

using Modest Maps and tiles from OpenStreetMap. GPS traces were mono-colored and represented nothing but location; there was a circle at the end so that the user would know where the trip began and ended.

This worked to a certain extent, but we soon had to visualize more data, so we changed the format. We colored traces based on impact and exposure values. The color scheme used five shades of red. Higher levels of, say, carbon impact were darker shades of red. Similarly, trips that had lower carbon impact were lighter shades of red.

The running metaphor is that the more impact the user has on the environment, the more the trip should stand out on the map. The problem with this implementation was that the traces on the map did not stand out (Figure 1-1). We tried using brighter colors, but the brightly colored trips clashed with the existing colors on the map. Although we want traces to stand out, we do not want to strain the user's eyes. To solve this problem we tried a different mapping scheme that again made all trips on the map mono-color, but used circles to encode impact and exposure. All traces were colored white, and the model values were visually represented with circles that varied in size at the end of each trip. Greater values were displayed as circles larger in area while lesser values were smaller in area. This design scheme was short-lived.

FIGURE 1-1. We experimented with different visual cues on a map to best display location data with impact and exposure values. The above shows three iterations during our preliminary design. The left map shows GPS traces color-coded by carbon impact; in the center map, we encoded impact with uni-color area circles; on the right, we incorporated GPS data showing when the user was idle and went back to using color-coding. (See Color Plate 1.)

One problem with representing values only at the end of a trace was that users thought the circles indicated that something happened at the very end of each trip. However, this is not the case. The map should show that something is happening during the entirety of a trip. Carbon is emitted everywhere you travel, not collected and then released at a destination.

We switched back to color-coding trips and removed the scaled area circles representing our models' values. At this point in the design process, we now had two types of GPS data: traveling and stationary. Traveling trips meant that the user was moving, whether on foot or in a vehicle; stationary chunks are times when the user is not moving. She might be sitting at a desk or stuck in traffic. To display stationary chunks, we did not completely abandon the idea of using area circles on the map. Larger circles mean longer duration, and smaller circles mean shorter duration. Similar to traveling trips, which are represented by

lines, area circles are color-coded appropriately. For example, if the user chooses to color-code by particulate matter exposure, a stationary chunk that was spent idle on the freeway is shown as a brightly colored circle.

However, we are again faced with same problem as before: trying to make traces stand out on the map without clashing with the map's existing colors. We already tried different color schemes for the traces, but had not yet tried changing the shades of the actual map. Inspired by Trulia Snapshot, which maps real estate properties, we grayscaled map tiles and inverted the color filters so that map items that were originally lightly colored turned dark and vice versa. To be more specific, the terrain was originally lightly colored, so now it is dark gray, and roads that were originally dark are now light gray. This darkened map lets lightly colored traces stand out, and because the map is grayscale, there is less clashing (Figure 1-2). Users do not have to try hard to distinguish their data from roads and terrain. Modest Maps provided this flexibility.

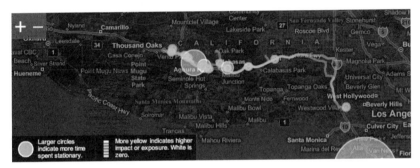

FIGURE 1-2. In the current mapping scheme, we use color filters to highlight the data. The map serves solely as context. Linked histograms show impact and exposure distributions of mapped data. When the user scrolls over a histogram bar, the corresponding GPS data is highlighted on the map. (See Color Plate 2.)

Choosing a color scheme

Once we established map tiles as the dark background and represented trips in the light foreground, we decided what colors to use. This is important because users recognize some colors as specific types of events. For example, red often means to stop or that there is danger ahead, whereas green means progress or growth, especially from an environmental standpoint.

It is also important to not use too many contrasting colors. Using dissimilar colors without any progression indicates categorical data. Model values, however, are on a continuous scale. Therefore, we use colors with a subtle gradient. In the earlier versions we tried a color scale that contained different shades of green. Users commented that because green usually means good or environmentally friendly, it was strange to see high levels of impact and exposure encoded with that color. Instead, we still use shades of green but also incorporate yellows. From low to high values, we incrementally shift from green to yellow, respectively. Trips that have impact or exposure values of zero are white.

Making trips interactive

Users can potentially map hundreds of trips at one time, providing an overview of traveling habits, impact, and exposure, but the user also needs to read individual trip details. Mapping a trip is not enough. Users have to be able to interact with trips so that they know the context of their travels.

When the user scrolls over a trip on the PEIR map, that trip is highlighted, while all other trips are made less prominent and blend in with the background without completely disappearing. To be more specific, transparency of the trip of interest is decreased while the other trips are blurred by a factor of five. Cabspotting, a visualization that maps cab activities in San Francisco, inspired this effect. When the user clicks on a trip on the map, the trip log automatically scrolls to the trip of interest. Again, the goal is to provide users with as much context as possible without confusing them or cluttering the screen.

These features, of course, handle multiple trips only to a certain extent. For example, if there are hundreds of long trips in a condensed area, they can be difficult to navigate due to clutter. This is an area we plan to improve as we incorporate user-contributed metadata such as tags and classification.

Displaying distributions

PEIR provides histograms on the right side of the map to show distributions of impact and exposure for selected trips. There are four histograms, one for each microenvironment model. The histograms automatically update whenever the user selects a trip from the trip log. If trips are mostly high in impact or exposure, the histograms are skewed to the right; similarly, if trips are mostly low in impact or exposure, the histograms are skewed to the left.

We originally thought the histograms would be useful since they are so widely used in statistics, but that proved not to be the case. The histograms actually confused more than they provided insight. Although a small portion of the test group thought they were useful, most expected the horizontal axis to be time and the vertical axis to be the amount of impact or exposure. People seemed more interested in patterns over time than overall distributions. Therefore, we switched to time-based bar charts (Figure 1-3). Users are able to see their impact and exposure over time and browse by week.

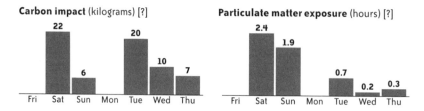

FIGURE 1-3. Time series bar charts proved to be more effective than value-based histograms.

Sharing personal data

PEIR lets users share their impact and exposure with Facebook friends as another way to compare values. It is through sharing that we get around the absolute scale interpretation of axes and shift emphasis onto relative numbers, which better helps users make inferences. Although 1,000 kilograms of carbon might seem like a lot, a comparison against other users could change that misconception. Our Facebook application shows aggregated values in users' Facebook profiles compared against other Facebook friends who have installed the PEIR Facebook application (Figure 1-4).

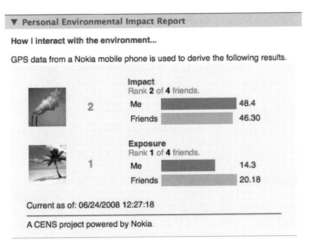

FIGURE 1-4. PEIR's Facebook application lets users share their impact and exposure findings as well as compare their values with friends. (See Color Plate 3.)

The PEIR Facebook application shows bar graphs for the user's impact and exposure and the average of impact and exposure for his or her friends. The application also shows overall rank. Those who have less impact or exposure are higher in rank. Icons also provide more context. If impact is high, an icon with a chimney spouting a lot of smoke appears. If impact is low, a beach with clear skies appears.

Shifting attention back to the PEIR interface, users also have a network page in addition to their personal profile. The network page again shows rankings for the last week of impact and exposure, but also shows how the user's friends rank. The goal is for users to try to climb in the rankings for least impact and exposure while at the same time encouraging their friends to try to improve. Although actual values in units of kilograms or hours for impact or exposure might be unclear at first, rankings are immediately useful. When users pursue higher ranking, values from PEIR microenvironment models mean more in the same way that a score starts to mean something while playing a video game.

The reader should take notice that no GPS data is shared. We take data privacy very seriously and make many efforts to keep certain data private, which is why only impact and exposure aggregates are shown in the network pages.

YFD

Whereas PEIR deals with data that is not immediately relatable, YFD is on the opposite side of the spectrum. YFD helps users track data that is a part of everyday conversation. Like PEIR, though, YFD aims to make the little things in our lives more visible. It is the aggregate of small choices that have a great effect. The visualization had to show this.

To begin, we go back to one of the challenges mentioned earlier. We want users to tweet frequently and work personal data collection into their daily Twitter routine. What are the motivations behind data collection? Why does a user track what he eats or his sleep habits? Maybe someone wants to lose weight so that he feels more confident around the opposite sex, or he wants to get more sleep so that he does not fall asleep at his desk. Another user, however, might want to gain weight, because she lost weight when she was sick, or maybe she sleeps too much and always feels groggy when she gets up. Others just might be curious. Whatever the motivation, it is clear that everyone has his or her own reasons for personal data collection. YFD highlights that motivation as a reminder to the user, because no matter what diet system someone is on or sleep program he is trying, people will not change unless they really want to. Notice the personal words of motivation in large print in the middle of the screen in Figure 1-5.

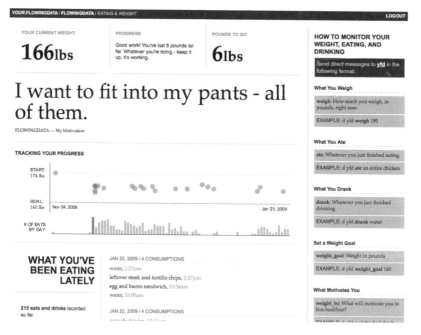

FIGURE 1-5. People track their weight and what they eat for different reasons. YFD places motivation front and center. (See Color Plate 4.)

It is also worth noting that each tracker's page shows what has happened most recently at the top. This serves a few purposes. First, it will update whenever the user tweets a data point, so that the user can see his status whenever he logs in to YFD. Second, we do not want to stray too far from the feel of Twitter, again to reinforce working YFD tweets into

the Twitter routine. Finally, the design choice largely came out of the experience with PEIR. Users seem to expect time-based visualization, so most YFD visualization is just that.

There is one exception, though—the feelings and emotions tracker (Figure 1-6). As anyone can tell you, emotions are incredibly complicated. How do you quantify happiness or sadness or nervousness? It did not seem right to break emotions down into graphs and numbers, so a sorted tag cloud is used instead. It somehow feels more organic. Emotions of higher frequency are larger than those that occur rarely. The YFD trackers are all modular at these early stages of development, but I do plan to eventually integrate all trackers as if YFD were a dashboard into a user's life. The feelings tracker will be in the center of it all. In the end, everything we do is driven by how we feel or how we want to feel.

FIGURE 1-6. Users can also keep track of how they feel. Unlike the other YFD trackers, the page of emotions does not have any charts or graphs. A word cloud was chosen to provide more organic-feeling visualization.

The Point

Data visualization is often all about analytics and technical results, but it does not have to be—especially with personal data collection. People who collect data about themselves are not necessarily after the actual data. They are mostly interested in the resulting information and how they can use their own data to improve themselves. For that to come through, people have to see more than just data in the visualization. They have to see themselves. Life is complex, data represents life, and users want to understand that complexity somehow. That does not mean we should dumb down the data or the information. Instead, we use the data visualization to teach and to draw interest. Once there is that interest, we can provide users with a way to dig deeper and explore their data, or more accurately, explore and understand their lives in that data. It is up to the statistician, computer scientist, and designer to tell the stories properly.

How to Participate

PEIR and YFD are currently by invitation only, but if you would like to participate, please feel free to visit our sites at *http://peir.cens.ucla.edu* or *http://your.flowingdata.com*, respectively. Also, if you are interested in collaborating with the PEIR research group to incorporate new models, strategies, or visualization, or if you have ideas on how to improve YFD, we would love to hear from you.

The Beautiful People: Keeping Users in Mind When Designing Data Collection Methods

Jonathan Follett and Matthew Holm

Introduction: User Empathy Is the New Black

ALWAYS KEEP THE WANTS AND NEEDS OF YOUR AUDIENCE IN MIND. THIS PRINCIPLE, WHICH GUIDES THE FIELD known as user experience (UX) design, seems painfully obvious—enough to elicit a roll of the eyes from any professional creating new, innovative digital technologies or improving upon already existing systems. "Yes! Of course there's a person using the product!"

But, while the benefits of following a user-centered design process can be great—like increased product usability and customer satisfaction, and reduced 800-number service calls—this deceptively simple advice is not always followed, especially when it comes to collecting data.

What Is UX?

UX is an emerging, multidisciplinary field focused on designing products and services that people can easily understand and use. Its primary concern is making systems adapt to and serve the user, rather than the other way around. (See Figure 2-1.) UX professionals can include practitioners and researchers in visual design, interaction design, information architecture, user interface design, and usability. And the field, which is strongly related to human factors and computer-human interaction, draws upon ethnography and psychology as well: UX professionals operate as user advocates. Generally, UX design techniques

are applied to desktop and web-distributed software, although proponents may use the term more broadly to describe the design of any complex experience—such as that of a museum exhibit or retail store visit.

The Benefits of Applying UX Best Practices to Data Collection

When it comes to data collection, user experience design is more important than ever. Data—that most valuable digital resource—comes from people and their actions, so designers and developers need to be constantly thinking about those people, and not just about the data they want to collect. The key method for collecting data from people online is, of course, through the use of the dreaded form. There is no artifact potentially more valuable to a business, or more boring and tedious to a participant.

As user experience practitioners, we regularly work with data collected from large audiences through the use of web forms. And we've seen, time and again, that the elegant visual design of forms can assist greatly in the collection of data from people. The challenge presented by any form design project is that, although it's easy enough to collect data from people, it can be exceptionally difficult to collect good data. Form design matters (see Figure 2-1), and can directly affect the quality of the data that you receive: better-designed forms gather more accurate and more relevant data.

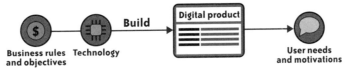

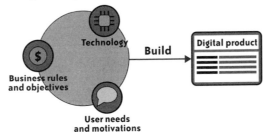

FIGURE 2-1. Rather than treating audience needs as an afterthought, the UX design process addresses audience needs, business requirements, and technical feasibility during the design stage.

So, what is it that drives people to fill in forms and create the data we need? And how can we, as designers and developers, encourage them to do it more efficiently, effectively, and accurately?

We'll take a look at a case study here, showing an example of simple form design using UX best practices and principles to increase the completion rate of unsolicited questionnaires.

The Project: Surveying Customers About a New Luxury Product

Our project was an online survey for a marketing consulting firm, Urban Wallace Associates, that was trying to gauge consumer interest in a new luxury product. (To maintain confidentiality, we've had to change some of the details throughout this chapter relating to the content of the survey questions.) The survey audience was the same demographic as the product's eventual retail audience: wealthy individuals between the ages of 55 and 75.

An email survey was not our client's first choice. Urban Wallace Associates had already attempted a telephone survey of the target group. "Normally, we get about 35% answering machines," says UWA President, Roger Urban. "In this group, we got more than 80% answering machines. When someone did pick up, it was usually the housekeeper!"

Unable to get a satisfactory sample of the target audience on the phone, our client turned to email. One of the reasons our client chose this communication method is because, for this affluent group, email is a near-universal utility. And while email faces its own set of gatekeepers—namely, automated junk mail filters—very few people, as of yet, hire others to read it for them. Even the wealthy still open their own emails.

Urban Wallace Associates secured an email marketing firm to help generate and prequalify the recipient list, and to deliver and track the outgoing messages. Our firm was brought in to design and build the survey landing page, which would open in the recipient's web browser when he clicked a link in the body of the email, and to collect the results into a database. Our primary focus in this task was maintaining an inviting atmosphere on the questionnaire web page, so that respondents would be more willing to complete the form. A secondary task was creating a simple interface for the client so that he could review live reporting results as the data came in.

Specific Challenges to Data Collection

Data collection poses specific challenges, including accessibility, trust, and user motivation. The following sections discuss how these issues affected our design.

Challenges of Accessibility

Advocates of web accessibility—designing so that pages and sites are still useful for people with special needs and disabilities—often say that designing a site that is accessible will also create a site that is more usable for everyone. This was not just a theoretical consideration in our case, since, with a target audience whose members were approaching or past retirement, age-related vision impairment was a real concern. Some 72% of Americans report vision impairment by the time they are 45 years of age.

The other side of the age issue—one rarely spoken of, for fears of appearing discriminatory—is that older people use computers and the Internet in fewer numbers and with less ease than younger people who grew up with computers in their lives. (Individuals with higher incomes generally use computers and the Internet more, however, so those age-related effects were mitigated in our sample group.) Respondents who are stymied by a confusingly designed survey are less likely to give accurate information—or, indeed, to complete the survey at all. In our case, as in all such projects, it pays to recall that essential adage: know your audience.

Challenges of Perception

While accessibility is a functional issue—a respondent cannot complete a survey if she can't read it—our project faced other challenges that were more emotional in nature, and depended on how the respondent perceived the questioner and the questions.

Building trust

Internet users are well aware that giving out information to people online can have serious consequences, ranging from increased spamming, phone solicitation, and junk mail all the way up to fraud and identity theft. Therefore, for those looking to do market research online, building trust is an important factor. Although the response to the product and our survey was ultimately quite positive overall (as we'll describe in more detail later on), there were several participants who, when asked why they were not interested in the product, responded with statements such as:

> "Don't trust your firm"
> "Unknown Offeror"
> "Don't believe what [the product] claims to deliver"
> "can't afford it…don't trust it…too good to be true so it probably isn't. PLEASE DO NOT CONTACT ME ABOUT THIS PRODUCT ANY MORE"

These responses illustrate the lengths to which we must go in order to build trust online. It was more important, in our case, because we were explicitly *not* selling anything—we were conducting research. "I don't want anything that sounds like a sales lead," our client, Roger Urban, told us at the outset. It would be necessary to provide clear links back to information about Urban Wallace Associates, so people could see what kind of firm was asking them questions, and to post clear verbiage that we were not collecting their personal data, and that we were not going to contact them again. The only wrinkle was that our client's research required knowing the U.S. state in which each respondent was living. So we would have to figure out a way to capture that information without violating the spirit of the trust we were trying to build.

Length of survey

Keeping the respondent from disengaging was one of our biggest concerns. The client and we agreed early on to keep the survey to a single screen. Multiple screens would not only require more patience from the respondent, but they might require additional action

(such as clicking a "go on to the next question" button). Any time a survey requires an action from the respondent, you're inviting him to decide that the extra effort is not worth it, and to give up. Further, we wanted to avoid intimidating the respondent at any point with the *perceived* length of the survey. Multiple screens, or the appearance of too many questions on a single screen, increase the likelihood that a respondent will bail out.

Accurate data collection

One particularly important problem we considered during the design stage of this survey was that the data we collected needed to be as accurate as possible—perhaps an obvious statement, but difficult nonetheless. Our form design had to elicit responses from the participants that were honest, and not influenced by, say, a subconscious desire to please the questioner (a common pitfall for research of this type). The difference between collecting opinion data and information that might be more administrative in nature, such as an address for shipping, is that shipping data can be easily validated, whereas opinion data, which is already subjective, has a way of being more slippery. And although the science of designing opinion polls and measuring the resulting data is not something we'll cover in depth in this chapter, we will discuss some of the language and other choices our team made to encourage accurate answers.

Motivation

Finally, although we've talked about concerns over how to make it *possible* for respondents to use the form, as well as the problems of getting them to trust us enough to keep participating, avoiding scaring them off with a lot of questions, and making sure we didn't subconsciously influence their answers, we haven't mentioned perhaps the most important part of any survey: why should the person want to participate at all? For this type of research survey, there is no profit motive to participate, unlike online forums such as Amazon's Mechanical Turk, in which users complete tasks in their spare time for a few dollars or cents per task. *But when there is no explicit profit to be made, how do you convince a person to take the time to answer your questions?*

Designing Our Solution

We've talked about some of the pitfalls inherent in a data-collecting project; in the next few sections, we discuss the nuts and bolts of our design, including typography, web browser compatibility, and dynamic form elements.

Design Philosophy

When we design to elicit a response, framing the problem from a user's perspective is critical. It's easy to get caught up in the technical constraints of a project and design for the computer, rather than the person using it. But form data is actively generated by a person (as opposed to being passively generated by a sensor or other input), and requires the participant to make decisions about how and whether to answer your questions. So, the way in which we collect a participant's data matters a great deal.

As we designed the web form for this project, we focused on balancing the motivations of survey participants with the business objectives of the client. The client's primary business goal—to gather data determining whether the target audience would be interested in purchasing a new luxury product—was in line with a user-centered design perspective. By placing the person in the central role of being both advisor and potential future customer, the business objectives provided strong justification for our user-centered design decisions.

Here are a couple of guidelines we used to frame our design decisions:

Respect the user

Making our design people-centered throughout the process required thinking about our users' emotional responses. In order to convince them to participate, we had to first show them respect. They're not idiots; they're our potential customers. We all know this instinctively, but it's surprising how easily we can forget the principle. If we approach our users with respect, we'll naturally want the digital product we build for them to be accessible, usable, and easily understood. This perspective influences the choices we make for everything from language to layout to technology.

Make the person real

In projects with rapid timelines or constrained budgets, we don't always have the resources to sculpt a complete user profile or persona based on target market research, or to observe users in their work environments. In these situations, a simple "guerilla" UX technique to create empathy for the user and guide design decisions is to think of a real person we know in the demographic, whom we'd legitimately like to help. We had several such stand-in personas to guide our thinking, including our aging parents and some former business mentors whom we know very well. Of course, imagining these people using our digital product is only a first step. Since we knew them well, we were also able to enlist some of them to help in preliminary testing of our design.

In the end, people will adapt their own behavior to work with just about any design, if they have to. The purpose of UX is to optimize those designs so people will want to use a product or service, and can use it more readily and easily, without having to adapt their behavior.

Designing the Form Layout

Generally, no matter how beautiful our form design, it's unlikely that it will ever rise to the level of delighting users. There is no designers' holy grail that can make people enthusiastic about filling out a form. However, form aesthetics do matter: clear information and visual design can mitigate users' boredom by clearly guiding their eyes and encouraging them to make it to the end, rather than abandoning the task halfway through. Good form design doesn't draw attention to itself and should be nearly invisible, always honoring its primary purpose, which is to collect accurate information from people. While form design needs to be both pleasing and professional in tone, in most cases, proper visual treatment will seem reserved and utilitarian in comparison to most other kinds of web pages. Form visual design can only be judged by how effectively it enables users to complete the task. For this project, the areas where we focused our design efforts were in the typography, page layout, and interaction design.

Web form typography and accessibility

In general, older readers have difficulty seeing small type. And survey participants are not so generous that they're willing to strain their eyes to read a form. Because the target audience for our survey project was older (55–75 years of age), we knew that overall legibility would be an issue.

We chose the sans serif typeface Arial (a close cousin via Microsoft of the modern workhorse Helvetica), which is standard-issue on nearly 100% of web browsers, and we set headers and body copy large at 20 pixels and 14 pixels, respectively. Although larger type caused the page to be slightly longer, the improvements in legibility were well worth it. Line spacing was not too tight, and was left-justified with a rag right. Line length was roughly 85 characters. And we set the majority of the text with the high contrast combination of black type on a white background, also for legibility considerations. While we did use color strategically to brighten the page and emphasize the main headers, we did not rely on it to provide any additional information to the user. We did this because, for the male audience, roughly 7–8% has some type of color blindness.

Giving them some space

A densely designed form with no breathing room is guaranteed to intimidate the user. So, leaving some open whitespace in a layout is key.

In our survey, the first section included a text description of the luxury product, which we asked participants to read and evaluate. Web readers are notorious for their short attention spans and tendency to skim text rather than read it all the way through. So, following web writing best practices, we separated the 250-word product description into subsections with headers, pulling out key bullet points and dividing it into easily digestible chunks (see Figure 2-2).

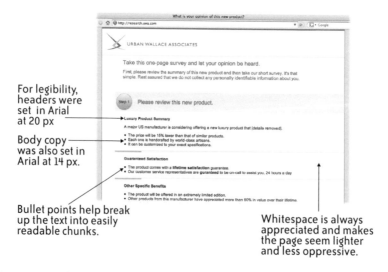

For legibility, headers were set in Arial at 20 px

Body copy was also set in Arial at 14 px.

Bullet points help break up the text into easily readable chunks.

Whitespace is always appreciated and makes the page seem lighter and less oppressive.

FIGURE 2-2. *Designing for legibility. (See Color Plate 5.)*

Accommodating different browsers and testing for compatibility

To make sure the form was usable by our audience, we designed the form page so it could be viewed easily in a variety of screen sizes, from an 800-pixel width on up. To accomplish this, we centered the form in the browser, using a neutral gray background on the right and left margins to fill the remaining space of widescreen monitors and ensure that the form wouldn't appear to be disembodied and floating. We also tested in all major web browsers, including the legacy IE6, to ensure that the dynamic form looked good and functioned well.

Interaction design considerations: Dynamic form length

Dynamic forms can "soften the blow" of having many questions to answer. Using Java-Script or other methods can create a soft reveal that allows the form to be subtly altered—or lengthened—based on user input (see Figures 2-3 and 2-4). These techniques allowed us to balance not scaring users off with a form that is too long on the one hand, and not infuriating them because they had been "deceived" about the form length on the other.

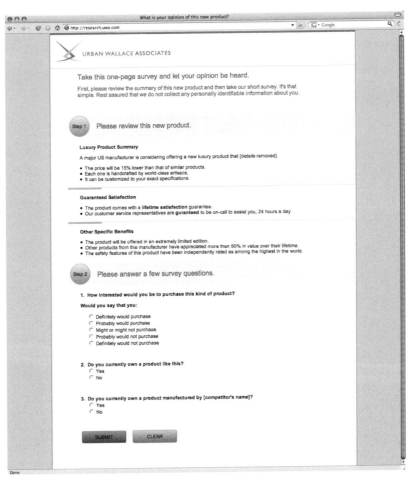

FIGURE 2-3. The survey starts with only three questions. (See Color Plate 6.)

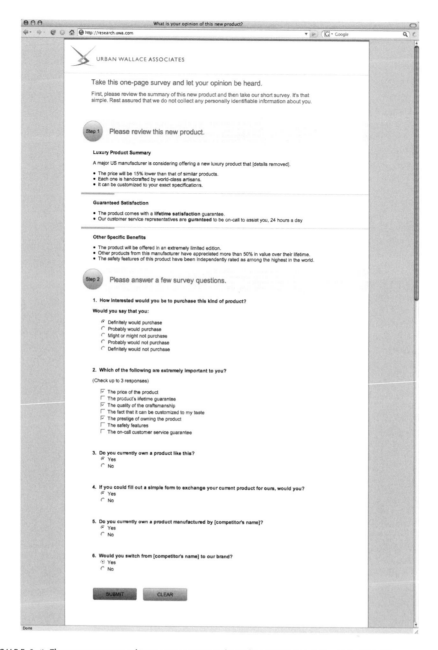

FIGURE 2-4. The survey may expand to up to six questions depending on user input. (See Color Plate 7.)

For our project, the readers, in effect, built the survey as they answered each question. We used a very simple piece of JavaScript code to make sure each new question was conditional upon an answer to previous questions. The idea for this solution came from another website we were working on at the time. In that project—a portfolio site for a designer— we used JavaScript to hide and reveal details about different projects, making it possible to take in all of the designer's work at a glance and then dive deeper into areas of interest, all

without leaving the home page. This idea—not overwhelming the user with too much information, yet making that information quickly accessible at the same time—was on our minds when we approached the survey design. Here is the code we used:

```
<script language="JavaScript">
//This finds the word "Yes" in an input value and displays the designated hiddenElement
(or hides it if "Yes" is not found)
function switchem(switchElement,hiddenElement) {
if (switchElement.value.search("Yes") > -1)
    document.getElementById(hiddenElement).style.display = '';
else
    document.getElementById(hiddenElement).style.display = 'none';
}
</script>

<script language="JavaScript">
//This finds the word "No" in an input value and displays the designated hiddenElement
(or hides it if "No" is not found)
function switchem2(switchElement,hiddenElement) {
if (switchElement.value.search("No") > -1)
    document.getElementById(hiddenElement).style.display = '';
else
    document.getElementById(hiddenElement).style.display = 'none';
}
</script>

...

<li id="survey1" class="surveynum">How interested would you be to purchase this kind of
product?
    <p><b>Would you say that you:</b></p>
    <ul class="nobullet">
        <li><input
onclick="switchem(this,'survey2');switchem2(this,'survey3');document.
getElementById('surveytextarea').value=''" type="radio" name="q1" value="Yes,
Definitely would purchase"> Definitely would purchase</li>
        <li><input
onclick="switchem(this,'survey2');switchem2(this,'survey3');document.
getElementById('surveytextarea').value=''" type="radio" name="q1" value="Yes, Probably
would purchase"> Probably would purchase</li>
        <li><input
onclick="switchem(this,'survey2');switchem2(this,'survey3');document.
getElementById('surveytextarea').value=''" type="radio" name="q1" value="Yes, Might or
might not purchase"> Might or might not purchase</li>
        <li><input
onclick="switchem(this,'survey2');switchem2(this,'survey3');document.
getElementById('q2a').checked=false;document.getElementById('q2b').
checked=false;document.getElementById('q2c').checked=false;document.
getElementById('q2d').checked=false;document.getElementById('q2e').
checked=false;;document.getElementById('q2f').checked=false;
document.getElementById('q2g').checked=false" type="radio" name="q1" value="No,
Probably would not purchase"> Probably would not purchase</li>
```

```
        <li><input
onclick="switchem(this,'survey2');switchem2(this,'survey3');document.
getElementById('q2a').checked=false;document.getElementById('q2b').
checked=false;document.getElementById('q2c').checked=false;document.
getElementById('q2d').checked=false;document.getElementById('q2e').
checked=false;;document.getElementById('q2f').checked=false;
document.getElementById('q2g').checked=false" type="radio" name="q1" value="No,
Definitely would not purchase"> Definitely would not purchase</li>
    </ul>
</li>
<li id="survey2" style="display:none" class="surveynum">Which of the following are
extremely important to you?
    <p>(Check up to 3 responses)</p>
    <ul class="nobullet">
        <li><input type="checkbox" name="q2" id="q2a" value="The price of the product">
The price of the product </li>
        <li><input type="checkbox" name="q2" id="q2b" value="The product's
lifetime guarantee"> The product's lifetime guarantee</li>
        <li><input type="checkbox" name="q2" id="q2c" value="The quality of
the craftsmanship"> The quality of the craftsmanship </li>
        <li><input type="checkbox" name="q2" id="q2d" value="The fact that it can be
customized to my taste"> The fact that it can be customized to my taste </li>
        <li><input type="checkbox" name="q2" id="q2e" value="The prestige of
owning the product"> The prestige of owning the product </li>
        <li><input type="checkbox" name="q2" id="q2f" value="The safety features"> The
safety features </li>
        <li><input type="checkbox" name="q2" id="q2g" value="The on-call customer
service guarantee"> The on-call customer service guarantee</li>
    </ul>
</li>
<li id="survey3" style="display:none" class="surveynum">Why are you not interested in
this product?
    <ul class="nobullet">
        <li><textarea id="surveytextarea" name="q3"></textarea></li>
    </ul>
</li>
```

The result is that selecting any of the three positive responses on the 5-point scale in Question 1 revealed a checklist that helped further identify what the respondent liked about the product (Figure 2-5). Selecting either of the two negative responses revealed a text area in which the respondent could explain, precisely, what he disliked about the product (Figure 2-6).

As programming goes, this is child's play and hardly worth mentioning. But the impact from the user's standpoint is subtle and powerful. It meant that we could "listen" and "respond" to the user's input in a very conversational manner. It also meant that the psychological impact of the form length is much lower, as users are facing only a three-question survey at the start. The survey potentially could expand to six questions, but all of this happens without the user ever leaving the survey landing page, and without forcing the user to actively click some sort of "Next page" button.

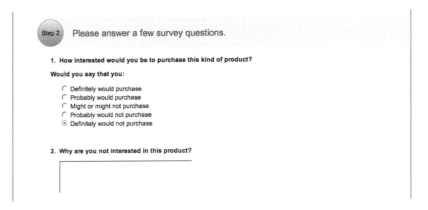

FIGURE 2-5. Detail of survey when the user answers "Yes" to Question 1. (See Color Plate 8.)

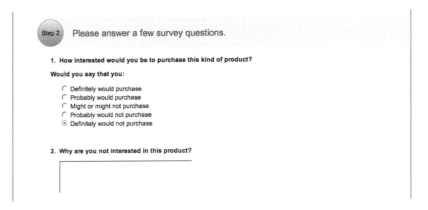

FIGURE 2-6. Detail of survey when the user answers "No" to Question 1. (See Color Plate 9.)

Designing trust

We did some concrete things to try to establish trust with the respondents and indicate that this was a legitimate survey, not a phishing expedition. First, we prominently displayed the client's company logo at the top of the web survey page. The logo itself linked back to the "About Us" area on Urban Wallace Associates' main website, so survey participants could see who they were communicating with. Additionally, we hosted the survey page on a subdomain of our client's main site, not on some third-party host.

As previously mentioned, our client's research needed the U.S. state of residence of each respondent. But, since we told respondents, "we do not collect any personally identifiable information about you," it would have been awkward to then start asking questions about where the person lived. Our solution was to record the visitor's IP address automatically, which would satisfy the U.S. state location requirement but not violate the respondent's privacy. After all, a user's IP data is logged anytime he or she visits *any* website, and, at

most, it can only be used to determine the city of that otherwise anonymous user's Internet Service Provider.

We then purchased an inexpensive data set of IP-to-State information. With it, we were able to match each IP address collected with the U.S. state in which it resided. Although we could have scripted our pages to access this database and match the numbers at the time of data collection, we chose to do the matching semi-automatically after the fact. For starters, the project budget and timeframe did not warrant purchasing the additional server power to handle the task. But more important, from a user perspective, was the delay this matching would have inevitably built into the survey completion process. Although it might have been more convenient for us to receive finalized data at once, it would have created an additional inconvenience for our user. When designing a data collection experience, it's important to think about what server tasks must take place during the survey in order for the user's needs to be met, and what tasks can be delayed until after data collection. Don't ask the user to do what you can do—or discover—on your own.

All of this leads us back to the central point of this chapter, which is also the final, and core, aspect of building trust: treat the respondent with respect. By demonstrating that you value the respondent and her time and intelligence, by interacting with her in a conversational manner (despite the fact that all survey questions are being delivered by a preprogrammed machine), and showing her that you've been "listening" to her answers (don't, for example, ask slight variations of the same question over and over again, which makes it seem as though you didn't pay attention to her original response), you'll increase trust, encourage real answers, and keep the respondent from disengaging.

Designing for accurate data collection

This sort of talk can seem a little touchy-feely at times, especially to people who only work with the hard numbers retrieved from data collection, and not the human beings who generated that data. But all of this user-centered focus is not just a matter of politeness—it's also crucial for the reliability of the data that we actually get. "For a survey like this," says Roger Urban, whose firm specializes in measuring market interest and customer satisfaction through face-to-face, mailed, telephone, and email surveys just like this, "you're dealing with extremely thin data sets, so the quality of that data is *really* important." In other words, when important decisions are being based on the answers given by only a few hundred people, those answers had better be *great.*

But great answers do not mean *positive* answers. After all, this is research, and just like scientists, we want to measure reality (Do customers care about price that much when it comes to this product? Is safety really their top concern, or not? *Are* they, in fact, happy with our service?), to see where our assumptions are wrong. "Techniques of persuasion are a disaster when it comes to research," says Roger Urban. People will, subconsciously, try to please researchers by answering in the way that they feel they are *supposed* to answer. Introducing persuasive techniques, whether implicit or explicit, will skew your research data. "If you want an artificially high positive," says Urban, "I can get it for you every time." But if you're making real business or policy decisions, what good is such data?

Motivation

You can't use persuasive techniques during the act of data collection, but you *do* need to persuade your respondents to participate in the first place. With no money involved, what is their motivation?

"There should always be some benefit," says Roger Urban, "even if that benefit is just 'voicing your opinion.'" Human beings are interesting creatures; where cold, hard cash may not be able to compel us, far more nebulous benefits may do the trick—for example, some well-placed flattery. We all like to be thought of as experts; validation that our opinion *is* important may be enough to convince us to spend time talking to a stranger. So, too, can the allure that we may be receiving "inside information" by participating, that we are glimpsing what the future holds. For example, what techie wouldn't be interested in participating in a survey that allowed us to glimpse the design of Apple's next i-gadget?

In our project's case, we knew that we were dealing with an older audience. The language in the initial email was important in terms of engaging the recipient, and our team went with an appeal to the respondent's expertise. In our first mailing, we tested two different headlines on equal-sized groups of recipients:

> "You can shape the face of [product information removed] for future generations."
> "We're seeking the voice of experience."

As it turned out, the first headline, though offering the respondent the power to steer the very direction of the future, apparently proved slightly more ephemeral and altruistic (after all, it implies that the benefit may be solely for future generations, not necessarily for the respondent) than the ego-stroking one that turns their age into a positive ("experience"). For the first headline, 12.90% of those who opened the email clicked through, and 16.22% of those completed the survey. For the second headline, 14.04% of those who opened the email clicked through, with 29.5% of those people completing the survey. When the second mailing was conducted two weeks later, with the "voice of experience" headline on all messages, it generated a click-through rate of 27.68% and a completion rate of 33.16%. This second email went to people on the list who did not open the first mailing. (One of the secrets of email surveys is that the second mailing to the same list generally receives just as many responses as the first.)

This is another aspect of UX philosophy that's worth remembering: test everything. In this case, test even your testing methods! When you have the time and resources, test different copy, test different layouts, and test different types of interaction design—all with actual users.

Reporting the live data results

In our project, one special consideration was that the recipient of the final data, the client, would also be a user of the system—with drastically different needs from those of the survey participants.

Because the project was time sensitive, the client needed to see the survey results quickly to determine whether the product was generally well received. For this use case scenario, our solution was an HTML page, accessible to the client, which displayed the data, crudely sorted with minimal formatting. The live, raw survey results were sorted first by mailing (two mailings of each headline were sent to two age segments—55 to 64 and 65 to 75) and then by people's Yes/No answers to the first question about their interest in the product.

Unlike the survey participants, who needed to be convinced to participate and encouraged to complete the form, the client was motivated by a desire to see the data as quickly as it was generated. For the client, speed and immediate access to the live results as they came in were more important than any other factors. Thus, his user experience reflected those priorities (see Figure 2-7).

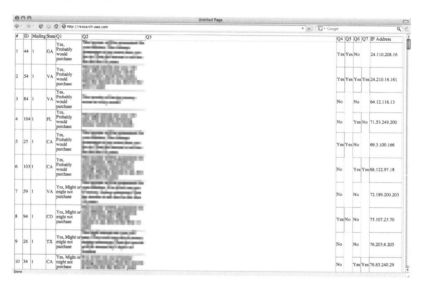

FIGURE 2-7. On this live data reporting screen, the client was able to see the survey results as they came in.

The raw data display was not, of course, the final deliverable. Upon the project conclusion we presented the client with fully sortable Excel spreadsheets of all the data we had collected (from eight total mailings, sent in two batches), including the U.S. state data that had not yet been generated at the time of the survey.

Results and Reflection

In the end, was all of this effort worth it? It's just a web form, right? People fill out millions of these things every day. Some might think that we don't need to put any more thought into how to design one—that the "problem" of creating a usable web form has already been solved, once and for all. But you should never underestimate the lack of effort that has been given to solving the most common design problems, particularly online. Most forms today are not much different than the ones that rolled out in the early 1990s.

Moreover, if there's one thing a good designer, especially one following UX principles, should know, it's that there is no such thing as a one-size-fits-all solution. Customization for your user group will almost always improve the experience—and, in this type of exercise, your data collection.

The results in our client's case appear to have been well worth the effort. We learned that, for this email marketing company's previous campaigns, normal rates of opened emails were in the 1–2% range; our mailing hit 4%. The normal click-through rate was 5–7% of opened emails; ours reached 21%. Most relevant, the normal rate of those who click through to the web page and then take action (i.e., complete the form) is usually 2–5%; for our design, that completion rate was 29%. (See Figure 2-8.)

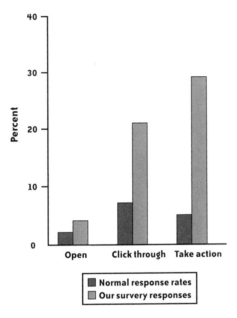

FIGURE 2-8. The response rates for our survey were significantly higher than the norm, which could be attributed to a better overall user experience.

There are, of course, other possible reasons why this survey performed so much better than this company's previous mailings. It's possible that the product was simply far more compelling than other products or topics on which the company had conducted surveys, and that the excitement generated by this product carried more people through to the end. It's also possible that the recipient pre-screening was far more accurate than usual, and this group was particularly well fitted to the product. There may even be an age bias at work—are older computer users more likely to open emails, read them, click through, and complete surveys than younger users, who may be more savvy and cautious about unsolicited emails? We're not aware of any studies on the subject, but it is a possibility. Indeed, although we can't rule out *any* of these explanations completely, the email company does

not appear to have been doing anything differently for our survey than it does for the hundreds of other surveys it regularly sends out. It's probably safe to conclude that our form design had something to do with the project's success.

Oh, and although it has no relevance to the survey design, we thought you might be interested to know that the reception of the product itself was extremely positive. While our client tells us that the product would have been viable to launch with a 10% positive response rate (answering "Yes" to the first survey question), it turned out that more than 16% of the respondents were interested in potentially buying it. What is the product? Unfortunately, confidentiality agreements preclude us from saying anything more about it.

If you want a glimpse, you'll just have to hope you're part of the next email survey. Don't be so quick to throw those emails in the trash; at the very least, you might learn something new about good—or bad—form design.

CHAPTER THREE

Embedded Image Data Processing on Mars

J. M. Hughes

Abstract

SPACECRAFT ARE UNIQUE ENGINEERING PROJECTS, WITH CONSTRAINTS AND REQUIREMENTS NOT found in earth-bound artifacts. They must be able to endure harsh temperature extremes, the hard vacuum of space, and intense radiation, and still be lightweight enough for a rocket to loft them into space and send them to their destination. A spacecraft is an exercise in applied minimalism: just enough to do the job and no more. Everything that goes into the design is examined in terms of necessity, weight, and cost, and everything is tested, and then tested again, before launch day, including the embedded computer system that is the "brains" of the spacecraft and the software that runs on it. This chapter is an overview of how the image processing software on the *Phoenix* lander acquired and stored image data, processed the data, and finally sent the images back to Earth.

Introduction

When designing and programming an embedded system, one is faced with a variety of constraints. These include processor speed, execution deadlines, allowable interrupt latency, and memory constraints, among others. With a space mission, the constraints can be severe. Typically the computer onboard a space vehicle will have only enough expensive

radiation-hardened memory to fulfill the mission objectives. Its central processing unit (CPU) will typically be a custom-made device designed to withstand the damaging effects of high-energy cosmic rays. By commercial standards, the CPU isn't fast, which is typical of radiation-hardened electronics. The trade-off here is speed versus the ability to take a direct hit from an interstellar particle and keep on running. The dual-core CPU in a typical PC, for example, wouldn't last long in space (nor would much of the rest of the PC's electronics, for that matter).

Then there are the science objectives, which in turn drive the software requirements for functionality and performance. All must be reconciled within the confines of the spacecraft's computing environment, and after numerous trade-off decisions, the final product must be able to operate without fatal errors for the duration of the mission. In the case of a robotic spacecraft, any fault may be the end of the mission, so there are requirements for getting things right before the rockets light up and everything heads off into the wild blue yonder.

On May 25, 2008, the *Phoenix* Mars Lander touched down safely in the northern polar region of Mars. Figure 3-1 shows an artist's impression of what *Phoenix* might look like after landing. Unlike the rovers that moved about in the relatively warm regions near the Martian equator, *Phoenix* was a stationary lander sitting in a barren, frigid landscape where the atmospheric pressure is equivalent to being at an altitude of about 100,000 feet on Earth. The thin atmosphere on Mars is also mostly carbon dioxide. Not exactly an ideal vacation spot, but a good place to look for ancient frozen water.

FIGURE 3-1. Artist's impression of Phoenix on Mars (Image credit: NASA/JPL). (See Color Plate 10.)

The lander's mission was to look for direct evidence of water, presumably in the form of ice just below the surface (it found it, by the way), and possibly for indications that Mars could have once provided a habitat suitable for life. Because of the location of its landing site, the spacecraft had a limited lifespan; when the Martian winter set in, it would almost certainly be the end of *Phoenix*. At the high latitude of the landing site, the odds of the lander surviving a totally dark, frigid (−90° C or colder) winter under a blanket of carbon dioxide snow would be very, very slim, at best.

I was the principle software engineer for the imaging software on *Phoenix*, and in this chapter I will attempt to share with you some of the thinking that went into the various data-handling design decisions for the imaging flight software for the *Phoenix* Mars Lander. In JPL/NASA jargon it is called the "imaging flight software" because it was responsible for handling all the imaging chores on the surface of Mars, and it was qualified as "flight software" for the mission.

With the *Phoenix* Mars Lander, the challenge was to capture and process data from any of four different charge-coupled device (CCD) imagers (similar to what's in a common digital camera) simultaneously, and do it all in a very limited amount of pre-allocated memory in the spacecraft's main computer. Not only that, but the images might also need to be compressed prior to transmission back to Earth using one or more of several different compression methods. Just for good measure, some of the final data products (that is, the images) had to be chopped up into small segments, each with its own sequentially numbered header, to allow for efficient storage in the spacecraft's flash memory and reduce the amount of lost data should something happen to a packet during its journey from Mars to Earth. The resulting embedded code acquired and processed over 25,000 images during the operational lifetime of the *Phoenix* lander.

Some Background

But before we delve into the data handling, it would be a good idea to briefly introduce the main actors in the drama: the imagers (also referred to as the cameras) and the spacecraft's computer.

The primary computer on *Phoenix* was built around a RAD6000 CPU running at a maximum clock rate of 20 MHz, although it could also be operated at slower clock rates to conserve battery power. No cutting-edge technology here; this was basically a radiation-hardened, first-generation PowerPC with a mix of RAM and flash memory all crammed onto a set of VME circuit boards. After dealing with the landing chores, its primary functions involved handling communications with Earth (uplink and downlink in jargon-speak; see the sidebar "Uplink and Downlink" on page 38), monitoring the spacecraft's health, and coordinating the activities of the various science instruments via commands sent up from the ground. It used WindRiver's VxWorks real-time operating system (RTOS) with numerous extensions provided by the spacecraft contractor, Lockheed Martin. All of the flight software was written in C in accordance with a set of specific coding rules.

UPLINK AND DOWNLINK

In the jargon of space missions, the terms *uplink* and *downlink* refer to the transfer of data or commands to and from controllers on Earth to a spacecraft. Uplink refers to commands or data transferred to the spacecraft. Downlink occurs when the spacecraft sends data back to Earth.

Like many things in life, it's almost never a straightforward matter of pointing an antenna on the roof at the spacecraft and pressing the "Push To Talk" button. Commands or data to be uplinked must first pass through a review, and perhaps even some simulations, to make sure that everything is correct. Then, the commands and data are passed to mission controllers who will schedule when the uplink occurs (or is "radiated," in space-speak). And finally, it goes into NASA's Deep Space Network (DSN) communications system and gets radiated out into space. But that wasn't the final step, because in the case of *Phoenix* it had to be relayed by one of the orbiters now circling Mars, since *Phoenix* did not have the ability to talk to Earth directly. When the orbiter rose over the horizon on Mars, *Phoenix* would listen for any new uplink data.

Downlink was just as convoluted. Again, the orbiter would act as a relay, receiving the data from *Phoenix* and then passing it on to one of NASA's DSN antennas back on Earth. Then, it would make its way through various processing and relay steps until finally arriving at JPL. If it was image data, then the Mission Image Processing Laboratory (MIPL) at JPL would reassemble the images and make them available to the science teams eagerly awaiting the pictures at the science operations center at the University of Arizona.

Phoenix carried three primary cameras for surface science imaging: the Stereo Surface Imager (or SSI, with two CCDs), the Robotic Arm Camera (the RAC, with a single CCD), and the MECA Optical Microscope (OM) camera (again, a single CCD identical to the one used in the RAC). Figure 3-2 shows the flight model of the SSI, and Figure 3-3 shows the RAC attached to the robotic arm. The OM was tucked away inside the enclosure of the MECA instrument, which itself resembled a black box mounted on the upper deck surface of the lander.

The challenge was to devise a way to download the image data from each of the cameras, store the data in a pre-allocated memory location, process the data to remove known pixel defects, crop and/or scale the images, perform any commanded compression, and then slice-and-dice it all up into packets for hand-off to the main computer's downlink manager task for transmission back to Earth.

Each $1,024 \times 1,024$ pixel CCD in the SSI was capable of generating 2 megabytes of data, or 1 megapixel of 12-bit pixel values. Because it was a true stereo camera, the imagers in the SSI were often referred to as "eyes." Plus, it did look a bit like an old-fashioned robot's

FIGURE 3-2. *The Stereo Surface Imager (Image credit: University of Arizona/NASA/JPL). (See Color Plate 11.)*

head. The RAC and OM cameras each contained a single 512×256 pixel CCD imager, and each generated 131,072 pixel values (or 262,144 bytes) of data (from now on I'll refer to both as the RAC/OM, because from the imaging software's point of view, they were identical imagers). Only 12 bits were actually used for each pixel worth of data from the CCD imagers, and what to do with the remaining 4 unused bits in a standard 16-bit "word" of memory generated some interesting discussions during the design phase, which I'll address in the next section. All of the images generated by SSI, RAC, and OM were monochrome, not color. Color was synthesized during processing back on Earth using separate images taken with either filters or special illumination.

I should note here that while the imaging software controlled the OM CCD to acquire images, it had nothing to do with the control of the MECA instrument and the electromechanical control of the optical microscope itself. That was handled by a separate realtime task written by the MECA team at JPL.

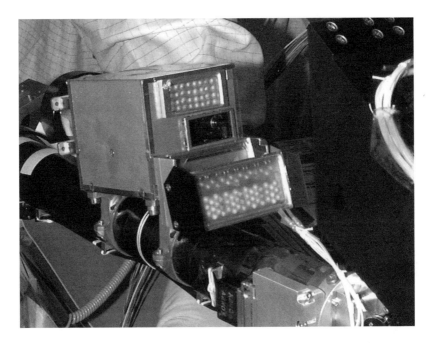

F I G U R E 3 - 3 . The Robotic Arm Camera (Image credit: University of Arizona/Max Planck/NASA/JPL).

Although 1 megapixel doesn't sound like much by the standards of today's consumer digital cameras, the CCD imagers used on *Phoenix* were custom-made for science imaging. Each CCD in the cameras cost tens of thousands of dollars, and only a limited number were ever made. They were reliable, robust, and precise, and each individual CCD was exhaustively tested and characterized pixel-by-pixel for sensitivity, noise, and defects, among other things. It is this level of characterization, and the reference data it generates, that sets a scientific CCD apart from the devices used in consumer cameras. Accurate characterization is what allows a researcher to have a high level of confidence that the image data accurately represents the scene that the camera captured. It is also a major contributor to the cost.

To Pack or Not to Pack

As with any highly constrained embedded system, the software needed to meet both its operational requirements and the constraints of its execution environment. As one might expect, these were not always complementary conditions, so trade-off decisions had to be made along the way. Both the SSI and the RAC/OM cameras utilized 12-bit conversion for the pixel data, which led to the first major trade-off decision: data packing. For a general high-level overview of binary data, see the sidebar "Binary Data" on page 41.

During the early design phase of the mission, the notion of packing the 12-bit pixel data came up and generated some interesting discussions. Given that only a limited amount of memory was available for image data storage, the concept of packing the 12-bit pixel data

into 16-bit memory space was appealing. By *packing*, I'm referring to storing the 12-bit pixel data contiguously, without any "wasted" bits in between—in effect ignoring 16-bit memory boundaries. But more efficient data storage came at the cost of increased processing time (unpacking, shifting, repacking). A digital image is an array (whether it's treated as a 1-D array or a 2-D array depends on what is being done to it), so any operation on an image involved handling the image data utilizing one or more algorithmic loops working through the array. The amount of data we were planning to push through the RAD6000 was significant, and even at the full-out clock rate of 20 MHz it was going to be painfully slow, so every CPU cycle counted.

In the end it was decided to "waste" a bit of memory and store each 12-bit pixel in a 16-bit memory location to keep things simple and avoid using any more CPU time than necessary. This decision was also driven by the desire, established early on, to avoid the use of multiple large processing buffers or result arrays by doing all image processing and compression in-place. Data packing would have made this rather challenging, and the resulting code would have been overly complex and could have shot down the whole in-place processing concept we wanted to implement.

BINARY DATA

Data is information. In computer systems it is represented numerically, since that it what the CPU in a computer deals with. Data can represent text, wherein each character has a unique numeric value, or it can represent images by encoding each pixel, or picture element, in an image with a numeric value representing its intensity, its color, or a combination of both characteristics. Given an appropriate numerical encoding scheme, a computer can process any type of data one might care to imagine, including audio, electrical potentials, text, images, or even the set of characteristics that define the differences between dogs and cats. But no matter what it represents, to the computer it's all just numbers. We supply the rules for how it will be encoded, processed, displayed, and interpreted.

Data also comes in a variety of sizes, depending on what it represents. For example, a window or door switch in a burglar alarm system needs only a single bit (or binary digit) to represent its two possible states: open or closed, 0 or 1. To represent a character in the English alphabet and punctuation, one needs about 100 numbers or so, each represented by 8 bits of data. Modern computers work in base 2, so 8 bits could represent any number from 0 to 255 ($11001000_2 = 200_{10}$, for example). In many computers there are preferred sizes for values expressed in base 2, typically in multiples of either 8 or 16 bits. In a 16- or 32-bit CPU, like the one used on *Phoenix*, memory can be efficiently accessed in "words" of 16 bits. Trying to access fewer bits than this (such as 8 bits) may actually be inefficient, so data that is greater than 8 bits in size but less than 16 bits is often stored in a 16-bit memory location along with some unused bits. This is how the image data on *Phoenix* was handled, because the electronics for the CCD imagers produced 12-bit-per-pixel data, but the spacecraft's memory was organized as either 16- or 32-bit storage locations.

The Three Tasks

In the VxWorks RTOS environment used for *Phoenix*, there really isn't anything that is synonymous to what a typical computer user might think of as individual programs. Nothing is loaded from a disk (there are no disks), and everything the computer will ever do is loaded into memory when the system first starts. It's actually all just one big program with a lot of smaller subprograms running more or less at the same time. These smaller subprogram activities are referred to as *tasks*, or *threads*, and they execute based on the availability of resources such as timed events or I/O (input/output) devices, and their assigned priority in the greater scheme of things (high-priority tasks get the chance to run more often than low-priority activities).

It was obvious from the outset that a minimum of two tasks would be needed for the surface image processing, one for each of the cameras. The SSI and RAC/OM were very different beasts, with different command sets and different operating characteristics. The SSI used all new controller hardware and incorporated CCD imagers identical to those used on the Mars Rovers. The RAC and OM imagers were originally built by the Max Planck Institute in Germany, and had been around for a while (one of the original designs was flown on the Huygens probe that landed on Titan). The RAC/OM controller hardware was actually a flight spare unit from the ill-fated Mars '98 mission, which apparently met a tragic end when its descent engines shut off prematurely a few hundred feet above the surface of Mars. But the data from each camera still needed to be processed, compressed, and then downlinked, and these operations weren't dependent on the physical data source. The image data was all 12 bits per pixel, and all that really varied was the geometry (height and width), and consequently how much image data would need to be handled.

Although there was a desire on the part of the spacecraft integration team (Lockheed Martin) to try to keep the number of science instrument tasks to a minimum, it became obvious early on that it didn't make much sense to duplicate the same image compression and downlink functions in both camera tasks. This would be wasteful in terms of limited program storage space, and it would effectively double the effort necessary to make changes in the code and then verify those changes. Consequently, a decision was made to use three tasks: one task would handle the SSI, one would deal with the RAC and OM cameras (one or the other, but not both at the same time, because the interface hardware wouldn't allow it), and a third would act as a shared resource to perform image compression and downlink processing using the data generated by the two camera control tasks, and it would run asynchronously. So while the SSI and RAC/OM tasks interfaced with the control electronics to acquire image data, control the internal temperature of the cameras, and perform motion control, the third task would do nothing but image data processing and downlink.

The image processing task was called the ICS, which stood for Image Compression SubSystem, although it ended up doing more than just compressing image data. A block diagram of the three tasks and the communications among them is shown in Figure 3-4.

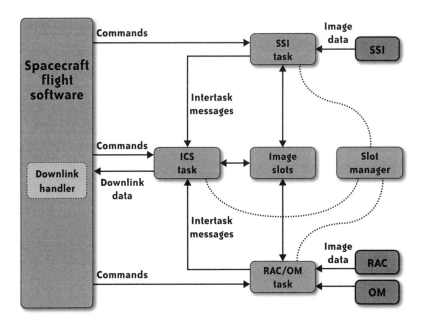

FIGURE 3-4. Imaging flight software tasks.

The decision to use three tasks did increase the level of complexity in the system, but it also reduced the amount of program storage space required. As an added bonus, having a third independent task made it much easier to make a change to a particular ICS processing function, and then test the functionality with data from either of the imaging tasks using real camera hardware or from a simulated image data source. This turned out to be a boon when doing extensive compression testing later on in the project, when over 15,000 test images were processed back-to-back through the ICS to verify its operation using an automated test setup.

The ICS also included two source modules, which contained shared functions for static memory management (known as the "slot manager") and image manipulation (decimation, subframing, pixel defect correction, and so on). These were not actually part of the ICS task, but rather served as thread-safe pseudolibraries to support the two camera control tasks and the ICS task. The reality was that there really wasn't any other convenient place to put this code, given the architecture constraints imposed on the instrument software, so it ended up with the ICS.

Slotting the Images

I mentioned earlier that the amount of memory available to each of the various instrument tasks was limited, but just how limited may be surprising to some, given that it is now commonplace to find 500 megabytes or even a gigabyte (or more) in a desktop PC. The initial memory allocation to both the SSI and RAC/OM tasks for image data storage was 230K short of a full 10 megabytes (10,255,360 bytes, to be exact). There was discussion of

increasing this after the spacecraft landed, which meant that any memory management scheme had to be flexible, but this was the design baseline. The default storage scheme needed to be able to handle at least four SSI images (or two pairs, consisting of one image for each "eye") and at least four RAC/OM images, all in the same memory space. The odd size meant that it wouldn't be possible to squeeze in more than four full-size SSI images, at least not initially.

In embedded systems, the use of dynamic memory allocation is usually considered to be a Really Bad Idea. To avoid issues with fragmented memory, memory leaks, null pointers, mystery crashes, and the possibility of losing the mission completely, the use of dynamic memory allocation (C's malloc function and its kin) was forbidden by the flight software coding rules. This meant that the imaging software had to manage the image data itself within whatever amount of memory was assigned to it, and it had to be robust and reliable.

The solution was the use of a set of functions that acted as a memory manager for the pre-allocated memory assigned to the ICS at boot-time. The memory manager was the key component of the image data processing. To prevent collisions, blocking semaphores were used to control shared access by each of the three imaging tasks (actually, any task in the spacecraft software could have used the shared memory, but only the cameras did so).

The static memory allocation was divided up into "slots," which could be either large enough to hold a full-size SSI image, or a smaller size for RAC/OM images. Figure 3-5 shows the default organization of the ICS image storage space.

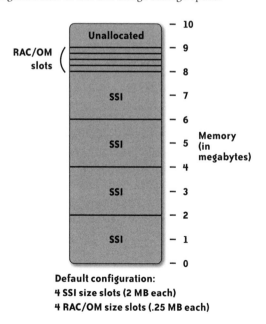

Default configuration:
4 SSI size slots (2 MB each)
4 RAC/OM size slots (.25 MB each)

FIGURE 3-5. Default image slot assignments.

This is only one possible configuration, and the number of each type of slot could be changed on the fly via commands uplinked from Earth.

Each image also had an associated structure containing header data. The image header recorded things such as a code defining the camera that generated the image, the exposure time, the image processing options selected, the image dimensions, optical filters that may have been used, and how the image was compressed (if compression was used). Part of the header was filled in by the instrument task that generated the image, and the remainder was filled in by the ICS prior to sending the image data to the spacecraft downlink handler. Because the header data was not image data per se, it was stored in a separate set of slots until it was time to do the downlink operation. Each image slot and its associated header data had to be tracked and processed in tandem.

The memory manager was basically just a set of functions that operated on a set of arrays of structures, as shown in Figure 3-6. The current state of the memory slots was maintained by the arrays, which, in essence, constituted a dynamic model of the physical memory space and its contents.

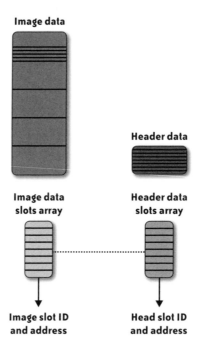

FIGURE 3-6. Memory slot manager arrays.

One of the arrays contained structures for image data, one per image slot. The C typedef for the structure is:

```
typedef struct {
    uint16_t    slot_status;      /**< Owned or unowned            */
    int16_t     slot_owner;       /**< -1 if slot is unowned       */
    int16_t     slot_size;        /**< either RAC/OM or SSI sized  */
    uint16_t    *slot_address;    /**< address of data space of slot */
} ics_img_slot_entry_t;
```

The second array contained structures pointing to header data entries, and its definition is:

```
typedef struct {
    uint16_t    slot_status;                /**< Owned or unowned               */
    int16_t     slot_owner;                 /**< -1 if unowned                  */
    int16_t     img_id;                     /**< associated image data slot number */
    uint16_t    hdr_data[ICS_HDR_SLOT_SZ];  /**< array for header data          */
} ics_hdr_slot_entry_t;
```

Notice that the header structure contains an entry for the image ID. This was essential, since slots could be allocated and released in any order, and there was no guarantee that the index of an image slot entry would be the same index for its associated header slot. Rather than rely on the index offset into the arrays always being in sync, the image ID was used to bind image and header data entries together.

The ability to dynamically reconfigure the image slot assignments allowed the memory manager to be tailored to specific mission activities. If the plan for a particular day on Mars (or a Sol, as it was called) involved imaging with the SSI, then one could configure the slots to minimize the number of RAC/MECA size allocations, which was the default configuration. If, on the other hand, the plan involved a lot of RAC or OM images, the memory could be configured to handle no SSI images and up to 39 of the smaller image sizes.

Passing the Image: Communication Among the Three Tasks

Image data fresh from one of the cameras was written into a slot by one of the camera tasks. After performing any required pixel correction or subframe operations, the camera task notified the ICS that a new image was available for processing. The ICS would then perform any commanded compression (either lossy or lossless) in place on the image within its slot, and then package and hand off the data for downlink. Only after the downlink was complete would the slot be released and become available for a new image. The sequence of events from exposure to image hand-off for the SSI camera is shown in Figure 3-7.

The entire sequence of events shown in Figure 3-6 was contingent on the availability of an image slot. If a slot was not available, the camera task would wait for a configurable period of time to allow the ICS to finish compressing and downlinking an image, which would result in a slot becoming available. If the ICS didn't release a slot within that period of time, the instrument task would generate an error message for the operators back on Earth and drop the image on the floor (there really wasn't any place else to drop it).

Once one of the camera instrument tasks obtained a slot, it "owned" that slot until it was handed off to the ICS, which then became the owner. Ownership verification was based on the slot ID (its number) assigned by the slot manager when the slot was initially allocated, an image ID code, and the camera instrument task ID. When a hand-off was made to the ICS, it verified that the ID codes presented matched those already recorded for that particular image slot.

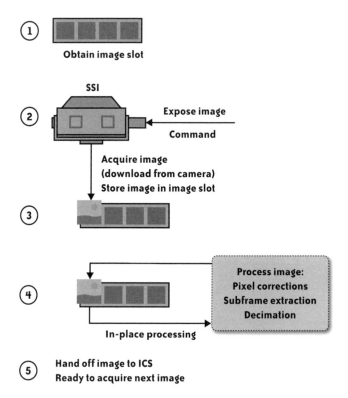

① Obtain image slot

SSI

② Expose image
Command

Acquire image
(download from camera)
Store image in image slot

③

④ Process image:
Pixel corrections
Subframe extraction
Decimation

In-place processing

⑤ Hand off image to ICS
Ready to acquire next image

FIGURE 3-7. Image acquisition and hand-off sequence.

As mentioned earlier, the ICS ran asynchronously and was not tightly bound to either of the camera tasks. It was able to do this by leveraging the built-in message queue system in VxWorks, and through the use of the shared functions in the memory slot manager. Figure 3-8 shows a message sequence chart (MSC) type of representation of the steps involved along the way in getting data from a camera to finally sending it to downlink.

The use of the internal message queue (the S/C FSW process line, which stands for *spacecraft flight software*) allowed either camera task to issue a command to the ICS using the same mechanism as the commands uplinked from Earth. The command would sit in the queue until the ICS was done with its current activity. The cameras could continue to acquire images as long as there were slots available to store the image data, and the ICS would retrieve and process the data in turn until the queue was empty, without regard for what the cameras might be doing.

Note that Figure 3-8 doesn't show the error checking that went on during imaging activities. All in all, the number of lines of code dedicated to error checking and fault handling was roughly equal to the lines of code that actually processed or otherwise handled the data. Failure Mode, Effects, and Criticality Analysis (FMECA) techniques were employed early in the design life cycle and provided guidance during the implementation of the software and its fault-handling capabilities.

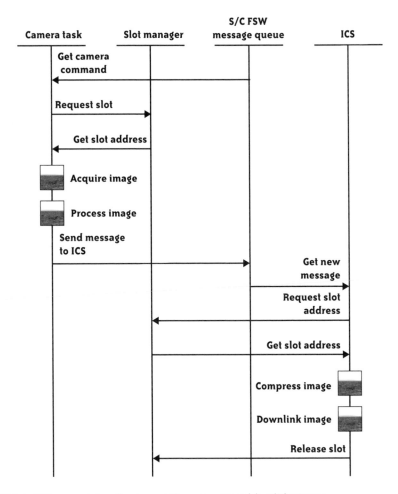

FIGURE 3-8. MSC representation of image acquisition, processing, and downlink activities.

The ICS serialized the data stream, but the use of the image slots and the command message queue allowed sets of images to be acquired in rapid (relatively speaking) succession. It also meant that there was some timing margin available for image acquisition that reduced the chances of operations being suspended while waiting for an image to be downlinked. Early test command sequences demonstrated that it was possible to do things like creating short "movies" (well, sort of, since it took about six seconds to download each image from one of the SSI cameras), or generate a large (30+ images) data set using the RAC or OM at different focal lengths.

Getting the Picture: Image Download and Processing

A lot went on between the time an image exposure occurred and the eventual hand-off to the ICS. Each camera in the system had its own control electronics to process commands, convert the analog signals from a CCD into 12-bit digital values, and then store the data in a hardware buffer until the flight software could download it into an image slot.

All this occurred under the control of logic embedded in radiation-hardened programmable gate array devices.

Once an image was acquired from a camera and written into an image slot, it was subjected to various forms of processing, all of which occurred in-place within the confines of an image slot. No additional large (image-sized) buffers were used for the processing or the results thereof, and only a few small buffers were necessary to hold intermediate results. The use of in-place processing was a key factor in the design of the imaging software, and allowed the three tasks to maintain a small memory footprint in the overall system. Figure 3-9 shows a comparison between a multiple-buffer approach and the single buffer (i.e., slot) in-place design used for the *Phoenix* imaging flight software.

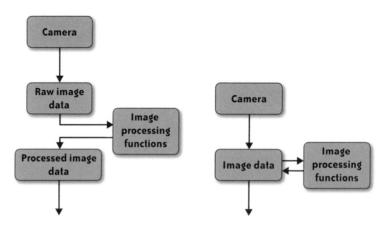

FIGURE 3-9. *Multiple data buffers versus a single data buffer.*

This was another design trade-off that was made early on in order to meet the image processing requirements and still stay within the amount of memory allocated to the cameras. Although it did meet the memory requirements, the downside was that there would be no "undo" operation. As shown in Figure 3-10, if an error occurred during image processing, either the entire image would be lost or a partially garbled image might be returned.

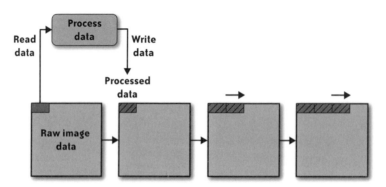

FIGURE 3-10. *In-place data processing.*

The processing algorithms walked through the data in an image slot, reading, processing, and then writing the data back. Some of the algorithms, such as pixel corrections, didn't change the geometry of the image but instead simply modified a single pixel value based on an uplinked table of known "bad" pixels (a pixel might be bad because it is not as sensitive as its neighbors, or it might be too sensitive). In the environment of space, it was expected that the odd cosmic ray could possibly blast through a pixel on a CCD and render it defective. Other operations, such as subframing, extracted a region from the original image, wrote it back into the slot, and adjusted the height and width parameters accordingly. Decimation employed a mathematical averaging technique to reduce image size by processing pixels in groups of 4, 9, or 16 to generate a single result pixel. The resulting images were reduced by 1/2, 1/3, or 1/4 in size, respectively, while minimizing the "stair-step" effect often seen with images that have been reduced using a subsampling technique wherein every 2nd, 3rd, or 4th pixel is retained and the rest discarded. This operation also wrote the modified data back into the image slot and adjusted the geometry parameters accordingly.

After an imaging task had completed the commanded processing, it would then send a message to the ICS (as described previously) and move on to the next command in the message queue. If an image slot was available, this could result in acquiring yet another image.

Image Compression

Just as the data produced by a robotic mission is precious, so is the communications bandwidth needed to return that data. For smaller images, such as those reduced by subframe or decimation operations, it could be acceptable to just downlink the image without compression. Larger images, such as the full-size SSI images, would consume a lot of downlink bandwidth, so compression was always considered as an option in such cases.

The ICS provided two forms of compression and two forms of size reduction using pixel mapping and scaling. Which type of compression or reduction would be used for a particular image depended largely on the level of image fidelity deemed necessary for the object of interest. In some cases, 8 bits per pixel would suffice; in other cases, the loss of fidelity inherent with JPEG compression was acceptable; and for the cases where the image had to retain as much fidelity as possible, there was a lossless compression method available.

In the ICS, a JPEG compressor, using all integer math and in-place operations, provided so-called "lossy" compression. JPEG is considered lossy because it discards some of the image data as a result of the compression process. It could compress image data to varying degrees by command. The final code was loosely based on the JPEG compressor flown on the Mars '98 mission, although only a part of that original code survived in the ICS for *Phoenix*. The original JPEG compressor used floating-point math, multiple full-size image arrays as buffers, and dynamic memory allocation. How that ever managed to make it into flight software is still a mystery to me, but it did. The use of floating-point values to represent

pixel data in the compression code also meant that it consumed four times as much memory per image as the native 16-bit integer representation of the original image.

A second form of compression, known as Rice Lossless or just Rice compression, used an algorithm developed by Robert Rice of the Jet Propulsion Laboratory. The Rice algorithm could compress image data by almost 2:1 with no data loss, whereas the JPEG algorithm discarded data during the compression. The Rice compression also operated on the image in-place in the image slot.

The two noncompression reduction methods used either a lookup table to map 12-bit pixel values to 8-bit values, or a bit reduction method that shifted the pixel data right by 4 bits to yield an 8-bit-per-pixel image. Both the JPEG and Rice compression functions would accept either 12- or 8-bit image data.

The decision to use the lossy JPEG compression or not typically came down to weighing various factors such as how accurate the data needed to be, how much bandwidth would be available, how much downlink storage was available in the spacecraft's main computer, and how much time was available to perform the compression (recall that the RAD6000 had a top speed of 20 MHz, so compressing a megapixel of image data could take over a minute).

When using the JPEG compression, the amount of compression to be applied was determined by a command parameter that specified the worst-case reduction ratio for the final data. In other words, instead of specifying a "quality" factor (which is typically how one tells a JPEG compressor how hard to work on an image), the ICS used a scaling factor and worked out the required compression level on its own. This was based on a quick-look analysis of the overall image entropy. The image entropy was an estimate of how "busy" the image was, and images with a higher level of entropy (lots of details and changes in brightness, such as a pebble-strewn patch of ground with sharp shadows) would require a higher compression setting to meet the final size goal. Images with low entropy, such as the Martian sky with a few clouds drifting by, wouldn't have a whole lot going on, and so would require a lesser amount of compression to meet the size target.

The scaling factor for JPEG compression was also used to divide the original image into segments. These segments were then fed into the JPEG compressor one at a time, and the output was written back into the image slot. The final result in the image slot prior to downlink was a set of small, self-contained JPEG images, the total size of which was equal to or less than the commanded size reduction ratio for the original image.

The Rice compressor included its own embedded method of segmentation, and it was downlinked by simply reading out the compressed data in the form of small packets sized to fit neatly into the flash memory in the spacecraft's main computer. The output of the lookup table and bit-reduction methods was also simply read out in flash-sized packets for downlink.

Downlink, or, It's All Downhill from Here

The last step in the process was the hand-off to the downlink manager in the spacecraft flight software. Some science instruments could simply pass their data to downlink and be done with it, but because of the large amount of data and the use of packetization, the ICS ended up doing a lot of downlink preprocessing on its own.

For the JPEG data, this meant handling each of the compressed segments individually. The first and last segments in a sequence always included a full-sized image data header. The intermediate segments got a smaller form of the header data, which included an image ID code and a sequence number. As each segment was read from the image slot, the header data was applied. The use of a sliding window form of readout allowed the segments to be packed end-to-end while assembling a flash-sized packet. This in turn allowed the downlink handler to maximize the use of the temporary flash storage space, because some of the compressed segments could be smaller than others if the part of the image corresponding to a segment had a low entropy. In fact, it was common to see compressed segment sizes vary widely, so packing them end-to-end avoided wasting any of the on-board flash memory.

Because the data consisted of uniquely identified segments, the loss of a downlink packet wouldn't consign the entire image to the garbage. The reconstruction and decompression software back on the ground at JPL could figure out what segments were missing and simply fill in the missing part of the image with black zero-value pixel data. If the missing data showed up later (which was possible, considering the rather torturous route the data took on its way down), then it could be placed into the image to fill in the missing pixels.

Once the data was passed to the downlink handler, the ICS was done, and it would release the image data slot. The entire process—from image exposure to completion of downlink hand-off—took between 3 to 10 minutes, depending on the CPU speed and what other additional imaging activities where slated to occur, such as auto-exposure and sun-finding (which are complex topics in their own right, so I haven't discussed them here).

Conclusion

The instrument software did much more than just take pictures and process image data. It also managed motion control with three degrees of freedom for the SSI, and the focus and viewport cover motors in the RAC. The RAC also supported multiple banks of red, blue, and green LEDs to illuminate whatever might be in the robotic arm scoop and create color images. Both the SSI and the RAC incorporated active thermal control, achieved either through the use of special heaters or by intentionally stalling a stepper motor to achieve self-heating. On top of all this, there was the error-checking and fault-recovery code. All in all, it was very busy software.

If I had it to do all over again, I suppose the main thing I would want to see changed would be that the cameras use their own embedded processors rather than rely on the spacecraft CPU. This would have made things much easier all around for everyone. Apart from that, I always felt that there was too much crammed into each of the instrument tasks. In other words, the thermal control should have been a separate task for each camera. This would have greatly reduced the complexity of each of the tasks, albeit at the expense of increasing the overall complexity of the intertask communications. At the outset, however, there wasn't enough evidence to build a compelling case for this, so the design was already firm (not really frozen, just very inflexible) by the time some new thermal requirements popped up that needed to be accommodated.

And, finally, I really had issues with the method chosen for performing a "heartbeat" check. I didn't know going in that the command message queue was going to be used for this purpose. What this did was impose a requirement on the instrument tasks to be able to drop whatever they were doing in order to check the command message queue on a regular basis for a "ping" message. I believe that a much better approach would have been for the instrument to register a callback function with the spacecraft flight software that could be used to check the value of a continuously updated counter variable on an asynchronous basis. If the value didn't change after some amount of time, the instrument task was probably hung. There was indeed a rather big squabble over this, but in the end the ping message was used simply because that's what had always been done and that's what the existing test systems were designed to handle. So even though the system wasn't designed to deal with tasks that could take minutes to process large amounts of image data, it wasn't going to be changed.

The *Phoenix* SSI and RAC/OM imaging software was a lot of work to design, implement, and test, and in the end it did what it was supposed to do for the entire life of the mission. Figure 3-11 is one of the first images (SS001EDN896308958_10D28R1M1) returned from the SSI on Sol 1, the spacecraft's first full day on Mars.

FIGURE 3-11. Image returned from the SSI on Sol I (Image credit: NASA/JPL/University of Arizona).

LEARNING MORE ABOUT PHOENIX

If you would like to know about the *Phoenix* mission, these are the primary places to start:

- *Phoenix* website at the University of Arizona: *http://phoenix.lpl.arizona.edu*
- *Phoenix* website at the Jet Propulsion Laboratory: *http://www.jpl.nasa.gov/news/phoenix/main.php*
- NASA's *Phoenix* website: *http://www.nasa.gov/mission_pages/phoenix/main/index.html*

At JPL, the MIPL folks do a lot of image processing for a variety of missions. You can learn more about what they do here:

- JPL's Mission Image Processing Laboratory: *http://www-mipl.jpl.nasa.gov/*

And if you would like to learn more about the RAD6000 CPU, image processing, or embedded systems, be sure to check out Wikipedia at *http://www.wikipedia.org*.

CHAPTER FOUR

Cloud Storage Design in a PNUTShell

Brian F. Cooper, Raghu Ramakrishnan, and Utkarsh Srivastava

Introduction

YAHOO! RUNS SOME OF THE WORLD'S MOST POPULAR WEBSITES, AND EVERY MONTH OVER HALF A BILLION people visit those sites. These websites are powered by database infrastructures that store user profiles, photos, restaurant reviews, blog posts, and a remarkable array of other kinds of data. Yahoo! has developed and deployed mature, stable database architectures to support its sites, and to provide low-latency access to data so that pages load quickly.

Unfortunately, these systems suffer from some important limitations. First, adding system capacity is often difficult, requiring months of planning and data reorganization, and impacting the quality of service experienced by applications during the transition. Some systems have a hard upper limit on the scale they can support, even if sufficient hardware were to be added. Second, many systems were designed a long time ago, with a single datacenter in mind. Since then, Yahoo! has grown to a global brand with a large user base spread all over the world. To provide these users with a good experience, we have to replicate data to be close to them so that their pages load quickly. Since the database systems did not provide global replication as a built-in feature, applications had to build it themselves, resulting in complex application logic and brittle infrastructure. Because of all the effort required to deploy a large-scale, geographically replicated database architecture, it was hard to quickly roll out new applications or new features of existing applications that depended on that architecture.

PNUTS is a system that aims to support Yahoo!'s websites and application platforms and address these limitations (Cooper et al. 2008). It is designed to be operated as a storage cloud that efficiently handles mixed read and write workloads from tenant applications and supports global data replication natively. Like many other distributed systems, PNUTS achieves high performance and scalability by horizontally partitioning the data across an array of storage servers. Complex analysis or decision-support workloads are not our focus. Our system makes two properties first-class features, baked in from the start:

Scale-out
> Data is partitioned across servers, and adding capacity is as easy as adding new servers. The system smoothly transfers load to the new servers.

Geo-replication
> Data is automatically replicated around the world. Once the developer tells the system at which colos* to replicate the data, the system takes care of the details of making it happen, including the details of handling failures (of machines, links, and even entire colos).

We also set several other goals for the system. In particular, we want application developers to be able to focus on the logic of their application, not on the nuts and bolts of operating the database. So we decided to make the database hosted, and to provide a simple, clean API to allow a developer to store and access data without having to tune a large number of parameters. Because the system is to be hosted, we wanted to make it as self-maintainable as possible.

While all of these goals are important to us, building a database system that could both scale-out and globally replicate data was the most compelling and immediate value proposition for the company. And as we began to design the system, it became clear that this required us to rethink many well-understood and long-used mechanisms in database systems (Ramakrishnan and Gehrke 2002).

The key idea we use to achieve both scale-out and geo-replication is to carry out only simple, cheap operations synchronously, and to do all the expensive heavy lifting asynchronously in the background. For example, when a user in California is trying to tag a photo with a keyword, she definitely does not want to wait for the system to commit that tag to the Singapore replica of the tag database (the network latency from California to Singapore can be as high as a second). However, she still wants her friend in Singapore to be able to see the tag, so the Singapore replica must be updated asynchronously in the background, quickly (in seconds or less) and reliably.

As another example of how we leverage asynchrony, consider queries such as aggregations and joins that typically require examining data on many different servers. As we scale out, the probability that some of these servers are slow or down increases, thereby adversely affecting request latency. To remedy this problem, we can maintain materialized

---

* *Colo*cation facility, or data center. Yahoo! operates a large number of these, spread across the world.

views that reorganize the base data so that (a predetermined set of) complex queries can be answered by accessing a single server. Similar to database replicas, updating each view synchronously would be prohibitively slow on writes. Hence, our approach is to update views asynchronously.

In the rest of this chapter, we explore the implications of focusing on scale-out and geo-replication as first-class features. We illustrate the main issues with an example, explain our basic approach, and discuss several issues and extensions. We then compare PNUTS with alternative approaches. Our discussion concentrates on the design philosophy, rather than the details of system architecture or implementation, and covers some features that are not in the current production version of the system in order to highlight the choices made in the overall approach.

Updating Data

As users interact with websites, their actions constantly result in database updates. The first challenge we examine is how to support this massive stream of updates while providing good performance and consistency for each update.

The Challenge

Imagine that we want to build a social networking site. Each user in our system will have a profile record, listing the user's name, hobbies, and so on. A user "Alice" might have friends all over the world who want to view her profile, and read requests must be served with stringent low-latency requirements. For this, we must ensure that Alice's profile record (and similarly, everyone else's) is globally replicated so those friends can access a local copy of the profile. Now say that one feature of our social network is that users can update their status by specifying free text. For example, Alice might change her status to "Busy on the phone," and then later change it to "Off the phone, anybody wanna chat?" When Alice changes her status, we write it into her profile record so that her friends can see it. The profile table might look like Table 4-1. Notice that to support evolving web applications, we must allow for a flexible schema and sparse data; not every record will have a value for every field, and adding new fields must be cheap.

TABLE 4-1. User profile table

Username	FullName	Location	Status	IM	BlogID	Photo	...
Alice	Alice Smith	Sunnyvale, CA	Off the phone, anybody wanna chat?	Alice345			...
Bob	Bob Jones	Singapore	Eating dinner		3411	me.jpg	...
Charles	Charles Adams	New York, New York	Sleeping		5539		...
...							

How should we update her profile record? A standard database answer is to make the update atomic by opening a *transaction*, writing all the replicas, and then closing the transaction by sending a commit message to all of the replicas. This approach, in line with the

standard ACID* model of database transactions, ensures that all replicas are properly updated to a new status. Even non-ACID databases, such as Google's BigTable (Chang et al. 2006), use a similar approach to synchronously update all copies of the data. Unfortunately, this approach works very poorly if we have geo-replication. Once Alice enters her status and clicks "OK," she may potentially wait a long time for her response page to load, as we wait for far-flung datacenters to commit the transaction. Moreover, to guarantee true atomicity, we would have to exclusive-lock Alice's status while the transaction is in progress, which means that other users will potentially be unable to see her status for a long time.

Because of the expense of atomic transactions in geographically separated replicas, many web databases take a *best-effort* approach: the update is written to one copy and then asynchronously propagated to the rest of the replicas. No locks are taken or validation performed to simulate a transaction. As the name "best-effort" implies, this approach is fraught with difficulty. Even if we can guarantee that the update is applied at all replicas, we cannot guarantee that the database ends in a consistent state. Consider a situation where Alice first updates her status to "Busy," which results in a write to a colo on the west coast of the U.S., as shown in Table 4-2.

TABLE 4-2. An update has been applied to the west coast replica

West coast		East coast	
Username	**Status**	**Username**	**Status**
Alice	Busy	Alice	--

She then updates her status to "Off the phone," but due to a network disruption, her update is directed to an east coast replica, as shown in Table 4-3.

TABLE 4-3. A second update has been applied to the east coast replica

West coast		East coast	
Username	**Status**	**Username**	**Status**
Alice	Busy	Alice	Off the phone

Since update propagation is asynchronous, a possible sequence of events is as follows: "Off the phone" is written at the east coast before the "Busy" update reaches the east coast. Then, the propagated updates cross over the wire, as shown in Table 4-4.

---

* A transaction's changes are Atomic, Consistent, Isolated from the effects of other concurrent transactions, and Durable.

TABLE 4-4. The two updates cross during propagation

West coast	
Username	Status
Alice	Busy

"Busy"
"Off the phone"

East coast	
Username	Status
Alice	Off the phone

The "Busy" status overwrites the "Off the phone" status on the east coast, while the "Off the phone" status overwrites the "Busy" status on the west coast, resulting in the state shown in Table 4-5.

TABLE 4-5. Inconsistent replicas

West coast	
Username	Status
Alice	Off the phone

East coast	
Username	Status
Alice	Busy

Depending on which replica her friends look at, Alice's status will be different, and this anomaly will persist until Alice changes her status again.

To deal with this problem, some web-scale data stores implement *eventual consistency*: while anomalies like that described earlier may happen temporarily, eventually the database will resolve inconsistency and ensure that all replicas have the same value. This approach is at the heart of systems such as S3 in Amazon's Web Services. Eventual consistency is often achieved using techniques such as gossip and anti-entropy. Unfortunately, although the database will eventually converge, it is difficult to predict which value it will converge to. Since there is no global clock serializing all updates, the database cannot easily know if Alice's last status update was "Busy" or "Off the phone," and thus may end up converging the record to "Busy." Just when Alice is ready to chat with her friends, all of them think that she is busy, and this anomaly persists until Alice changes her status again.

Our Approach

We have struck a middle ground between strong consistency (such as ACID transactions) with its scalability limitations, and weaker forms of consistency (such as best effort or eventual consistency) with their anomalies. Our approach is timeline consistency: all replicas will go through the same timeline of updates, and the order of updates is equivalent to the order in which they were made to the database. This timeline is shown in Figure 4-1. Thus, the database will converge to the same value at all replicas, and that value will be the latest update made by the application.

FIGURE 4-1. Timeline of updates to Alice's status.

Timeline consistency is implemented by having a master copy where all the updates are made, with the changes later propagated to other copies asynchronously. This master copy serializes the updates and ensures that each update is assigned a sequence number. The order of sequence numbers is the order in which updates should be applied at all replicas, even if there are transient failures or misorderings in the asynchronous propagation of updates. We have chosen to have a master copy per record since many Yahoo! applications rely on a single table in which different records correspond to different users, each with distinct usage patterns. It is possible, of course, to choose other granularities for mastership, such as a master per partition (e.g., based on a key) of records.

Even in a single table, different records may have master copies located in different servers. In our example, Alice, who lives on the west coast, has a record that is mastered there, whereas her friend Bob, who lives in Singapore, has his record mastered in the Asian replica. The mastership of the record is stored as a metadata field in the record itself, as shown in Table 4-6.

TABLE 4-6. Profile table with mastership and version metadata

Username	_MASTER	_VERSION	FullName	...
Alice	West	32	Alice Smith	...
Bob	Asia	18	Bob Jones	...
Charles	East	15	Charles Adams	...
...				

Of course, a master copy seems at odds with our principle that only cheap operations should be done synchronously. If Alice travels to New York and updates her status from there, she must wait for her update operation to be forwarded to the west coast, since her profile record is mastered there; such high-latency cross-continental operations are what we are trying to minimize. Such cross-colo writes do occur occasionally, because of shifting usage patterns (e.g., Alice's travel), but they are rare. We analyzed updates to Yahoo!'s user database and found that 85% of the time, record updates were made to the colo containing the master copy. Of course, Alice may move to the east coast or to Europe, and then her writes will no longer be local, as the master copy for her record is still on the west coast. Our system tracks where the updates for a record are originating, and moves mastership to reflect such long-standing shifts in access patterns, in order to ensure that most writes continue to be local. (We discuss mastership in more detail in the next section.)

When an application reads a record, it typically reads the local replica. Unless that replica is marked as the master copy, it may be stale. The application knows that the record instance is some consistent version from the timeline, but there is no way for the application to know from the record itself whether it is the most recent version. If the application absolutely must have the most recent version, we allow it to request an *up-to-date read*; this request is forwarded to the master to get the latest copy of the record. An up-to-date read is expensive, but the common case of reading the local (possibly stale) replica is cheap, again in line with our design principles. Luckily, web applications are often tolerant of stale data. If Alice updates her status and her friend Bob does not see the new status right away, it is acceptable, as long as Bob sees the new status shortly thereafter.

Another kind of read that the application can perform is a *critical read*, to make sure that data only moves forward in time from the user's perspective. Consider a case where Alice changes her avatar (a picture representing the user). Bob may look at Alice's profile page (resulting in a read from the database) and see the new avatar. Then, Bob may refresh the page, and due to a network problem, be redirected to a replica that has not yet seen Alice's avatar update. The result is that Bob will see an older version of the data than the version he just saw. To avoid these anomalies for applications that want to do so, the database returns a version number along with the record for a read call. This version number can be stored in Bob's session state or in a cookie in his browser. If he refreshes Alice's profile page, the previously read version number can be sent along with his request, and the database will ensure that a record that is no older than that version is returned. This may require forwarding to the master copy. A read that specifies the version number is called a "critical read," and any replica with that version, or a newer version, is an acceptable result. This technique is especially helpful for users that update and then read the database. Consider Alice herself: after she updates her avatar, she will become confused if we show her any page with her old avatar. Therefore, when she takes an action that updates the database (like changing her avatar), the application can use the critical read mechanism to ensure that we never show her older data.

We also support a *test-and-set* operation that makes a write conditional upon the read version being the same as some previously seen version (whose version number is passed in as a parameter to the test-and-set request). In terms of conventional database systems, this provides a special case of ACID transactions, limited to a single record, using optimistic concurrency control.

More on mastership

We employ various techniques to ensure that read and write operations go on smoothly and with low latency, even in the presence of workload changes and failures.

For example, as we mentioned earlier, the system implements *record-level* mastership. If too many writes to the record are originating from a data center other than the current master, the mastership of the record is promptly transferred to that data center, and subsequent writes are done locally there. Moreover, transferring mastership is a cheap operation and happens automatically, thereby allowing the system to adapt quickly to workload changes.

We also implement a mechanism that allows reads and writes to continue without interruption, even during storage unit failures. When a storage unit fails, an *override* is issued (manually or automatically) for that storage unit, signifying that another data center can now accept writes on behalf of the failed storage unit (for records previously mastered at the failed storage unit). We take steps (details omitted here) to ensure that this override is properly sequenced with respect to the updates done at the failed storage unit. This is done to guarantee that timeline consistency is still preserved when the other data center starts accepting updates on behalf of the failed storage unit.

In PNUTS, all read and write requests go through a routing layer that directs them to the appropriate copy (possibly the master) of the record. This level of indirection is a key to how we provide uninterrupted system availability. Even when a storage unit has failed and its data is recovered on to another storage unit, or record masters are moved to reflect usage patterns, these changes are transparent to applications, which still continue to connect to routers and enjoy uninterrupted system availability, with requests seamlessly routed to the appropriate location.

Supporting ordered data

Our system is architected to support both hash-partitioned and range-partitioned data. We call the hash version of our database *YDHT*, for Yahoo! Distributed Hash Table, and the ordered version is called *YDOT*, for Yahoo! Distributed Ordered Table. Most of the system is agnostic to how the data is organized. However, there is one important issue that is sensitive to physical data organization. In particular, hash-organized data tends to spread load out among servers very evenly. If data is ordered, portions of the key space that are more popular will cause hotspots. For example, if status updates are ordered by time, the most recent updates will be of most interest to users, and the server with the data partition at the end of the time range will be the most loaded. We cannot allow hotspots to persist without compromising system scale-out.

Logically ordered data is actually stored in partitions of physically contiguous records, but with partitions arranged without regard to order, possibly across physical servers. We can address the hotspot issue by moving partitions dynamically in response to load. If a few hot partitions are on the same server, we can move them to servers that are less loaded. Moreover, we can also dynamically split partitions, so that the load on a particularly hot single partition can be divided amongst several servers.* This movement and splitting of partitions across storage units is distinct from the mechanism mentioned previously for changing the location of the master copy of a record: in this case, changing the record master affects the latency of updates that originate at a server, but does not in general reduce the cumulative read and write workload on a given partition of records. A particular special case that requires splitting and moving partitions is when we want to update or insert a large number of records. In that case, if we are not careful we can create a sever load imbalance by sending large batches of updates to the same few servers. Thus, it is necessary to understand something about how the updates are distributed in the key space, and if necessary, preemptively split and move partitions to prepare for the upcoming onslaught of updates (Silberstein et al. 2008).

We insulate applications from the details of the physical data organization. For single record reads and writes, the use of a routing layer shields applications from the effects of partition movement and splitting. For range scans, we need to provide a further abstraction: imagine

---

* The observant reader may have noticed that if all updates affect the partition containing the end of the time range, splitting this partition will not solve the problem, and some measure such as sorting by a composite key, e.g., user and time, is required.

that we want to scan all registered users whose age is between 21 and 30. Answering this query may mean scanning a partition with several thousand records on one server, then a second partition on another server, and so on. Each partition of several thousand records can be scanned quickly, since they are sequentially ordered on disk. We do not want the application to know that we might be moving or splitting partitions behind the scenes. A good way to do this is to extend the *iterator* concept: when an application is scanning, we return a group of records, and then allow the application to come back when it is ready to ask for the next group. Thus, when the application has completed one batch and has asked for more, we can switch them to a new storage server that has the partition with the next group of records.

Trading off consistency for availability

Timeline consistency handles the common case efficiently and with clean semantics, but it is not perfect. Occasionally, an entire datacenter will go down (e.g., if the power is cut) or become unreachable (e.g., if the network cable is cut), and then any records mastered in that datacenter will become unwriteable. This scenario exposes the known trade-off between consistency, availability, and partition tolerance: only two of those three properties can be guaranteed at all times. Since our database is global, partitions will happen and cannot cause an outage, and thus in reality we only have a choice between consistency and availability. If a datacenter goes offline, possibly with some new updates that have not yet been propagated to other replicas, we can either preserve consistency by disallowing updates until the datacenter comes back, or we can preserve availability by violating timeline consistency and allowing some updates to be applied to a nonmaster record.

Our system gives the application the ability to make this choice on a per-table basis. If the application has chosen availability over consistency for a particular table, and a datacenter goes offline, the system temporarily transfers mastership of any unreachable records in that table. This decision effectively forks the timeline to favor availability. An example is shown in Figure 4-2. After the lost colo is restored, the system automatically reconciles any records that have had conflicting updates, and notifies the application of these conflicts. The reconciliation ensures that the database converges to the same value everywhere, even if the timeline is not preserved. On the other hand, if the application has chosen consistency over availability, mastership is not transferred and the timeline is preserved, but some writes will fail.

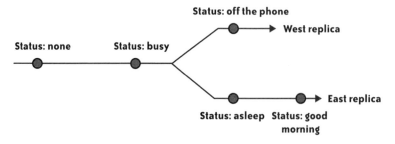

FIGURE 4-2. The west datacenter is offline, so the update timeline forks.

For certain operations, this trade-off between consistency and availability can be easier to manage. For example, imagine that an application wants to include polls, where users vote on various questions (like "What is your favorite color?") and the poll results are stored as counters in our database. Counter operations (like increment) are commutative, and can therefore be applied even to the nonmaster copy without breaking timeline consistency. Normally our replication mechanism transfers the new version of the record between replicas, but for commutative operations we would actually have to transmit the operation (e.g., increment). Then, whenever the master received the operation (either during normal operation or after a datacenter failure), it could apply it without worrying about whether it is out of order. The one restriction in this scheme is that we cannot mix commutative and noncommutative operations: setting the value of the counter at any time after the record inserted is forbidden, since we do not know how to properly order an increment and an overwrite of the value.

Another extension to our approach is to allow updates to multiple records. Many web workloads involve updates to a single record at a time, which is why we focused on timeline consistency at a per-record basis. However, it is occasionally desirable to update multiple records. For example, in our social networking application we might have binary friend links: if Alice and Bob are friends, then Alice appears in Bob's friend list and Bob appears in Alice's. When Alice and Bob become friends, we thus need to update two records. Because we do not provide ACID transactions, we cannot guarantee this update is atomic. However, we can provide *bundled writes*: with one call to the database, the application can request both writes, and the database will ensure that both writes eventually occur. To accomplish this, we log the requested writes, and the system retries the writes until they succeed. This approach preserves per-record timeline consistency, and since the retries can be asynchronous, preserves our performance goals.

In summary, timeline consistency provides a simple semantics for how record updates are propagated, and flexibility in how applications can trade-off read latency for currency. However, it does not support general ACID transactions—in particular, transactions that read and write multiple records.

Complex Queries

As web applications become more complex and interesting, they need to retrieve and combine information from the database in new and different ways. Next, we examine how to support those queries at a massive scale.

The Challenge

Our system is optimized for queries that touch one or just a few records. In particular, we can look up records by primary key; once we know Alice's username, it is straightforward to determine which partition contains her profile record and read it while loading her page. Also, our system can store data as hash-partitioned or range-partitioned tables. For range-partitioned tables, we can conduct range scans over ordered ranges of primary keys.

For example, we might store Alice's friends list by having one record per connection, where the primary key of each connection is the pair of user IDs for Alice and the friend (Table 4-7).

TABLE 4-7. Friends table

User1	User2	...
Alice	Bob	...
Alice	Charles	...
Alice	Dave	...
...		

In a range-partitioned table, all of the records prefixed with "Alice" will be clustered, and a short-range scan will be able to pick them up.

Now imagine that we want to add another feature to our social network site. Users can post photos and then comment on one another's photos. Alice might comment on Bob's photo, Charles's photo, and Dave's photo. When we display a photo, we want to show the set of comments associated with that photo. We also want to show Alice the set of comments she has made on other people's photos. We specify the primary key of the comments table as (PhotoID,CommentID) and store it as an ordered YDOT table (Table 4-8), so that all comments for the same photo are clustered and can be retrieved by a range query.

TABLE 4-8. Photo comments table

PhotoID	CommentID	Comment	Commenter
Photo123	18	Cool	Mary
Photo123	22	Pretty	Alice
Photo123	29	Interesting	Charles
...			

How can we collect the set of comments that Alice has made? We have to perform a join between Alice's profile record (which contains her username as a key) and the comment records (which have Alice's username as a foreign key). Because of our scale-out architecture, data is partitioned across many servers, so computing the join can require accessing many servers. This expensive operation drives up the latency of requests, both because multiple servers must be contacted and because a single query generates a great deal of server load (which slows down other requests).

Another type of query that can be expensive to compute in a scale-out system is group-by-aggregate queries. Imagine that users specify hobbies, and we want to count the number of users who have each hobby so that we can show Alice which hobbies are most popular. Such a query requires scanning all of the data and maintaining counts. The table scan will place prohibitive load on the system and certainly cannot be done synchronously, as Alice's page will take forever to load.

These examples show that while point lookups and range scans can be executed quickly, more expensive join and aggregation queries cannot be executed synchronously.

Our Approach

Our key principle for handling expensive operations is to do them asynchronously, but expensive queries cannot really be handled this way; we do not want to make Alice come back repeatedly to check whether the asynchronous query collecting all of her comments has completed.

Materialized views (Agarawal et al. 2009) can, however, be maintained asynchronously, and when Alice logs in she can quickly (and synchronously) query the view.* Although an asynchronously maintained view can be stale compared to the base data, the application already must be built to cope with stale replicas, so dealing with stale view data is usually acceptable. In fact, we treat a materialized view as a special kind of replica that both replicates and transforms data. By using the same mechanism that updates replicas to also update views, we ensure that views have similar reliability and consistency guarantees as replicated base data, without having to design and implement a second mechanism.

Even though view maintenance is done in the background, we still want to make it cheap. If view maintenance takes too many system resources, it will either disrupt synchronous read and write requests (adding latency to every query), or we will have to throttle it to run slowly, at which point the view will be so stale as to possibly be unusable. Thus, we have to find ways to make view maintenance efficient. Consider the earlier example where we want to show Alice all of the comments she has made on other people's photos. We will create a materialized view where comment data is reorganized to be clustered by the foreign key (username of the commenter) rather than the primary key. Then, all of the comments made by Alice will be clustered together. We can also place Alice's profile record in the view, keyed by her username, so that her profile and her comments are clustered. Computing the key/foreign key join is as easy as scanning the set of view records prefixed with "Alice", and then joining them. The result is shown in Table 4-9.

TABLE 4-9. Co-clustering joining profile and comment records

Alice	West	32	Alice Smith	...	← Profile record
Alice	Photo123	22	Pretty	...	← Comment records
Alice	Photo203	43	Nice	...	↓
Alice	Photo418	33	OK	...	
...					

Note that we do not prejoin the profile and comment records in the view. By merely co-locating records that would join, we make join maintenance cheap: whenever there is an update to a base record, we only have to update a single view record, even if that view record would join with multiple other records.

---

* Materialized views are not currently in the production version of the system.

How can we store profile and comment records in the same table? In a traditional database it would be difficult, since the two records have different schemas. However, a core feature of PNUTS is its ability to represent flexible schemas. Different records in the same table can have different sets of attributes. This feature is very useful in web applications since web data is often sparse; a database of items for sale will have different attributes (e.g., color, weight, RAM, flavor) depending on what kind of item it is. It turns out that flexible schemas are also key to implementing materialized join views so that we can colocate joining records from different tables.

The asynchronous view approach is useful for helping to answer other kinds of queries as well. A group-by-aggregation query can be effectively answered by a materialized view that has pregrouped, and maybe even preaggregated, the data. There are even "simple" queries, such as a selection over a nonprimary key attribute, that can be most effectively answered by a materialized view. Consider a query for users who live in Sunnyvale, California. Since our user table is keyed by username, this query normally requires an expensive table scan. However, we can use the materialized view mechanism to build a secondary index over the "location" field of the table, store the index in an ordered YDOT table, and then conduct a range scan over the "Sunnyvale, California" index records to answer our query (Table 4-10).

TABLE 4-10. Location index

Location	Username
Sunnyvale, CA	Alice
Sunnyvale, CA	Mary
Sunnyvale, CA	Steve
Sunnyvale, CA	Zach
...	

As with materialized views in other systems, we can create them effectively only if we know in advance what kinds of queries to expect. Luckily, in web-serving workloads, the queries are usually templates known in advance with specific parameters (such as the location or username) bound at runtime. As such, application developers know in advance which queries are complex enough to require materializing a view. To ask ad hoc queries over data stored in PNUTS, developers have to use our plug-ins to pull data out of our system into a compute grid running Hadoop, the open source implementation of MapReduce.

Once we have a few different mechanisms for handling complex queries, it will be useful to implement a query planner to help execute queries effectively. A planner helps remove some of the burden from the application developer, who can write declarative queries without worrying too much about how they will be executed. However, an effective query planner at our scale will require sophisticated statistics collection, load monitoring, network monitoring, and a variety of other mechanisms to make sure the planner has enough information about all the possible bottlenecks in the system to make the most effective query plan.

Comparison with Other Systems

When we began thinking about PNUTS, two other massive scale database systems from Google and Amazon had recently been announced, and a third from Microsoft would later be made public. As we developed our designs, we examined these other systems carefully to see whether some or all of their ideas could be useful to us. Some of the ideas from these systems influenced us, but we decided to build a new system with an architecture that was different in many ways. We now look at each of these systems and discuss why we decided to depart from their design principles.

Google's BigTable

BigTable (Chang et al. 2006) is a system designed to support many of Google's web applications. The system is based on horizontally partitioning a "big table" into many smaller tablets, and scattering those tablets across servers. This basic approach to scalability, as well as features such as flexible schema and ordered storage, are similar to the approach we took. However, there were several design decisions where we diverged from BigTable.

The first major difference was in our approach to replication. BigTable is built on top of the Google File System (GFS; Ghemawat et al. 2003), and GFS handles the replication of data by synchronously updating three copies of the data on three different servers. This approach works well in a single colo, where interserver latencies are low. However, synchronously updating servers in three different, widely dispersed colos is too expensive; Alice might wait a long time for her status to be updated, especially if her friends access a datacenter with a poor connection to the Internet backbone. To support cross-colo replication, we developed the timeline consistency model, and the associated mechanisms for mastership, load balancing, and failure handling.

We also decided not to enforce the separation between database server and filesystem that is enforced between BigTable and GFS. GFS was originally designed and optimized for scan-oriented workloads of large files (for example, for MapReduce). BigTable uses GFS by keeping a version history of each record, compacted into a file format called *SSTables* to save space. This means that on record reads and updates, the data must be decoded and encoded into this compressed format. Moreover, the scan-oriented nature of GFS makes BigTable useful for column-oriented scans (such as "retrieve all the locations of all the users"). In contrast, our primary workload is to read or update a single version of a single record or a small range of records. Thus, we store data on disk as complete records organized into a B-tree. This approach is optimized for quickly locating, and updating in-place, individual records identified by primary key.

PNUTS differs from BigTable in other ways as well. For example, we support multiple tables for an application, instead of one large table, and we support hash as well as ordered tables. A follow on to BigTable, called MegaStore (Furman et al. 2008), adds transactions, indexes, and a richer API, but still follows the basic architectural tenets of BigTable.

Amazon's Dynamo

Dynamo (DeCandia et al. 2007) is one of the systems Amazon has built recently for large-scale data workloads, and is the one most closely aligned with our goals of a highly available, massive scale structured record store. (Records in Dynamo are referred to as objects.) Dynamo provides write availability by allowing applications to write to any replica, and lazily propagating those updates to other replicas via a gossip protocol (explained next).

The decision to lazily propagate updates to deal with slow and failure-prone networks matches our own; however, our mechanism for replication is quite different. In a gossip protocol, an update is propagated to randomly chosen replicas, which in turn propagates it to other randomly chosen replicas. This randomness is essential to the probabilistic guarantees offered by the protocol, which ensures that most replicas are updated relatively quickly. In our setting, however, randomness is decidedly suboptimal. Consider an update Alice makes to her status in a colo on the west coast of the U.S. Under gossip, this update may be randomly propagated to a replica in Singapore, which then randomly propagates the update to a replica in Texas, which then randomly propagates the update to a replica in Tokyo. The update has crossed the Pacific Ocean three times, whereas a more deterministic approach could conserve scarce trans-Pacific backbone bandwidth and transfer it (and other updates) only once. Moreover, gossip requires the replica propagating the update to know which servers in which other colos have replicas, which makes it hard to move data between servers for load balancing or recovery.

Another key difference with Dynamo is the consistency protocol. Gossip lends itself to an eventual consistency model: all data replicas will eventually match, but in the interim, while updates are propagating, replicas can be inconsistent. In particular, replicas can have a state that is later deemed "invalid." Consider, for example, Alice, who updates her status from "Sleeping" to "Busy" and then updates her location from "Home" to "Work." Because of the order of updates, the only valid states of the record (from Alice's perspective, which is what matters) are (Sleeping,Home), (Busy,Home), and (Busy,Work). Under eventual consistency, if the two updates are made at different replicas, some replicas might receive the update to "Work" first, meaning that those replicas show a state of (Sleeping,Work) temporarily. If Alice's boss sees this status, Alice might be in trouble! Applications that rely on the application of multiple updates to a record in the proper order need a stronger guarantee than eventual consistency. Although our timeline consistency model allows replicas to be stale, even stale replicas have a consistent version that reflects the proper update ordering.

There are various other differences with Dynamo: Dynamo provides only a hash table and not an ordered table, and we have opted for a more flexible mapping of data to servers in order to improve load balancing and recovery (especially for ordered tables, which might have unpredictable hot spots). Amazon also provides other storage systems besides Dynamo: S3 for storing blobs of data, and SimpleDB for executing queries over structured, indexed data. Although SimpleDB provides a richer API, it requires that the application come up with a partitioning of the data such that each partition is within a fixed size limit. Thus, data growth within a partition is restricted.

Microsoft Azure SDS

Microsoft has built a massive scale version of SQL Server (called SQL Data Services or SDS) as part of its Azure services offering (*http://hadoop.apache.org*). Again, the focus is on scalability through horizontal partitioning. A nice feature of SDS is the enhanced query capabilities made available by extensively indexing data and providing SQL Server as the query-processing engine. However, SDS achieves this query expressiveness by rigidly enforcing partitioning: applications create their own partitions and cannot easily repartition data. Thus, although you can ask expressive queries over a partition, if a partition grows or becomes hot, the system cannot easily or automatically relieve the hotspot by splitting the partition. Our decision to hide partitioning behind the abstraction of a table allows us to make and change partitioning decisions for load and recovery reasons. While this means that our query model is less expressive (since we do not support complex queries which cross partitions), we are continuing to look at ways to enhance our query functionality (for example, through views, as described earlier).

Another difference with SDS is that PNUTS has geographic replication built in as a first-class feature of the system. In at least the first release of SDS, the workload is expected to live within a single datacenter, and remote copies are only used in case of a total failure of the primary replica. We want Alice's friends in Singapore, Berlin, and Rio de Janeiro to have their own local, first-class copies of Alice's updates.

Other Related Systems

A variety of other systems have been built by companies who have scalability and flexibility needs similar to ours. Facebook has built Cassandra (Lakshman et al. 2008), a peer-to-peer data store with a BigTable-like data model but built on a Dynamo-like infrastructure. Consequently, Cassandra provides only eventual consistency.

Sharded databases (such as the MySQL sharding approach used by Flickr [Pattishall] and Facebook [Sobel 2008]) provide scalability by partitioning the data across many servers; however, sharding systems do not typically provide as much flexibility for scaling or globally replicating data as we desire. Data must be prepartitioned, just like in SimpleDB. Also, only one of the replicas can be the master and accept writes. In PNUTS, all replicas in different data centers can accept writes (although for different records).

Other Systems at Yahoo!

PNUTS is one of several cloud systems that are being built at Yahoo!. Two other components of the cloud are also targeted at data management, although they focus on a different set of problems than PNUTS. Hadoop (*http://hadoop.apache.org*), an open source implementation of the MapReduce framework (Dean and Ghemawat 2007), provides massively parallel analytical processing over large datafiles. Hadoop includes a filesystem,

HDFS, which is optimized for scans, since MapReduce jobs are primarily scan-oriented workloads. In contrast, PNUTS is focused on reads and writes of individual records. Another system is MObStor, which is designed to store and serve massive objects such as images or video. MObStor's goal is to provide low-latency retrieval and inexpensive storage for objects that do not change. Since many applications need a combination of record storage, data analysis, and object retrieval, we are working on ways to seamlessly integrate the three systems. A survey of our efforts to integrate these systems into a comprehensive cloud is at (Cooper et al. 2009).

Conclusion

When we embarked on the PNUTS project, we had in mind a system that could seamlessly scale to thousands of servers and multiple continents. Building such a system required more than clever engineering; it required us to reopen many settled debates in the database field. Although it was a relatively easy decision to jettison ACID, we soon realized we had to develop something to replace it, and thus developed the timeline consistency model. Although the model is relatively simple by design, handling complex corner cases, developing an efficient implementation mechanism, and mapping application use cases to the model required deep thinking and many iterations. Another point to note is that at first our customers and we were relatively blasé about restricting ourselves to a simple query language. However, as developers began trying to build real applications on top of PNUTS, we realized that the small fraction of the query workload that was more complex than we could handle would be a major stumbling block to the system's adoption. If we did not develop a mechanism to handle these queries, developers would have to resort to complicated workarounds, either implementing expensive operations (such as nested loop joins) in their application logic or frequently exporting data to external indexes to support their workload.

The field is in the early stages of cloud data management, and this is reflected in the many alternative system designs being built and deployed. We hope the ideas embodied in the PNUTS system can help us get closer to the goal of easily manageable, broadly applicable, multitenanted cloud database systems that provide applications with elastic, efficient, globally available, and extremely robust data backends.

Acknowledgments

PNUTS is a collaborative effort among many different people at Yahoo!. Leading the engineering effort are P.P.S. Narayan and Chuck Neerdaels. Other researchers on the project include Adam Silberstein and Rodrigo Fonseca. Brad McMillen and Pat Quaid help with the architecture of PNUTS and its place in Yahoo!'s cloud offerings. Other designers and developers of the system have included Phil Bohannon, Ramana Yerneni, Daniel Weaver, Michael Bigby, Nicholas Puz, Hans-Arno Jacobsen, Bryan Call, and Andrew Feng.

References

Azure Services Platform. *http://www.microsoft.com/azure/*.

Hadoop. *http://hadoop.apache.org*.

Agrawal, P., A. Silberstein, B. F. Cooper, U. Srivastava, and R. Ramakrishnan. "Asynchronous View Maintenance for VLSD Databases." In *SIGMOD*, 2009.

Chang, F. et al. "Bigtable: A distributed storage system for structured data." In *OSDI*, 2006.

Cooper, B. F., E. Baldeschwieler, R. Fonseca, J. J. Kistler, P.P.S. Narayan, Chuck Neerdaels, Toby Negrin, Raghu Ramakrishnan, Adam Silberstein, Utkarsh Srivastava, and Raymie Stata. "Building a cloud for Yahoo!" *IEEE Data Engineering Bulletin*, 32(1): 36–43, 2009.

Cooper, B. F., R. Ramakrishnan, U. Srivastava, A. Silberstein, P. Bohannon, H.-A. Jacobsen, N. Puz, D. Weaver, and R. Yerneni. "PNUTS: Yahoo!'s hosted data serving platform." In *VLDB*, 2008.

Dean, J. and S. Ghemawat. "MapReduce: Simplified data processing on large clusters." In *OSDI*, 2004.

DeCandia, G. et al. "Dynamo: Amazon's highly available key-value store." In *SOSP*, 2007.

Furman, J. J., J. S. Karlsson, J.-M. Leon, A. Lloyd, S. Newman and P. Zeyliger. "Megastore: A Scalable Data System for User Facing Applications." In *SIGMOD*, 2008.

Ghemawat, S., H. Gobioff, and S.-T. Leung. "The Google File System." In *SOSP*, 2003.

Lakshman, A., P. Malik, and K. Ranganathan. "Cassandra: A Structured Storage System on a P2P Network." In *SIGMOD*, 2008.

Pattishall, D. V. "Federation at Flickr: Doing Billions of Queries Per Day." *http://www.scribd.com/doc/2592098/DVPmysqlucFederation-at-Flickr-Doing-Billions-of-Queries-Per-Day*.

Ramakrishnan, R. and J. Gehrke. Database Management Systems. McGraw-Hill, New York, NY, 2002.

Silberstein, A., B. F. Cooper, U. Srivastava, E. Vee, R. Yerneni, and R. Ramakrishnan. "Efficient bulk insertion into a distributed ordered table." In *SIGMOD*, 2008.

Sobel, J. "Scaling out." Facebook Engineering Blog, August 2008.

Information Platforms and the Rise of the Data Scientist

Jeff Hammerbacher

Libraries and Brains

AT THE AGE OF 17, I WAS FIRED FROM MY JOB AS A CASHIER AT SCOTT'S GROCERY STORE IN FORT Wayne, Indiana. With only two months remaining before my freshman year of college, I saw in my unemployment an opportunity. Instead of telling my parents that I had been fired, I continued to leave the house every afternoon in my cashier's outfit: black pants, black shoes, white shirt, and smock. To my parents, I looked ready for some serious coupon scanning; in reality, I was pulling 10-hour shifts reading at the public library.

All reasonably curious people wonder how their brain works. At 17, I was unreasonably curious. I used my time at the library to learn about how brains work, how they break, and how they are rebuilt. In addition to keeping us balanced, regulating our body temperature, and making sure we blink our eyelids together every now and again, our brains ingest, process, and generate massive amounts of information. We construct unconscious responses to our immediate environment, short-term plans for locution and limb placement, and long-term plans for mate selection and education. What makes brains interesting is not just their ability to generate reactions to sensory data, but their role as repository of information for both plan generation and the creation of new information. I wanted to learn how that worked.

One thing about brains, though: they remain stubbornly housed within a single body. To collect information from many brains, we build libraries. The field of library science has evolved numerous techniques for herding the information stored in libraries to enable future consumption; a fun read on the topic is Alex Wright's *Glut* (Joseph Henry Press). In addition to housing information for future retrieval, libraries play a critical role in the creation of new information. As philosopher Daniel Dennett puts it, "a scholar is just a library's way of making another library."

Libraries and brains are two examples of Information Platforms. They are the locus of their organization's efforts to ingest, process, and generate information, and they serve to accelerate the process of learning from empirical data. When I joined Facebook in 2006, I naturally started to build an Information Platform. Because of the tremendous growth in the number of users on Facebook, the system our team built ended up managing several petabytes of data. In this chapter, I'll recount the challenges faced in building out Facebook's Information Platform and the lessons learned while constructing our solution from open source software. I'll also try to outline the critical role of the Data Scientist in using that information to build data-intensive products and services and helping the organization formulate and accomplish goals. Along the way, I'll recount how some other businesses have approached the problem of building Information Platforms over the decades.

Before we get started, I should point out that my clever plan to visit the library instead of the grocery store did not work out as intended. After a few blissful days of reading, I came out of the library one evening and couldn't locate my car. It was not uncommon for me to lose my car at the time, but the lot was empty, so I knew something was up. It turns out that my mom had figured out my scheme and gotten my car towed. During the long walk home, I internalized an important lesson: regard your own solutions with skepticism. Also, don't try to outsmart your mother.

Facebook Becomes Self-Aware

In September 2005, Facebook opened to non-college students for the first time and allowed high school students to register for accounts. Loyal users were outraged, but the Facebook team felt that it was the right direction for the site. How could it produce evidence to justify its position?

In addition, Facebook had saturated the student population at nearly all of the colleges where it was available, but there were still some colleges where the product had never taken off. What distinguished these laggard networks from their more successful peers, and what could be done to stimulate their success?

When I interviewed at Facebook in February 2006, they were actively looking to answer these questions. I studied mathematics in college and had been working for a nearly a year on Wall Street, building models to forecast interest rates, price complex derivatives, and hedge pools of mortgages; I had some experience coding and a dismal GPA. Despite my potentially suboptimal background, Facebook made me an offer to join as a Research Scientist.

Around the same time, Facebook hired a Director of Reporting and Analytics. The director had far more experience in the problem domain than me; together with a third engineer, we set about building an infrastructure for data collection and storage that would allow us to answer these questions about our product.

Our first attempt at an offline repository of information involved a Python script for farming queries out to Facebook's tier of MySQL servers and a daemon process, written in C++, for processing our event logs in real time. When the scripts worked as planned, we collected about 10 gigabytes a day. I later learned that this aspect of our system is commonly termed the "ETL" process, for "Extract, Transform, and Load."

Once our Python scripts and C++ daemon had siphoned the data from Facebook's source systems, we stuffed the data into a MySQL database for offline querying. We also had some scripts and queries that ran over the data once it landed in MySQL to aggregate it into more useful representations. It turns out that this offline database for decision support is better known as a "Data Warehouse."

Finally, we had a simple PHP script to pull data from the offline MySQL database and display summaries of the information we had collected to internal users. For the first time, we were able to answer some important questions about the impact of certain site features on user activity. Early analyses looked at maximizing growth through several channels: the layout of the default page for logged-out users, the source of invitations, and the design of the email contact importer. In addition to analyses, we started to build simple products using historical data, including an internal project to aggregate features of sponsored group members that proved popular with brand advertisers.

I didn't realize it at the time, but with our ETL framework, Data Warehouse, and internal dashboard, we had built a simple "Business Intelligence" system.

A Business Intelligence System

In a 1958 paper in the *IBM Systems Journal*, Hans Peter Luhn describes a system for "selective dissemination" of documents to "action points" based on the "interest profiles" of the individual action points. The author demonstrates shocking prescience. The title of the paper is "A Business Intelligence System," and it appears to be the first use of the term "Business Intelligence" in its modern context.

In addition to the dissemination of information in real time, the system was to allow for "information retrieval"—search—to be conducted over the entire document collection. Luhn's emphasis on action points focuses the role of information processing on goal completion. In other words, it's not enough to just collect and aggregate data; an organization must improve its capacity to complete critical tasks because of the insights gleaned from the data. He also proposes "reporters" to periodically sift the data and selectively move information to action points as needed.

The field of Business Intelligence has evolved over the five decades since Luhn's paper was published, and the term has come to be more closely associated with the management of structured data. Today, a typical business intelligence system consists of an ETL framework pulling data on a regular basis from an array of data sources into a Data Warehouse, on top of which sits a Business Intelligence tool used by business analysts to generate reports for internal consumption. How did we go from Luhn's vision to the current state of affairs?

E. F. Codd first proposed the relational model for data in 1970, and IBM had a working prototype of a relational database management system (RDBMS) by the mid-1970s. Building user-facing applications was greatly facilitated by the RDBMS, and by the early 1980s, their use was proliferating.

In 1983, Teradata sold the first relational database designed specifically for decision support to Wells Fargo. A few years later, in 1986, Ralph Kimball founded Red Brick Systems to build databases for the same market. Solutions were developed using Teradata and Red Brick's offerings, but it was not until 1991 that the first canonical text on data warehousing was published.

Bill Inmon's *Building the Data Warehouse* (Wiley) is a coherent treatise on data warehouse design and includes detailed recipes and best practices for building data warehouses. Inmon advocates constructing an enterprise data model after careful study of existing data sources and business goals.

In 1995, as Inmon's book grew in popularity and data warehouses proliferated inside enterprise data centers, The Data Warehouse Institute (TDWI) was formed. TDWI holds conferences and seminars and remains a critical force in articulating and spreading knowledge about data warehousing. That same year, data warehousing gained currency in academic circles when Stanford University launched its WHIPS research initiative.

A challenge to the Inmon orthodoxy came in 1996 when Ralph Kimball published *The Data Warehouse Toolkit* (Wiley). Kimball advocated a different route to data warehouse nirvana, beginning by throwing out the enterprise data model. Instead, Kimball argued that different business units should build their own data "marts," which could then be connected with a "bus." Further, instead of using a normalized data model, Kimball advocated the use of dimensional modeling, in which the relational data model was manhandled a bit to fit the particular workload seen by many data warehouse implementations.

As data warehouses grow over time, it is often the case that business analysts would like to manipulate a small subset of data quickly. Often this subset of data is parameterized by a few "dimensions." Building on these observations, the CUBE operator was introduced in 1997 by a group of Microsoft researchers, including Jim Gray. The new operator enabled fast querying of small, multidimensional data sets.

Both dimensional modeling and the CUBE operator were indications that, despite its success for building user-facing applications, the relational model might not be best for constructing an Information Platform. Further, the document and the action point, not the

table, were at the core of Luhn's proposal for a business intelligence system. On the other hand, an entire generation of engineers had significant expertise in building systems for relational data processing.

With a bit of history at our back, let's return to the challenges at Facebook.

The Death and Rebirth of a Data Warehouse

At Facebook, we were constantly loading more data into, and running more queries over, our MySQL data warehouse. Having only run queries over the databases that served the live site, we were all surprised at how long a query could run in our data warehouse. After some discussion with seasoned data warehousing veterans, I realized that it was normal to have queries running for hours and sometimes days, due to query complexity, massive data volumes, or both.

One day, as our database was nearing a terabyte in size, the `mysqld` daemon process came to a sudden halt. After some time spent on diagnostics, we tried to restart the database. Upon initiating the restart operation, we went home for the day.

When I returned to work the next morning, the database was still recovering. To get a consistent view of data that's being modified by many clients, a database server maintains a persistent list of all edits called the "redo log" or the "write-ahead log." If the database server is unceremoniously killed and restarted, it will reread the recent edits from the redo log to get back up to speed. Given the size of our data warehouse, the MySQL database had quite a bit of recovery to catch up on. It was three days before we had a working data warehouse again.

We made the decision at that point to move our data warehouse to Oracle, whose database software had better support for managing large data sets. We also purchased some expensive high-density storage and a powerful Sun server to run the new data warehouse.

During the transfer of our processes from MySQL to Oracle, I came to appreciate the differences between supposedly standard relational database implementations. The bulk import and export facilities of each database used completely different mechanisms. Further, the dialect of SQL supported by each was different enough to force us to rewrite many of our queries. Even worse, the Python client library for Oracle was unofficial and a bit buggy, so we had to contact the developer directly.

After a few weeks of elbow grease, we had the scripts rewritten to work on the new Oracle platform. Our nightly processes were running without problems, and we were excited to try out some of the tools from the Oracle ecosystem. In particular, Oracle had an ETL tool called Oracle Warehouse Builder (OWB) that we hoped could replace our handwritten Python scripts. Unfortunately, the software did not expect the sheer number of data sources we had to support: at the time, Facebook had tens of thousands of MySQL databases from which we collected data each night. Not even Oracle could help us tackle our scaling challenges on the ETL side, but we were happy to have a running data warehouse with a few terabytes of data.

And then we turned on clickstream logging: our first full day sent 400 gigabytes of unstructured data rushing over the bow of our Oracle database. Once again, we cast a skeptical eye on our data warehouse.

Beyond the Data Warehouse

According to IDC, the digital universe will expand to 1,800 exabytes by 2011. The vast majority of that data will not be managed by relational databases. There's an urgent need for data management systems that can extract information from unstructured data in concert with structured data, but there is little consensus on the way forward.

Natural language data in particular is abundant, rich with information, and poorly managed by a data warehouse. To manage natural language and other unstructured data, often captured in document repositories and voice recordings, organizations have looked beyond the offerings of data warehouse vendors to various new fields, including one known as enterprise search.

While most search companies built tools for navigating the collection of hyperlinked documents known as the World Wide Web, a few enterprise search companies chose to focus on managing internal document collections. Autonomy Corporation, founded in 1996 by Cambridge University researchers, leveraged Bayesian inference algorithms to facilitate the location of important documents. Fast Search and Transfer (FAST) was founded in 1997 in Norway with more straightforward keyword search and ranking at the heart of its technology. Two years later, Endeca was founded with a focus on navigating document collections using structured metadata, a technique known as "faceted search." Google, seeing an opportunity to leverage its expertise in the search domain, introduced an enterprise search appliance in 2000.

In a few short years, enterprise search has grown into a multibillion-dollar market segment that is almost totally separate from the data warehouse market. Endeca has some tools for more traditional business intelligence, and some database vendors have worked to introduce text mining capabilities into their systems, but a complete, integrated solution for structured and unstructured enterprise data management remains unrealized.

Both enterprise search and data warehousing are technical solutions to the larger problem of leveraging the information resources of an organization to improve performance. As far back as 1944, MIT professor Kurt Lewin proposed "action research" as a framework that uses "a spiral of steps, each of which is composed of a circle of planning, action, and fact-finding about the result of the action." A more modern approach to the same problem can be found in Peter Senge's "Learning Organization" concept, detailed in his book *The Fifth Discipline* (Broadway Business). Both management theories rely heavily upon an organization's ability to adapt its actions after reflecting upon information collected from previous actions. From this perspective, an Information Platform is the infrastructure required by a Learning Organization to ingest, process, and generate the information necessary for implementing the action research spiral.

Having now looked at structured and unstructured data management, let's get back to the Facebook story.

The Cheetah and the Elephant

On the first day of logging the Facebook clickstream, more than 400 gigabytes of data was collected. The load, index, and aggregation processes for this data set really taxed the Oracle data warehouse. Even after significant tuning, we were unable to aggregate a day of clickstream data in less than 24 hours. It was clear we'd need to aggregate our logfiles outside of the database and store only the summary information for later querying.

Luckily, a top engineer from a large web property had recently joined our team and had experience processing clickstream data at web scale. In just a few weeks, he built a parallelized log processing system called Cheetah that was able to process a day of clickstream data in two hours. There was much rejoicing.

Despite our success, Cheetah had some drawbacks: first, after processing the clickstream data, the raw data was stored in archival storage and could not be queried again. In addition, Cheetah pulled the clickstream data from a shared NetApp filer with limited read bandwidth. The "schema" for each logfile was embedded in the processing scripts rather than stored in a format that could be queried. We did not collect progress information and we scheduled Cheetah jobs using a basic Unix utility called cron, so no sophisticated load-sharing logic could be applied. Most importantly, however, Cheetah was not open source. We had a small team and could not afford the resources required to develop, maintain, and train new users to use our proprietary system.

The Apache Hadoop project, started in late 2005 by Doug Cutting and Mike Cafarella, was a top candidate to replace Cheetah. Named after the stuffed elephant of Doug's son, the Hadoop project aimed to implement Google's distributed filesystem and MapReduce technologies under the Apache 2.0 license. Yahoo! hired Doug Cutting in January 2006 and devoted significant engineering resources to developing Hadoop. In April 2006, the software was able to sort 1.9 terabytes in 47 hours using 188 servers. Although Hadoop's design improved on Cheetah's in several areas, the software was too slow for our needs at that time. By April 2008, however, Hadoop was able to sort 1 terabyte in 209 seconds using 910 servers. With the improved performance numbers in hand, I was able to convince our operations team to stick three 500-gigabyte SATA drives in the back of 60 unused web servers, and we went forward with our first Hadoop cluster at Facebook.

Initially, we started streaming a subset of our logs into both Hadoop and Cheetah. The enhanced programmability of Hadoop coupled with the ability to query the historical data led to some interesting projects. One application involved scoring all directed pairs of interacting users on Facebook to determine their affinity; this score could then be used for search and News Feed ranking. After some time, we migrated all Cheetah workflows to Hadoop and retired the old system. Later, the transactional database collection processes were moved to Hadoop as well.

With Hadoop, our infrastructure was able to accommodate unstructured and structured data analysis at a massive scale. As the platform grew to hundreds of terabytes and thousands of jobs per day, we learned that new applications could be built and new questions could be answered simply because of the scale at which we were now able to store and retrieve data.

When Facebook opened registration to all users, the user population grew at disproportionately rapid rates in some countries. At the time, however, we were not able to perform granular analyses of clickstream data broken out by country. Once our Hadoop cluster was up, we were able to reconstruct how Facebook had grown rapidly in places such as Canada and Norway by loading all of our historical access logs into Hadoop and writing a few simple MapReduce jobs.

Every day, millions of semi-public conversations occur on the walls of Facebook users. One internal estimate put the size of the wall post corpus at 10 times the size of the blogosphere! Before Hadoop, however, the contents of those conversations remained inaccessible for data analysis. In 2007, a summer intern with a strong interest in linguistics and statistics, Roddy Lindsay, joined the Data team. Using Hadoop, Roddy was able to single-handedly construct a powerful trend analysis system called Lexicon that continues to process terabytes of wall post data every night; you can see the results for yourself at *http://facebook.com/lexicon*.

Having the data from disparate systems stored in a single repository proved critical for the construction of a reputation scoring system for Facebook applications. Soon after the launch of the Facebook Platform in May of 2007, our users were inundated with requests to add applications. We quickly realized that we would need a tool to separate the useful applications from those the users perceived as spam. Using data collected from the API servers, user profiles, and activity data from the site itself, we were able to construct a model for scoring applications that allowed us to allocate invitations to the applications deemed most useful to users.

The Unreasonable Effectiveness of Data

In a recent paper, a trio of Google researchers distilled what they have learned from trying to solve some of machine learning's most difficult challenges. When discussing the problems of speech recognition and machine translation, they state that, "invariably, simple models and a lot of data trump more elaborate models based on less data." I don't intend to debate their findings; certainly there are domains where elaborate models are successful. Yet based on their experiences, there does exist a wide class of problems for which more data and simple models are better.

At Facebook, Hadoop was our tool for exploiting the unreasonable effectiveness of data. For example, when we were translating the site into other languages, we tried to target users who spoke a specific language to enlist their help in the translation task. One of our Data Scientists, Cameron Marlow, crawled all of Wikipedia and built character trigram frequency counts per language. Using these frequency counts, he built a simple classifier

that could look at a set of wall posts authored by a user and determine his spoken language. Using this classifier, we were able to actively recruit users into our translation program in a targeted fashion. Both Facebook and Google use natural language data in many applications; see Chapter 14 of this book for Peter Norvig's exploration of the topic.

The observations from Google point to a third line of evolution for modern business intelligence systems: in addition to managing structured and unstructured data in a single system, they must scale to store enough data to enable the "simple models, lots of data" approach to machine learning.

New Tools and Applied Research

Most of the early users of the Hadoop cluster at Facebook were engineers with a taste for new technologies. To make the information accessible to a larger fraction of the organization, we built a framework for data warehousing on top of Hadoop called Hive.

Hive includes a SQL-like query language with facilities for embedding MapReduce logic, as well as table partitioning, sampling, and the ability to handle arbitrarily serialized data. The last feature was critical, as the data collected into Hadoop was constantly evolving in structure; allowing users to specify their own serialization format allowed us to pass the problem of specifying structure for the data to those responsible for loading the data into Hive. In addition, a simple UI for constructing Hive queries, called HiPal, was built. Using the new tools, non-engineers from marketing, product management, sales, and customer service were able to author queries over terabytes of data. After several months of internal use, Hive was contributed back to Hadoop as an official subproject under the Apache 2.0 license and continues to be actively developed.

In addition to Hive, we built a portal for sharing charts and graphs called Argus (inspired by IBM's work on the Many Eyes project), a workflow management system called Databee, a framework for writing MapReduce scripts in Python called PyHive, and a storage system for serving structured data to end users called Cassandra (now available as open source in the Apache Incubator).

As the new systems stabilized, we ended up with multiple tiers of data managed by a single Hadoop cluster. All data from the enterprise, including application logs, transactional databases, and web crawls, was regularly collected in raw form into the Hadoop distributed filesystem (HDFS). Thousands of nightly Databee processes would then transform some of this data into a structured form and place it into the directory of HDFS managed by Hive. Further aggregations were performed in Hive to generate reports served by Argus. Additionally, within HDFS, individual engineers maintained "sandboxes" under their home directories against which prototype jobs could be run.

At its current capacity, the cluster holds nearly 2.5 petabytes of data, and new data is added at a rate of 15 terabytes per day. Over 3,000 MapReduce jobs are run every day, processing 55 terabytes of data. To accommodate the different priorities of jobs that are run on the cluster, we built a job scheduler to perform fair sharing of resources over multiple queues.

In addition to powering internal and external reports, a/b testing pipelines, and many different data-intensive products and services, Facebook's Hadoop cluster enabled some interesting applied research projects.

One longitudinal study conducted by Data Scientists Itamar Rosenn and Cameron Marlow set out to determine what factors were most critical in predicting long-term user engagement. We used our platform to select a sample of users, trim outliers, and generate a large number of features for use in several least-angle regressions against different measures of engagement. Some features we were able to generate using Hadoop included various measures of friend network density and user categories based on profile features.

Another internal study to understand what motivates content contribution from new users was written up in the paper "Feed Me: Motivating Newcomer Contribution in Social Network Sites," published at the 2009 CHI conference. A more recent study from the Facebook Data team looks at how information flows through the Facebook social graph; the study is titled "Gesundheit! Modeling Contagion through Facebook News Feed," and has been accepted for the 2009 ICWSM conference.

Every day, evidence is collected, hypotheses are tested, applications are built, and new insights are generated using the shared Information Platform at Facebook. Outside of Facebook, similar systems were being constructed in parallel.

MAD Skills and Cosmos

In "MAD Skills: New Analysis Practices for Big Data," a paper from the 2009 VLDB conference, the analysis environment at Fox Interactive Media (FIM) is described in detail. Using a combination of Hadoop and the Greenplum database system, the team at FIM has built a familiar platform for data processing in isolation from our work at Facebook.

The paper's title refers to three tenets of the FIM platform: Magnetic, Agile, and Deep. "Magnetic" refers to the desire to store all data from the enterprise, not just the structured data that fits into the enterprise data model. Along the same lines, an "Agile" platform should handle schema evolution gracefully, enabling analysts to work with data immediately and evolve the data model as needed. "Deep" refers to the practice of performing more complex statistical analyses over data.

In the FIM environment, data is separated into staging, production, reporting, and sandbox schemas within a single Greenplum database, quite similar to the multiple tiers inside of Hadoop at Facebook described earlier.

Separately, Microsoft has published details of its data management stack. In papers titled "Dryad: Distributed Data-Parallel Programs from Sequential Building Blocks" and "SCOPE: Easy and Efficient Parallel Processing of Massive Data Sets," Microsoft describes an information platform remarkably similar to the one we had built at Facebook. Its infrastructure includes a distributed filesystem called Cosmos and a system for parallel data processing called Dryad; it has even invented a SQL-like query language called SCOPE.

Three teams working with three separate technology stacks have evolved similar plat-forms for processing large amounts of data. What's going on here? By decoupling the requirements of specifying structure from the ability to store data and innovating on APIs for data retrieval, the storage systems of large web properties are starting to look less like databases and more like dataspaces.

Information Platforms As Dataspaces

Anecdotally, similar petabyte-scale platforms exist at companies such as Yahoo!, Quant-cast, and Last.fm. These platforms are not quite data warehouses, as they're frequently not using a relational database or any traditional data warehouse modeling techniques. They're not quite enterprise search systems, as only some of the data is indexed and they expose far richer APIs. And they're often used for building products and services in addi-tion to traditional data analysis workloads. Similar to the brain and the library, these shared platforms for data processing serve as the locus of their organization's efforts to ingest, process, and generate information, and with luck, they hasten their organization's pace of learning from empirical data.

In the database community, there has been some work to transition the research agenda from purely relational data management to a more catholic system for storage and query-ing of large data sets called a "dataspace." In "From Databases to Dataspaces: A New Abstraction for Information Management" (*http://www.eecs.berkeley.edu/~franklin/Papers/dataspaceSR.pdf*), the authors highlight the need for storage systems to accept all data for-mats and to provide APIs for data access that evolve based on the storage system's under-standing of the data.

I'd contend that the Information Platforms we've described are real-world examples of dataspaces: single storage systems for managing petabytes of structured and unstructured data from all parts of an organization that expose a variety of data access APIs for engi-neering, analysis, and reporting. Given the proliferation of these systems in industry, I'm hopeful that the database community continues to explore the theoretical foundations and practical implications of dataspaces.

An Information Platform is the critical infrastructure component for building a Learning Organization. The most critical human component for accelerating the learning process and making use of the Information Platform is taking the shape of a new role: the Data Scientist.

The Data Scientist

In a recent interview, Hal Varian, Google's chief economist, highlighted the need for employees able to extract information from the Information Platforms described earlier. As Varian puts it, "find something where you provide a scarce, complementary service to something that is getting ubiquitous and cheap. So what's getting ubiquitous and cheap? Data. And what is complementary to data? Analysis."

At Facebook, we felt that traditional titles such as Business Analyst, Statistician, Engineer, and Research Scientist didn't quite capture what we were after for our team. The workload for the role was diverse: on any given day, a team member could author a multistage processing pipeline in Python, design a hypothesis test, perform a regression analysis over data samples with R, design and implement an algorithm for some data-intensive product or service in Hadoop, or communicate the results of our analyses to other members of the organization in a clear and concise fashion. To capture the skill set required to perform this multitude of tasks, we created the role of "Data Scientist."

In the financial services domain, large data stores of past market activity are built to serve as the proving ground for complex new models developed by the Data Scientists of their domain, known as Quants. Outside of industry, I've found that grad students in many scientific domains are playing the role of the Data Scientist. One of our hires for the Facebook Data team came from a bioinformatics lab where he was building data pipelines and performing offline data analysis of a similar kind. The well-known Large Hadron Collider at CERN generates reams of data that are collected and pored over by graduate students looking for breakthroughs.

Recent books such as Davenport and Harris's *Competing on Analytics* (Harvard Business School Press, 2007), Baker's *The Numerati* (Houghton Mifflin Harcourt, 2008), and Ayres's *Super Crunchers* (Bantam, 2008) have emphasized the critical role of the Data Scientist across industries in enabling an organization to improve over time based on the information it collects. In conjunction with the research community's investigation of dataspaces, further definition for the role of the Data Scientist is needed over the coming years. By better articulating the role, we'll be able to construct training curricula, formulate promotion hierarchies, organize conferences, write books, and fill in all of the other trappings of a recognized profession. In the process, the pool of available Data Scientists will expand to meet the growing need for expert pilots for the rapidly proliferating Information Platforms, further speeding the learning process across all organizations.

Conclusion

When faced with the challenge of building an Information Platform at Facebook, I found it helpful to look at how others had attempted to solve the same problem across time and problem domains. As an engineer, my initial approach was directed by available technologies and appears myopic in hindsight. The biggest challenge was keeping focused on the larger problem of building the infrastructure and human components of a Learning Organization rather than specific technical systems, such as data warehouses or enterprise search systems.

I'm certain that the hardware and software employed to build an Information Platform will evolve rapidly, and the skills required of a Data Scientist will change at the same rate. Staying focused on the goal of making the learning process move faster will benefit both organizations and science. The future belongs to the Data Scientist!

The Geographic Beauty of a Photographic Archive

Jason Dykes and Jo Wood

PHOTOGRAPHS CAN BE BEAUTIFUL. IT SEEMS ALMOST DEMEANING TO CONSIDER SOMETHING THAT CAN
capture experience, kindle emotion, and invoke the sublime merely as data. Yet once
stored digitally, we can process a photograph's binary digits just as we might any other
stream of numeric data. But we can go further: by collecting those photographic representations together, by arranging them, by describing them, we can create *context* and a new
beauty emerges, something that is fed by the beauty of the images that comprise the collection, but which is so much more than the sum of its parts.

In this chapter we explore the beauty that emerges when we consider the *geography* of a
photographic collection, and we examine that geography visually with maps and other
graphics. By geography we mean the information that allows us to associate something
with a *place* or *location* (two quite distinct concepts). And when we're dealing with data,
there's a lot of geography about. Some estimates suggest that up to 80% of data is geographic (MacEachren and Kraak 2001). This information might be recorded directly
through latitude and longitudinal coordinates, or indirectly though association with a
postal code, a name, or some other notion of place. This geography can be a useful way of
organizing, filtering, and interpreting data. The geography recorded in the growing number
of large contributed data sets may be a particularly useful source of information about perspectives of *place*.

Geography can be assigned to data in a number of ways. It may be part of the data collection process (for example, through satellite remote sensing). It may emerge during data query and interpretation (for example, through location-based services such as Google Local). Or it may be generated through more sophisticated spatio-temporal analysis as part of a process of sensemaking, as typified by the current interest in *geovisual analytics* (Andrienko et al. 2008). Here, we will use as our starting point data that has been made geographic as part of the collection process through specific locations, but that contains additional, less-explicit descriptions of *place*. The Geograph archive contains over one million photographs that have been pinned to a precise latitude and longitude, either automatically by GPS-enabled devices such as the iPhone, or by individuals who have manually located their photos on a map. Additionally, the geography of these photos has also been described by their owners as freeform text, perhaps by naming nearby locations, or by describing features or activities captured by the photo. There is complexity and subtlety here, and as we shall see, beauty can emerge when we try to visualize this to enhance our knowledge of the interplay between location and descriptions of place.

When writing beautiful code, it is frequently the case that the code has a very specific purpose, such as sorting a list, solving a system of linear equations, or performing a Fourier transform. The beauty of the code can result from the effectiveness in meeting that purpose (Kolawa 2007). When dealing with beautiful data, such a purpose might not be quite so precise. *Exploration* of data is an important part of the scientific endeavor and can lead to insights, hypotheses to be tested, and validation of prior theory. Beautiful data warrants exploration. It contains patterns, structures, and anomalies that are not immediately apparent but emerge as reward for mining the hidden depths within. In our work we build upon two long traditions for exploring data in a visual manner. *Cartography* has developed robust techniques for visually representing geographic data to communicate information and support knowledge discovery. Over the centuries it has innovatively and successfully combined the objective rigor of science with more subjective skills of interpretation design and critique. Maps themselves can be things of beauty as well as their referents. *Information visualization* encapsulates the process of visual exploration of data that may not have any geographic component, through the design and generation of graphs, charts, and associated interactions. Here we report on approaches to exploring beautiful geographic data that combine elements of cartography and information visualization.

Beauty in Data: Geograph

We consider Geograph a beautiful data set for a whole host of reasons. An engaging combination of valued data source, online community, game, and motivation for exploring the countryside, this rapidly expanding archive of georeferenced and annotated photographs of the landscape of the British Isles gives ample scope for considering beauty in the big picture and in myriad small details.

Originally conceived by Gary Rogers, and supported by Paul Dixon, Barry Hunter, and a growing team of moderators, Geograph is an effort to collect "geographically representative photographs and information" (Geograph 2009) for each 1 km grid cell in Great Britain and

Ireland. At the time of writing, this process has involved over 8,500 contributors collecting and documenting more than one and a quarter million photographs, with over 90% of the 244,000 1 km grid squares in Britain *"geographed."* Figure 6-1 provides an example. This number will undoubtedly have been augmented over time—the British countryside is being geographed as you are reading!

FIGURE 6-1. *Minor road near Aberuchill. Bioran Dalchonzie in the distance. This is the 1,000,000th image to appear on the Geograph website (http://www.geograph.org.uk/photo/1006884). Image © Dr. Richard Murray; licensed for reuse under a Creative Commons License (http://creativecommons.org/licenses/by-sa/2.0/). (See Color Plate 12.)*

Contributors to Geograph are free to select their representative view, but the geographic features should be indicative of the typical human and physical geography in the 1 km grid cell:

> [T]hink what a child looking at a map in a geography lesson might find useful when trying to make sense of what the human and physical geographical features in a given grid square actually look like (Hawgood et al. 2007).

We see beauty in various aspects of Geograph:

- The objective of producing an open archive of purposefully selected and annotated images has an engaging blend of simplicity (the idea), complexity (the process, which is structured in a manner that also has some beauty), and utility (the resource). The organization and devotion of those running the project to maintain the collection and make it usable are admirable and impressive.

- There is beauty in the "collective effort" approach used in generating the archive from the "bottom-up" and the way in which technology and person-power are used to achieve the aims. The collective beauty in the collaborative "citizens as sensors" (Goodchild 2007) nature of the project, which relies upon common understanding and broad cooperation with little individual gain, is considerable.

- The implementation and presentation of the idea in an engaging, accessible, and stimulating website that provides access to the information in so many ways also embodies aesthetic and technical qualities.

- The maps generated from geographs at a range of scales to provide insights into the various processes involved in generating the collection have aesthetic quality (see, for example, Figure 6-2). These include a number of innovative cartographic representations and interactive features that provide access to this mass of information and change as the collection is updated, such as geograph densities and distribution maps of contributors and their contributions.

- The individual contributions have aesthetic appeal as representations of human and physical landscape determined by those who inhabit and visit the locations depicted. This is formalized by the Geograph community, as candidates for the geograph of the year (GOTY) are chosen on a weekly basis from the photographs contributed.

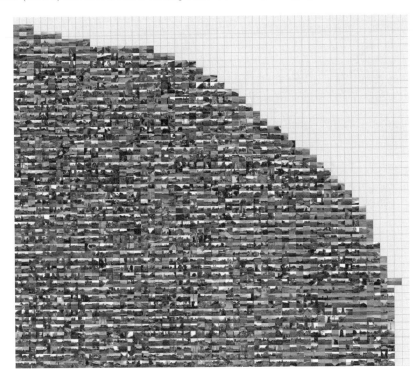

FIGURE 6-2. Example Geograph photomosiac of the Norfolk coast. Each photo is mapped at its geographic location and represents a 1 km square of the landscape. Images licensed for reuse under a Creative Commons License (http://creativecommons.org/licenses/by-sa/2.0). (See Color Plate 13.)

Geograph is somewhat typical of the broad user-generated georeferenced data sets that are becoming available, but these various qualities make it particularly notable. There are real opportunities for exploring the Geograph data and generating new knowledge that may further accentuate its beauty. We provide some examples in the sections that follow that describe some of our visual exploration of the geographies represented in the collection.

Visualization, Beauty, and Treemaps

Before we delve into the Geograph archive itself, it is worth considering some of the motivations and visual techniques that might be usefully applied to exploring the collection. The cartographic tradition has understandably focused predominantly on static products that are reproduced using traditional media. Most of our work in the last 15 years has been interactive—drawing on digital technologies to reconsider the nature and role of maps and redeploying them as responsive graphical means of querying for exploration (Fisher 1998). We have aimed to ensure aesthetic quality in the smoothness of the interactions, and satisfaction, by developing informed views and dynamic behaviors that provoke thought and discovery. However, some of our recent work has re-emphasized *data density* and focused back on the fundamental cartographic design decisions associated with generating layouts and symbolism (data encodings) that use space efficiently and effectively. This work has been partially motivated by hardware advances that have made processing and displaying large data-dense graphics more feasible. It is, in effect, a response to the need for new effective and aesthetically pleasing methods for graphically representing the kinds of larger data sets that are increasingly available as we follow Tufte's advice to "present many numbers in a small space" (Tufte 1983).

What Is Beauty in Visual Data Exploration?

We regard beauty to be a subjective quality associated with some stimulus that results in a positive perceptual experience. In visualization, beauty is often in the eye of the developer or designer. Apposite calls have been made to the community to formally critique visualization work in an effort to consider aesthetics more collectively (e.g., Kosara 2007). However, until a usable body of knowledge is developed, we are reliant upon broad principles and rules of thumb when developing aesthetically pleasing graphics.

A number of these are used in *Beautiful Code* (Oram and Wilson 2007) and can be usefully applied to data visualization. For example, Brian Kernighan (Kernighan 2007) identifies characteristics of beautiful code that include compactness, elegance, efficiency, and utility, and informally quantifies compactness by indicating, "Ideally the code would fit onto a single page." Yukihiro Matsumoto deems code to be less than beautiful if it is difficult to understand, and has used this principle to inform his approach to developing the Ruby programming language (Matsumoto 2007). But "difficult to understand" should not be confused with complexity. A simple graphic that is easy to understand but shows very little data is not beautiful in the way we define it here. Rather, beautiful data visualization shows things that are complex but in a way that makes them easier to understand—perhaps by focusing attention on certain aspects of the data or emphasizing particular perspectives. It may follow Kernighan's principle of aiming to do so on a single "page."

In our case, we endeavor to use space efficiently to show multiple (spatial and other) relationships by augmenting and synthesizing existing approaches to cartography and information visualization. We seek to do so in ways that are compact enough to fit onto a single page or screen and sufficiently elegant to reveal both overall structure (*Gestalt*) and local detail (*details on demand*) concurrently. We aim to design and develop interpretable

and useful graphics in the context of the needs of any particular data set with real users who can understand and use the graphics to address known information needs.

Tufte (1983) conceived of the notion of the *data/ink ratio*—a heuristic that encourages the designer of a graphic to evaluate the proportion of the ink on a page that is used directly to represent data. The larger the ratio, the more efficient is the use of graphic symbolization and the greater the depth of information that can be revealed. This metric of form and function may contribute to the beauty of a data graphic. We can likewise consider the idea of *data/location ratio*—the degree to which the position of a graphical element on a page reflects characteristics of the data it represents. Traditional cartographic maps score highly in this respect since the location of a symbol on the page usually identifies the geographic location of its referent. Many information graphics are perhaps less efficient in this regard, as are some maps (such as cartograms and schematics), often for good reason. We would argue that the efficient use of space is an important aspect of beautiful visualization in that it supports the process of visual discovery of geographic (and other) patterns. This is increasingly true in the context of the massive volumes of data with a geographic component, such as large volunteered collections. In short, there is beauty in using and representing space efficiently—particularly to reveal geography.

Making Treemaps Beautiful: A Geographic Perspective

Treemaps are space-filling representations of hierarchies (Shneiderman 1992), as seen in Figure 6-3. Like many beautiful ideas, the treemap is based on an elegantly simple concept. An item of data is represented as a rectangle. If that data item itself contains a collection of other data items (a defining feature of any hierarchy), each is represented as a smaller rectangle that sits inside the "parent" rectangle. In turn, these smaller rectangles can themselves contain even smaller "children" that sit inside them, and so on. The rectangles are arranged such that they fill the entire graphical space without any gaps. Each rectangle, or *node*, can be sized according to some characteristic of the data it represents. It can also be colored in response to the data and be labeled in some meaningful way. All rectangles are visible; they do not overlap. There is elegance in the compactness of the representation (a single colored and labeled rectangle can simultaneously show three or more independent characteristics of some data). The simple geometric form of each node (a rectangle) lends itself to the representation of large data sets since a treemap can simultaneously show almost as many nodes as there are pixels on a screen. There is also some cognitive elegance in that the semantic containment relationships of the hierarchy are represented directly as geometric containments in the treemap (parent nodes enclose child nodes).

We saw opportunities for employing treemaps to represent large quantities of information recorded as geographical and thematic hierarchies. And by constructing new hierarchies we saw the possibility for the large numbers of records in the Geograph data set to be explored in this way.

However, treemaps have been widely critiqued for a number of reasons. Ironically, the aesthetic quality of treemaps has been criticized (Cawthon and vande Moere 2007), although we would argue this is more a function of implementation than design *per se*.

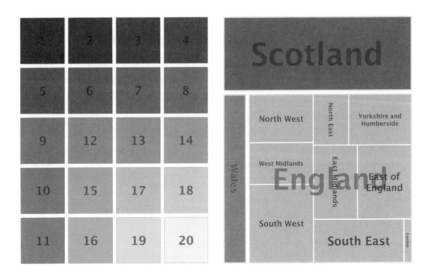

FIGURE 6-3. Two simple treemaps. (Left) The placement of 20 ordered nodes using a conventional squarified layout (colored by order). Note the inconsistent use of location to represent the ordered sequence 1 to 20. (Right) A spatial treemap where nodes are placed according to their approximate geographic location (colored by category).

More significantly, the arbitrary placement of nodes in a treemap significantly lowers the data/location ratio. Most existing treemap layout algorithms locate nodes in order to maximize their aspect ratios (making nodes as square as possible is important for aesthetics and size comparison tasks) and to aid readability (maximizing horizontal linear continuity). Very few are concerned with using graphical location to represent some aspect of the data. As a result, treemaps contain linear discontinuities and arbitrary node placement (e.g., Figure 6-3). This counters established best practice in cartography and statistical graphics, whereby locations on the plane are regarded as the primary means of representing relational information (Bertin 1983). Arbitrary location of nodes within treemaps fails to take advantage of the "first law of cognitive geography" (Fabrikant et al. 2002), whereby near things are regarded as more similar than distant things.

We saw scope for ordering nodes at all levels of a two-dimensional treemap according to one- or two-dimensional orderings in the data (Wood and Dykes 2008). In doing so we address one of the key problems associated with the treemap, namely that the primary information-carrying dimensions are not fully utilized, by mapping one (or more) data dimensions to them. In short, we use space within the treemap to represent one dimensionally ordered or two dimensionally spatially arranged relationships in our data.

A Geographic Perspective on Geograph Term Use

The concept of *place* is a complex one that is not well described with simple latitude-longitude coordinate pairs. It is more than simply *location*, in that it also says something about the nature of features that create a sense of place. It can rely on intangible, subjective, and sometimes contradictory characteristics that traditionally are not well represented in digital data sets. Volunteered, or community contributed, geographic information

such as the personal descriptions of place available in Geograph gives us access to new and multiple perspectives. These may reflect a range of viewpoints and enable us to begin to consider alternative notions of place as we attempt to describe it more effectively.

Consequently, Ross Purves and Alistair Edwardes have been using Geograph as a source of descriptions of place in their research at the University of Zurich. Their ultimate objective involves improving information retrieval by automatically adding indexing terms to geo-referenced digital photographs that relate to popular notions of place, such as "mountain," "remote," or "hiking." Their work involves validating previous studies and forming new perspectives by comparing Geograph to existing efforts to describe place and analyzing term co-occurrence in the geograph descriptions (Edwardes and Purves 2007).

A popular approach in the literature involves identifying basic levels or scene types through which place is described. Such summative descriptions of place have been traditionally derived through human subject tests. These are difficult to coordinate and usually involve small numbers of participants, making it hard to generalize from the results or repeat the experiments. Edwardes and Purves evaluated the way in which Geograph contributors use and rank scene types such as *mountain*, *hill*, *valley*, *river*, *rock*, *lake*, *canyon*, *cliff*, *ocean*, and *cave*, and found significant correlations with the terms reported in participant studies and the degree to which they are used (Edwardes and Purves 2007).

With the terms used in the collection validated to an extent, we collectively identified opportunities for exploring the nature, structure, and geography of some of these relationships in Geograph. In particular, we wished to understand the relationship between photographic content, photographic location, and textual description of place as recorded in contributors' annotations of their photographs. A visualization approach seemed appropriate, and the treemap techniques enabled us to explore these characteristics of Geograph.

The examples that follow document some of the ways in which spatial treemaps and other graphics were used in our exploration of Geograph as we developed our shared knowledge of the collection to inform our understanding of the descriptions of *place*.

Representing the Term Hierarchy

The Geograph archive was processed in April 2008 when approximately 750,000 images had been geolocated with a title and textual description. We focused on images that related to six basic levels, or scene types, deemed particularly interesting through Edwardes's and Purves's analysis: *beach*, *village*, *city*, *park*, *mountain*, and *hill*. For each of these scene types we then selected the most popular descriptive terms occurring in three different *facets*: *activities* (predominantly verbs), *elements* (predominantly nouns), and *qualities* (predominantly adjectives). This resulted in a term co-occurrence hierarchy of six scene types, each containing three facets, each containing a number of descriptors associated with the scene type. A treemap reflecting this hierarchy contains nodes for each of the co-occurrences of our selected scene types with a popular descriptor and reveals some structure in the descriptions used in Geograph. The treemap shown in Figure 6-4 uses an

ordered squarified layout algorithm to optimize shape and locational consistency of nodes (Wood and Dykes 2008). Leaf nodes (individual geographs) are of unit size.

FIGURE 6-4. Treemap of terms occurring in geograph titles and comments for six selected scene types. Node sizes represent term occurrence. Colors emphasize the scene type/facet/descriptor hierarchy with an inherited random scheme. Layout uses an "ordered squarified" approach to maintain square shapes amongst nodes. (See Color Plate 14.)

Each node in Figure 6-4 is colored using an inherited random scheme where scene types are randomly colored, and children (facets, descriptors, and the geographs themselves) inherit this color with a minor mutation. Although the colors have no independent meaning, this coloring scheme is used to emphasize the hierarchical structure of the classification. This combination of layout and color encoding helps us in our exploration of the data by revealing structure and encouraging visual comparison. For example, we can see that *hill* is a more popular term than *park*, *village*, *city*, *beach*, or *mountain* as it occupies a larger area in the treemap. The elements facet is consistently more popular than qualities or activities across these scene types. The activity facet is particularly strongly associated with *park*. The descriptor *road* dominates four of the scene types, but not *beach* or *mountain*. Descriptors such as *valley* and *path* are used more frequently with *hill* than *mountain*, although in relative terms these descriptors are more commonly related with *mountain* than *hill*. *Loch* is used more frequently with *mountain* than *hill*. *Footpath* is popular as a descriptor of *hill* but not *mountain*. One important aspect of the beauty of this kind of data-dense information is that many other relationships are displayed concurrently and might equally be reported. We could go on and describe our pictures in many more than 1,000 words.

We have taken a number of design decisions here based upon our experience of interpreting various Geograph graphics. A useful alternative involves employing a "slice and dice" layout algorithm. The result is a mosaic plot that makes the proportions of each scene type and facets within them easier to relate, as lengths are compared rather than areas (Figure 6-5, top). However, the elongated nodes that result mean that labeling and size estimation between descriptors are more difficult. A compromise involves applying the ordered squarified algorithm to arrange leaf nodes (Figure 6-5, bottom). Experimenting with layout and color in this way at different levels of the hierarchy helps us emphasize and explore the various salient qualities of the data set.

FIGURE 6-5. Treemap of terms occurring in geograph titles and comments for six selected scene types. Node sizes represent term occurrence. Colors emphasize the scene type/facet/descriptor hierarchy with an inherited random scheme. Layouts uses a "slice and dice" approach to aid comparison of magnitudes (top) and "slice and dice/ordered squarified" approaches to aid legibility of labels (bottom). (See Color Plate 15.)

Representing Absolute Location with Color

While the treemaps in Figures 6-4 and 6-5 provide some indication of how *place* is described, they say little about its relationship with *location*. We explored a couple of ways of adding locational information to the treemap. The first involved using color to provide an indication of absolute location within the British Isles. Geograph locations are stored as projected coordinate pairs with "eastings" and "northings" recording the distances to the east and north of the origin of the British National Grid.

The challenge was to represent the two dimensions of photo location (easting and northing) with a color that distinguished it from other photos in different locations. Most color spaces are defined using three components (for example, red, green, and blue; or hue, saturation, and value), so selecting just two components to represent coordinate pairs is problematic. Additionally, most color schemes are perceptually nonuniform; in other words, the perceived similarity of two colors a fixed distance apart from each other varies across the color space. We therefore chose to use the CIELab color model, which provides a more perceptually consistent color gamut. By representing eastings and northings of each photo's location with the *a* and *b* components of the color space, we were able to produce a geographic map of color where southwesterly locations were colored orange, southeasterly locations were green, northeasterly were blue, and northwesterly were purple. Central locations tended toward brown, and the degree of color similarity between two nodes provided an indication of locational similarity of the photos they represent. Figure 6-6 colors nodes in the ordered squarified treemap (compare with Figure 6-4) in this way.

Some locational influences on descriptions of place are apparent from this view that may inform our exploration of the Geograph archive from a spatial perspective. For example, *track*, *summit* and *cairn*, exhibit different geographies to *downs*, *chalk*, *barrow*, and *junction* within *hill*; *mountain*, *beach*, and *village* have different locational characteristics; *activities* and *qualities* have distinct geographies within *beach*. Some of the complexities associated with the relationship between location and place are also apparent.

Representing Relative Location with Spatial Treemaps

The use of color to show location has some aesthetic appeal and provides some insight into location-place relationships, but it is limited in its effectiveness. In particular, it requires of the reader a memory of how color is related to location. The treemap shown in Figure 6-6 also fails to use node position in any meaningful way. So instead, we can map the geographic location of each photo to node position within the treemap such that northerly photos appear toward the top of an enclosing node's space, westerly toward the left, and so on. Because the treemap will fill the space with nonoverlapping rectangles, we cannot provide an *exact* spatial mapping of location, but this form of layout does give an indication of *relative* location of nodes and so increases the data/location ratio. If we are concerned with exploring the locational aspects of the place descriptors, we can use CIELab coloring to emphasize absolute location, or we can represent some other aspect of the data with color

FIGURE 6-6. "Ordered squarified" treemap with colors showing absolute locations through a CIELab color space in which perceived differences in color relate closely to differences in location. (See Color Plate 16.)

(such as term importance) while retaining a strong cartographic metaphor. Figure 6-7 retains our ordered squarified layout to show the term hierarchy but rearranges nodes within each descriptor according to geography.

Here, the pinks, purples, and browns in *mountain* show us that this term is used in the north and west, although terms such as *pen*, *trig*, *cwm*, and *black* defy this pattern, reflecting their distinct geography. The vivid colors of *beach* reflect the peripheral, coastal nature of this scene type, whereas the more muted colors of *city* show that this is a more central base level.

Figure 6-8 goes one step further by arranging all nodes using the spatial ordering approach. As such, it therefore shows the geography and hierarchy of our six scene types.

Representing Location Displacement

Although we can identify some spatial patterns in our hierarchical structure, the degree to which nodes have been displaced from their true geographic location in order to be tessellated within the treemap space is not always clear. CIELab coloring can give some indication of this displacement; note the different colors within the quality and activity facets in *beach* or the discontinuities in *city* / *element* / *hall* and *hill* / *element* / *farm* in Figure 6-8. We can improve things further, however, by indicating graphically how a photo or group of photos has been translated from geographic coordinates during the tessellation. Doing so follows the advice of Skupin and Fabrikant (2003), who recommend that cognitively plausible cartography should use appropriate methods for communicating this form of positional error.

FIGURE 6-7. "Ordered squarified" treemap with colors showing absolute locations through a CIELab color space. Leaf nodes within descriptor nodes are arranged to relate to locations using a spatial ordering algorithm. (See Color Plate 17.)

Figure 6-8 superimposes a collection of lines on the treemap. These join each node's treemap position to its geographic location—the longer the line, the greater the displacement. See, for example, the displacement vectors associated with the *quality* and *activity* facets in *beach,* which confirm the different geographies that we have already noted despite their juxtaposition in the spatial treemap. The design goal behind the creation of these lines was to provide additional spatial context to the treemap while retaining the ability to explore the term hierarchy. Thicker lines are used to show *scene type* displacements rather than *facet* displacements in Figure 6-8. Very thin lines were thus used when showing geograph displacement, as many hundreds of thousands of lines may be drawn between geographic photo locations and positions of leaf nodes in the treemap. Figure 6-9 provides an example in which displacement vectors are curved more sharply at their node position end than their geographic location end. This helps to emphasize any spatial clustering of nodes, as is the case in many instances in Figure 6-9, as well as providing an overview of the general trends in displacement.

This concurrent view of term hierarchy and both relative and absolute geography allows us to consider the geographies that we noted of *track, summit,* and *cairn* in *hill* and compare them with those of *downs, chalk, barrow,* and *junction* simultaneously.

This spatial arrangement may draw our attention to new *relationships*. For example, *bridleway, path,* and *track* have similar functions but different geographies when used with *hill; fishing* and *cricket* are *activities* with different geographies in *village;* compare *chapel* and

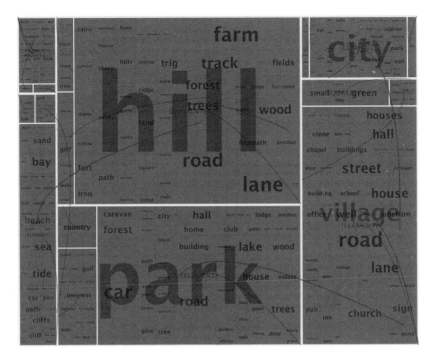

FIGURE 6-8. Spatial treemap of terms occurring in geograph titles and comments for six selected scene types. Node sizes represent term occurrence, and colors represent absolute spatial locations with CIELab scheme. Displacement vectors show absolute locations of non-leaf nodes (scene types, facets, and descriptors). (See Color Plate 18.)

church in *village*, or *golf* with *hill* to *golf* with *park*. Figure 6-10 shows some elements of *beach* in close-up, allowing us to see, amongst other things, aspects of the coastline of Britain through the clustered absolute locations of *tide*, the southern emphases of *path* and *cliffs* within *beach*, and particular geographic clusters associated with *beach / element / pier* in the southeast and *beach / element / harbour* in the central northwest.

Beauty in Discovery

We consider spatially ordered and spatial treemaps of large hierarchical data sets that have high *data/location ratios* to be aesthetically pleasing, and offer the figures presented in this chapter as candidate beautiful depictions of beautiful data. But things of beauty should be lucid, usable, and ultimately satisfying as well as elegant. Matsumoto (2007) expresses this in the context of computer code through his belief that beautiful code is readable. Just as maps make complex geospatial data readable in a fit-for-purpose manner that enables multiple spatial relationships to be determined and tasks such as navigation, geographic comparison, and pattern detection to be achieved, so our efforts aim to make analytical sense of the geography of the language of Geograph through readable graphics. Can we read Geograph? We contend that these and other graphics mean that we're well on our way toward interpreting some of the complexity of this rich and beautiful example of the kinds of geospatial data sets that are emerging, and using the kinds of relationships between description and location identified through our analysis to act upon this knowledge.

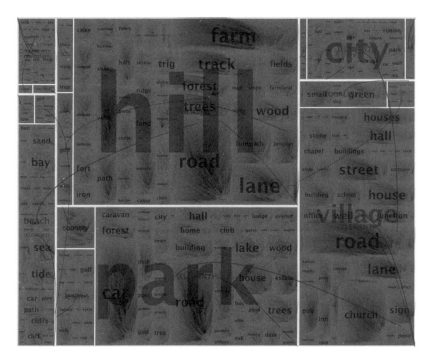

FIGURE 6-9. Spatial treemap of terms occurring in geograph titles and comments for six selected scene types. Displacement vectors show absolute locations of leaf nodes (co-occurring terms) and provide information about spatial clustering and spatial trends in displacement required to meet the space-filling objectives of the treemap. (See Color Plate 19.)

The spatial relationships depicted in these views are dependent upon aspect ratios and the average locations of nodes within leaves. We may be interested in more precise geographies than those described here, and the data-dense treemaps have been useful in selecting candidate facets and descriptors for more traditional mapping. Maps of term co-occurrence derived through the treemaps have enabled us to identify quantifiable spatial differences in term use. For example, we have found that *valley* is used with *hill* more frequently than might be expected in the south and southwest, while *summit* is used more frequently in the north. These relationships persist at different scales and when using alternative viable means of term selection from Geograph. They may reflect a bias in selecting particular aspects of the landscape to be recorded, regional geography, linguistic differences, personal preferences of individuals contributing in particular places, or likely a combination of these factors. Whatever the explanation, our reading of the treemaps draws attention to these geographic characteristics of some places in the light of others. Also note the somewhat rustic terms used to describe *village* here. These trends may not be due to conscious bias, but may relate to the selection of aspects of landscape that are aesthetically pleasing for Geograph—meaning that our reading of the data reinforces our contention that we are dealing with beautiful data. We intend to continue our exploration and analysis of the geography of such terms with maps and more formal spatial methods. These and other aspects of the geography of user-selected descriptive terminology are contributing to the development of an ontology for describing place.

FIGURE 6-10. Spatial treemap of terms occurring in geograph titles and comments for selected element descriptors in the beach base level. Displacement vectors show absolute locations of leaf nodes in this enlarged section of Figure 6-9. (See Color Plate 20.)

Our graphics and our exploration are incomplete. We are investigating the effects of systematic bias in community-contributed geographic information and developing strategies to mitigate this. We are developing notations to describe the visual design space and interactive applications through which this can be explored. We are yet to consider whether the geographically varying relationships that we are able to identify in Geograph are consistent over time. Nevertheless, the methods described here help us move toward achieving knowledge…against all the odds when the size, structure, diversity, and complexity of data are considered. But who better to contribute to our understanding of place than a large group of volunteers who inhabit places working collectively? And how better to explore the notions of place contained within their descriptions than through carefully designed multivariate graphics that reveal structure and aid discovery?

Reflection and Conclusion

We have argued that the beauty in data lies in its depth. Beauty emerges as previously hidden structures and patterns are revealed. These patterns prompt new thoughts and questions about the data. They inspire. They encourage exploration. They provide insight. Where they are spatial, *geographic beauty* may emerge.

Beautiful data encourages beautiful visualization, as it also encourages exploration and rewards the viewer who explores. Visualization is particularly apt for exploring geographic patterns, as centuries of cartography have demonstrated.

The examples we present here show how we can use beautiful data such as the geographs of Geograph to address the description of place with a view to using such descriptions in an applied context for information management and retrieval. Sophisticated and data-dense graphics with aesthetic appeal are an important part of this process.

We broadly consider beauty to be a characteristic of an entity that provides pleasure, meaning, or satisfaction. In terms of data and its representation, various aspects of Geograph have these qualities. Our visualization of some facets of Geograph in space-filling graphics with high data/location ratios is innovative, creative, and has a problem-solving basis. It has helped inform our colleagues' work and opened new analytical avenues. We would put forward these data-dense depictions of the people's descriptions of the human and physical geography of the British Isles in time and place as being among the most beautiful that we have created.

Acknowledgments

We gratefully acknowledge Barry Hunter and contributors to Geograph British Isles (*http://www.geograph.org.uk/credits/2008-04-31*), whose work is made available under the following Creative Commons Attribution-ShareAlike 2.5 License (*http://creativecommons.org/licenses/by-sa/2.5/*).

Ross Purves's and Alistair Edwardes's work on Geograph is also gratefully acknowledged. This has been undertaken as part of the project TRIPOD, supported by the European Commission under contract 045335.

References

Andrienko, G., N. Andrienko, J. Dykes, S. Fabrikant, and M. Wachowicz. 2008. "Geovisualization of dynamics, movement and change: key issues and developing approaches in visualization research." *Information Visualization*, v. 7: 173–180.

Bertin, J. 1983. *Semiology of graphics* (W.J. Berg, trans.). Madison: University of Wisconsin Press. (Original work published 1973.)

Cawthon, N., and A. vande Moere. 2007. "The Effect of Aesthetic on the Usability of Data Visualization," Proceedings of the 11th International Conference Information Visualization, IEEE Computer Society Washington, DC: 637–648.

Edwardes, A., and R. Purves. 2007. "A theoretical grounding for semantic descriptions of place." M. Ware and G. Taylor (eds.). LNCS: Proceedings of 7th Intl, Workshop on Web and Wireless GIS, W2GIS: 106–120.

Fabrikant, S., M. Ruocco, R. Middleton, D. Montello, and C. Jörgensen. 2002. "The first law of cognitive geography: Distance and similarity in semantic space." Proceedings of GIScience 2002: 31–33.

Fisher, P.F. 1998. "Is GIS hidebound by the legacy of cartography?" *The Cartographic Journal*, v. 35: 5–9.

Geograph. "Geograph British Isles - photograph every grid square." *http://www.geograph.co.uk/* (accessed April 9, 2009).

Goodchild, M. 2007. "Citizens as sensors: the world of volunteered geography." *GeoJournal*, v. 69: 211–221.

Hawgood, D., D. Dunford, R. Farrow, B. Hunter, and P. Mayes. "Geograph or supplemental." *http://www.geograph.org.uk/article/Geograph-or-supplemental/* (accessed April 9, 2009).

Kernighan, B.W. 2007. "A Regular Expression Matcher," in *Beautiful Code: Leading Programmers Explain How They Think,* ed. Andy Oram and Greg Wilson, 1–9. Sebastopol, CA: O'Reilly.

Kosara, R. 2007 "Visualization Criticism-The Missing Link Between Information Visualization and Art." Proceedings of the 11th International Conference Information Visualization, IEEE Computer Society Washington, DC: 631–636.

MacEachren, A.M., and M.J. Kraak. 2001. "Research challenges in geovisualization." *Cartography and Geographic Information Science*, v. 28: 3–12.

Matsumoto, Y. 2007. "Treating Code as an Essay," in *Beautiful Code: Leading Programmers Explain How They Think,* ed. Andy Oram and Greg Wilson, 477–481. Sebastopol, CA: O'Reilly.

Oram, A. and G. Wilson, eds. 2007. *Beautiful Code: Leading Programmers Explain How They Think.* Sebastopol, CA: O'Reilly.

Shneiderman, B. 1992. "Tree visualization with tree-maps: 2-d space-filling approach." *ACM Transactions on Graphics* (TOG), v. 11: 92–99.

Skupin, A. and S. Fabrikant. 2003. "Spatialization Methods: A Cartographic Research Agenda for Non-geographic Information Visualization." *Cartography and Geographic Information Science*, v. 30: 99–119.

Tufte, E.R. 1983. *The Visual Display of Quantitative Information* (First Edition). Cheshire, CT: Graphics Press.

Wood, J. and J. Dykes. 2008. "Spatially Ordered Treemaps." *IEEE Transactions on Visualization and Computer Graphics*, v. 14: 1348–1355.

CHAPTER SEVEN

Data Finds Data

Jeff Jonas and Lisa Sokol

Introduction

NEXT-GENERATION "SMART" INFORMATION MANAGEMENT SYSTEMS WILL NOT RELY ON USERS DREAMING UP smart questions to ask computers; rather, they will automatically determine if new observations reveal something of sufficient interest to warrant some reaction, e.g., sending an automatic notification to a user or a system about an opportunity or risk.

An organization can only be as smart as the sum of its perceptions. These perceptions come in the form of observations—observations collected across the various enterprise systems, such as customer enrollment systems, financial accounting systems, and payroll systems. With each new transaction an organization learns something. It is at the moment something is learned that there exists an opportunity, in fact an obligation, to make some sense of what this new piece of data means and respond appropriately. For example, does the address change on the customer record now reveal that this customer is connected to one of your top 50 customers? If an organization cannot evaluate how new data points relate to its historical data holding in real time, the organization will miss opportunities for action.

When the "data can find the data," there exists an opportunity for the insight to find the user.

How data finds data is a statement about *discoverability*, the degree to which previous information can be located and correlated with the new data. Discoverability requires the ability to recall related historical data so that an arriving piece of data can find its place, similar to the way each jigsaw puzzle piece is assessed relative to a work-in-progress puzzle. Each new puzzle piece incrementally builds upon what is knowable, at each given point in time relative to the evolving puzzle picture. Often new pieces, although important to building out the bigger picture, do not themselves bring new critical information. (On the other hand, some pieces may change the shape of the puzzle in a way that warrants ringing the bell—finding that one piece that connects the palm tree scene to the alligator scene.) It is at this moment in time, when the new puzzle piece presents the opportunity to reshape the picture, that discoveries are made. Real-time discovery replaces the need for users to think up and pose the right question at just the right time.

Organizations that are unable to switch to the "data finds data" paradigm will be less competitive and less effective.

The Benefits of Just-in-Time Discovery

Advanced information management systems that play this "data finds data" game will not rely on users to dream up the correct, relevant, timely questions to ask computers. While this technology will initiate new policy debates, such as which data will be permitted to find which data and who is notified of what relevance, here are some examples of what a "data finds data" system can do:

Guest convenience
> After tossing and turning in bed all night in a hotel room, the guest finally decides at 7 a.m. to call for a late checkout and schedule a wake-up call at noon. Shortly after the guest sinks into a deep sleep, disaster strikes when the maid carelessly knocks on the door to clean the room. Regrettably for hotel travelers worldwide, this most basic inconvenience occurs all too often. When the data finds the data, the late checkout and wake-up call requests converge with maid scheduling information. This "data finds the data" instance would trigger an automatic text message, notifying the maid *not* to clean this room until after 2 p.m.

Customer service
> With interest in a soon-to-be-released book, a user searches Amazon for the title, but to no avail. The user decides to check every month until the book is released. Unfortunately for the user, the next time he checks, he finds that the book is not only sold out but now on back order, awaiting a second printing. When the data finds the data, the moment this book is available, this data point will discover the user's original query and automatically email the user about the book's availability.

Improved child safety
> A parent wants to ensure that her young children are safe while walking to school. The parent might search the community website to ensure that no registered sex offenders

are living along her children's walking route to school. Will the parent check this website every day, to determine whether a new address of an offender is added to a street on the route? Using the "data finds the data" paradigm, should a new sex offender register an address on the children's walking route, the new data will immediately connect with the earlier query. The parent will be instantly notified of the relevant discovery.

Cross-compartment exploitation

The government uses "compartments" to intentionally isolate data. Isolating data helps prevent highly sensitive data from escaping. Despite new mandates for information sharing, the traditional data protection practices for highly classified data prevent the government from discovering that two such compartments are dealing with the same subject or have subject overlap. An example of this might be one unit that is working on counterterrorism and another on counternarcotics. The government has hundreds of compartments, and the practicality of locating relevant data in another compartment is remote, because one never knows who has what information. When the data finds the data, the moment a record is added to the counternarcotics database of relevance to the counterterrorism unit (e.g., data involving the same person), notification is immediately published to the appropriate user.

Corruption at the Roulette Wheel

This is a true story where bad-guy data finds good-guy data—causing an unexpected discovery and resulting in a surprise outcome.

In the mid-1990s, riverboat gaming became legalized in many new jurisdictions, Louisiana being one of them. One of the challenges of a new gaming jurisdiction is the lack of available local employee candidates with deep gaming experience. New jurisdictions must therefore train the local workforce in a wide range of specialty job categories, ranging from dealers to surveillance room operators. Bossier City, Louisiana is one such community that had to make the transition from no casino business to casino riverboat operations.

Today is like any other day in any other casino. The dealers are watching the players. The floor supervisors are watching the dealers and the players. The casino manager is watching the floor supervisors, the dealers, and the players. And the surveillance room is watching everyone—even the casino executives. The surveillance room has an obligation to watch gaming transactions, not only to protect the house but also to protect the customers. Surveillance focuses both on gambling transactions as well as evidence of other criminal activity. For example, a purse-snatcher is bad for business because he interferes with the customer experience.

Surveillance is the last line of defense.

Hundreds of cameras (thousands in the Vegas mega-casinos) are piped into a remarkably tiny surveillance room. Twenty, thirty, maybe forty monitors cover an entire wall like a scene out of *CSI*. So how is it that only a few operators cleared for access to this room make sense of this information overload? Answer: *tripwires* and *attentive browsing*.

Tripwires come in many forms, ranging from a tip on a hotline to a floor supervisor asking for the surveillance room to evaluate the play of a customer (e.g., to determine whether she is counting cards).* On this day, the surveillance operator is browsing—performing what might be called a random audit—zeroing in on one table after another, watching a short while to see if anything seems out of place, and then moving on.

Wait! What is that? Can't be. The attentive surveillance operator has just observed a player blatantly cheating on the roulette table. Today the observed scam is known as "past posting"—a player who is placing bets after the roulette ball has already landed in its number. Past posting occurs when the player notices the ball has landed on a number (e.g., 32) and seeing this outcome, quickly places a late, sure-to-win bet on that number. Unlike card counting, which is legal but discouraged, "past posting" is actually cheating and is definitely illegal.

What is so peculiar today is that the table has one dealer and one player. Usually the "past posting" scam involves a team of players—players working together to prevent the dealer from detecting the late bet. Such team activity might involve two or more "players" at the table who appear completely unrelated (e.g., acting like they don't know each other). After the ball finds its number, one player (e.g., a nice lady with a grandma disposition) will reach all the way across the board as if to place a bet. The dealer, of course, says, "Madam, it is too late to place your bet." Nonetheless, the reach across the table (toward a losing number) has enabled the other team member (say, a punk-rock-looking dude with a mohawk) to place a late bet on the winning number—hidden from the view of the dealer.

There is no such team on the table today. This is curious and warrants immediate inspection. The tapes are rewound. There it is! The dealer seems a bit distracted and misses the past post event. At this point it would be common to start looking backward in time by reviewing the earlier moments of the game. (And at the same time, maybe another room operator will begin watching the game go forward live.) Bang! Again and again the player makes late bets, the careless dealer missing this each time—and each time, paying the customer for the win.

Security is notified. The troops mobilize. The player is confronted and detained for arrest by law enforcement. How could this happen?

The dealer is obviously quite embarrassed. Being in a new jurisdiction, this employee is also new to gaming and really only has had classroom training. The dealer makes it clear that she has only heard about this type of scam. She then points out that security has really done a good job today. She is very embarrassed and is quick to guarantee it will never happen again on her watch.

Enter "data finds data."

---

* Notably, the role of casino surveillance is intelligence. They report their observations and findings, but perform no enforcement; enforcement is the role of the security department.

When the cheater is apprehended, he is required to identify himself. The cheater today, like any other day, presents his name, address, phone number, and some other information. This information is collected on a standard form, with a signature if they can get one, and thereafter is data-entered into the corporate security arrest processing systems.

Of course, the cheater's last name is not the same as the dealer's; that would make life too simple. The address is also not that of the dealer. The phone number, however, happens to be the same as the phone number that the dealer used on her employment application! At this exact moment that the arrest information is presented to the arrest processing system, a secondary system performing data finds data* makes this vital discovery and produces an immediate alert that basically says, "Employee #5764 has the same phone number as Arrestee #44-00321!"

Long story short, the dealer is confronted, she confesses, and they are both processed and handed over to law enforcement for prosecution.

To be clear: the users did not take identity attributes (e.g., name, address, phone number) of the "past posting" cheater and attempt to search the wide array of operational systems (call this a federated search). The applicant, employee, loyalty club, and arrest processing systems, among others, cannot even be searched by address or phone number—they were not designed for that.

Using a "data finds the data" environment, the users do not have to proactively search or pose relevant questions. The users in the security department enter what they have learned into their system, and this new information is then assessed against other enterprise information assets. The new information is found to relate to existing data, and this relationship meets a prespecified condition of interest: when a "bad" guy is related to an employee. Because this condition is met, an alert is triggered because the bad guy and the employee share a phone number (thus, bad guy knows employee). If the cheater arrest data had perhaps found an association with a hotel visitor of three years ago, this noninteresting discovery would not have resulted in an alert.

To drive this point home, let's now imagine the phone number provided by the "past poster" had no relationship to that of the dealer. In this case, no alert would have been produced. The dealer may have been questioned with some suspicion, but there simply would not be enough evidence to make any claim. Might corporate security have opened an investigation of the dealer, or hired a private investigator to determine whether these two individuals were in fact close friends? Who knows?

But what if? What if the phone number does not match and no connection is made? The dealer continues to deal. Time marches on. What if, six months later, the dealer changes

---

* This technology, formerly known as Non-Obvious Relationship Awareness (NORA), was developed by Systems Research & Development (a company founded by Jeff Jonas) for the Las Vegas gaming industry. SRD has since been acquired by IBM and is now part of IBM's Entity Analytics group. Some additional information is available here: IEEE Paper: Threat & Fraud Intelligence – Las Vegas Style (*http://jeffjonas.typepad.com/jeff_jonas/2006/11/ieee_paper_thre.html*).

her home address in the employment system—and the new information is the same as the cheater's address? How would the organization know this? In truth, no organization will ever know this unless it can play this important game called "the data finds the data." The moment this new information connects the dealer with the closed case, such a system detects an alert condition: bad guy related to an employee.

Alerts, by the way, do not necessarily mean there is criminal activity. Alerts do, however, play an important role in focusing an organization's finite investigatory resources—in this case, a condition of sufficient interest to warrant a closer (human) look.

Other examples: this riverboat casino operation also found a scam involving a marketing person who figured out a system hack to cash-back comp (a marketing activity whereby the more you play, the more points you get, and points can be redeemed for cash!) his roommate. And in another case, it discovered that the person pulling out the "car a day" winner ticket happened to "select" her sister (of a different last name), with the family members acting as if they had never met.

All three of these scams were revealed as the data became known using "data finds data"—and all three scams were detected in the first 90 days of operation!

The reason why data finds data is essential is that the order in which information arrives is uncertain. Systems and processes that take the order of events for granted have a fatal flaw: out-of-order facts may provide the organization with important knowledge that never gets acted upon. More about this later.

One large retailer with thousands of physical storefronts across the United States analyzed its historical data holdings and was shocked to discover that two out of every thousand employees had in fact already been arrested for stealing from them. Worse yet, these employees were caught stealing from the same store that hired them! Despite the order in which the data is presented, the moment the enterprise has such evidence there is no time to waste. The store should know this immediately.

Traditional remedies to address out-of-order data points are cumbersome. How can corporate security take advantage of new enterprise data that reveals an employee may be a known shoplifter? When should updates to an employee record in the human resource system cause corporate security to reevaluate all its earlier investigations? How can the reevaluation be structured so that the organization can't miss instances when new or modified records in the internal investigations database are related to employees? One strategy is to periodically test the investigations database against the entire employee database. Another strategy is for corporate security to reinvestigate every employee on some recurring basis. But both of these strategies will miss important discoveries because timing is critical.

Even perfect algorithms running against perfectly reengineered operational systems (e.g., the human resources system and the internal investigations system) will still miss certain discoverable events. What if the data needed to determine that two people are the same or connected exists in an entirely unrelated system? For example, imagine a third record

arriving from an unrelated system, such as a loyalty club enrollment system, which reveals a previously unknown linkage between a home address and a home phone number. What kind of enterprise systems would be required to detect this condition, a condition we will characterize as a nonobvious relationship?

Data finds data, including nonobvious relationships, requires that one first solve the problem of "enterprise discoverability."

Enterprise Discoverability

When new information arrives in the organization, whether that is a new employee, a change to an employee record, shoplifter information, or a loyalty club enrollment, one needs to know what other organizational data relates to this information.

One common approach to enterprise discovery involves a technique known as "federated search," the passing of a query to every relevant operational system. As we shall demonstrate, this does not work for data finds data systems. Discoverability, especially within large-scale, real-time environments, necessitates directories.

Federated Search Ain't All That

Organizations have numerous operational systems, each with its own dedicated business function, tailored information structure, analytics, and reports. Secondary aggregations of data are common, and include such things as data warehouses, operational data stores, and data marts. There are countless information silos, each particular to its mission or function.

Traditional federated search systems involve the user querying the database of each silo for relevant content. More sophisticated federated search systems use intelligent middleware to broker the individual queries to each database, a model where the middleware processes the query by engaging the myriad of information silos automatically and compiling the findings, returning the collective results to the inquirer.

Federated search assembles cross-silo data "just-in-time," at the point information is needed. Although this type of federated search is applicable in some settings, it is not well suited to high-performance enterprise discoverability, which is required to deliver on data finds data.

There are *two* primary reasons federated search does not scale:

- Existing systems generally do not have the indexes necessary to enable the efficient location of a record. Payroll systems, for example, will often have prebuilt indexes (defined pointers into the data) to facilitate searches on employee number, tax ID number, and name. Rarely would a payroll system have an efficient way to locate records on address or phone number. Suppose our newly discovered gambling cheat discloses his address and phone number. Our payroll system keeps track of all of the employees' phone numbers and addresses. (It has to send out paychecks, after all.) This same payroll system would not be able to easily generate (if it can at all) a list of any

employees who share an address or phone number with our previously mentioned gambling cheat. Even if an index were created on employee phone numbers within the payroll system, this still would not allow one to locate the emergency contact phone number in this same system. If we can't compare the gambling cheat's identification data against all relevant employee data, we miss the discovery of the *connection* between employee and cheat.

If a field is not in an index, the method for locating a record in a database is known as a "table scan." In a table scan, the value being searched for is compared against every single row in the table—the first record in the database, then the second, and so on. Therefore, the larger the database, the longer each search takes, and the greater the computational burden placed on the host system.

- To make matters worse, federated search requires recursive processing (some conditions necessitate repeating steps), which is a nightmare for distributed query environments. Suppose you perform a federated query to discover enterprise records related to a specific person—say, starting with a specific person's name and date of birth. If the federated query returns some new attributes for this person, e.g., a few addresses and phone numbers, then you have learned something new. To be thorough, one should leverage the new data learned about this person, i.e., initiate another enterprise-wide federated query in case there are additional records that can now be located based on these new data points. Now, what if this second federated query discovers another address, a few more ways to spell the name, and an alias or two? To be thorough, each time something is learned that might enable the discovery of a previously missed record, the discovery process must perform another enterprise-wide federated query.

Here is a real use case that underscores this point. An organization (a commercial entity, not a government) had 2,000 databases under its control. User queries were directed across these databases to gather related records. Brilliant middleware designed to optimize the search process was created over many years and at the cost of millions of dollars. This very smart system would know which databases could process which queries, determine the ideal order of database access, simulcast queries to all relevant sets, and assemble what has been learned. However, no amount of engineering on this federated search approach could overcome one serious design flaw: every time something was discovered (e.g., an alias or a new phone number), the brilliant middleware had to reissue the queries to many databases. This recursive process, being run on very large computers, eventually had to be programmed to stop processing at eight minutes! Note that the next recursive inquiry might have finally revealed an essential record.

But wait, eight minutes! This means a human or a system is now standing by, unable to act in the moment, as no answer is available for all these minutes. However, when data finds data, *the data is the question*. This now means every piece of new data arriving may see up to eight minutes of latency before processing the next piece of data. Imagine how impractical it would be to use a federated approach at the scale of hundreds or thousands of federated queries a second (real transactional volumes) submitted across the enterprise network, bouncing around and executing recursively through countless operational systems!

If these mentioned factors are not compelling enough, the death blow to federated search is that all the systems that must be searched have to be physically switched on and available, not undergoing maintenance or backups, or in the middle of periodic nightly or month-end batch processes. Connectivity must of course be fully operational as well. Contemplate these mandates in conjunction with an organization composed of hundreds or thousands of systems spread across buildings, time zones, and continents.

Federated search cannot support the "data finds data" mission, because it has no ability to deliver on enterprise discoverability at scale.

Directories: Priceless

Think about a library. Think of the library's floors, hallways, and shelves as silos of information. Valuable information is tucked away, waiting to be discovered. No one roams the halls when looking for a specific book. Instead, one uses the card catalog—cross-referenced on subject, title, and author—to facilitate discovery of relevant documents.

Let's say that directories, indices, and catalogs are all basically the same thing: a thing used to locate other things. Some examples of locators include the card catalog at the library, phone directories, Google, eBay, and so on. In each case, the directories are equivalent to locator services: they return reference information (pointers) after being provided one or more search terms. At the library, the card catalog is a special-purpose directory used to enable efficient enterprise discovery, providing the user a specific pointer to a document (e.g., using the Dewey Decimal system). After the user is provided a pointer, the activity becomes "federated fetch." Note the difference between federated *search* (not useful) and federated *fetch* (useful).

A Google search does not scour the planet for the results; rather, a specialty directory created by Google is searched and the results, pointers to the real documents (e.g., URLs) are returned to the inquirer.

It would follow that the *only* scalable solution to enterprise-wide discoverability involves the use of directories. No surprise there; a special-purpose directory is therefore a fundamental component that permits "data finds data" systems to handle discoverability at scale and determine relevance in real time.

All directories are not created equal. There is a big difference between traditional "context-less" directories versus directories capable of accumulating and persisting context. Contextualized directories enable data to find data in remarkably unexpected (nonobvious) ways, in real time, at great volume, and with extraordinary efficiency.

Context-less directories are the most common type of directory: each document is indexed indifferent to all other documents. In other words, new enterprise transactions (documents) update the directory without any attention to how this transaction (metadata for the index) might relate to any other transaction. Context-less directories are designed to provide users with the most basic ability to locate documents (e.g., all books related to "Billy the Kid").

Semantically reconciled* directories are directories that attempt to exploit synonyms, things that use different words to mean that same things. This means users looking for one thing (e.g., "Billy the Kid") should find other "same" things (e.g., "William Antrim," one of his aliases). Semantically reconciled directories recognize when a newly reported entity references a previously observed entity. Directories that contain semantically reconciled data can be thought of much like a library card file, with one big difference: cards relating to like entities are rubber-banded together. This means if a search locates one card, as a bonus, all other related cards are discovered without any additional effort. Most notably, some of the cards in the rubber-banded clump of library cards may not even contain the original data item being searched.

Quite frankly, this can look like magic. When attempting to discover what the enterprise knows about an email address, one can discover a record with the email address as well as other records in the enterprise about the same person—for example, loyalty club activity, despite the fact that the loyalty club record never contained an email address. Algorithms that semantically reconcile identities (for example, people or organizations) are sometimes referred to as *identity resolution.*[†] Algorithms that determine when multiple entities are in fact the same entity require a deeply nuanced discussion, and as such are beyond the scope of this chapter.

Semantically reconciled and relationship-aware directories[‡] are a type of directory that provide an even higher degree of context by allowing users to discover additional documents, such as those related by intimate association (e.g., Billy the Kid aka William Antrim). It may also be important to understand there was a real William Antrim, who happened to be Billy the Kid's stepfather. The way to visualize this is to picture in your mind's eye a library card catalog with some cards already bundled in rubber bands as described earlier, plus threads that connect some bundles to other cards and other bundles. One can search any single set of terms and locate a bundle, and at that instant learn how that bundle is associated (related) to other bundles. Some association threads are thicker than others, indicating a stronger association. By following a thread to another bundle, one can then instantly see what threads lead from the next bundle. In this manner one can observe degrees of separation, as in the six degrees of Kevin Bacon.

When contemplating "data finds data" systems, keep in mind that the moment a new transaction is placed in context, possibly adding to the context of an existing entity, there is the potential that the new information may change the shape of the picture as the bundles and the threads reorganize.

---

* Defined as *"Recognizing when two objects are the same despite having been described differently."*

† Don't confuse identity resolution with a quasi-related set of methods sometimes referred to as match/merge or merge/purge. More about the distinction here: "Entity Resolution Systems vs. Match Merge/Merge Purge/List De-duplication Systems" (*http://jeffjonas.typepad.com/jeff_jonas/2007/09/entity-resoluti.html*).

‡ The NORA (Non-Obvious Relationship Awareness) is an example of a semantically reconciled and relationship-aware directory.

Persistent context is the term used to refer to the current state of the reconciled and relationship-aware index—essentially, the present status of the ever-changing and incrementally improving puzzle. Persistent context is the memory of how things relate, and it trumps the just-in-time context that is delivered in federated search systems.

Persistent context (semantically reconciled and relationship-aware directories) enables high-performance discovery, streaming contextualization, and the opportunity to detect relevance in real time. It is also worth noting that the detection of relevance is computationally cheapest if it can be assessed at the moment the data ingestion is taking place. In this respect, the librarian (the function that stitches the new data into the directory) is the first to notice if arriving data is of enough relevance to be published (e.g., to a user).

Sense-making on streams beats boiling the ocean. A clear way to envision this is imagining an organization with 4 exabytes of historical data that receives 5 terabytes a minute. Do you think they run a process over the weekend to reveal what has been learned? There may not be enough computers or energy on Earth to do this. (Note: Envisioned behavior at scale proves to be very helpful when designing highly efficient systems.)

Relevance: What Matters and to Whom?

Now we have lots of data coming at us. Take a moment to assess all the sights and sounds in your immediate environment: the background hum of the computer, the music playing, the cartoons on the TV, and the kids trying to steal one another's toys. As humans, we have internal relevance-detection algorithms that assess all of the presented data, and alert us when some observations cause us to take notice and possibly react. Sort of like ignoring the kids and their ongoing bickering until it threatens to escalate into violence. It's that one move, by one kid, that alerts us that it is time to intercede.

How one exploits technology to calculate relevance and when to allow it to automatically register an alarm is crucial. On the technology side, the objective is a state in which the very next item in an alarm queue is the next most important item for review. There is also no reason to produce more alarms than there are available resources (for example, analysts, systems) to deal with them. Risk-assessment engines, for example, must be configured to produce alarms appropriate to one's individualized risk, staffing, and ability to respond. If resources increase, one can increase alarm sensitivity.

Components and Special Considerations

Our intelligent "data finds data" environment must contain eight essential building blocks:

- The existence of, and availability of, observations
- The ability to extract and classify features from the observations
- The ability to efficiently discover related historical context
- The ability to make assertions (same or related) about new observations
- The ability to recognize when new observations reverse earlier assertions

- The ability to accumulate and persist this asserted context

- The ability to recognize the formation of relevance/insight

- The ability to notify the appropriate entity of such insight

The Existence of, and Availability of, Observations

If there is no data, then there is no chance one can make sense of it. And if there is data, it has to be "sensed" (collected) by some sensor system for it to ever be of potential use. And even if data is collected, one must have access to it to have any hope of making sense of it.

The Ability to Extract and Classify Features from the Observations

For the sake of argument, let's say a grain of sand contains too few features to extract and classify. Grains of sand are frequently the same color, size, weight, shape, and so on. Therefore, the lack of discriminating features would prevent one from identifying the same piece (semantic reconciliation) later. The point being, for data to be placed into context, one must be able to extract and classify its key features. Structured data is rather easy when address information is contained in one column and first and last name are in another. Unstructured data, such as newspapers and blogs, take a lot more work; extracting the right names and addresses is a challenging field, often called *entity extraction*. Feature extraction from video, such as car license plate readers, can be done in certain cases.

Long story short, one must be able to extract and classify the key features of observations if one hopes to stitch observations together into context.

The Ability to Efficiently Discover Related Historical Context

As new observations arrive, the extracted and classified key features are used to look into the contextualized historical data (what we have called persistent context) to discover how this new piece fits. For this to occur in real time in support of high-volume data streams, this discovery requirement must be extremely fast.

The Ability to Make Assertions (Same or Related) About New Observations

When a new observation is contextualized with respect to the historical data holdings, the algorithms must make one of several assertions: (a) this is a new entity, the first of its kind (e.g., a new person); (b) this is a known entity (e.g., this is an observation about somebody we already know), in which case the new entity is "resolved" with the existing entity; or (c) how this entity (the new one or known one) now relates to other entities.

There comes a point, just the same as when people put jigsaw puzzles together, where one concludes that nothing more can be done. It is at this point that one abandons the current item wherever it has been placed and moves one's attention to the next puzzle piece (observation). Note that you may have made the last assertion in error, but at this point it is unlikely you will ever discover this unless a new piece arrives to reveal this potentiality.

The Ability to Recognize When New Observations Reverse Earlier Assertions

Sometimes an observation contains new information that provides the evidence that an earlier assertion should be reversed. Possibly this new information proves that entities previously deemed not the same are in fact the same entity. Conversely, a new observation may reveal that two entities previously determined to be the same are now believed to not be the same at all (for instance, the new data point indicates that two Bob Joneses in our database are not the same person, and instead are a case of junior versus senior).

Using new observations to reverse earlier assertions is one of the most complicated aspects of semantic reconciliation algorithms. But without this important feature, databases drift from the truth over time. The disadvantage of this is that periodic database reloads are used to correct for this phenomenon. And for very large data sets, obviously this presents a scalability nightmare.

The Ability to Accumulate and Persist This Asserted Context

When the assertion process is complete—in other words, when new observations are reduced to assertions (new, same, or related entities) and new observations are used to remedy these same earlier assertions—the newly learned knowledge must be captured in a database so that the very next transaction can benefit from the new knowledge. In some respects, this begins to feel like a very basic incremental learning system.

The Ability to Recognize the Formation of Relevance/Insight

Only after a new observation is applied to the historical data such that no more computation is warranted, this is the moment the system must ask itself, "Have I learned something that matters?", much in the same way a person will incrementally look to see what has been revealed after each puzzle piece is placed onto the board.

The work we have done involves the detection of prespecified patterns of interest. For example, it is relevant to discover whether the good guys know bad guys or if the cash transactions for one person exceed $10,000 per day.

However, new relevance parameters can be set based on external processes, which might include human insight or secondary pattern-discovery/data-mining engines.

The Ability to Notify the Appropriate Entity of Such Insight

When insight is detected, who or what system should be notified? In our existing implementations this is trivial, as each relevance rule (for example, if a prospect is a close associate of one of my top 50 customers) and the dissemination rule (i.e., send a courtesy message about this to the casino host) is established at the same time.

Privacy Considerations

Smarter systems, like those capable of performing "data finds data," require very close attention to privacy and civil liberties protections. How these next-generation systems are built and deployed, and what policies (including accountability and oversight) govern their use deserves close attention and vigorous debate. Some of the core issues include: defining what data should be indexed for discoverability, how the data will be stitched together (e.g., what constitutes a relationship?), what constitutes relevance, what relevance is disclosed to whom, who can search the index, how the system will be monitored for unauthorized use, and how errors will be detected and corrected.

Fortunately, the directory-based model has a number of nice privacy-enhancing characteristics, including:

- Urges to share more data with more parties are replaced by transferring less information to fewer places (card catalogs).

- Who searches for what and what they found can be logged (for instance, using tamper-resistant logs) in a consistent manner, thus facilitating better accountability and oversight.[*]

- Information sharing between parties is now reduced to just the records that they need to know and to share (sharing less by sharing only the information that must be shared).

- It is now possible to make the index anonymized, which means the risk of unintended disclosure of even the limited metadata in the index is drastically reduced.[†]

Conclusion

"Data finds data" systems determine how new observations relate to what is known and detect relevance/insight worth special attention. Such insight ideally occurs in real time, thus enabling real-time reaction.

This emerging technology will ultimately differentiate one organization from another across a spectrum of enterprise interests, ranging from better recognition of opportunity to better estimation of risk.

Data finds data will likely become yet another building block from which next generations of advanced analytics will benefit. This new paradigm will inevitably lead to the emergence of even smarter systems, potentially even contributing to advances in cognitive computing.

---

[*] Tamper-resistant logs are also often called *immutable audit logs*. An interesting paper published by the Markle Foundation on the subject as related to national security, especially in relation to nontransparent government systems, is located here: *http://www.markle.org/downloadable_assets/nstf_IAL_020906.pdf*.

[†] More about anonymized directories can be found in a chapter entitled "Anonymized Semantic Directories. A Privacy–Enhancing Architecture for Enterprise Discovery," by Jeff Jonas and John Karat, in a book entitled *Emergent Information Technologies and Enabling Policies for Counter-Terrorism*. Robert L. Popp (editor), John Yen (editor), published in 2006 by Wiley-IEEE Press (*http://www.wiley.com/WileyCDA/WileyTitle/productCd-0471776157.html*).

CHAPTER EIGHT

Portable Data in Real Time

Jud Valeski

Introduction

APPLICATION DATA HAS BEEN LOCKED AWAY FOR A LONG TIME. INITIALLY IT WAS CONFINED IN APPLICATIONS running on disconnected systems siloed around the world. Enter the combination of CAT-5 Ethernet cabling, IP, routers, DNS, and sockets. Once machines were connected to one another, data was able to move more freely between applications, and subsequently it became more interesting. Data became enveloped in a variety of new contexts, beyond the application from which it originated. Overnight, client-server computing took off with the advent of the Internet, and suddenly wildly disconnected machines were talking to one another. With HTTP as the communication medium, and text the language, data started flowing.

The major types of mainstream data that have been moving around over the past 15 years can be categorized as pornography and general consumer commerce (including advertisements by proxy), and both conform nicely to the delivery model provided by traditional "web browsers" and their server counterparts, introduced in the early 1990s. More recently, a third category of data has started moving around *en masse*: social data. People have moved their socializing onto the network, and it's creating a new type of data, as well as new access needs that don't conform well to the patterns that have become

ingrained thanks to the browser. Social data is here, and its needs are now. A January 14, 2009 PEW report, *Adults and Social Network Websites*,* stated that well over 50% of online adults between the ages of 18 and 34 have social networking profiles.

In this chapter I discuss this evolution and our current approaches to solving the inherent issues in consuming today's trendy information: social data. Although leaps and bounds have been made to get us to where we are, some fundamental programming principles were lost along the way: event-driven architectures and predictability of data structure. Often solutions to modern problems are right under our noses, and Occam's razor suggests they're usually simple. By literally shifting HTTP 180 degrees and awakening the POST method giant, "real time" can legitimately become part of the industry's vocabulary. The introduction of an intermediary broker, Gnip (*http://www.gnip.com*), provides a convenient bridge between heterogeneous social data and consuming applications.

The State of the Art

Today's social data is being contorted to fit a delivery and formatting landscape that doesn't map well to the behavioral needs end users prefer. This is often the case when a platform becomes established over time; people find new ways to leverage it, even if sacrifices must be made in order to do so. Illustrating the major underpinnings of today's framework is the best way to describe this contorted leverage.

Transport

There are many ways to connect two sockets together and move data between them. However, for the foreseeable future, there is only one that matters: HTTP. There will always be specialized cases wherein more performant protocols can be used to optimize data transmission for said special case, but HTTP is ubiquitous, and has punched more holes in more firewalls, across Earth and its satellites, than anything else. Therefore, it is the one. If something can't be done over HTTP, that something needs to be reconsidered. To illustrate this point, consider consumer electronic devices. Many of them are cool, but only the amazing devices have HTTP clients on them (e.g., iPhone, or Android-based devices). Truly amazing devices have HTTP servers on them as well (Nokia's S60 can run an HTTP server). As with any good rule, there are exceptions. HTTP is both state-less and heavyweight, and both of these traits can get in the way when you're trying to do things that need to be fast and state-full. The following protocols exemplify the kind of exceptions I'm talking about.

XMPP

AOL's Instant Messenger product was the industry's first crack at a real-time social messaging product, and it took off like a rocket. People wanted to "chat." It didn't take long for people to want to chat P2P, or through other services, thus XMPP was born. Starting as a

---

* *http://www.pewinternet.org/Reports/2009/Adults-and-Social-Network-Websites.aspx*

standardized framework of transports and formats for social conversation and presence data, XMPP has been cobbled into a general messaging framework that allows for a wide variety of uses, from IM to general message PubSub. In mid-2008, Cisco bought Jabber.com (the leader in commercialized XMPP installations), and the network's routers will soon have slim, specialized XMPP handlers burned into silicon for all the world to use.

BitTorrent

When your use case is highly specialized, it's best to tune your pipeline to be "perfect." Cutting out the cruft and overhead to negotiate data transfer between arbitrary clients and servers is only natural when the clients and servers are tightly coupled and well known to each other. BitTorrent is phenomenal at moving large binary chunks of data to and fro across a distributed set of nodes, and is a great example of optimizing for a very specific use case.

Proprietary/P2P

One of HTTP's weaknesses is that effectively each request/response pair includes the same set of headers as the previous one, even when the pair may be the nth negotiation between a specific client and specific server. Wouldn't it be smarter to manage the client-server negotiation out of band and upfront, and leave the data channel alone to do nothing but move bits around? Yes. This reason, amongst many others, drives many Point-2-Point (or Peer-2-Peer) protocol implementations that move vast amounts of data around every day.

HTTP being the tube of choice leaves the question: what is its format counterpart? Surely if a transport protocol has become ubiquitous over the years, the data moving across it must have distilled along the way as well.

Formats

XML has provided the basis for data formatting going forward. The question as to which base-level format something should be communicated in has largely gone away. Now discussions over XML-derived formats are where the conversation takes place. Although most developers take XML for granted these days, it is worth noting how heavy and bloated it is. It's a text-based format that is rather descriptive, by definition, and therefore it is generally not the most optimized format for communicating. Whenever I get into modern protocol and format discussions, I'm reminded of AOL's proprietary FDO model. FDO is a binary, tightly bit-packed protocol/format combination optimized for 300-baud modem connections. Thankfully, connections have evolved to the point that broadband speeds have become the norm.

All that said, just like HTTP, XML's weaknesses are also its strengths. If we have learned anything over the past 15 years, it is that ubiquity follows human-readable protocols and formats—and I mean that literally. The further a format gets from being decipherable by a human, the further down the innovation stack it gets pushed. When the only way to debug something is via decoding tools that transform data into something I can interpret using my puny brain, a significant hurdle has been put in place between human

creativity and communication. "Winning data" is readable by a programmer. "Losing data" can be consumed only by machines.

Note that there's a difference between payload formats and metadata formats (usually XML). High-definition video data (e.g., the latest blockbuster movie in HD) takes up vast amounts of physical space, and is not human-readable; I call this a payload format. The descriptive information surrounding said video, its metadata, is relatively compact. Payload formats overwhelm metadata transmission across the network (just ask your favorite ISP what its ratio looks like), yet they are relatively dumb and uninteresting until they are decoded by a machine.

APIs

This is where things start to get interesting. Once everyone realized that the gazillions of HTTP transactions flying around looked like traditional API calls, REST gave us the foundation to use the Web as a giant distributed application. Roy Fielding, one of HTTP 1.1's contributors, gave us the mental framework to describe things as REST (REpresentational State Transfer; thank you, Mr. Fielding).

Developers could finally stop grappling with CORBA and DCOM to distribute their logic and data across networked machines, and instead use the standard HTTP and text-based tools to get their applications to talk to one another on levels lower than traditional web applications.

This has led to an explosion of APIs across nearly every web application you can think of, as shown in Figure 8-1. An API became the thing every product manager had to have. This was both a good thing and a bad thing. On the bright side, thousands of products have opened up their data for all the world to use. Programmable Web (*http://www.programmableweb.com/*) has hundreds of them documented and ready to use. On the dark side, many APIs were hastily produced with no consideration for how they might be used. The result has been a surge in API calls being made across the WAN to disparate endpoints that may or may not meet your expectations, as the API caller, in terms of performance or functional characteristics. Very few web APIs offer service-level agreements (SLAs), for example, and when they do, the terms are usually deplorable.

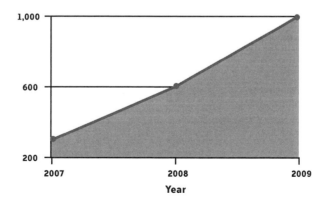

FIGURE 8-1. Public API growth over the past few years, as derived from Programmable Web.

The need, real or imagined, for an application's data and functionality to be available via an API has created some interesting challenges on the network.

If you look at how APIs are being used across the network today, they are providing data with seemingly arbitrary delivery characteristics and SLAs. For the first time, at scale, we have software being integrated with other software with extreme regularity. These kinds of integrations have been dubbed "mashups," as they "mash" data from various services together. More and more, end user expectations are that the data in their social applications arrives in real time, yet the infrastructure to support real-time data transmission is far from prolific. In our pursuit of real-time applications, the infinitely complex creativity of software developers has yielded many different models in an attempt to provide real-time notification (e.g., "Comet," "Web Hooks," various "PubSub" messaging systems) to applications. Some of these have worked well, and others have not. No matter your approach, fundamentally there's no real magic going on in the solution; rather, age-old frameworks are always at play behind the curtain.

There are two basic time-flow-processing primitives in software: polling and events. Software executes across time, and user-interactive software needs to consume input from a user or another service. That input makes its way into the running application via either polling or events. It's worth noting that you can implement either using the other, but that's a subtle trick left for a computer science classroom, and I'll avoid it here. What are important are the higher-level notions that define how an application collects its relevant input. It's easiest to convey the two models using examples.

Polling

Polling is accomplished by the software constantly asking an interrupt whether there has been a change. If a change is detected, the program can take a defined action as a result. An often-used analogy is the bartender. Imagine a bar setting, one bartender, and 10 patrons. If the bartender is a polling bartender, he will repeatedly ask each patron if he or she would like a drink. "Would you like a drink?" "Would you like a drink?" "Would you like a drink?" and on and on down the bar. Every now and then, one of the patrons being asked will respond "yes," and the bartender will change his behavior and make the patron a drink. Polling is beautifully simple, but can often be horribly inefficient (as the analogy illustrates) for both the client and the server.

Rate limiting

Frontending your online service with an API for developers to access can usually be done fairly easily. Slapping some framework on top of your application and wiring up data access doesn't take much. However, once you've done so and made the API public, you are no longer in control of how your API will be used. That very control has protected running code for thousands of years. Building a "web API" (aka "Web Service") at scale takes real thinking, engineering, and operations.

If one is lucky enough to build an API interesting to developers, and subsequently one that is heavily polled, likely the easiest way to deal with the increased load on their application is to block access at the IP, or header, level and to limit their API's use. Although that solves the scaling issues, it interrupts the desired program flow for those integrating the needed API in order to keep their users happy. Developers don't want to build throttling layers in their applications; they just want to make the calls they're used to making and have them "just work." Actually solving the data access problem in your system takes more energy than IP-based rate-limiting (aka "throttling"), yet we often don't have the luxury of time to invest in the true solutions. Some social data applications have invested in getting this right, and their APIs accommodate heavy load (e.g., Digg). Most, however, have not.

Getting it right

Having a popular social application with lots of social data shouldn't require a massive investment in infrastructure and horizontally scalable applications, however. Both of those things inhibit innovation at the product level, and eat money for breakfast. Instead, leveraging the time-tested "event" primitive, described shortly, is in order. The law of large numbers illustrates that 90%+ of calls to access social data are wasted. The vast majority of the time, the data sought isn't even available. Continuing with the bartender example, eventually the patrons are going to become irritated with being asked the same question over and over again when their answer is always the same: "no."

Constantly asking Flickr for photo updates that a given user has made is a waste. Instead, Flickr telling your application when that user has updated his photostream is significantly more efficient and, more importantly to users, more timely.

Zero miles per gallon efficiency

I'll use what has become known as the "Flickr, Friendfeed example" to highlight the inefficiency inherent in polling for social data. Social data, by and large, is user-generated. That means social applications that leverage social data are based on the behavior of humans, not on the more predictable and manageable behavior of computers. When we build software, the value of which is purely a function of human activities, things get interesting. This example is useful because both a publisher (Flickr) and a consumer (Friendfeed) compared notes, yielding valuable insight into the problem inherent in "off-box," heterogeneous notification transmission via polling.

In July of 2008, Even Henshaw-Plath and Kellan Elliot-McCrea presented "Beyond REST?" (*http://www.slideshare.net/kellan/beyond-rest*) at OSCON (O'Reilly's Open Source Convention) in Portland, Oregon. In the presentation, they revealed that Friendfeed polled Flickr's API 2.9 million times in order to determine whether any of Friendfeed's 46,000 Flickr accounts had uploaded photos over a 24-hour period. Of those 46,000 users, only 7,000 of them even visited Flickr over the time period and could have potentially uploaded a photo.

A well-known social application rule, called the "1, 9, 90" rule, has emerged over the past few years. The gist is that if you consider 100% of a social application's user base, 1% of the users contribute to the core data (e.g., "upload a photo"), 9% of the users engage with the data (e.g., "mark a photo as favorite"), and 90% of the users just view the data (e.g., "view photos"). Conservatively applying this rule to the Flickr/Friendfeed example would suggest that of the 7,000 users that visited Flickr on that fateful day, 700 of them would have uploaded photos. That means Friendfeed polled Flickr 2.9 million times to learn that 700 of their users actually did something. That's a "hit" percentage of 0.02%, or 4,000 polls to find a single update.

Blending the Flickr/Friendfeed example with the bartender analogy would mean that the polling bartender would need to ask a patron whether she wanted a drink 4,000 times before the patron said "yes" in order to ensure that the patron received her drink in real time.

It's one thing for an application making local "on-box" API calls to absorb such inefficiencies. It's quite another for software making API calls across the Web to behave so inefficiently. When you consider this one example in light of all the social applications in use today, the overhead is truly appalling.

Event-driven software drives software to real time, and social data, by definition, needs to be communicated in real time. Seeing that a check cleared my checking account via my online banking software can be "off" by a day or two, but a teenager seeing the pictures his best friend took on spring break needs to happen immediately.

Events

An event-driven architecture, in contrast to polling, takes a different approach. As opposed to the bartender asking patrons over and over again whether they'd like a drink, the bartender just stands behind the bar waiting for patrons to tell him that they'd like another drink. Though event handling is often more efficient, it does require some extra overhead in terms of the discrete "event" notion itself. Events have to be fired, and captured; a framework for event handling has to exist, which leads to complexity. Polling can be done very simply in a linear, procedural loop, and that simplicity is one of the contributing reasons to its overuse.

Ever since the Jurassic period, these two execution-flow paradigms formed the foundation of software development. Both client and server software relied on them to control execution flow and the behavior of applications. Operating systems leveraged them appropriately to provide fluid user input and interactivity. As a developer, your choice of one over another often boiled down to the language you were using, or the functionality provided by whatever library or framework you happen to be using. Although the performance characteristics between the two are often not terribly interesting in local, "on-box" applications, the performance characteristics between them when doing remote, "off-box" operations can be crippling to an application. Note that when dealing with UI and graphics rendering, local performance differences can make or break an application.

Once programmers started injecting remote API calls into local applications *en masse*, the differences between polling and event handling became clear. The difference between local I/O calls and remote I/O calls is exponential. All the work that went into making disk, memory, and chipset interfaces faster to speed up applications became moot. Figure 8-2 illustrates the relative I/O performance difference between local types of data access and remote data access. To keep things simple, I've implied the inherent IP connection setup/teardown latency, and just illustrate the point as a function of bandwidth/throughput. If you do, however, consider the actual protocol negotiation as a function of total data transfer overhead, the latency issue becomes even more severe.

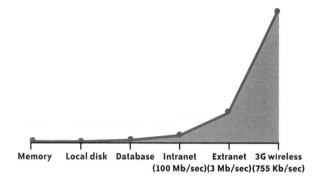

FIGURE 8-2. *Relative throughput of file descriptors operating on various connection types.*

As you can see, the differences are intense. When remote versus local data access times are on such extremes, the differences between using polling or events to drive your application will compound latency issues even further. When your software needs to know whether something has changed in a service across the network, in order to take some action, you don't have time for inefficient polling. If the bartender gets an affirmative response to the "do you want a drink?" question, one in every 4,000 requests, the time wasted in querying blows up when the bartender has to ask the question of patrons sitting across town.

The differences between polling and events are all well and good, but only one of these models is easy over the Web: polling. Client-server programming via HTTP/REST never provided a formal event-driven framework for web application development, and as a result, the Web is littered with social data–driven applications that suffer from innate timing inefficiencies that are further highlighted by the inherent timeliness of social data. If my friend is going to be in town tomorrow, I don't want to find out too late. The very applications we want to be "real time" are built on a house of cards that started crumbling just as the walls were going up.

HTML 5 events

It is worth noting that the HTML 5 specification outlines an event model and "Web Socket" framework that exposes bidirectional communication at a high level. XMLHttpRequest has

taken GUI web applications to a new level, and I suspect that "Web Sockets" will have a major impact on web app development in the coming years. Allowing a browser-based application to access data in a more socket-like manner will only lead to great things.

WAN Scale Events

Distributed event handling and notification is not a new problem, and neither are its solutions. In fact, the enterprise space has produced incredibly robust and efficient, albeit proprietary, solutions in the form of "message buses." Tibco comes to mind as a leader in enterprise message bus solutions. However, enterprise message buses are focused on the criticality of the data they're usually transferring, as opposed to diverse sets of endpoint connections across an even more diverse connection stack. Stock trades need to be guaranteed in delivery and privacy. Guarantees at this level come at a cost, and that cost gets translated into high licensing fees, which do not translate well to the Internet at large. Social data is created, and consumed by applications that are free to end users. Subsequently, expensive, proprietary, hard-to-integrate message bus solutions from the enterprise space are not welcome on the Web.

Leveraging the technologies that yielded the explosion of social data itself to provide event-driven notification schemes generously provides solutions based on technology the system is already familiar with. HTTP POSTs can be used to push events across the WAN between arbitrary services, using standard formats (XML), and the latency gap in execution control flow can be closed. Jeff Lindsay is doing a great job evangelizing the embodiment of this HTTP POST event transmission model in what he's dubbed "Web Hooks" (*http://blog.webhooks.org/*). To reiterate, HTTP isn't the most optimized protocol for transmitting these events, nor is XML the most optimized format, but the two provide the most prolific, pragmatic mechanism to solve the problem within the context of real-time server-to-server communication.

If social data becomes any more latent, one of two things will happen: either we, as consumers, will continue to suffer and our behavior patterns and expectations will have to conform to an inferior model, or we'll stop using the products because their usefulness degrades to the point of not having enough value to bother. The former has plenty of precedent (Beta versus VHS) as we regularly accept less-than-great solutions to problems we want solved. The latter happens every day as burgeoning industries and products regularly collapse due to timing and last-mile refinement issues. Until a framework becomes standard, an intermediary event gateway can broker events and the data itself across a variety of protocols and formats, from social data publishers to social data consumers. Providing the mechanism can be done fairly cheaply and generically, while eliminating detrimental latency around social data. Real-time social data ubiquity, at "web scale," is dependent upon an event-driven model.

Gnip was founded on the notion that event-driven architectures around social data consumption are the only way to deliver real-time access patterns. However, recognizing that polling is here to stay, and at times the preferred model, Gnip can still be polled for social data activities.

Single API integrations are generally straightforward. However, when you go to wire up many endpoints, the inefficiencies start piling up. Gnip does the work of multi-API integration for its data consumers, who then have to integrate with only a single point: Gnip.

Social Data Normalization

Assume we've solved the data access latency issue by using HTTP POSTs, à la Web Hooks, to handle events across the WAN. This resolves general API access issues, but not the diverse nature of the data itself. XML provides structure for data, but it does nothing for commonality. Social data aggregation applications today are stricken with one-off understandings of each social data API they integrate with. The overhead in understanding the intricacies of the data structure that comes back from a particular API is high—too high. While protocol muxing gateways have existed for a long time, generally only strict XML transformation translators exist for consolidating common, normalized data from disparate sources. Unfortunately, strict parsing of data rarely works, as the set of services actually creating the data is so diverse. Their understanding of the standards, encodings, and escape sequences all varies. In addition, the software creating the XML for consumption inevitably contains bugs, which result in poorly formatted output, further complicating its consumption.

We learned from strict HTML-parsing web browsers that standards unfortunately do not result in perfectly formatted data that software adhering to those standards can flawlessly consume. The reality is that standards are interpreted differently, software is buggy, and the most powerful de facto standard is what users are already doing. The power of the people can never be denied.

If you've ever spent time looking at data from various social sources, you'll notice that it starts looking the same. Although the commonality is clear for a human to interpret, it is much harder for a machine to interpret. Human editorial guidance in mapping data setA to data setB is required.

Consider the two following examples of XML from two different "social bookmarking" services. Although they're both clearly XML, representation of the "bookmark" is wildly different, and yet they both provide a similar service to the end user.

From Delicious:

```
<item>
  <title>Fractals derived from Newton-Raphson iteration</title>
  <pubDate>Mon, 19 Jan 2009 20:02:05 +0000</pubDate>
  <guid isPermaLink="false">http://delicious.com/url/7549fded443f#joe</guid>
  <link>http://www.chiark.greenend.org.uk/~sgtatham/newton/</link>
  <dc:creator>iacovibus</dc:creator>
  <comments>http://delicious.com/url/7549fded443f</comments>
  <wfw:commentRss>http://feeds.delicious.com/v2/rss/url/a</wfw:commentRss>
  <source url="http://feeds.delicious.com/v2/rss/joe">joe's bookmarks</source>
  <category domain="http://delicious.com/joe/">mathematics</category>
  <category domain="http://delicious.com/joe/">newton-raphson</category>
  <category domain="http://delicious.com/joe/">fractals</category>
  <category domain="http://delicious.com/joe/">iteration</category>
</item>
```

From givealink.org:

```
<item>
  <title>Bus slams into shop houses after driver collapses behind wheel</title>
  <link>http://www.thaivisa.com/forum/Bus-Slams-Shop-Coll-t198228.html</link>
  <description>Bus slams into shop collapses behind wheel</description>
</item>
```

With thousands of services exposing their user-generated content (UGC) via APIs and feeds today, normalizing its structure and content so developers can anticipate commonality needs to be a priority. The DiSo project is a major catalyst in bringing relevant parties to the table, across APIs, in order to distill more consumable social data; see *http://diso-project. org/wiki/activity-streams*.

Gnip was designed to act as an intermediary between data producers and data consumers. As such, it is in a unique position to translate, and normalize, social data's meaning into a canonical understanding and structure. Leveraging the collective input and knowledge around industry's desire for more readily consumable social data, Gnip acts as a funnel. Taking in a plethora of different protocols and formats and outputting consistent, more homogeneous data provides easier access to data.

Business Value of Data

The debate around whether or not open source software is good or bad is largely over. There are fairly clear lines between when it is a good idea for a business to open source its software, or parts of it, and when it is not. In a nutshell, if your software is "one of a kind" intellectual property that sets you apart from the rest of the world, you should consider keeping it under lock and key. Otherwise, it's a candidate for open sourcing so the community can overlay its experience and expertise into the code and make the world a better place. Unfortunately, similar decision frameworks aren't as mature when it comes to data. The explosion of APIs has caught the data publishers off guard, and subsequently their understanding of the value of their data is as clear as mud.

Some traditional content publishers have hardened the value of their data. Weekly periodicals give the content away for free, and have advertisers support the production of the content (commentary) and the product (the magazine). Some trade magazines charge a premium for subscriptions, and leave advertising models at the door. Traditional media/ content publishers on the Internet have largely adopted the advertising model to support the distribution of their data (content). However, access to social data via APIs doesn't have a mature model. Should providers charge for access, for the data itself, or should everything just be free? Unless you're a "freegan," none of these answers are clear. Unless the data in question has intrinsic value, appraising it becomes very difficult and convoluted. Should acquiring that microblogging message cost you, as a data consumer, $0.10? Should that message be licensed, or should the access method be leased? The difference between an item's value and the shipping/handling around it comes to the fore. Should the user actually generating the content on the publisher's service receive a cut of any revenue derived from it? Who actually owns the data to begin with? As you can see, these are loaded questions with no clear answers.

Until a social data marketplace emerges, the industry will be left with some publishers claiming their data is priceless, while others consider theirs free. Consumers have been trained to believe that most data is free, so if social data is ever actually priced, they will have to evolve to be tangibly part of the value chain.

Public versus private

Some data is considered public, whereas other data is private. The distinction between the two is defined by the service providing the data, and is usually outlined in the Terms of Service for a given service. While the social understanding of the two is an interesting topic in and of itself, I'll consider the technical implications of accessing the two in this section.

Let's start with the easier of the two, public. Accessing public data is relatively straightforward. The majority of today's data APIs are accessed via unauthenticated REST interfaces. This means that they are no different than any other URL on the network; they're easily consumable by arbitrary users and applications. Accessing these API endpoints requires little, if any, form of authentication, and authorization is all handled behind the scenes in a generally opaque manner to the API consumer. The two more prolific authentication patterns are the use of HTTP Basic-Auth and "API keys" embedded in URLs. Both allow the API service to control access to the data and API functionality based on the "authentication" credential. Surprise, surprise, both work very well with HTTP. Regardless of whether any authentication is required for a public API's access, the underlying social data being accessed is still "public" in most cases.

Private data opens a can of worms. As more and more applications start leveraging oft-considered "private" data available from other applications, end users demand control over that access. Data providers also overlay their own notions of access rights, using a variety of technologies. Both of these realities make aggregated access to private data highly complex.

Ensuring that end users' data is protected from a storage standpoint is only part of the battle. Storage redundancy and encryption have allowed applications to flourish, generally without the loss or compromise of user information. In fact, users feel so safe that they freely hand out their usernames and passwords to third-party applications in order to allow deeper levels of API integration. The practice is incredibly insecure, yet it illustrates the degree to which users will sacrifice their private information in order to get the functionality they desire. There are two effective alternatives to sharing private login credentials: OAuth and blind URLs.

OAuth (*http://oauth.net/*) provides a simple solution to allow various services to interact, all while giving end users ultimate control over their information without sharing their username and password with third parties. The interaction passes users off to the desired integration point and asks them to enable the level of access requested by the integrating service. If the end user approves the interaction, a token is shared between the two services, and the user can revoke its abilities if she ever chooses to do so.

Blind URLs are an even simpler way to share information across services and among users, yet they're not technically "secure," so they're often lent little credibility. Flickr's "Guest Pass" sharing functionality masterfully leverages blind URLs to allow a user to share "private" photos with users who lack a Flickr account and therefore aren't part of the Flickr user's "friends" or "family" sharing matrix. Blind URLs don't require any work on behalf of the consuming service to obtain URL consumption permission, but they technically can be guessed, which can lead to private information being leaked.

Gnip currently plays exclusively with public data. Drawing the boundaries between which controls should be provided to end users, and which should not, isn't always clear when discussing intermediary infrastructure. For example, you don't know, or care, what internal traffic routing services credit card companies use to ensure secure financial transactions, yet controlling who can see your vacation pictures is critical. Gnip is working to draw its line between public and private data, as well as how it will ultimately support the same services for private data as it does for public.

Conclusion: Mediation via Gnip

Amidst raging tides bringing more heterogeneous APIs ashore every day, some consistency is warranted. As a message-oriented middleware service, Gnip promises to "deliver the Web's data" using a middleman data brokerage approach. Representing the data publisher's desire to share via an array of inbound transport protocols, Gnip shuttles normalized data from those publishers to Gnip consumers in real time (sub-60-second latency from message receipt to rebroadcast). Regardless of inbound data format inconsistencies, Gnip "cleans" and normalizes the data into a canonical format as a service to the Gnip consumer. The result is a single integration with Gnip's API, and consistently formatted data for the consuming application.

You can access many social data APIs through Gnip's single interface, all in "real time." Gnip's framework is biased toward the event-driven model described earlier, in order to promote a more efficient data flow across the network and between applications at large. However, polling is supported as well. Requiring polling-based applications to switch to an event-based model in order to leverage the normalizing benefits Gnip provides would be too heavy handed. Without simultaneous, wholesale adoption of yet-to-be-completed standards around Publish/Subscribe frameworks and format consistencies, a broker in the middle is necessary.

The current infrastructure has done a great job carrying things thus far, and online commerce has boomed. However, continually morphing use cases and end-user needs to conform to existing frameworks will keep us bound to their limitations. The needs of real-time social data require a change in the underlying control-flow shape, upon which our applications are built. I'm looking forward to event-driven architectures spanning the Web.

CHAPTER NINE

Surfacing the Deep Web

Alon Halevy and Jayant Madhaven

What Is the Deep Web?

THE TERM "DEEP WEB" REFERS TO WEB CONTENT THAT LIES HIDDEN BEHIND HTML FORMS. IN ORDER
to get to such content, a user has to perform a form submission with valid input values.
Take, for example, the store locator form in Figure 9-1. Searching for stores in the zip code
94043 results in a web page with a listing of stores. The result page is an example of a web
page in the Deep Web.

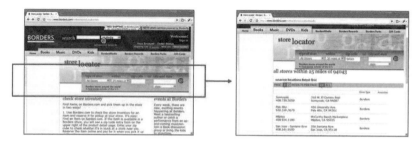

FIGURE 9-1. The Borders Store Locator form and a deep-web page resulting from a particular form submission. (See Color Plate 21.)

The Deep Web has been acknowledged as a significant gap in the coverage of search engines. This is because search engines employ web crawlers to discover web pages that will be included in their index, and traditionally these web crawlers were believed to rely exclusively on hyperlinks between web pages to discover new web content. They lacked the ability to automatically perform form submissions, and hence web pages behind forms were not included in the index of a search engine. The web page with the form typically carries very little information about the content of the pages behind the form; thus, common web users could get to Deep Web content only if they already knew of the existence of the corresponding HTML form or if search engines somehow led them to the form. They then had to perform the correct form submission to get to the underlying content. In fact, the very name Deep Web (alternately, Invisible Web or Hidden Web) arises from the observation that such content was not easily accessible to web users through search engines.

Various accounts have hypothesized that the Deep Web has much more data than the currently searchable World Wide Web (Bergman 2001, He 2007, Raghavan 2001). Our recent study (Madhavan 2007) estimated that there are tens of millions of HTML forms with potentially useful deep-web content, and that the Deep Web spans every conceivable domain. Popular domains include used car sales, real estate listings, rental apartments, job listings, products, and food recipes. There are a number of forms that provide access to government or public-sector information, such as laws and regulations, court rulings, environmental reports, etc. But there are also forms that let users search for more esoteric content, such as shade trees, taxes paid for park access, resin statues of horses, etc.

When considering the Deep Web, we must keep in mind that HTML forms are used for a variety of tasks on the Web, not all of which constitute accessing deep-web content. For example, they are used in login forms that require a username and a password, in feedback forms where user input is posted to forums and blogs, in shopping carts to execute purchases, etc. Such forms require private information or lead to changes in backend state, and are not considered to be part of the Deep Web. Instead, we are primarily concerned with forms that simply let users anonymously search for information.

Given the nature and amount of deep-web content, it is natural that search engines would like to include such content in their web indexes. They would then be able to lead users to new content that they would not be able to get to otherwise. This has led to a lot of interest, in both academia and industry, in the problem of offering access to deep-web content. However, a vast majority of the research and technology has focused on addressing the problem in narrow domains. The most prominent such approach has been in the context of *vertical* search engines that each focus on content within a single narrow domain. For example, there are used car search or job search sites that let users search over multiple underlying sites from a single portal. These solutions, while offering access to some part of the Deep Web, are very limited in their reach and omit large amounts of form-based sites that do not fit into narrowly defined domains.

Our goal is to offer access to the Deep Web to users of a general-purpose search engine. From the point of view of the search engine, we would like to include content from the

Deep Web at large, i.e., reach as many of the millions of HTML forms as possible. Hence, we require a solution that works in all possible languages and domains and needs no human supervision, i.e., one that is completely automatic. From the point of view of the host of a deep-web site, the solution should not overwhelm the host's resources; in other words, it should drive only truly relevant user traffic to the site.

In this chapter, we present an overview of a solution that meets the criteria just listed. Our approach, called surfacing, precomputes, for each HTML form, a set of queries that are likely to retrieve useful contents from the underlying site. URLs are assembled for each of the precomputed queries and are inserted into the search engine index. At a high level, our approach addresses two challenges: to decide which form inputs to fill when submitting queries to a form, and to find appropriate values to fill in these inputs. At its core, the approach relies on probing an HTML form with intelligently chosen sample queries and analyzing the distinctness of the web pages that are retrieved. We believe our solution, while extremely simple and elegant, is very efficient and is able to effectively open up a large fraction of the Deep Web to web search users. Our surfacing approach can be applied to any HTML form on the Web that uses the get method (overviewed later in this chapter). This primarily excludes forms that we would not want to be crawled anyway, e.g., forms that require user information or result in product purchases; such forms typically use the post method.

Our deep-web surfacing system has been deployed on the Google search engine. We have successfully crawled several million sites in several hundred domains and in over 50 languages. Currently, over 1,000 queries per second on Google.com see a result from the Deep Web on the first page of results. On the whole, search engine users find these results about as useful as regular search results. More details about our solution and experimental analyses are presented in (Madhavan 2008) and (Madhavan 2009).

In the rest of this chapter, we first take a closer look at alternative solutions for offering access to deep-web sites. We then describe a conceptual model for thinking about our problem. We then describe our approach to predicting the useful inputs (and input combinations) in a form and to predicting the values that are appropriate for text inputs. We conclude with some remarks about our experience in deploying our solution.

Alternatives to Offering Deep-Web Access

There are two common approaches to offering access to deep-web content. The first approach, popular with vertical search engines, is to create mediators for specific domains (e.g., cars, books, or real estate). In this approach we could create a single master form (the mediator) and then create semantic mappings between individual forms and the mediator. For each query over the mediator, the relevant underlying forms are selected based on some precomputed form summaries. The semantic mappings are used to construct queries over each individual form. Content is then retrieved from each of the selected forms and then combined before presenting them to a user. At a high level, this approach is very similar in spirit to the implementation of modern comparative shopping portals that retrieve offers from multiple underlying sites using web services.

Although adequate for vertical search, which focuses on homogenous collections of forms within a single domain, this approach is unsuitable for a general-purpose search engine. First, the human cost of building and maintaining the many different mediators and mappings is high. Second, identifying the forms that are most relevant to a search engine keyword query is extremely challenging. Only a small number of forms have to be identified; otherwise, the underlying forms can receive user traffic more than they can possibly handle. To achieve this, at the extreme, the form summaries might need to be almost as large as the underlying content itself. Finally, and more fundamentally, data on the Web is about everything, and boundaries of domains are not clearly definable. Hence, creating a mediator for the Web would be an epic challenge, and it would need to be done in over 100 languages. Thus, such an approach is unsuitable for use when the goal is to cover a large number of forms across many domains.

The second approach is *surfacing*, which precomputes the most relevant form submissions for any interesting HTML form. Each form submission generates a unique URL that can then be indexed by a search engine like any other HTML page. This approach enables leveraging existing search engine infrastructure. Further, it leads to a seamless inclusion of deep-web pages into web searches, i.e., they can be inserted directly into the ranked list of result pages in response to search queries. In addition, user traffic is directed to deep-web content when a user clicks on such a search result, which he presumably already believes to be relevant based on its snippet.

There are two main challenges in implementing the surfacing approach: to decide which form inputs to fill when submitting queries to a form and to find appropriate values to fill in these inputs. First, HTML forms typically have more than one input, and hence a naive strategy of enumerating the entire Cartesian product of all possible values of all inputs can result in a very large number of URLs being generated. Crawling too many URLs will drain the resources of the web crawler, which has to crawl each of the generated URLs, and will in all likelihood pose an unreasonable load on web servers hosting the HTML forms. Furthermore, when the Cartesian product is very large, it is likely that a large number of the result pages are empty and hence useless from an indexing standpoint. As an example, a particular search form on Cars.com has five inputs and a Cartesian product yields over 240 million URLs, though there are only 650,000 cars for sale (*http://www.cars.com*). Not surprisingly, the vast majority of the form submissions will have no records at all, and hence are useless to a search engine.

Second, HTML forms typically have text inputs and might also expect a reasonable value to be provided in the input before any results can be retrieved. The text inputs can be of two types: generic inputs that accept arbitrary words, e.g., a keyword search box, and typed inputs that only accept values from a specific well-defined set, e.g., a zip-code input in the store locator in Figure 9-1.

The solution that we will describe in the rest of this chapter addresses these challenges as follows: first, we devised what we call the *informativeness test*, which we use to evaluate query templates, i.e., combinations of form inputs. For any template, we probe the form

with different sets of values for the inputs in the template, and check whether the HTML pages we obtain are sufficiently distinct from one another. Templates that generate distinct pages are deemed good candidates for surfacing. Second, we designed an algorithm that efficiently traverses the space of query templates to identify those suitable for surfacing. The algorithm balances the trade-off between trying to generate fewer URLs and trying to achieve high coverage of the site's content. Third, we designed an algorithm for predicting appropriate input values for text boxes. The algorithm extends previous algorithms (Barbosa 2004, Ntoulas 2005) for selecting keywords for generic text inputs, and applies the informativeness test to indicate typed inputs that recognize values from common data types, such as zip codes, prices, and dates.

Basics of HTML Form Processing

Here we present a brief overview of form processing. More information can be found in the HTML form specification (*http://www.w3.org/TR/html401/interact/forms.html*).

An HTML form is defined within a form tag (see Example 9-1). The action identifies the server that will perform the query processing in response to the form submission. Forms can have several input controls, each defined by an input tag. Input controls can be of a number of types, the prominent ones being text boxes, select menus (defined in a separate select tag), checkboxes, radio buttons, and submit buttons. Each input has a name, which is typically not the name that the user sees on the HTML page. Users select input values either by entering arbitrary keywords into text boxes or by selecting from predefined options in select menus, checkboxes, and radio buttons. In addition, there are hidden inputs whose values are fixed and are not visible to users interacting with the form. These are used to provide the server additional context about the form submission (e.g., the specific site from which it came). In this chapter, we focus on the select menus and text boxes in a form. Checkboxes and radio buttons can be treated in the same way as select menus.

EXAMPLE 9-1. HTML code that includes a form that lets users search for jobs

```
<form action="http://jobs.com/find" method="get">
  <input type="hidden" name="src" value="hp"/>
  Keywords: <input type="text" name="kw"/>
  State: <select name="st"> <option value="Any"/><option value="AK"/>
                            <option value="AL"/> ... </select>
  Sort By: <select name="sort"> <option value="salary"/>
                      <option value="startdate"/> ... </select>
  <input type="submit" name="s" value="go"/>
</form>
```

When a form is submitted, the web browser sends an HTTP request with the inputs and their values to the server using one of two methods: get or post. With get, the parameters are appended to the action and included as part of the URL in the HTTP request (e.g., *http://jobs.com/find?src=hp&kw=chef&st=Any&sort=salary&s=go* in Example 9-1). With post, the parameters are sent in the body of the HTTP request and the URL is simply the action (e.g., *http://jobs.com/find* in Example 9-1). Hence, the URLs obtained from forms that use get are unique (and dependent on submitted values), whereas the ones obtained with post are not.

Since search engines identify web pages based on their URLs, the result pages from a post are indistinguishable and hence cannot be directly inserted into a search engine index. Furthermore, as per the HTML specification, post forms are to be used whenever submission of the form results in state changes or side effects (e.g. for shopping carts, travel reservations, and logins). As already mentioned, such sites are typically not informational in nature. For these reasons, we restrict our attention to get forms that tend to produce content more suitable for web search.

Forms that require any kind of personal information have to be excluded, for example, by filtering away forms that include any password inputs and any words such as username, login, etc., that are typically associated with personal information. Likewise, forms that simply record user feedback or comments can be excluded by ignoring those containing text area inputs.

Finally, we note that handling JavaScript events is beyond the scope of our approach (as described in this chapter). Forms and inputs can have onselect, onclick, and onsubmit attributes where arbitrary JavaScript code can be included. Handling these events involves simulating JavaScript execution on all possible events. In principle, we can take advantage of the JavaScript engines such as SpiderMonkey and V8 (see "References" on page 147) by harnessing a web browser to perform form submissions on our behalf, thereby extending our algorithms to handle such forms as well. Such simulations are more expensive to process, and hence the challenge here lies in quickly identifying JavaScript forms that are likely to yield deep-web content that can be added to the search engine index, i.e., the eventual web page has an idempotent URL like a get request.

Queries and Query Templates

We can think of a form as an interface that lets users pose queries over a backend database. Each form submission is a query that takes values for each of the inputs and returns a subset of the records from the database. The queries belong to a restricted language as determined by constraints on the form inputs and their values. Further, at the outset the contents of the form site are unknown. Thus, the problem of selecting form submissions for surfacing is essentially one of selecting a set of queries from the restricted language over a database with unknown contents.

Some of the challenges in selecting the right set of queries arise from the ambiguous nature of form inputs. Specifically, inputs can be of two types. First, there are *selection* inputs that impose selection conditions on the database records, e.g., kw (keywords in job descriptions) and st (state) in Example 9-1. The values for selection inputs can either be drawn from a predefined list (through a select menu) or entered into a text input. Text inputs may only accept values of a particular type, but in general that type is unknown to us. Selection inputs can often be assigned a wildcard value that matches all the records in the database. For select menus, the wildcard has to be one of the menu's options, e.g., the input state has the value Any. For text inputs, the wildcard is the empty string.

Second, there are *presentation* inputs that do not affect the selection of records, but only control presentation aspects, such as the sort order or the HTML layout of the result page, e.g., sort in Example 9-1. Distinguishing between selection and presentation inputs is one of the challenges that a surfacing solution has to address.

Formally, suppose we were to use SQL to pose queries. We can model the contents of a form site as a database with a single table D of m attributes. Each form submission is then the query select * from D where P, where P represents the selection predicates expressed by the selection inputs.

For example, suppose the form in Example 9-1 were used to pose queries over the job table Jobs(position, city, state, desc), the submission to retrieve chef positions in the state of California will correspond to the query select * from Jobs where state = 'CA' and desc like '%chef%'. Note that we are assuming here that the other inputs in Example 9-1 are presentation inputs.

The problem of surfacing is fundamentally a problem of selecting a good set of queries (form submissions). However, it is impractical, or even infeasible, to reason about the properties of individual submissions. Millions of distinct form submissions might be possible from an individual form, but testing each submission separately might drain the resources of the underlying site. Instead, in order to reason about collections of submissions, we define the notion of *query templates*. A query template designates a subset of the inputs in the form as *binding inputs* and the rest as *free inputs*. Multiple form submissions can be generated by assigning different values to the binding inputs. Thinking in terms of SQL queries, the query template concisely represents all queries of the form select * from D where P', where P' includes only the selection predicates imposed by the binding inputs in the form. The number of binding inputs is the *dimension* of a template. Table 9-1 shows three examples of query templates for the form in Example 9-1.

TABLE 9-1. Examples of query templates, each with different binding inputs and the corresponding collection of form submission URLs and SQL queries over the underlying Jobs database

Binding inputs	Form submission URLs and SQL queries
st	URL: *http://jobs.com/find?src=hp&kw=&st=S&sort=salary&s=go* Query: select * from Jobs where state = S
kw	URL: *http://jobs.com/find?src=hp&kw=K&st=Any&sort=salary&s=go* Query: select * from Jobs where desc like '%K%'
st, kw	URL: *http://jobs.com/find?src=hp&kw=K&st=S&sort=salary&s=go* Query: select * from Jobs where state = S and desc like '%K%'

Note that, in practice, values have to be assigned to the free inputs in a template in order to generate valid form submissions. Ideally, we would like these values not to add any additional selection condition to SQL queries for the template. For text inputs, we can assign the empty string; for select menus, we assign the default value of the menu in the

hope that it is a wild card value. We note that, in the interest of easing the interaction burden on their users, forms typically support wildcard values for most, if not all, of their inputs.

The problem of surfacing a deep-web site can now be divided into two subproblems:

- Selecting an appropriate set of query templates.
- Selecting appropriate input values for the binding inputs, i.e., instantiating the query template with actual values. For a select menu, we use all values in the menu, but for a text input, the values have to be predicted, and we cannot assume *a priori* knowledge of the domains of the values to be considered.

We assume for simplicity of exposition that the set of values with which an input is instantiated is the same for all templates in which the input is binding. However, in practice some inputs may be correlated. For example, the values for one input (e.g., cityName) may be dependent on the value chosen for another input (e.g., state), or multiple inputs (e.g., salaryMax and salaryMin) might restrict the same underlying attribute.

Selecting Input Combinations

We first describe how we can determine the inputs and combinations of inputs in the form that are useful for surfacing. For now, we assume that we know the values for each input in the form, i.e., text inputs and select menus are treated uniformly. The problem of selecting values for text inputs is addressed in the next section.

As we have seen, we can model the surfacing problem as one of selecting an appropriate set of query templates. We start by identifying some of the objectives that we should pursue in selecting the right set of query templates. As we outlined earlier, a naive strategy of enumerating the Cartesian product of all possible input values can be both wasteful (by imposing heavy loads on the web crawler and the server hosting the form) and unnecessary (since a large fraction of URLs might not have any data records).

Since we would like to expose as much of the deep-web content as possible, a natural goal for a strategy would be to maximize the coverage of the underlying database (i.e., the total number of records retrieved), while limiting the total number of form submissions. However, given that we are generating pages that are to be placed in a search engine index, we must address several other considerations as well.

First, it might seem that the best strategy would be to determine a few form submissions that would each contain a large number of results. However, a web page with a large number of results might not be the best one to be placed in a search engine index. For example, for a used car site, it is not useful to have a single web page that has all the Hondas in the inventory for sale. Instead, it would be preferable to have pages for each model of Honda or for different price ranges. Thus, we would like to generate URLs that have neither too few nor too many records in each page.

Second, although the size of the main index of a search engine is quite large, it is still not nearly enough to store all the pages that can possibly be extracted from the Deep Web. Since the overarching goal of a search engine is to direct users to relevant websites in response to their queries, we would much rather have diverse and important content coming from many sites. In a sense, the number of URLs generated need not be complete, but good enough to drive relevant traffic to the underlying sites.

Third, it is actually unnecessary for our surfacing of a website to strive for complete coverage. It suffices to seed the web index with enough diverse content from the site. The regular web crawler eventually will crawl the hyperlinks on the surfaced pages (e.g., links to more results for the same query or to results of related queries), thereby eventually increasing the coverage for the site.

In summary, our objective is to select queries for millions of diverse forms such that we are able to achieve good (but perhaps incomplete) coverage through a small number of submissions per site, and the surfaced pages are good candidates for selection into a search engine's index.

Quality of query templates

We can think of each of the stated objectives as a criterion for query templates. For example, we would definitely not want a template that includes a presentation input as a binding input. The records retrieved by such templates can just as easily be retrieved by the queries in a template that does *not* include the presentation input (since they do not affect the selection of records), and this also generates fewer URLs.

Templates with a large dimension are not preferable, as they generate too many URLs, many of which will retrieve no records. However, larger templates are likely to ensure retrieval of many more records.

Templates with a smaller dimension are preferable, as they generate fewer URLs, but it is also likely that each of their queries will retrieve far too many records. As outlined earlier, pages with too many records do not make good candidates for placement in the index. Further, sites might place practical limitations on the number of actual records displayed on each page, thereby reducing the actual number of records retrieved.

Thus, we would prefer templates that (a) do not include any binding presentation inputs, and (b) do not have too large or too small a dimension. Intuitively, the dimension of templates should be dependent on the size of the underlying database.

We now define a single test that tries to capture the criterion just stated. Before we describe it, we consider an example that tries to illustrate the intuition. Consider two templates in the form in Example 9-1, T_1 with single binding input st (State) and T_2 with single binding input sort (Sort by), and consider the set of form submissions generated by them (Table 9-2).

TABLE 9-2. Templates can be determined to be informative or uninformative by analyzing the similarity in content for the form submissions they generate

Query template (binding inputs)	Template form submissions informative/uninformative
T_1 (st)	http://jobs.com/find?src=hp&kw=&st=Any&sort=salary&s=go
	http://jobs.com/find?src=hp&kw=&st=AK&sort=salary&s=go
	http://jobs.com/find?src=hp&kw=&st=AL&sort=salary&s=go
	...
	web page contents are different → template is informative
T_2 (sort)	http://jobs.com/find?src=hp&kw=&st=Any&sort=salary&s=go
	http://jobs.com/find?src=hp&kw=&st=Any&sort=startdate&s=go
	...
	web page contents are similar → template is uninformative

Observe that each of the submissions for T_1 retrieves job listings in a different state. As a result, the records retrieved will be different, and hence the resulting web pages will have very different content. We call such templates that generate web pages with very different content *informative templates*. On the contrary, since there are no keywords, the records retrieved by each of the submissions in T_2 will all be the same (all jobs). Hence, the resulting web pages are likely to be very similar to one another. We call such templates that generate web pages with similar content *uninformative templates*. In essence, our goal is to select templates that are informative and exclude those that are uninformative.

Thus, we can evaluate a template based on the distinctness of the web pages resulting from the form submissions it generates. We estimate the number of distinct web pages the template generates by clustering them based on the similarity of their content.

If the number of distinct web pages is small in comparison to the number of form submissions, it is very likely that either (1) the template includes a presentation input and hence multiple sets of pages essentially have the same records, (2) the template dimension is too high for the underlying database and hence there are a number of pages with no records, all of which resemble one another, or (3) there is a problem in the template (or the form) that leads to error pages that again resemble one another. If the template does not fall into one of these categories but still generates pages with indistinct content, then it is likely to be of only marginal value to the search engine index, and hence is unlikely to have any impact on search engine queries.

Informativeness test

We consider the URLs generated by a given template and download the contents of the web pages. We compute a signature for the contents of the web page resulting from each submission and deem templates to be uninformative if they compute much fewer signatures than the number of possible submissions.

Informativeness is defined with respect to a threshold τ that can be experimentally determined. Suppose Sd is the set of distinct signatures, and St is the set of all signatures. Then, we say that T is informative if $|Sd|/|St| > \tau$.

While the exact details of the content signature are less important, we enumerate the important properties we want from such a function. First, the signature should be agnostic to HTML formatting, since presentation inputs often simply change the layout of the web page. Second, the signature must be agnostic of term ordering, since result reordering is a common presentation operation. Third, the signature must be tolerant to minor differences in page content. A common source of differences is advertisements, especially on commercial sites. These advertisements are typically displayed on page margins. They contribute to the text on the page but do not reflect the content of the retrieved records and hence have to be filtered away. Finally, the signature should not include the input values themselves. A used car search site that has no red Honda Civics for sale in the zip code 94107 is likely to have an error message like "No search results for Red Honda Civic in 94107!" Likewise, the result page for a large fraction of the {color make model zip} queries will be "No search results for {color make model} in {zip}". The only differences between these pages are the search terms themselves, and a signature that does not exclude the search terms is likely to deem them different and hence deem the corresponding template informative.

In practice, it might not be necessary to analyze all the contents of all the submissions generated by a template. It should suffice to test a large enough sample set of all possible submissions.

Searching for informative query templates

Our goal now is to search for the informative query templates in a form. We can adopt a very naive strategy of considering all possible templates in a form and applying the informativeness test for each one. However, given a form with n inputs, there are $2^n - 1$ possible templates, and it will be computationally expensive and also unnecessary to test each possible template. Hence, an incremental strategy can be adopted instead to traverse the space of all templates and to test only those that are likely to be informative.

Our strategy is to search through the space of templates in a bottom-up fashion, beginning from templates with a single binding input. The main intuition leading to this strategy is that the informativeness of a template is very likely to be dependent on templates that it extends, i.e., has one additional binding input. If template T has dimension k and none of the k smaller templates (of dimension k–1) that it extends is informative, then T is unlikely to be informative.

We start by considering all templates of dimension 1. We test each of the candidate templates for informativeness. If any template of dimension 1 is deemed informative, we augment it, i.e., construct templates of dimension 2 that have a superset of its binding inputs.

Thus, the candidate templates are such that at least one of the templates they extend is known to be informative (but not necessarily both). Each of the new candidate templates is then tested to determine whether it is informative. From the informative ones of dimension 2, we continue in a similar fashion to build candidate templates of dimension 3, and so on. We terminate when there are no informative templates of a given dimension.

We note that all candidate inputs are considered while augmenting a template. We could choose a more aggressive strategy where we consider only informative inputs, i.e., their corresponding template of dimension 1 was deemed informative. However, we believe that in practice such a strategy will (erroneously) omit some informative templates. It is not uncommon to have forms with one primary input that is required to retrieve any results and other inputs that are essentially refinements. For example, a form with make and color can be such that the default value for make ensures that no records are returned by simply selecting a color. Hence, the template with binding input color is uninformative, whereas the one with make and color is informative.

Once our search terminates, we can add the URLs generated by all the informative templates to the search engine index. A number of practical refinements can be considered to fine-tune the search. For example, we found that we never have to consider templates with more than three binding inputs or ones that generate too many submissions. They are unlikely to be informative and can be pruned away easily. It is not necessary to analyze all the URLs generated by a template. It typically suffices to consider a large enough sample.

Our experimental analyses indicate that our algorithm generates far fewer URLs than other simpler alternate strategies. Specifically, we find that we are able to generate two orders of magnitude fewer URLs in general over the best reasonable heuristic strategy that does not use the informativeness test. We also found that our approach can efficiently determine the informative templates for the form—both the number of templates tested and the total number of form submissions downloaded during analysis are small in number. Importantly, we anecdotally found that the number of URLs we generate is dependent on the size of the underlying database rather than the number of inputs in the form.

Predicting Input Values

A large number of HTML forms have text inputs. In addition, some forms with select menus require values in their text inputs before any results can be retrieved.

We note that text inputs are typically used in two different ways. First, there are generic inputs that practically accept any reasonable value, and the words entered in the inputs are used to retrieve all documents in a backend text database that contain those words. Common examples of this case are searching for books by title or by author. Second, there are typed inputs. Such inputs only accept values from a well-defined finite set or datatype (e.g., zip codes), or belong to some continuous but well-defined datatype (e.g., dates or prices). Invalid entries in typed text boxes generally lead to error pages, and hence it is

important to identify the correct data type. Badly chosen keywords in generic text boxes can still return some results, and hence the challenge lies in identifying a finite set of words that extracts a diverse set of result pages.

The two types of text inputs can be treated separately. In what follows, we first describe an algorithm to generate keywords for a generic input before considering the case of typed inputs.

Generic text inputs

Before we describe how good candidate keywords can be identified for generic inputs, let us consider (and dismiss) a possible alternative. Conceivably, we could have designed word lists in various domains to enter into text inputs and tried to match each text input with the best-fitting word list. However, we quickly realized that there are far too many concepts and far too many domains. Furthermore, for generic inputs, even if we identified inputs in two separate forms that correspond to the same concept in the same domain, it is not necessarily the case that the same set of keywords will work on both sites. The best keywords often turn out to be very site-specific. Since our goal was to scale to millions of forms and multiple languages, we required a simple, efficient, and fully automatic technique.

We adopt an iterative probing approach. At a high level, we assign an initial seed set of candidate keywords as values for the text input and construct a query template with the text box as the single binding input. We generate the corresponding form submissions, download the contents of the corresponding web pages, and extract additional keywords from the resulting documents. The extracted keywords are then used to update the candidate values for the text box. We repeat the process until either we are unable to extract further keywords or we have reached an alternate stopping condition, e.g., a sufficient number of candidate keywords. On termination, a subset of the candidate keywords is chosen as the set of values for the text box.

Iterative probing has been proposed in the past as a means to retrieve documents from a text database (Barbosa 2004, Callan 2001, Ipeirotis 2002, Ntoulas 2005). However, these approaches had the goal of achieving maximum coverage of specific sites. As a consequence, they employ site-aware techniques, and the approaches are not applicable across all domains.

At a high level, we customize iterative probing as follows:

- To determine whether the text input is in fact a generic input, we apply the informativeness test on the template in the first iteration using the initial candidate set. Our results indicate that generic text inputs are likely to be deemed informative, but others inputs are not.

- To select the seed set of candidate values, we analyze the contents of the web page that has the form. We select words from a page by identifying the words most relevant to its contents. Any reasonable word scoring measure, e.g., the popular TF-IDF measure (Salton 1983), can be used to select the top few words on the form page.

- To select new candidate values at the end of each iteration, we consider the set of all words found on all form submission pages analyzed for the template. We exclude words that appear on too many pages, since they are likely to be part of the boilerplate HTML that appears on every page. We also exclude words that appear on one page, since they are likely to be nonsensical or idiosyncratic words that are not representative of the contents of the form site.

- To select the final set of values for the text input, we consider all the candidate values extracted from the form page or the submission pages and select from the set in the order of their ability to retrieve the most diverse content (by analyzing the content of the pages resulting from form submissions).

We note that placing a single maximum limit on the number of keywords per text input is unreasonable because the contents of form sites might vary widely from a few to tens to millions of results. We use a back-off scheme to address this problem. We start with a small maximum limit per form. Over time, we measure the amount of search engine traffic that is affected by the generated URLs. If the number of queries affected is high, then we increase the limit for that form and restart the probing process.

Our experimental analyses indicate that iterative probing as outlined here is effective in selecting input values for generic inputs. The corresponding form submissions are able to expose a large number of records in the underlying database. Interestingly, we found that text inputs and select menus in the same form often expose different parts of the underlying data. We were also able to establish that a web crawler can, over time, expose more deep-web content starting with the URLs generated by our system.

Typed text inputs

Our work indicates that there are relatively few types that, if recognized, can be used to index many domains, and therefore appear in many forms. For example, a zip code is used as an input in many domains, including store locators, used cars, public records, and real estate. Likewise, a date often is used as an input in many domains, such as events and article archives.

To utilize this observation, we build on two ideas. First, a typed text input will produce reasonable result pages only with type-appropriate values. We use this to set up informativeness tests using known values for popular types. We consider finite and continuous types. For finite types (e.g., zip codes and state abbreviations in the U.S.), we can test for informativeness using a sampling of the known values. For continuous types, we can test using sets of uniformly distributed values corresponding to different orders of magnitude. Second, popular types in forms can be associated with distinctive input names. We can use such a list of input names, either manually provided or learned over time (e.g., as in [Doan 2001]), to select candidate inputs on which to apply our informativeness tests.

Conclusion and Future Work

We described an approach to surfacing content from the Deep Web, thereby making that content accessible through search-engine queries. The most significant requirement from our system is that it be completely automatic (and hence scale to the Web), and retrieve content from *any* domain in *any* language. Interestingly, these stringent requirements pushed us toward a relatively simple and elegant solution, thereby showing that simplicity is often the key in solving hard problems.

There are many directions for future work on surfacing the Deep Web. In particular, there are certain patterns in forms that can be identified to broaden the coverage of our crawl. For example, pairs of fields are often related to each other (e.g., MinPrice and MaxPrice), and entering valid and carefully chosen *pairs* of values can result in surfacing more pages.

References

Barbosa, L. and J. Freire. "Siphoning Hidden-Web Data through Keyword-Based Interfaces." *SBBD* 2004: 309–321.

Bergman, M. K. "The Deep Web: Surfacing Hidden Value." *Journal of Electronic Publishing*, 2001.

Callan, J. P. and M. E. Connell. "Query-based sampling of text databases." *ACM Transactions on Information Systems*, 19(2): 97–130, 2001.

Doan, A., P. Domingos, and A. Y. Halevy. "Reconciling Schemas of Disparate Data Sources: A Machine-Learning Approach." SIGMOD Conference 2001: 509–520.

"Forms in HTML documents." *http://www.w3.org/TR/html401/interact/forms.html*.

He, B., M. Patel, Z. Zhang, and K. C.-C. Chang. "Accessing the Deep Web: A survey." *Communications of the ACM*, 50(5): 95–101, 2007.

Ipeirotis, P. G. and L. Gravano. "Distributed Search over the Hidden Web: Hierarchical Database Sampling and Selection." *VLDB* 2002: 394–405.

Madhavan, J., L. Afanasiev, L. Antova, and A.Y. Halevy. "Harnessing the Deep Web: Present and Future." *CIDR* 2009.

Madhavan, J., S. Jeffery, S. Cohen, X. Dong, D. Ko, C. Yu, and A. Y. Halevy. "Web-scale Data Integration: You can only afford to Pay As You Go." *CIDR* 2007.

Madhavan, J., D. Ko, L. Kot, V. Ganapathy, A. Rasmussen, and A. Y. Halevy. "Google's Deep-Web Crawl." *PVLDB* 1(2): 1241–1252 (2008).

Ntoulas, A., P. Zerfos, and J. Cho. "Downloading textual hidden web content through keyword queries." *JCDL* 2005: 100–109.

Raghavan, S. and H. Garcia-Molina. "Crawling the Hidden Web." *VLDB* 2001: 129–138.

Salton, G. and M. J. McGill. *Introduction to Modern Information Retrieval*. New York: McGraw-Hill, 1983.

SpiderMonkey (JavaScript-C) Engine, *http://www.mozilla.org/js/spidermonkey/*.

V8 JavaScript Engine, *http://code.google.com/p/v8/*.

CHAPTER TEN

Building Radiohead's House of Cards

Aaron Koblin with Valdean Klump

THIS IS THE STORY OF HOW THE GRAMMY-NOMINATED MUSIC VIDEO FOR RADIOHEAD'S "HOUSE OF Cards" was created entirely with data. Before you read the chapter, you should watch the video. The definitive source for the video is the project's Google Code page: *http://code. google.com/radiohead*. On that site, you'll also find several other resources, including samples of the data we used to build the video, a Flash application that lets you view the data in 3-D, some code you can use to create your own visualizations, and a making-of video. Definitely check it out.

How It All Started

In September 2007, I received an email from James Frost asking me if I'd be interested in doing a music video based on data. James is a very talented music video director who has done work for Coldplay, Norah Jones, Pearl Jam, and loads of other popular artists. He had seen my Flight Patterns project (Figure 10-1), which used air traffic GPS data to visualize commercial flight patterns and density, and wanted to meet up to talk about doing a visualization for a music video.

A couple of months later, James, his producer Justin Glorieux, and I met up in LA for coffee and we tossed some ideas around. I showed them some of the projects I'd been working on and some technologies I thought would make nice visualizations. We discussed a

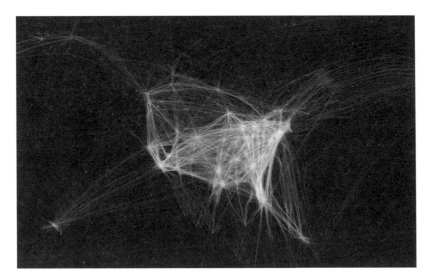

FIGURE 10-1. *Still image from "Flight Patterns" (2005). (See Color Plate 22.)*

couple of possibilities that involved Processing, a programming language widely used for data visualization. This direction eventually turned into the "Rest My Chemistry" video for the band Interpol, which came out in March of 2008. If you've never used Processing, I highly recommend you visit *http://processing.org/* and check it out. As far as I'm concerned, it is the best programming language for artists, designers, or anyone interested in dynamic data visualization.

The other possibility we discussed was visualizing laser sensor data. I first encountered this technology while working on a project for the Center for Embedded Network Sensing (CENS) at UCLA. CENS was using lasers to detect how light shines through forest canopies, and I was struck by the inherent beauty in the rendered images. James agreed after seeing some examples, and he was impressed by the concept of using lasers to create a piece of film. He said: "You mean you're shooting video without cameras? You're shooting video without video?" He immediately saw an opportunity to do something that hadn't been done before. Not too long afterward, he approached Radiohead with the concept.

Hopefully, you'll find the story of how this video was made to be an inspiration for your own work. In this chapter, I'll talk first about the equipment we used to capture the data. After that, I'll talk about the data itself, the video shoot, and the post-processing of the data. Finally, we'll take a look at the visualization code I provided for the Google Code site and discuss how you can play with it yourself.

The Data Capture Equipment

The video for "House of Cards" wouldn't have been possible without some sophisticated data capture equipment. When you watch the video, you'll notice that there's a variety of scenes, from static suburban landscapes to dynamic point clouds of vocalist Thom Yorke singing.

In order to get both the close-ups of Thom and the landscapes, we needed to use two different kinds of equipment: the Velodyne Lidar and the Geometric Informatics visualization system.

Velodyne Lidar

Velodyne is a company located just south of San Jose, California, that's run by two guys who compete in robot combat events like Battle Bots and Robot Wars in their spare time. The company produces loudspeakers, stereo equipment, and (naturally) powerful laser scanning devices, including the HDL-64E Lidar we used to capture the landscape and party scenes in "House of Cards." The HDL-64E's real claim to fame is that it was used successfully by several of the 2007 DARPA Urban Challenge vehicles, including the winning team, to achieve environment and terrain vision. In some cases, it was these vehicles' only vision system.

Velodyne's HDL-64E Lidar is a scanner with 64 laser emitters and 64 laser detectors. It spins in a circle, gathering data 360 degrees horizontally and 26.8 degrees vertically at a rate of over one million data points per second, which approximates to about 5 megabytes of raw data per second. By default, the Lidar rotates at 600 RPM (10 Hz), though this can be adjusted between 300 and 900 RPM by sending a text command through the system's computer serial port interface. We used the highest setting, 900 RPM, for maximum resolution when scanning the static landscapes.

The range of the Lidar varies based on the reflectivity of the environment. Pavement, for example, has a 50-meter range, while cars and foliage (which are more reflective) have a 120-meter range. The minimum range is 3 feet; anything closer, and the light reflects back into the detector too quickly for the device to measure it.

The emitter-detector pairs are divided into two 32-laser banks, as you can see in the diagram (Figure 10-2). The upper bank is directed at the higher half of the elevation angles; in other words, it scans the top half of the Lidar's vertical field of view. The lower bank, conversely, scans the lower half of the elevation angles. Because the upper bank is normally directed at higher elevations, and therefore at objects farther away from the Lidar, the distance traveled by the optical pulses is larger than the lower bank. Therefore, to obtain good resolution at longer distances, the lasers in the upper bank are triggered three times for every one trigger of the lower bank. You can see an example of how this affected our data in the still image from the video, shown in Figure 10-3.

The Lidar obtains a point of data by emitting a pulse of light (aka a laser beam) and then measuring the amount of light that comes back. As the unit runs, each of the 64 emitters releases an optical pulse that is five nanoseconds in duration. This pulse is then focused using a lens and is directed by mirrors out into the environment. When the light strikes something in the environment, a portion of the light reflects back toward the Lidar. This return light passes through the laser-receiving lens and a UV sunlight filter, which limits the amount of light introduced by the sun; without it, natural sunlight would decrease the system's sensitivity and create a lot of noise in the data.

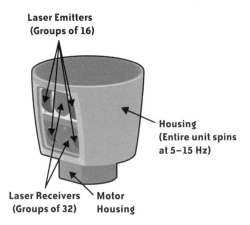

**Laser Emitters
(Groups of 16)**

**Housing
(Entire unit spins
at 5–15 Hz)**

**Laser Receivers
(Groups of 32)**

**Motor
Housing**

FIGURE 10-2. The Velodyne LIDAR (image courtesy of Velodyne, Inc.).

FIGURE 10-3. A still image of the party scene, shot with the Velodyne Lidar; notice the higher resolution at the top of this image, which was caused by the faster trigger rate of the lasers on the upper bank. (See Color Plate 23.)

After the return light has gone through the sunlight filter, the receiving lens focuses the return light on a photodetector called an Avalanche Photodiode (APD), which generates an output signal relative to the strength of the received light. The output signal from the APD is amplified and then converted from analog to digital. This data is then sent to a digital signal processor, which determines the time of the signal return. The strength and return time of the pulse creates one unit of data. As I said earlier, the HDL-64E model creates over one million data points every second, which is over 5 megabytes of raw data per second.

After the data is created, the sensor outputs it to the user through a standard 100BaseT Ethernet port. Data is continuously streamed out of this port at a frame rate equal to the rotation rate (600 RPM would produce a 10 Hz frame rate). Included in these Ethernet data packets are the distance, intensity, and angle data for each emitter-detector pair. The data is then captured using an Ethernet packet capture program and, in our case, saved to a hard drive.

Geometric Informatics

The Lidar is an incredible tool for visualizing outdoor scenery. It detects a point about the size of a nickel, depending on distance, which works fine for large spaces, but for the contours and details of a person's face, it's not good enough. For the close-ups of Thom Yorke singing, we needed something else. We needed something with finer vision.

While thinking about how to do the close-up shots, I happened to think back to an outfit called Geometric Informatics that I discovered at the 2005 SIGGRAPH conference. (Aside: if you have a cool data visualization technology, please go to every trade show possible on the chance that I may be attending…thank you.) It had a booth at the conference and a demo of its system, which it calls GeoVideo.

GeoVideo is a real-time motion capture system that is particularly suited for capturing the geometry of a person's face. It is significantly better than the Lidar system at close-ups, capable of discerning data points at 0.2 millimeters as opposed to 2 centimeters. With it we were able to capture the fine details of Thom Yorke singing. The point cloud data you see at the opening of the video was captured with GeoVideo.

If you think the drawing in Figure 10-4 looks a bit simple, that's because the device is not much to look at. The system looks like a beige box roughly a foot on either side with two lenses on it. One lens projects a field of light onto the subject in front of the box, while the other lens captures the data. The light field consists of a grid of 600,000 triangles, which, in effect, forms an instant contour map projected onto the subject in front of the sensor. The sensor then reads each triangle point as a point of data, which is then outputted raw to a computer at 54 megabytes per second. The sensor can capture 180 frames per second.

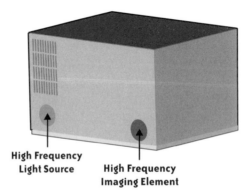

High Frequency
Light Source   High Frequency
Imaging Element

FIGURE 10-4. The Geometric Informatics system (image courtesy of Geometric Informatics). (See Color Plate 24.)

The advantage of the GeoVideo's method of projecting a light field onto the subject is that whatever is in front of the sensor isn't required to have a grid physically drawn onto it, wear a motion capture suit, or sit in front of a green screen with reference marks. The light projection creates an instant, portable reference map. It's incredibly easy.

The GeoVideo system is also capable of texture mapping, meaning that it can not only capture the data points, but also the textures between those data points. Combined together, this results in an eerily accurate 3-D representation of an object or a person's face. For the "House of Cards" video, we decided to forgo the textures and use only the data points. And even these we heavily downsampled. The result was the digital point cloud of Thom Yorke you see in the opening scene of the video. Rather than an exact likeness of him, he appears to be a digital avatar or soul—at least, that's how I see it. Having seen both versions of the data—with textures and without—I can say that the version we used without textures is much more interesting. With textures, he looked a bit like a character from a video game. Sometimes taking away data makes the visualization more beautiful.

The Advantages of Two Data Capture Systems

It's worth noting that, after working on this video, I became a big fan of using more than one data capture system on the same project. Mixing technologies can have a multiplier effect on creativity. We could have used just the Lidar or just the GeoVideo system to shoot the entire video, but I'm glad we didn't. It may have made the project more complex, but it allowed us to be more creative. It also gave us a lot more flexibility in regard to what we could capture.

There are a couple lessons too that you can draw from my experience of finding equipment. The first is that when it comes to finding equipment for data visualization, look everywhere. There are exciting sensing technologies being developed constantly that have never been used artistically. If you're about to embark on a visualization project, do some research online, at trade shows, or at your local university. Find out if there are new ways to capture your data that you hadn't considered before. A different piece of equipment might add a theme to your work or reveal data you didn't see previously. Always be looking for visualization techniques that will surprise people.

The second conclusion is a warning: if you only use one of piece of equipment, your work may be seen as just a demo of that piece of equipment. If we had only used the Lidar to create the "House of Cards" video, I have a slight suspicion that the video might have become "the Lidar video." By using both the GeoVideo system and the Lidar, the final product couldn't be slapped with a product label. No single tool defined the work. The mixture of two data capture systems made the story behind the video more interesting.

The Data

Before I talk about the shoot, I want to show you a sample of the data. It's really very simple. The following are three points I pulled arbitrarily from the data of Thom Yorke singing.

They're in the file *2067.csv*, which is the 1,067th frame in the video. Because each second is 30 frames and the first frame is *1001.csv*, these data points can be seen at around 0:36 in the video. You can find this datafile on the Google Code site, along with the other frames:

```
70.05, 162.48, -79.32, 122
70.23, 165.26, -78.82, 112
70.46, 168.00, -77.55, 95
```

The data are in the format *x, y, z, intensity*. All of the data we captured was eventually translated into this format.

The x, y, z values are relative distance measurements. The GeoVideo system, like the Lidar, has a 0, 0, 0 point upon which it bases all other points. What 70.46 means, therefore, is that the point is 70.46 units along the x-axis away from the 0 point. You can scale these numbers however you want. The intensity range is from 0 (0% white) to 256 (100% white).

You'll find 2,000 frames' worth of Thom singing on the Google Code site, comprising just over a minute from the video. The audio is available as well. We also included two static landscapes' worth of data: the city and the cul-de-sac. They are in the *HoC_DataApplications_v1.0.zip* archive that includes the viewer program.

The data you see on the site is in the same format as the data we delivered to the post-processing studio, with one minor difference. The studio wanted RGB values for each point, so we repeated the last value twice—in effect, using the intensity field as the color channel.

Capturing the Data, aka "The Shoot"

We recorded the points data for "House of Cards" in May 2008 over a weekend in Palm Beach County, Florida. Radiohead was on tour there at the time, and they like to shoot music videos while they're on tour to reduce their travel. For a behind-the-scenes look at what the production was like, check out the "Making Of" video at the Google Code site I mentioned at the beginning of this chapter.

The Outdoor Lidar Shoot

The first thing we did on arrival in Florida was set the Lidar up on the back of an old van the production crew had rented. We used the van to capture the static landscape data you see in the video, such as the city and the cul-de-sac.

Unlike the DARPA Urban Challenge vehicles, we did not put the Lidar on top of the vehicle. Instead, we tilted it 90 degrees and mounted it to the back of the van. This meant that the lasers would sweep the environment vertically. If picturing this is confusing, think of a lighthouse tipped on its side and sticking off the back of the vehicle, like a tail pipe. This meant that the lasers rotated from the street to the sky and back again. This happened 900 times per minute.

We did it this way because it gave us a very high-resolution scan of the area. And in fact, during post-processing, we isolated only one laser out of the 64, because all of them were effectively scanning the same thing. As the van was moved forward, then, the laser scanned a unique part of the environment with each revolution.

The landscape in Figure 10-5 was captured with this technique. Our van drove right down the middle of the street. Do you see how the lines on the street are perpendicular to the street itself? That's because the Lidar was hanging off the back and facing downward. You may notice as well that there are curved lines on the side of the apartment towers. This was caused by the movement of the van coupled with the rotation and angle of the Lidar.

FIGURE 10-5. Data captured by one laser from the Velodyne Lidar. (See Color Plate 25.)

The shoot went very smoothly. The production team had scouted the locations, so we simply drove to each scene and scanned them in order. When we reached an area we wanted to scan, we would slow the van down to around 10 mph and the driver would try to achieve as steady a speed as possible. Then we'd start recording.

Unlike a camera, the Lidar doesn't start and stop. Instead, when it's on, it's always rotating and always outputting data. So, we didn't have to turn it on and off, we just had to know when to start recording the data. When the moment came, our assistant director Larry Zience would shout "roll computer" as a signal to Rick Yoder, the Velodyne field engineer, to start collecting points. (This was mildly funny to some of the crew, because normally a director says "roll camera.") Rick would then hit a key on his laptop and the Lidar data would begin outputting to his hard drive. When Larry said "cut," we stopped recording.

Rick later sent me a note about what it was like to work with a film crew:

One of the things that stood out in my mind was how hard it was to break a photographer's habit of finding the right perspective for a shot. Conventional camera directors are not accustomed to building a model from scans and then manipulating the camera's perspective in post processing. They would say, "we want to dolly the camera from here to there and then move upward about 20 feet while panning about 45 degrees." We would then say, "Great! For now we'll just stick the scanner here in the middle of the scene and you can do that later in post."

Figure 10-6 shows another landscape. Notice how the power lines appear jagged? There's a simple reason for that: it's because the van was bumping up and down due to the uneven road and the natural bounce of the vehicle. Typically, these "errors" would be compensated for with gyroscopes, accelerometers, and other fancy pieces of equipment. In our case, we wanted the errors. Not only was it cheaper and easier to process, but (in my eyes, at least) it made the data more interesting. Perfection is an admirable goal, but not always the most creative.

FIGURE 10-6. Another landscape image captured by the Velodyne Lidar. (See Color Plate 26.)

The Indoor Lidar Shoot

We also used the Lidar indoors on a film set. It was used to capture the party scenes at 3:30 and 3:55 in the video. Unlike the landscape scenes, we used all 64 of the Lidar lasers' data for this part of the shoot rather than just one. That's because the party scenes are dynamic—the points change with every rotation of the Lidar—which means they change with each frame of the video. Therefore, you see the people in the scene moving. For this part of the shoot, we used the normal horizontal orientation for the Lidar, which is the reason the data appears in horizontal lines.

To create the party scene, we recruited some film students from a nearby school. Some of the students got very done up, thinking they would be in a Radiohead video and this was their time to shine; little did they realize, though, that all we really wanted was the form of their bodies. Sorry about that, guys!

If you count the horizontal lines in the image in Figure 10-7, you'll find that there are 64. And notice also how the top half of the image appears brighter? That's because the 32 lasers at the top of the Lidar trigger faster than the bottom. As I noted earlier, the Lidar is built this way because it normally scans large terrain spaces and requires a higher resolution for elevations approaching the horizon.

F I G U R E 1 0 - 7 . A still from the party scene, captured by the Velodyne Lidar; there are 64 lines of data, or one for each of the Lidar's lasers. (See Color Plate 27.)

Unfortunately, the resolution for the Lidar is very low, about 2 centimeters per point. That's why the figures look so hazy. To me, this added to the meaning of the video. Parties are often populated by people you don't know very well, and the visualization reflects this sense of alienation. However, the low resolution of the Lidar wasn't going to suffice for the close-ups on Thom Yorke. For this, we used the GeoVideo system.

The Indoor GeoVideo Shoot

The point clouds of Thom Yorke, his "lover" (played by actress Lauren Maher, who you first see at 1:05), and a couple of other scenes (such as the hand at 3:50) were all captured with Geometric Informatics' GeoVideo system.

The GeoVideo system is capable of an astonishing level of realism. If you watch the demo videos on Geometric Informatics' website, you'll notice that it achieves a much higher

quality image than the point clouds in our video. Its visualizations also don't suffer from the interference and errors that appear in our video.

The reason our video is lower quality is that we made it this way deliberately. James Frost, the director, didn't want a perfect visual avatar of Thom Yorke; he wanted a fragile, evanescent vision of him (see Figure 10-8). When watching the opening scene, to me this implies that this is not Thom Yorke the man, but something closer to the singer's soul. We are seeing the ghost in the machine.

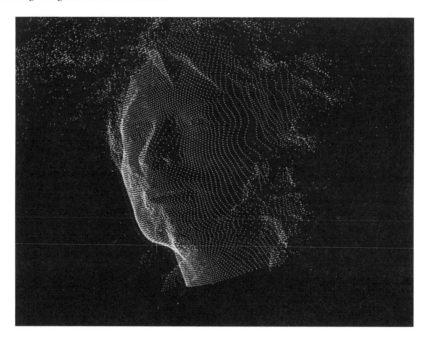

FIGURE 10-8. A still image from the video of Radiohead singer Thom Yorke. (See Color Plate 28.)

The low quality of the data and the frequent errors in the visualization also make it appear as if acquiring the data was difficult. This apparent difficulty enhances the story. A clearer image would not have conveyed the meaning we wanted.

The interference in the data was not done in post-processing; rather, it was created on set. The production company brought a number of props with them to break up the data, including little bits of mirror glued to a sheet of plexiglass, feathers that were dropped in front of the scanner, and running water that was poured on a piece of plexiglass in front of Thom. The mirrors ultimately worked the best to disrupt the data in a nonorganic way; the feathers didn't do a very good job of interrupting the data, and water absorbed the light, creating only empty points in the data set.

Including both the GeoVideo and Lidar portions, the interior shoot took about 10 hours. For all of Thom's scenes, we were careful to back up the data on multiple hard drives for fear that if we lost it, we might not be able to shoot it again.

Processing the Data

After all the data was captured, the processing work started. The first thing we did was send the raw Lidar data to 510 Systems, an engineering company in Berkeley, California that has a lot of experience processing this type of data. The company assigned the project to its in-house Lidar data guru, Pierre-Yves Droz. He's an expert at turning raw Lidar data into usable formats.

Pierre did two things for us after receiving the data, which we mailed to him on DVDs. First, for the landscape scenes, he isolated a single laser out of the 64 and created a data set of just that laser's points. Second, he converted all of the raw Lidar data, including the dynamic party scene data, into individual data points consisting of *x*, *y*, *z*, and *intensity*.

To convert the raw data, Pierre needed to know the precise position and orientation of each of the Lidar's laser emitter and detector pairs. This calibration information is provided by Velodyne, and the parameters are unique to each Lidar unit. Pierre also used the speed of the van to help calculate how far the Lidar moved in the real world as it rotated.

All told, we gave 510 approximately 4 gigabytes of raw data, which turned into almost 50 gigabytes of processed data in text *.obj* format.

Post-Processing the Data

Once we had the processed data, we took it to The Syndicate, a visual effects house in Santa Monica, California. It rendered the scenes in 2-D and added the particle flow effects you see in the video starting around the one-minute mark.

Brandon Davis, The Syndicate's particle specialist, worked on the project. He sent me an email describing why the project was unusual:

> From the start, the Radiohead project had very unusual possibilities from a visualization standpoint. With an animated data set, you get a strange paradox: view-dependent data that can be viewed independently. It really is a "second sight," being able to take what one sees and view it from different perspectives, revealing the gaps in that original sight. This opened the doors for some truly unique imagery.

He goes on to describe how he tackled the vaporization effect that you'll notice throughout the video:

> The client wanted to degenerate the data set over time as if the points were blowing away in a virtual wind. From the start we were looking at two distinct types of data—static Lidar point clouds of environments and dynamic animated point clouds of the singer Thom Yorke, the latter of which we knew would be the most challenging to manipulate. A static data set is relatively easy to manipulate because all you need to do is displace the points over time, so we knew it wouldn't be too difficult to selectively trigger portions of the data set to be affected by a velocity field, creating the effect of buildings and trees vaporizing away with noise-based turbulence. And as we predicted,

producing that effect on the static data sets was just a matter of moving bounding forms through the point cloud and doing a clipping test on a frame-by-frame basis. If a point was inside a bounding object on a specific frame, it was passed on to a particle system where it was free to move through a noise field, otherwise it remained static. This was very interactive and easy to control and generally fast to iterate.

The dynamic point cloud of Thom singing was another matter, however. Brandon continues:

> The dynamic point cloud was the biggest challenge on the project from my perspective. While you can try to apply the same methodology from the static data set, a dynamic data set creates a singular problem: it refreshes every frame! As soon as you release a point and pass it on to a particle system, the original source point pops right back into a new location, essentially re-spawning every frame. So while I could designate the points at the tip of his nose to release and blow away, every subsequent frame there was a new point to replace the one that blew away.

Eventually, The Syndicate figured out a simple way to add the decay effect to the dynamic point cloud using a 2-D mask: it added the mask with a layer of particles blowing away on top of the 3-D point cloud. This meant that there wasn't a perfect one-for-one particle decay like in the static landscapes, but I think the differences are imperceptible.

When I asked James, the director, why he added the particle decay effect in the first place, he said:

> "House of Cards" is essentially a love song, and as with love or friendships, in life there are points where relationships break down. They don't just stop; there is a series of events, a catalyst to start the demise or decline. For the video I wanted to explore this theme on a larger scale. It seems to me that in life we are very insular to what's going on in the world around us. The idea is that infrastructure can start to collapse on a large scale around us, but because we don't feel the effect of it, we as humans have reached a point where we don't care. But eventually that event will have a ripple effect and will finally reach us on a personal level. What's happening now with the financial institutions is a perfect example of this; a bank collapses, but unless your money is in that bank you don't think twice about it. Then your bank collapses.

When all of the post-processing was finished, the clips were edited together by Nicholas Wayman Harris at Union Editorial. At last, the video was complete.

Launching the Video

The "House of Cards" video was the first music video to be premiered by Google. It launched on July 11, 2008. The Google site includes some of the video's data, so that you may create your own visualizations, as well as a 3-D data visualization tool. Google's Creative Lab developed the site.

The visualization tool was written in Flash by myself and my friend Aaron Meyers. It allows the viewer to rotate the point cloud in real time while the video is playing. To me,

this is where the data becomes truly beautiful. The Flash application allows you to look at parts of the video from any angle you want in real time, something traditional video recording will never allow. You may even turn Thom Yorke's face so that it faces away from you, effectively holding his face as a mask up to yours and allowing you to look through his eyes. This effect is very powerful, in my opinion. It makes the music video tangible in a way I doubt many people have experienced before.

We also released some of the data itself—making it open source—along with a video creation tool written in the Processing programming language. We then encouraged people to download the data and create their own videos.

I want to share the source code for the video creation tool to show you how easy it is to create your own version of the video in Processing. This is the code that outputs frames of Thom Yorke singing:

```
import processing.opengl.*;

int frameCounter = 1;       //Declare a variable to store which frame we're dealing with
void setup(){               //Here we set up the program

  size(1024,768, OPENGL);     //This is the render size. We'll use OpenGL to draw as
                              //fast as possible

  //frameRate(30);            //Uncomment to watch the animation at 30 frames per second.

  strokeWeight(1);          //Draw lines at a width of 1, for now.

}

void draw(){                //Here we state the things we're going to do every frame

  background(0);              //We'll use a black background

  translate(width/2, height/2);   //The data has 0,0,0 at the center and we want to
                                  //draw that point at the center of our screen

  translate(-150,-150);       //Let's adjust our center slightly

  scale(2);                 //Let's draw things bigger

  //rotateY(frameCounter/50.0f);    //If uncommented, this makes the data rotate over
                                    //time

  //rotateY(mouseX/150.0);        //If uncommented, this uses the mouse's horizontal
                                  //location to adjust the rotation


  String[] raw = loadStrings(frameCounter+".csv");  //Here we load the current frame
                                                    //data into an array
```

```
for(int i = 0; i < raw.length;i++){        //Now we loop through each line of the
                                           //raw data

    String[] thisLine = split(raw[i],',');      //For each line we're going separate
                                                //each parameter

    float x = float(thisLine[0]);      //Now we make a decimal variable for each
                                       //parameter
    float y = float(thisLine[1]);
    float z = float(thisLine[2]);
    int intensity = int(thisLine[3]);

    stroke(intensity*1.1,intensity*1.6,200,255);      //We set the color of each point to
                                                      //correspond to the data's
                                                      //intensity value

    line(x,y,z,x+1,y+1,z+1);      //Here we draw a little line for each point; this
                                  //is much faster than a more complex object and
                                  //we'll be drawing a lot of them
}

frameCounter++;   //Add one to the frame variable to keep track of what frame we're
                  //currently on.

if(frameCounter>2101){       //If we get to the end of the data we'll exit the
                             //program
    exit();
    println("done");
}

//saveFrame("renderedFrames/"+frameCounter+".tga"); //This would be a way to save out
                                                    //a frame
//*remember you're saving files to your harddrive!*
}
```

It's not as beautiful as the data (this isn't *Beautiful Code,* after all), but it works great. As written, the code allows you to watch Thom Yorke sing the song head on, but with a couple of modifications, you can customize the experience. Here are two examples of modifications that are commented out in the previous code. The first is:

```
rotateY(frameCounter/50.0f);
```

Uncommenting this line at the beginning of the draw function causes Thom's face to turn around the y-axis as the frames increase.

The second modification is:

```
rotateY(mouseX/150.0);
```

Uncommenting this line at the beginning of the draw function allows you to make the rotation a function of the mouse. You may now move Thom's face as the frames are outputted.

I'm sure you can think of other things to modify; many people have done things I hadn't even considered, which is exactly what I hoped for. Once you've rendered out all the frames (by uncommenting the last line), you can put the frames together into a video with a program like QuickTime Pro, Final Cut, or After Effects. Some of the videos created by other people are really impressive. Check them out at the "House of Cards" YouTube group: *http://www.youtube.com/group/houseofcards*.

It really is quite easy. All it takes is some beautiful data with which to get started.

Conclusion

While writing this chapter, I came up with seven thoughts that you may find useful for capturing and presenting your own data in a beautiful way:

1. Looking at something ordinary in a new way can make it extraordinary.

   You don't need to scan the moon, a tropical island, or a fashion model to obtain data that looks beautiful. Looking at common objects in a new way can have the same effect. In the case of "House of Cards," we scanned a person's face and some common suburban architecture. By looking at these very common things in a new way and with new visualization techniques, we made them interesting.

2. Tell a story.

   Obviously it helps when you have an amazing song to work with, but do what you can to tell a story with your data. Just showing it to people isn't as cool as giving it some added meaning.

3. Using multiple visualization techniques is more interesting than using only one.

   As I mentioned previously, the "House of Cards" video was made stronger by using multiple technologies like the Velodyne Lidar, the GeoVideo system, and particle decay post-processing effects. If all we'd done was visualize raw Lidar data, it wouldn't have been as interesting.

4. Think about the data, not the real world.

   When we added bits of mirror to sheets of plexiglass and moved them in front of Thom's face as he was singing, we weren't thinking how it would look on a video camera. We were thinking about what it would do to the data. The data is the product. When you look at something you want to visualize, think about the data you will get from it.

   In other words, try making a bizarre reality, and then sensing that reality. This will make your story also weird and bizarre. Music videos often portray weirdness. Ask yourself, how can you manipulate your data to make it stranger, more interesting, different?

5. You don't have to use all the data.

   The GeoVideo system we used to scan Thom Yorke gave us much more data than we wanted. By downsampling it heavily, we produced a more interesting point cloud. We didn't want a photograph.

6. Set your data free.

   By allowing other people to have the data and create their own versions of the "House of Cards" video, we allowed each person to create the version he or she thought was the most beautiful. Everyone is always going to have an opinion as to what looks the best. Let people indulge that opinion. It'll be gratifying for you when you see their work and, you never know, someone out there might do something unexpected. That's a good thing. Over 100,000 people have already downloaded the data from the Google Code site and created some great videos.

7. Work with Radiohead.

   I'm being a bit tongue-in-cheek here, but there's no doubt that we were very lucky to work with one of the world's most innovative bands. And it wasn't just them—it was the whole crew. This video was made possible only with the cooperation of some incredibly talented people, including James Frost, Velodyne, Geometric Informatics, 510 Systems, and The Syndicate. Partner up with people who are more talented than you are, and your project will benefit enormously.

CHAPTER ELEVEN

Visualizing Urban Data

Michal Migurski

Introduction

WHAT MAKES DATA BEAUTIFUL, AND WHERE DOES IT COME FROM?

Beautiful data is interesting, useful, public, and free. Data must be of interest to someone, somewhere: its collector, an audience, a constituency. It must be useful to those whose interests demand its collection and maintenance, by helping them understand something about their environment. Data is most beautiful when it is public and free, and available for inspection and debate.

This is a story about Oakland Crimespotting (*http://oakland.crimespotting.org*), a research project of Stamen Design (*http://stamen.com*) in San Francisco. Crimespotting (see Figure 11-1) was developed as a response to the existing Oakland Police Department crime-reporting application, CrimeWatch (*http://gismaps.oaklandnet.com/crimewatch/*). As with many projects, Crimespotting didn't start with a concrete end goal in mind; it was born out of frustration, matured through basic technical research, and was finally made public after a traumatic crime in Oakland focused national attention on the city. It seems that this is a typical project arc: what starts with directed noodling often ends as a full-fledged informational project. This one in particular is an example of what Stamen advisor Ben Cerveny calls "things informationalize": a world of data is being moved onto the Internet piece by piece, exposed to and collided against an open source toolchain and methodology.

FIGURE 11-1. The logo for Oakland Crimespotting, a research project of Stamen Design.

There are three parts to the story. First, we crack the nut of Oakland Police data, extracting it from its home into a format that's more amenable to slicing and mixing. Next, we make it public by creating a dynamic website where it can be found and used by local citizens. Finally, we pay attention to how it behaves, revisit initial assumptions, and respond to public feedback.

Background

Applying modern practices in online data publishing to crime reporting is not a new idea. Current focus on crime can be traced back to journalist/developer Adrian Holovaty's 2005 project, Chicago Crime (*http://chicagocrime.org*). Chicago Crime was a prominent, early example of a Google Maps mashup, a website created by combining code and data from numerous other sources. In this case, the still-undocumented Google Maps API (*http://code.google.com/apis/maps/*) was repurposed as a base for Chicago Police Department crime report information. The police department's own site was a text-driven affair that happened to include street addresses or intersections for every report. Holovaty performed nightly collections of report data and published them on a dynamic, pan-and-zoomable, or "slippy," map. The service was an absolute coup, coming as it did hot on the heels of Google's early 2005 makeover of online mapping best practices. What had previously been limited to primitive line drawing and static images was transformed into an infinitely scrolling, reactive environment for geographic data.

Chicago Crime was not alone. Near the same time, developer Paul Rademacher created Housing Maps (*http://housingmaps.com*), an analogous combination of apartment rental data and visual browsing. The previous year, Michael Frumin and Jonah Perretti at the New York arts foundation Eyebeam (*http://eyebeam.org*) created FundRace (*http://fundrace.org*), a visualization of political contributions to presidential campaigns in the 2004 race for the White House. Rich Gibson, Schuyler Erle, and Jo Walsh released the book *Mapping Hacks* (O'Reilly), a technical guide to the new web-based cartography. A frenzy of online activity surrounded these events, as newly informationalized data sets were aggressively

cut with geographic context and republished online. The broader effect of all this was a realignment of expectations around maps: people now expected a new degree of multi-scale interactivity that author Steven Johnson calls "The Long Zoom," a new "way of seeing" that encompasses games, movies, and other media.

The impact of Google Maps on web mapping cannot be overstated, for two reasons. Google's decision to adopt a tile-based method for publishing its maps meant that it was possible to avoid the re-rendering cost for every view of its maps, which freed it up to generate significantly more visually sophisticated cartography. Other maps had to look good to compete. This decision also meant that the final visual presentation would be dynamically assembled by the user's browser, a technique made freshly relevant by Jesse James Garrett's coining of the term "AJAX" (Asynchronous JavaScript and XML), to describe a resurgence of interest in dynamic HTML and JavaScript made possible by the high quality and settling standards compliance of modern web browsers. The transmission of raw data was now happening on a separate channel from cartographic presentation, a departure from the previous practice of generating maps, address lookups, and directions on the server and delivering the entire package to the web visitor as a single image.

Map tiles and client-side interface and data assembly throw open the possibility of small developers creating geographical browsing applications of enormous sophistication, which is exactly what we've seen happening on the Web in the intervening four years.

All of this formed the background for a preliminary effort to extract manipulable, reusable data from Oakland's existing, commercially licensed crime-mapping product, CrimeWatch. This was an effort initially motivated by simple technical curiosity and an unexpected abundance of free time afforded by a Christmas holiday back injury.

Cracking the Nut

Oakland CrimeWatch is an application that serves crime report information in on-demand images with relatively primitive cartography and cartoon-like icons. CrimeWatch is optimized for data display, and follows from a development approach that focuses on predicting user needs rather than making raw ingredients available. The user experience of the application is informed by "wizards," user interfaces where the user is presented with a sequence of dialog boxes that lead through a series of steps, performing tasks in a specific sequence. The steps required by CrimeWatch are:

1. What: select the type or types of incidents.
2. Where: search near an address, within an administrative boundary, or near a feature, such as a school or park.
3. When: how far into the past to search.

CrimeWatch responds with a static image showing iconic representations of individual reports. These can be clicked for more information.

My interest in CrimeWatch was first piqued when I began to think about a way to reverse the server-side merging process, to start with a static image and extract crime report information with explicit location information attached: latitude and longitude values compatible with those used by other geographic software systems, commonly called *geolocation*. This kind of simple recognition problem is fairly well understood, and there are well-established techniques for visual feature extraction.

First, we need to get an image to work with. This is actually more complicated than it seems, and we must jump through a series of hoops to convince the server to generate a crime report map. CrimeWatch stores session state on the server, so it's necessary to simulate a complete set of wizard interactions by a fake user: accept terms and conditions with a form, proceed through the multiple steps of the interactive wizard while storing HTTP cookies and tokens along the way, and respond correctly to a series of nonstandard HTTP redirects. The process of reconstructing the steps necessary to arrive at a useful crime report image was the first serious hurdle for the project. The client-side HTTP proxy Charles (*http://charlesproxy.com/*) and the Mozilla plug-in LiveHTTPHeaders (*http://livehttpheaders.mozdev.org/*) made this process less painful than it needed to be. Interpreting the intermediate HTML pages themselves is greatly simplified by the use of a page-scraping library like Leonard Richardson's BeautifulSoup (*http://www.crummy.com/software/BeautifulSoup/*). BeautifulSoup is designed to make sense of the HTML "tag soup" frequently found online, correcting for such common problems as improperly nested tags or partial markup, and it allows us to read the HTML forms and JavaScript commands that establish a complete client/server session.

It's possible to mock up a first draft of the scraping process using simple Unix command-line tools such as shell scripts and cURL (*http://curl.netmirror.org/*). The key is carefully examining HTTP connections between the browser and server, looking for telltale bits of information to help you reconstruct the interaction: CGI variables in URLs and POST request bodies are the first step, showing exactly where the initial session is established upon acceptance of terms of use. Session-based applications such as CrimeWatch make heavy use of client-side state stored in cookies, so use of a cookie jar by your HTTP library is a must. CrimeWatch also relies heavily on client-side JavaScript smarts beyond simple form submissions, including the use of additional state variables, so intermediate response pages must be parsed with a tolerant HTML parser and regular expressions to search for details buried deep within page scripts. Finally, since many such older-generation web applications were built and released before cross-browser dynamic HTML became a common practice among developers, it's often necessary to spoof the User-Agent header and pretend to be either Internet Explorer or Mozilla Firefox; other browsers are turned away with compatibility warnings and no data.

At the end of this process, you are left with a medium-sized image bitmap, hopefully containing recognizable crime report icons. The first pass at extracting the pixel locations of each icon was simple, but slow: for every possible location in the image, compare its pixel colors to a known icon, and report positive matches wherever the amount of difference was below a certain threshold. Since we're dealing with predefined icons on a background

relatively free of conflicting noise, this is actually a completely bulletproof method. The crime icons used in CrimeWatch are unique, and easily identifiable even when partially occluded by other icons or map features. The tool I use to perform these image checks is NumPy (*http://numpy.scipy.org/*), the venerable and powerful Python array-manipulation library. Figures 11-2 and 11-3 show a portion of a sample image from CrimeWatch, with programmatically recognized icons outlined.

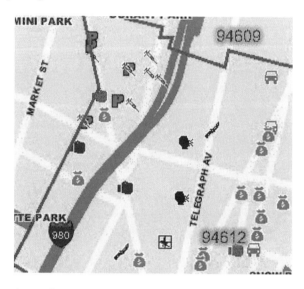

FIGURE 11-2. A sample image from CrimeWatch shows areas of theft, narcotics, robbery, vehicle theft, and other crimes. (See Color Plate 29.)

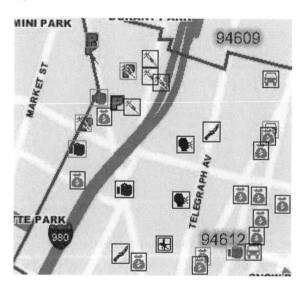

FIGURE 11-3. The same sample image from CrimeWatch with programmatically recognized icons outlined. (See Color Plate 30.)

The brute-force method is unfortunately quite slow on a typical CPU, but it's possible to speed it up with some knowledge of the kinds of maps you're likely to encounter. For example, many of the crime report icons have a significant characteristic color: theft is represented by a green bag of money, simple assault by a blue boxing glove, and prostitution by a pink letter "P". A simple preprocessing step is a cheap scan of the image to find pixel locations near one of these desired colors, which drastically cuts down on the number of locations to expensively check for a full-icon match. Figure 11-4 shows just the reddish parts of Figure 11-2 in white, an indication of likely places where the aggravated assault marker, a red boxing glove, can be found.

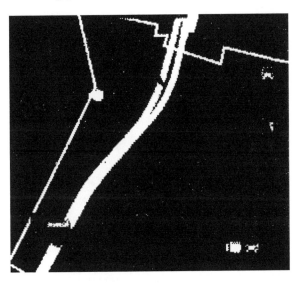

FIGURE 11-4. Again, the same sample image from CrimeWatch, this time with the reddish parts made white to show the red boxing glove icon (for aggravated assault) more clearly.

A slightly more complicated prepreprocessing step is a series of scans to search for proximity of characteristic icon colors. For example, burglary is represented by a small icon of a broken window rendered in black and white pixels. There is a lot of black on a typical map, and a lot of white, but only areas with icons and bits of text contain both black and white next to each other. We can find all pixels in close proximity to these two colors, and cut down the expensive search area to a limited number of candidate pixels.

The geolocation step requires determining a location for each crime report based on its detected pixel position in the rendered map. For this to be possible, it was helpful that CrimeWatch always returns a predictably sized and positioned map for a given set of inputs. For example, a map of Police Service Area #3 needs to always cover an identical area, regardless of whether the actual crime reports present at the time were concentrated in one corner of the area or spread out all over. CrimeWatch serves up maps with underlying geographical features such as streets or coastlines always in the same place. For each possible geographic layout, it's necessary to manually locate three widely spaced known reference points. Street intersections are great for this, as they can be easily picked out on

CrimeWatch for their (x, y) pixel locations and compared to a simple service such as Simon Willison's GetLatLon (*http://getlatlon.com*) for their (latitude, longitude) geographic locations. Six police service areas with three reference points apiece meant manually geolocating 18 known locations around Oakland. This needed to be done exactly once: all future icons found in each given Service Area could be compared to the known reference points using simple linear algebraic transforms to work out their geographic locations. Figure 11-5 shows a map for a downtown zip code, with three geographic reference points selected. Knowing these three points, it's possible to triangulate the location of any other point in the map.

FIGURE 11-5. A map of downtown Oakland showing three reference points for triangulation purposes. (See Color Plate 31.)

The only thing left to do was to simulate a user click on each crime icon to collect further details on the crime reports, such as its case number, date and time of day, and a simple textual description. The end product is a database containing 100 or so reports per day. One challenge to be found at this step is to decide what constitutes a unique report. I was collecting reports from a moving window, which meant that each individual report would be collected more than once, while multiple separate reports could be covered by a single case number provided by the police department. We ended up using a tuple of case number and text description, which was enough to cover most inconsistencies in data collection.

The code implementing this approach was executed in Twisted Python (*http://www. twistedmatrix.com/*), an event-driven networking engine that made it possible to open and maintain long-running simulated browser sessions with the CrimeWatch service. With this code library in hand, it was possible to transform a brittle process into an ongoing nightly collection run, and to eventually make the resulting data public in a form we believed more useful to Oakland residents than CrimeWatch.

Nightly collections of this data formed the basis of an initial eight months of collection and experimentation. Each evening, we'd run a web page scraper on a full combination of 13 types of crime and six Police Service Areas. Due to the one-at-a-time design of Crime-Watch, each individual report would require its own request/response loop with the server. We also added in considerable delays to each step—up to a minute or more between every individual step in the process—so as to not overload the CrimeWatch server with excessive requests. A single run would begin after midnight, and often last for six or more hours.

Frequently, there were errors. CrimeWatch often would lose its head completely, and cough up a map with no space, time, or type restrictions: all of Oakland, all crimes, for the past three months. We had no reliable way of detecting this case, and on frequent occasions reports in our database were geographically misplaced.

In this case, we felt that the occasional bad report was a small price to pay for an improved database browsing tool, and we continued to accumulate data over the first half of 2007, periodically releasing small experiments in visual presentation or publishing technique.

Making It Public

On August 2, 2007, journalist and *Oakland Post* editor-in-chief Chauncey Bailey was assassinated in broad daylight just a few blocks from my downtown apartment. Although the as-yet open case seemed an example of a political murder by a group Bailey was investigating, it refocused national attention on violent crime in Oakland. Around the same time, the *Oakland Tribune* published Sean Connelly and Katy Newton's award-winning Not Just A Number, an interactive map of Oakland homicides (*http://www.bayareanewsgroup.com/ multimedia/iba/njn/*). Connelly and Newton were particularly interested in the stories behind the city's murder statistics. Where a majority of victims had previously been identified by mug shots, Not Just A Number made a special effort to contact surviving family members, friends, and neighbors to put a face on the names in the news. We were interested in publishing a service complementary to these stories that offered hard facts and current data.

We budgeted two weeks of rapid development across three people: I transformed the collected data into a web-ready service, Stamen interaction designer Tom Carden developed an immersive visual interface using Flash, and creative director Eric Rodenbeck oversaw the visual direction and accompanying language.

Our first priority for publishing information is to show everything. The home page of the Crimespotting site is a map (Figure 11-6), and the map shows all crime reports from the past week. The map is positioned over most of West Oakland and downtown, with the iconic Lake Merritt included for visual recognition. Familiar "slippy map" pan and zoom controls make the rest of town immediately available, northwest toward Berkeley/Emeryville, northeast toward the affluent hills and Piedmont, and southeast toward San Leandro and beyond. This presentation is in sharp contrast to the existing wizard approach currently published by the City of Oakland. Where the existing application requires some prior knowledge of Oakland and assumes that the visitor is looking for crime information about some specific place, the Crimespotting slippy map requires no existing knowledge or particular search agenda, instead supporting a more exploratory, meandering form of search behavior.

Peter Morville describes the concept of "findability," a newly emerging concept that describes orientation in an information space and the ways in which data is made self-evident through interface and description. The dynamic web-based map has come a long way in the past four years. In 2005, one national newspaper experimenting with Google

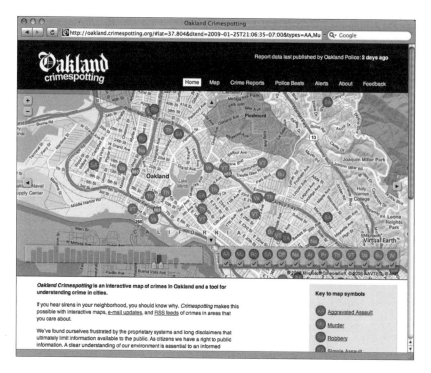

FIGURE 11-6. The Oakland Crimespotting home page shows a map of crime reports from the past week. (See Color Plate 32.)

Maps found that test subjects didn't know they could move a map; now organizations such as the *New York Times* routinely push the boundaries of information design and presentation online. With our crime database, we felt it was important to make the information more findable by creating a *data-first* user interface. Data first means that it's possible to start with a broad visual overview, and narrow down search results by type, time, or geography. We implemented the concept of "scented" widgets, introduced by UC Berkeley researchers Wesley Willett, Jeffrey Heer, and Maneesh Agrawala in a 2007 paper on embedded visualization (*http://vis.berkeley.edu/papers/scented_widgets/2007-ScentedWidgets-InfoVis.pdf*):

> While effective information scent cues may be based upon the underlying information content (e.g., when the text in a web hyperlink describes the content of the linked document, it serves as a scent), others may involve various forms of metadata, including usage patterns. In the physical world, we often navigate in response to the activity of others. When a crowd forms we may join in to see what the source of interest is. Alternatively, we may intentionally avoid crowds or well-worn thoroughfares, taking "the road less travelled" to uncover lesser-known places of interest. In the context of information spaces, such social navigation can direct our attention to hot spots of interest or to under-explored regions.

The date selector interface at the bottom-left corner of the main Crimespotting map interface shows a bar chart of reported crime over time (Figure 11-7), while the type selector at

the lower right includes discreet tooltips showing the total numbers of each report type in the currently selected time span (Figure 11-8). Both serve dual functions: filtering and feedback. The date selector in particular was inspired by a similar feature in blog statistics package Measure Map (*http://measuremap.com/*), designed by Jeffrey Veen at Adaptive Path, and later rolled into Google's own Analytics product. Measure Map's date slider in turn was inspired by interface features on Flickr, so this is truly a case of imitation being a sincere form of flattery. Our own enhancement is a color differentiation between bars showing days with already loaded data (dark) and those without (light).

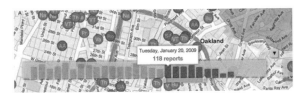

FIGURE 11-7. The date selector interface on the main Crimespotting map. (See Color Plate 33.)

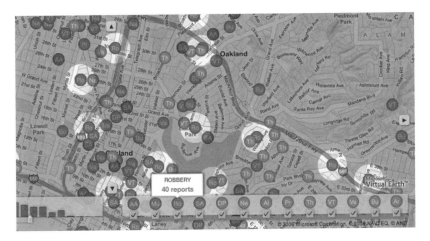

FIGURE 11-8. The type selector shows the total numbers of each report type in the selected time span. (See Color Plate 34.)

There's a flip side to showing everything, and that's information overload. We've introduced one form of visual report type filtering that's inspired by Apple's Spotlight feature in the Max OS X System Preferences dialog box: when a particular crime report on the map or in the type selector is hovered over by the mouse for an extra few seconds, the interface darkens, leaving brightly lit areas around mapped reports matching that type. A robbery may be covered up by a different type of crime and thus be invisible on the map, but it can be surfaced and accessed through the spotlight display.

One unexpected dividend of the design process was a clearer understanding of where data specialization could become an interface commodity. We chose Flash as an implementation environment for its visual sophistication, and early on realized that it would be necessary to implement our own slippy map interaction code rather than rely on one of the many available JavaScript implementations, like OpenLayers (*http://www.openlayers.org*).

COLOR PLATE 1 (FIGURE 1-1). We experimented with different visual cues on a map to best display location data with impact and exposure values. The above shows three iterations during our preliminary design. The left map shows GPS traces colorcoded by carbon impact; in the center map, we encoded impact with uni-color area circles; on the right, we incorporated GPS data showing when the user was idle and went back to using color-coding.

COLOR PLATE 2 (FIGURE 1-2). In the current mapping scheme, we use color filters to highlight the data. The map serves solely as context. Linked histograms show impact and exposure distributions of mapped data. When the user scrolls over a histogram bar, the corresponding GPS data is highlighted on the map.

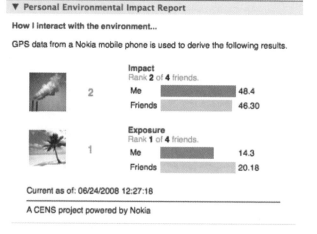

COLOR PLATE 3 (FIGURE 1-4). PEIR's Facebook application lets users share their impact and exposure findings as well as compare their values with friends.

COLOR PLATE 4 (FIGURE 1-5). *People track their weight and what they eat for different reasons. YFD places motivation front and center.*

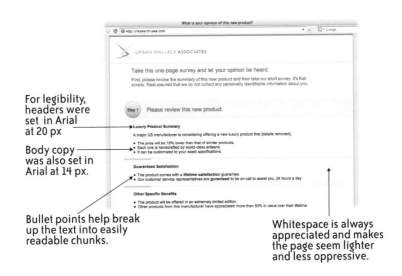

COLOR PLATE 5 (FIGURE 2-2). *Designing for legibility.*

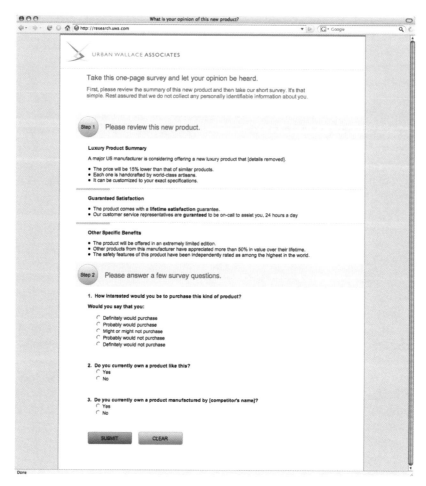

COLOR PLATE 6 (FIGURE 2-3). The survey starts with only three questions.

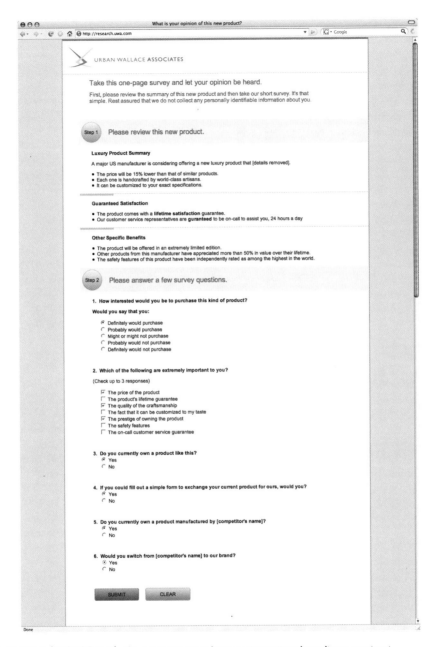

COLOR PLATE 7 (FIGURE 2-4). The survey may expand to up to six questions depending on user input.

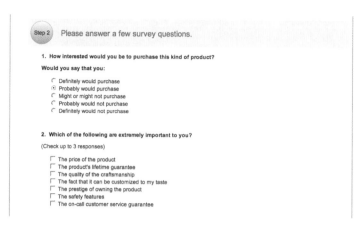

COLOR PLATE 8 (FIGURE 2-5). *Detail of survey when the user answers "Yes" to Question 1.*

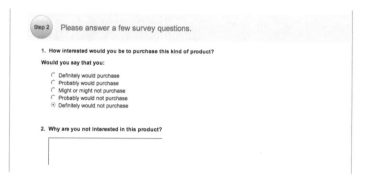

COLOR PLATE 9 (FIGURE 2-6). *Detail of survey when the user answers "No" to Question 1.*

COLOR PLATE 10 (FIGURE 3-1). *Artist's impression of Phoenix on Mars (Image credit: NASA/JPL).*

COLOR PLATE 11 (FIGURE 3-2). *The Stereo Surface Imager (Image credit: University of Arizona/NASA/JPL).*

COLOR PLATE 12 (FIGURE 6-1). *Minor road near Aberuchill. Bioran Dalchonzie in the distance. This is the 1,000,000th image to appear on the Geograph website (http://www.geograph.org.uk/photo/1006884). Image (c) Dr. Richard Murray; licensed for reuse under a Creative Commons License (http://creativecommons.org/licenses/by-sa/2.0/).*

COLOR PLATE 13 (FIGURE 6-2). Example Geograph photomosiac of the Norfolk coast. Each photo is mapped at its geographic location and represents a 1 km square of the landscape. Images licensed for reuse under a Creative Commons License (http://creativecommons.org/licenses/by-sa/2.0).

COLOR PLATE 14 (FIGURE 6-4). Treemap of terms occurring in geograph titles and comments for six selected scene types. Node sizes represent term occurrence. Colors emphasize the scene type/facet/descriptor hierarchy with an inherited random scheme. Layout uses an "ordered squarified" approach to maintain square shapes amongst nodes.

COLOR PLATE 15 (FIGURE 6-5). *Treemap of terms occurring in geograph titles and comments for six selected scene types. Node sizes represent term occurrence. Colors emphasize the scene type/facet/descriptor hierarchy with an inherited random scheme. Layouts uses a "slice and dice" approach to aid comparison of magnitudes (top) and "slice and dice/ordered squarified" approaches to aid legibility of labels (bottom).*

COLOR PLATE 16 (FIGURE 6-6). "Ordered squarified" treemap with colors showing absolute locations through a CIELab color space in which perceived differences in color relate closely to differences in location.

COLOR PLATE 17 (FIGURE 6-7). "Ordered squarified" treemap with colors showing absolute locations through a CIELab color space. Leaf nodes within descriptor nodes are arranged to relate to relative locations using a spatial ordering algorithm.

COLOR PLATE 18 (FIGURE 6-8). Spatial treemap of terms occurring in geograph titles and comments for six selected scene types. Node sizes represent term occurrence, and colors represent absolute spatial locations with CIELab scheme. Displacement vectors show absolute locations of non-leaf nodes (scene types, facets, and descriptors).

COLOR PLATE 19 (FIGURE 6-9). Spatial treemap of terms occurring in geograph titles and comments for six selected scene types. Displacement vectors show absolute locations of leaf nodes (co-occurring terms) and provide information about spatial clustering and spatial trends in displacement required to meet the space-filling objectives of the treemap.

COLOR PLATE 20 (FIGURE 6-10). Spatial treemap of terms occurring in geograph titles and comments for selected element descriptors in the beach base level. Displacement vectors show absolute locations of leaf nodes in this enlarged section of Figure 6-9.

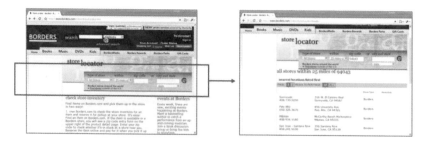

COLOR PLATE 21 (FIGURE 9-1). *The Borders Store Locator form and a deep-web page resulting from a particular form submission.*

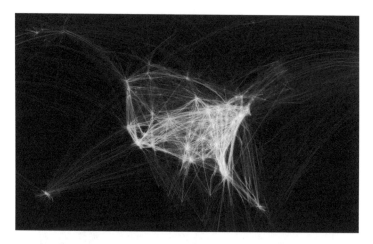

COLOR PLATE 22 (FIGURE 10-1). *Still image from "Flight Patterns" (2005).*

COLOR PLATE 23 (FIGURE 10-3). *A still image of the party scene, shot with the Velodyne Lidar; notice the higher resolution at the top of this image, which was caused by the faster trigger rate of the lasers on the upper bank.*

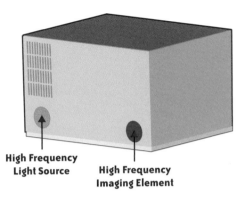

High Frequency
Light Source

High Frequency
Imaging Element

COLOR PLATE 24 (FIGURE 10-4). *The Geometric Informatics system (image courtesy of Geometric Informatics).*

COLOR PLATE 25 (FIGURE 10-5). *Data captured by one laser from the Velodyne Lidar.*

COLOR PLATE 26 (FIGURE 10-6). *Another landscape image captured by the Velodyne Lidar.*

COLOR PLATE 27 (FIGURE 10-7). A still from the party scene, captured by the Velodyne Lidar; there are 64 lines of data, or one for each of the Lidar's lasers.

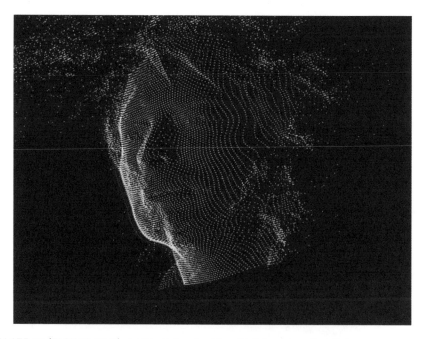

COLOR PLATE 28 (FIGURE 10-8). A still image from the video of Radiohead singer Thom Yorke.

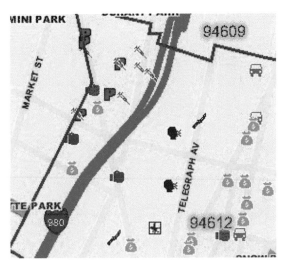

COLOR PLATE 29 (FIGURE 11-2). A sample image from CrimeWatch shows areas of theft, narcotics, robbery, vehicle theft, and other crimes.

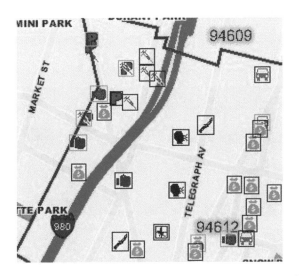

COLOR PLATE 30 (FIGURE 11-3). The same sample image from CrimeWatch with programmatically recognized icons outlined.

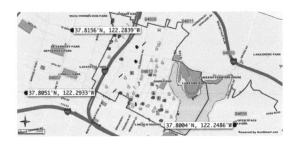

COLOR PLATE 31 (FIGURE 11-5). A map of downtown Oakland showing three reference points for triangulation purposes.

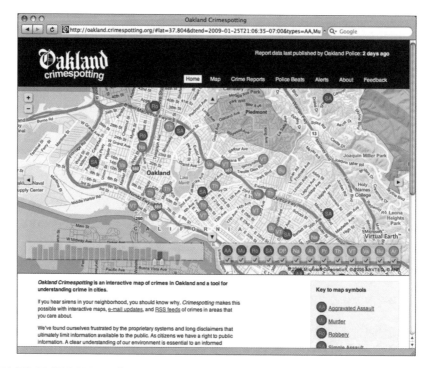

COLOR PLATE 32 (FIGURE 11-6). *The Oakland Crimespotting home page shows a map of crime reports from the past week.*

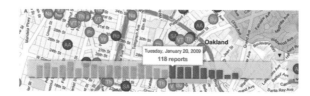

COLOR PLATE 33 (FIGURE 11-7). *The date selector interface on the main Crimespotting map.*

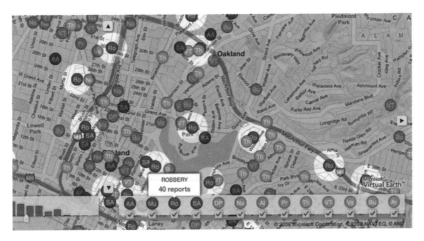

COLOR PLATE 34 (FIGURE 11-8). The type selector shows the total numbers of each report type in the selected time span.

COLOR PLATE 35 (FIGURE 11-10). A beat-specific page allows citizens to provide feedback to the officers who patrol their local areas.

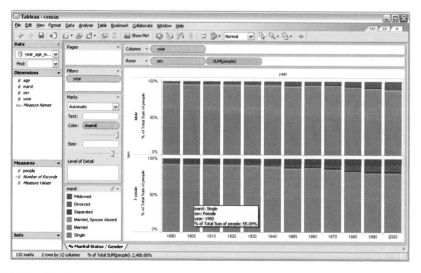

COLOR PLATE 36 (FIGURE 12-3). A prototype visualization built using Tableau showing the distribution of marital status over multiple decades.

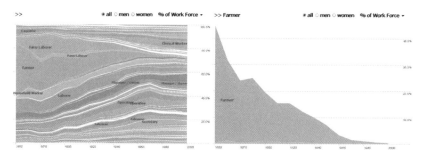

COLOR PLATE 37 (FIGURE 12-4). Job Voyager visualization: (left) an overview showing the constitution of the labor force over 150 years, and (right) a filtered view showing the percentage of farmers.

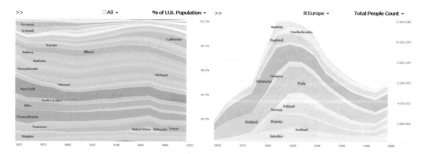

COLOR PLATE 38 (FIGURE 12-5). Birthplace Voyager visualization: (left) an overview showing the distribution of birthplaces over 150 years, and (right) a filtered view showing the total number of European immigrants.

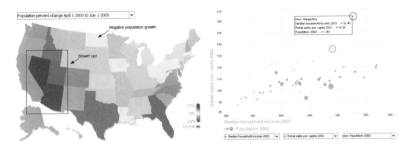

COLOR PLATE 39 (FIGURE 12-6). (Left) Interactive state map showing changes in each state's population from 2000 to 2005, and (right) scatterplot of U.S. states showing median household income (x-axis) versus retail sales (y-axis); New Hampshire and Delaware have the highest retail sales.

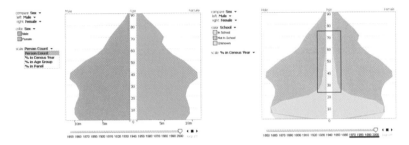

COLOR PLATE 40 (FIGURE 12-7). Population pyramid visualization: (left) a comparison of the total number of males and females in each age group in 2000, and (right) the distribution of school attendees in 2000 (an annotation highlights the prevalence of adult education).

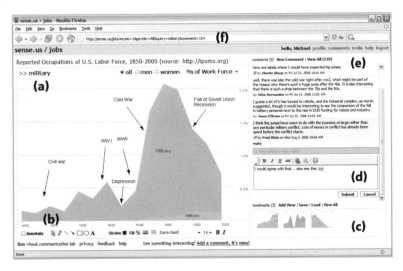

COLOR PLATE 41 (FIGURE 12-8). The sense.us collaborative visualization system: (a) An interactive visualization applet, with a graphical annotation for the currently selected comment. The visualization is a stacked time-series visualization of the U.S. labor force, broken down by gender. Here, the percentage of the workforce in military jobs is shown. (b) A set of graphical annotation tools. (c) A bookmark trail of saved views. (d) Text-entry field for adding comments. Bookmarks can be dragged onto the text field to add a link to that view in the comment. (e) Threaded comments attached to the current view. (f) URL for the current state of the application. The URL is updated automatically as the visualization state changes.

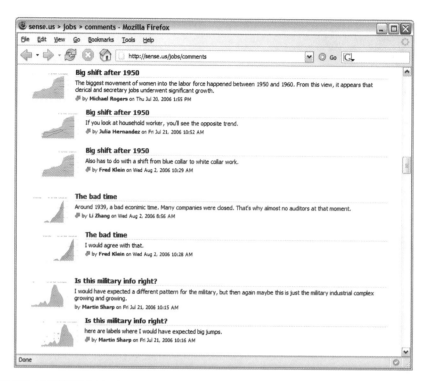

COLOR PLATE 42 (FIGURE 12-9). The sense.us comment listing page; comment listings display all commentary on visualizations and provide links to the commented visualization views.

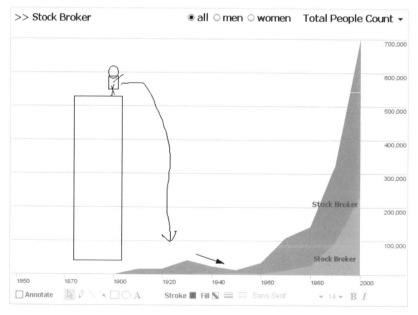

COLOR PLATE 43 (FIGURE 12-10). Annotated view of stockbrokers; the attached comment reads "Great depression 'killed' a lot of brokers."

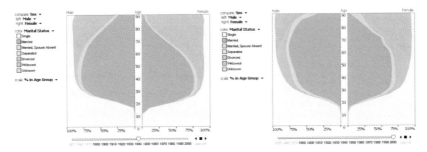

COLOR PLATE 44 (FIGURE 12-11). Population pyramid showing the distribution of marital status for each age group in (left) 1940, and (right) 2000.

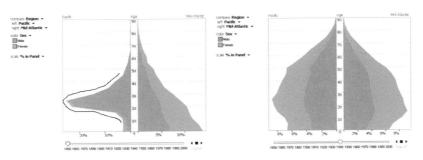

COLOR PLATE 45 (FIGURE 12-12). Population pyramid comparing the populations of the west coast and mid-Atlantic regions in (left) 1850, and (right) 1940.

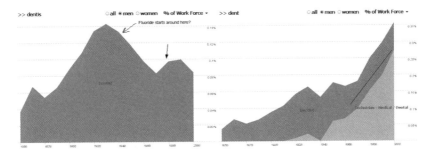

COLOR PLATE 46 (FIGURE 12-13). Annotated job voyager views highlighting (left) a decline in dentists after 1930, and (right) an overall increase in dentistry due to the rising ranks of dental technicians.

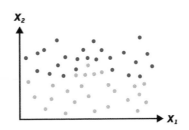

COLOR PLATE 47 (FIGURE 13-2). We can build models to discriminate between two sets of data.

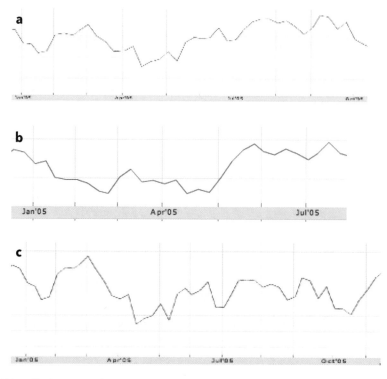

COLOR PLATE 48 (FIGURE 13-3). Performance of three securities (a, b, and c) in 2005.

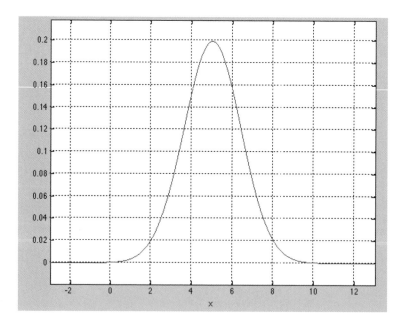

COLOR PLATE 49 (FIGURE 13-4). The normal distribution.

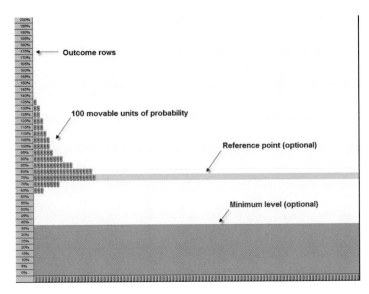

COLOR PLATE 50 (FIGURE 13-6). A tool by Goldstein et al. helps people understand a distribution as a set of outcomes.

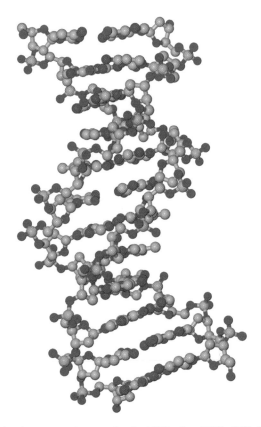

COLOR PLATE 51 (FIGURE 15-1). A short section of DNA, rendered in POV-Ray from PDB file 1BNA, doi: 10.2210/pdb1bna/pdb.

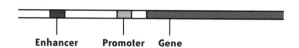

Enhancer   Promoter   Gene

COLOR PLATE 52 (FIGURE 15-2). A stretch of DNA containing a gene also contains nearby regions that interact with the cellular machinery to regulate its expression; here, a gene is preceded by a promoter element and an enhancer element, which "tag" the gene so the cell knows when it should be expressed.

COLOR PLATE 53 (FIGURE 16-1). Using free generic services to host the record of experimental work and processed data. (A) Part of the page of a single experimental measurement. (B) Images taken of the experiment hosted on Flickr. (C) A portion of the primary data store on a GoogleDocs spreadsheet.

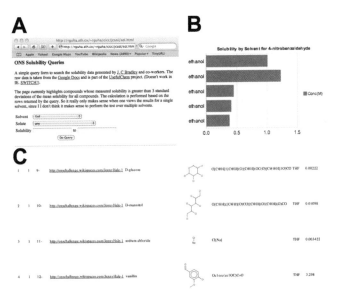

COLOR PLATE 54 (FIGURE 16-2). Visualization tools for examining the solubility data.(A) A simple form-based input uses JavaScript and the GoogleDocs API to generate (B) a graphical representation of the solubility values selected and (C) a tabular output of the data with rendered 2-D chemical structures. The service is available at http://toposome.chemistry.drexel.edu/~rguha/jcsol/sol.html. Note that these and other services described are dynamic and may not give the same results as those shown here for the same query.

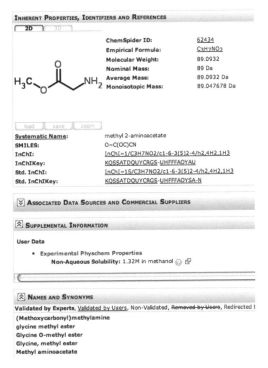

COLOR PLATE 55 (FIGURE 16-3). This example ChemSpider entry shows the solubility value and link to the original data.

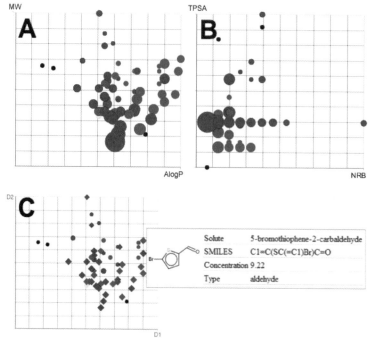

KEY: x-axis: ALOGP - y-axis: Weight
Pointsize is proportional to solubility value - Hover mouse over point to view data [Firefox].

COLOR PLATE 56 (FIGURE 16-5). *Graphical representation of solubility data in chemical space. Panels A and B show two visualizations of the same data plotted onto axes representing different chemical characteristics. The color of the spots represents the chemical type (red for aldehyde, blue for carboxylic acid, yellow for amine, and black for other) and the size the solubility. Panel C illustrates the clickable interface showing the chemical structure and value of the solubility for one data point.*

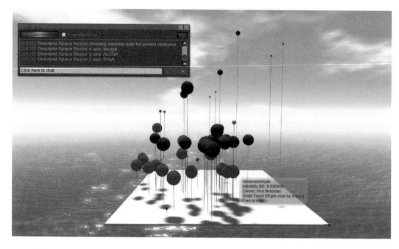

COLOR PLATE 57 (FIGURE 16-6). *Representing multidimensional data using Second Life. Three chemical descriptors are represented on the three spatial axes. The color of the balls indicates the type of chemical entity (as defined in the previous figure), and the size shows the solubility in the current solvent. The visualization is available at http://slurl.com/secondlife/Drexel/ 165/178/24 on Drexel Island, Second Life.*

COLOR PLATE 58 (FIGURE 17-1). The FaceStat judging interface.

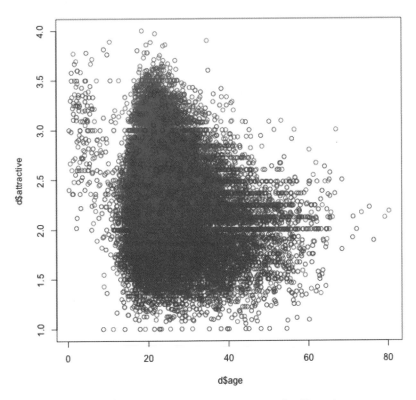

COLOR PLATE 59 (FIGURE 17-5). Scatterplot of attractiveness versus age, colored by gender.

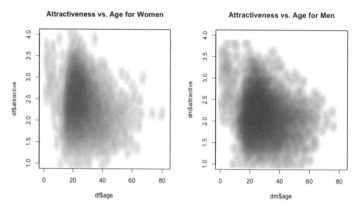

COLOR PLATE 60 (FIGURE 17-6). *Smoothed scatterplots for attractiveness versus age, one plot per gender.*

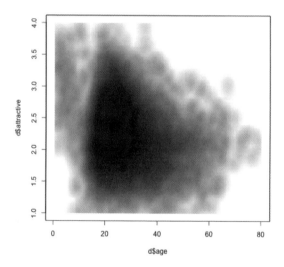

COLOR PLATE 61 (FIGURE 17-7). *Smoothed scatterplots for attractiveness versus age, colored by gender and overlaid on one plot.*

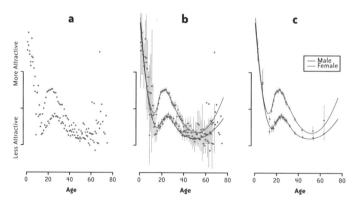

COLOR PLATE 62 (FIGURE 17-8). *Three iterations of plotting attractiveness versus age versus gender: (a) ages averaged within buckets per age year, (b) 95% confidence interval for each bucket, plus loess curves, and (c) larger buckets where the data is sparser.*

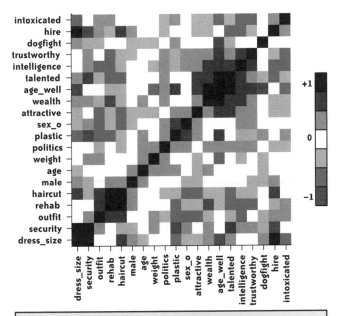

Text of questions

- **dress_size:** What is my dress size?
- **security:** If you were an airport security guard, would you search me?
- **outfit:** Do you like my outfit?
- **rehab:** Will I end up in rehab?
- **haircut:** Do you like my hairstyle?
- **age:** How old am I?
- **weight:** How much do I weigh?
- **political_affiliation:** What is my political affiliation? (Higher is more conservative)
- **plastic_surgery:** Have I had plastic surgery?
- **sexual_orientation:** What is my sexual orientation? (Higher is more gay)
- **attractive:** How attractive am I?
- **wealth:** How wealthy am I?
- **age_well:** Will/Have I age(d) well?
- **talented:** Am I talented?
- **intelligence:** How smart am I?
- **trustworthy:** How trustworthy am I?
- **dogfight:** Do you think I would win a fight with a medium sized dog?
- **hire:** Would you hire me?
- **intoxicated:** How intoxicated am I?

COLOR PLATE 63 (FIGURE 17-9). Pearson correlation matrix; attribute pairs with blue squares are positively correlated, while pairs with red squares are anticorrelated.

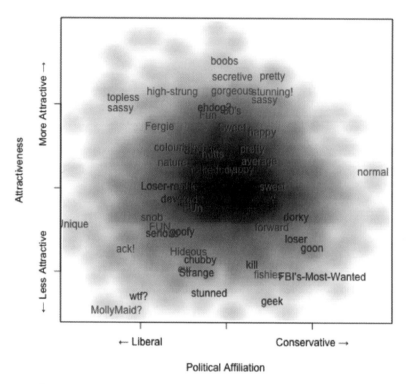

COLOR PLATE 64 (FIGURE 17-12). Tag sample plotted on a smoothed attractiveness versus age scatterplot.

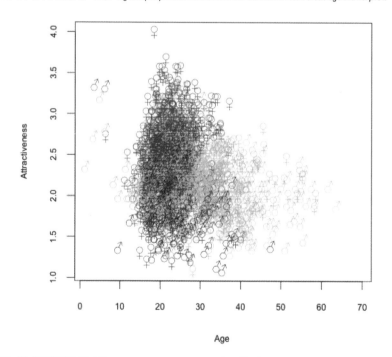

COLOR PLATE 65 (FIGURE 17-13). Attractiveness versus age, colored by cluster, showing a subsample of 2,000 points.

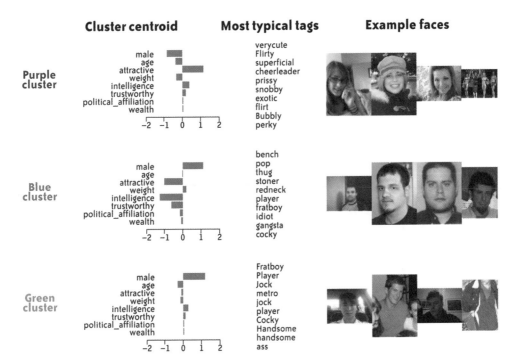

COLOR PLATE 66 (FIGURE 17-15). Cluster centroids, tags, and exemplars.

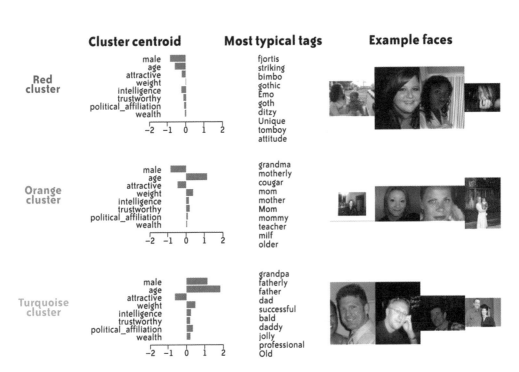

COLOR PLATE 67 (FIGURE 17-16). Cluster centroids, tags, and exemplars, continued.

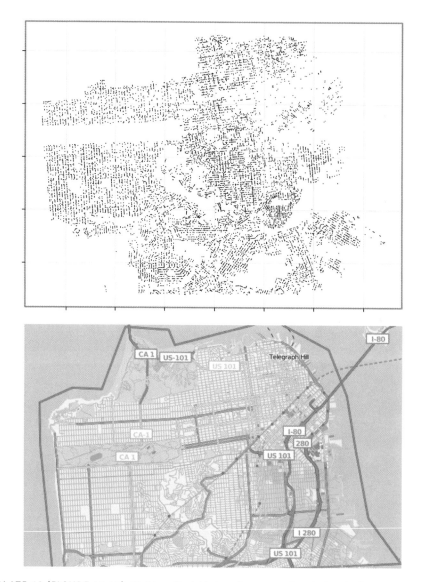

COLOR PLATE 68 (FIGURE 18-13). (Top) A small point is drawn for every residential sale in the data. It gives us a pretty good feel for the layout of San Francisco. (Bottom) For comparison, a street map of San Francisco from http://openstreetmap.com.

COLOR PLATE 69 (FIGURE 19-5). *Geographic partisanship in Pennsylvania. The base layer shows Pennsylvania counties shaded by their 2004 presidential election returns, with blue indicating higher support for the Democratic candidate John Kerry, red indicating higher support for the Republican candidate George W. Bush, and shades of purple in between. The scattered cylinders represent localized partisanship for 4,000 random registered voters in the state, defined as the percentage of people living within a 1-mile radius who are registered Democrats. Each cylinder is located on the voter's household and has a radius of 1 mile, thus replicating the region for the partisanship measure. Again, blue cylinders indicate highly Democratic regions—this time with regard to individual-level registration—red cylinders indicate highly Republican regions, and shades of purple indicate regions in the middle. The beauty of this graph is that it reveals complexity in the idea of red and blue regions of the country, of individual states, and even of individual counties.*

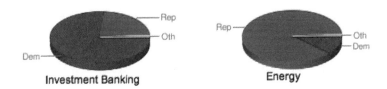

COLOR PLATE 70 (FIGURE 20-1). *Pie charts resulting from a data mashup of SEC industry data and Center for Responsible Politics political contribution data.*

Panning, zooming map interactions seemed like a useful feature to apply to other projects, so early work on crime data display resulted in a separate BSD-licensed software library called Modest Maps (*http://www.modestmaps.com/*). Modest Maps made it possible to see a clean break in functionality between data display and interaction metaphor, and the separation of the map-specific code library has assisted in rapid development for a significant number of unrelated projects, some from Stamen but many from outside designers and developers.

Our second priority was to introduce a public, shareable address space for the data we collect. Generally, there are just a few flavors of URL in Crimespotting:

- The map view, *http://oakland.crimespotting.org*, and a larger one at *http://oakland.crimespotting.org/map*
- The report list view, e.g., *http://oakland.crimespotting.org/crimes*, *http://oakland.crimespotting.org/crimes/Robbery*, *http://oakland.crimespotting.org/crimes/2009-01-09*, and *http://oakland.crimespotting.org/crimes/2009-01-09/Robbery*
- The individual report view, e.g., *http://oakland.crimespotting.org/crime/2009-01-09/Robbery/113569*
- The police beat view, e.g., *http://oakland.crimespotting.org/beat/04X*

Most of these URLs were designed before their associated content. In particular, they had to conform to the ideals described in Matt Biddulph's 2005 presentation, "Designing Data For Reuse" (*http://www.hackdiary.com/slides/xtech2005/*): human-readable, suggestive, hackable, opaque, permanent, and canonical. We have a hierarchy of addresses that makes sense when read aloud: "robberies on January 9th," "police beat 04X," and so on. Where there is potential ambiguity—for example, date-first "/crimes/2009-01-09/Robbery" versus type-first "/crimes/Robbery/2009-01-09" or singular "/crime/Robbery" versus plural "/crimes/Robbery"—we introduce an HTTP redirect to the proper, canonical form. The redirect makes the URL more shareable by ensuring that my list of thefts on a given day matches yours. One aspect of the individual report URLs that's an unfortunate compromise is the presence of a numeric primary key at the end of the address. PostgreSQL developer Josh Berkus has a special distaste for such keys, described in detail in his series on "Primary Keyvil" (*http://it.toolbox.com/blogs/database-soup/primary-keyvil-part-i-7327*):

> It didn't take long (about 2 months) to discover that there was a serious problem with having 'id' as the only unique column. We got multiple hearings scheduled on the calendar, in the same docket, on the same date or in the same place. Were these duplicates or two different hearings? We couldn't tell…. The essential problem is that an autonumber 'id' column contains no information about the record to which it's connected, and tells you nothing about that record. It could be a duplicate, it could be unique, it could have ceased to exist if some idiot deleted the foreign key constraint.

Our excuse for including such keys is connected to a fairly loose understanding of how the Oakland Police Department keeps its records. Although every report has a case number, case numbers are frequently shared between different reports, and appear to link clusters of individual charges into a single broader incident. An extreme example is case number

08-056061 (*http://oakland.crimespotting.org/crime/2008-08-01/murder/93014*), a combination of nine murder, theft, and aggravated assault reports from one night in August 2008. We've settled on the use of case number and text description (e.g., "ASSAULT W/SEMI-AUTOMATIC FIREARM ON PEACE OFFICER/FIREFIGHTER") as a unique identifier, too long for a comfortably readable URL. The numeric ID acts as a surrogate.

The outcome of this attention to URLs is to turn online crime information into a social object. With CrimeWatch, referring to a report entails a procedural description of actions to take: go to the wizard, select this, press that, click over here, and so on; finding specific information about a particular report requires approximately a dozen separate clicks. With exposed URLs, the address itself is a complete description of the crime information. Leonard Richardson identifies the address or URI as the primary technology that led to the WWW's supplantation of other popular 1990s Internet protocols. In his excellent 2008 talk "Justice Will Take Us Millions Of Intricate Moves" (*http://www.crummy.com/writing/speaking/2008-QCon/*), Richardson argues that a triangle of technologies makes up what we know as the Web: the URI to address things, HTTP to move them around, and HTML to help client software understand what to do with them. All three are critical components. URI design in particular is enjoying a flow of popular attention, but it's lowly old HTML with its links and forms that makes a connected web truly possible. This explanation is a crucial elaboration on Roy T. Fielding's 2000 PhD thesis introducing the idea of Representational State Transfer (REST) as an architectural style (*http://www.ics.uci.edu/~fielding/pubs/dissertation/top.htm*). Where possible, we try to follow these concepts by keeping the interactive flashy parts of Crimespotting firmly grounded in a supporting matrix of basic, 1993-vintage web page. Our API outputs XML for Flash, RSS and Atom for feed readers, and CSV for spreadsheets, all vital uses of information that constitute a complete API.

What launched in August 2007 included all the concepts described here, and relied on an expensive nightly scrape of CrimeWatch. We were fairly certain that someone in city government would eventually notice and complain, but we were lulled into a false sense of security by eight months of smooth sailing.

Revisiting

A short time after launch, our scraping bot began running into a wall. It was seemingly impossible to access the CrimeWatch site for any extended length of time, even with a regular browser. Conversations with the city information technology department suggested that once our access was publicly noted, it was considered unwelcome. The city offered some hints of an official method of accessing the data, but the wheels of bureaucracy grind slowly and nothing was forthcoming immediately. We regretfully took the site down, and spent a few months considering enhancements and strategies for bringing it back. There were two ideas we worked on during this time that ultimately never saw the light of day, and one new feature that we made public. An outcome of the revision process has been a more focused, pragmatic final data display.

In thinking about how best to represent the impact of local crime on a place, conversations with Adam Greenfield led to the idea of "violence as a force acting on a place." One way to envision the long-term impact of a murder or robbery on the surrounding neighborhood is as an aura (see Figure 11-9). My initial mental model of this was a space-time sphere, perhaps a quarter mile in space radius and a week in time radius. The visual display would be a small spot that grows into a large stain as a time slider is moved closer to the actual event time. Greenfield suggested inverting the sphere into a pair of cones: the actual crime is a point, with "light cones" spreading forward and backward through time. The visual display would be a large, diffuse circle that clarifies and focuses into a tiny point as the time slider is moved closer to the exact event time. This display concept might be a better fit for showing causality. The potential for a crime might be broad, spread throughout a neighborhood. As events unfold, the malignant potential collapses to a point where a neighbor is victimized and then subsequently spreads out again as news gets around and a feeling of personal safety falls away.

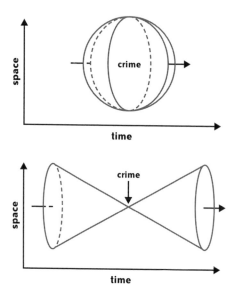

FIGURE 11-9. Two methods of envisioning the long-term impact of a murder or robbery on the surrounding neighborhood.

We made a number of interactive maps exploring the cone metaphor, and discovered a few interesting things. One thing we noticed was that certain report types have unique visual signatures that depend on their enforcement patterns. Prostitution in particular is a special case. Where most of the reports we display are driven by the event—a victim calling in—prostitution is driven by police department decisions and scheduled crackdowns. We routinely see weeks of quiet on the prostitution front interrupted by rapid, concentrated sweeps along San Pablo Avenue or International Boulevard. The cone display metaphor was unfortunately too esoteric for use on the primary website. The idea of time

navigation on maps is fairly novel, and it was important for us to make the relationship between report display and time control as unambiguous as possible. Cones would have to remain in the experimental bin.

Another possible enhancement that received a great deal of serious attention during our downtime was the concept of distributed page scraping. The reason our normal collection process was vulnerable to interruption was that all requests had to originate from the same Internet address, making them trivially easy to block when needed. We experimented with a distributed model implemented as a Firefox browser add-on, executed in JavaScript and controlled centrally. We hoped that a sufficient number of our technically savvy visitors would be willing to download a browser toolbar icon and help collect data when indicated. Requests to the CrimeWatch server would be spread over a large number of visiting IP addresses, at unpredictable hours of the day: a pattern effectively indistinguishable from normal site use. An added benefit of this process was the promise of human error correction at the end. The final screen in the mediated scraping process included an overview of all the reports the user had just assisted in collecting, with the possibility of marking certain matches as incorrect.

One feature developed during this time was beat-specific pages, such as this one for the commercial and residential area between downtown and Lake Merritt: *http://oakland. crimespotting.org/beat/04X* (see Figure 11-10). When we initially developed the service, we consciously decided to ignore the administrative divisions present in CrimeWatch. Police service areas, city council districts, zip codes, and beats all seemed to us a distraction from location and proximity. After our launch, we quickly learned that we were wrong about police beats. Our users informed us that citizen communication with the department occurred via beat officers, who had specific geographic patrols and regular meetings with local residents. The division of reports into beats was important, because it matched the area of concern and responsibility for any given officer. Furthermore, beat boundaries frequently follow obvious physical features of the city: major streets, creeks, freeways, and railroad tracks all serve to impart a sense of neighborhood self-identification. Beat pages are now home to a static overview map of the area showing its borders, as well as portions of the API likely to be maximally useful to nontechnical users comfortable with common spreadsheet software. The eventual feedback we received on this feature was invaluable. One resident said, "We have a Beat1X NCPC (Neighborhood Crime Prevention Council) meeting next week...I'll be able to show up more prepared than OPD...our experience has been that they seldom if ever have current statistics to share with us."

The Firefox browser plug-in and associated web service controller were completed and planned for limited, experimental rollout around the same time that the City of Oakland informed us that we would be provided with a nightly spreadsheet of complete citywide crime report information, along with street addresses or intersections where appropriate. Starting in January 2008 and lasting until the present day, our data collection process has evolved from a lengthy, error-prone affair to a rapid one blessed by the municipal creators and stewards of the data we were working with.

FIGURE 11-10. A beat-specific page allows citizens to provide feedback to the officers who patrol their local areas. (See Color Plate 35.)

Eventually, through the gracious assistance of Oakland CTO Bob Glaze, Program Manager Ahsan Baig, and the City's Julian Ware and Andrew Wang, we were granted a nightly Microsoft Excel spreadsheet of official crime report data. The difference was like night and day: where before it required hours of data processing and time lag to collect information, now it was a matter of just a few quick minutes. Location information also became significantly more reliable, featuring block-level street addresses and intersections in place of colored icons.

Conclusion

Have we been successful in maintaining a data service that conforms to the ideals of beauty we began with? The crime report data featured in Crimespotting is interesting, regularly eliciting mail from concerned residents and supporting a population of email alert subscribers several hundred strong. Crime is a serious issue for any urban resident, but it is especially relevant in a city with Oakland's reputation for trouble. Is our published data useful? We regularly hear from residents who use our news feeds and email alerts to stay abreast of neighborhood events or research new places to live. Are we sufficiently free or public?

All site information is made available in a variety of forms suitable for a wide range of technical proficiency, from the simple daily mail subscription or spreadsheet to the more advanced news feed or XML-based API. The project has been a productive success, resulting in what we believe is a data service maximally useful to local residents.

The core lesson that we've learned through the creation and continued upkeep of Oakland Crimespotting has been a social and political one. City and government information is being moved onto the Internet to match the expectations of a connected, wired citizenry. With it comes the idea that "data is the public good," as explained by FortiusOne CEO Sean Gorman in a vital blog post early this year (*http://blog.fortiusone.com/2009/01/28/ data-is-the-public-good-data-is-the-infrastructure-data-is-the-stimulus/*). The growth of software tools for "prosumer" visualization and analysis of data is making it increasingly important that predictable, trustworthy, and raw data be available online in preference to over-constrained web-based user interfaces. At the same time, emerging practices and conventions around the publication of raw data are also being slowly hammered out, and in many cases the intervention of an interested, capable outsider is required to direct attention to a problem in format or availability. Praxis talks, and change is best effected by taking the initiative to expose and improve data for the public good.

CHAPTER TWELVE

The Design of Sense.us

Jeffrey Heer

I MUST CONFESS THAT I DON'T BELIEVE IN BEAUTIFUL DATA. AT LEAST NOT WITHOUT CONTEXT.

Prior to World War II, the government of the Netherlands collected detailed civil records cataloging the demographics of Dutch citizenry. A product of good intentions, the population register was collected to inform the administration of government services. After the German invasion, however, the same data was used to effectively target minority populations (Croes 2006). Of the approximately 140,000 Jews that lived in the Netherlands prior to 1940, only about 35,000 survived.

Though perhaps extreme, for me this sobering tale underscores a fundamental insight: the "beauty" of data is determined by how it is used. Data holds the potential to improve understanding and inform decision-making for the better, thereby becoming "beautiful" in action. Achieving value from data requires that the right data be collected, protected, and made accessible and interpretable to the appropriate audience. The fiasco in which AOL released insufficiently anonymized search query data is a recent failure of protection.

Fortunately, most examples are not nearly as tragic as these tales. A more common occurrence is data wasting away: collected and stored in data warehouses—sometimes at great infrastructural cost—but left underutilized. For companies and governments alike, languishing data represents a lost opportunity and poor return on investment. The value of data is proportional to people's ability to extract meaning and inform action.

Somewhat paradoxically then, some data collections possess more (potential) beauty than others. Clearly the choice of data to collect and the design of storage infrastructures, schemas, and access mechanisms shape the potential of data to inform and enlighten while avoiding harm. However, the "last mile" in this climb toward beauty is the problem of human-information interaction: the means by which data is presented to and explored by people to support analysis and communication.

This chapter presents a case study on the use of interactive visualization to help foster beautiful data-in-action: the design of sense.us, a web application for collaborative exploration and sense-making of 150 years of United States census data. I will cover the steps we took in taking a large, government-collected data set—the U.S. census—and making it accessible to a general audience through a suite of interactive visualizations. I will also describe sharing and discussion mechanisms we devised to engage a community of data voyagers in social interpretation and deliberation. Our goal was to realize the potential beauty of data by fostering collective data analysis.

Visualization and Social Data Analysis

Visualizations are regularly used to construct meaning from data by facilitating comprehension, enabling exploration, and communicating findings. A large part of the human nervous system has evolved to process visual information; in the human brain, over 70% of the receptors and 40% of the cortex are implicated in vision processing (Ware 2004). Visualization design leverages the capabilities of this visual processing system to enable perception of the trends, patterns, and outliers residing within data.

Note that this is not an issue of crafting "fancy graphics." Often a simple table or bar chart (sans 3-D frills and specular highlights) can provide an effective presentation. The trick is choosing the right visual representation(s) for the data and tasks at hand.

An instructive example is Anscombe's Quartet, a collection of four data sets created by the statistician Francis Anscombe to illustrate the importance of visualizing data (Anscombe 1973). Each data set appears identical according to common descriptive statistics (Figure 12-1). However, plotting the data immediately reveals salient differences between the sets.

Other writers detail the ways in which effective visual design aids interpretation, communication, and decision-making. Tufte (1997) famously argues that the disaster of the space shuttle *Challenger* might have been avoided had engineers created better visual depictions of rocket damage data (though this is not without some controversy; see Robison et al. 2002).

Visualization researchers have catalogued the space of "visual variables"—such as position, length, area, shape, and color hue—that can be used to encode data in a visual display (Bertin 1967, Card et al. 1999). They have also studied how accurately humans decode these visual variables when applied to different data types, such as categorical (names), ordinal (rank-ordered), and quantitative (numerical) data (Cleveland & McGill 1984, Ware 2004). For instance, spatial position, as used in a bar chart or scatterplot, facilitates decoding

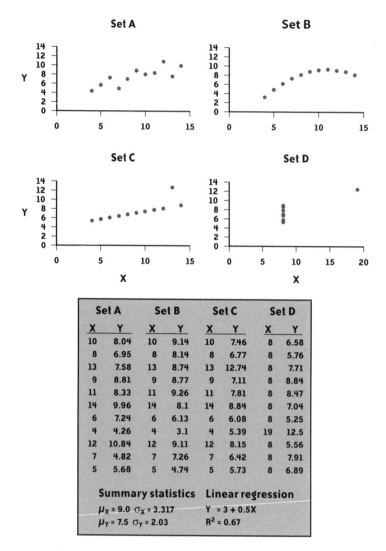

Set A

Set B

Set C

Set D

Set A		Set B		Set C		Set D	
X	**Y**	**X**	**Y**	**X**	**Y**	**X**	**Y**
10	8.04	10	9.14	10	7.46	8	6.58
8	6.95	8	8.14	8	6.77	8	5.76
13	7.58	13	8.74	13	12.74	8	7.71
9	8.81	9	8.77	9	7.11	8	8.84
11	8.33	11	9.26	11	7.81	8	8.47
14	9.96	14	8.1	14	8.84	8	7.04
6	7.24	6	6.13	6	6.08	8	5.25
4	4.26	4	3.1	4	5.39	19	12.5
12	10.84	12	9.11	12	8.15	8	5.56
7	4.82	7	7.26	7	6.42	8	7.91
5	5.68	5	4.74	5	5.73	8	6.89

Summary statistics   Linear regression

$\mu_X = 9.0$ $\sigma_X = 3.317$ $Y = 3 + 0.5X$

$\mu_Y = 7.5$ $\sigma_Y = 2.03$ $R^2 = 0.67$

FIGURE 12-1. Anscombe's Quartet, a collection of statistically similar data sets illustrating the use of visualization to aid understanding.

for each of these data types, while color hue ranks highly when used for category labels but poorly when used to convey quantitative values.

In this spirit, most visualization research focuses on the perceptual and cognitive aspects of visualization use, typically in the context of single-user interactive systems. In practice, however, visual analysis is often a social process. People may disagree on how to interpret data and may contribute contextual knowledge that deepens understanding. As participants build consensus, they learn from their peers. Moreover, some data sets are so large that thorough exploration by a single person is unlikely. This suggests that to fully support sense-making, visualizations should also support social interaction.

These observations led myself and my colleagues Martin Wattenberg and Fernanda Viégas of IBM Research to investigate how user interfaces for visualizing data might better enable the "social life of visualization." We embarked on a research project in which we designed and implemented a website, *sense.us*, aimed at group exploration of demographic data. The site provides a suite of visualizations of United States census data over the last 150 years, coupled with collaboration mechanisms to enable group-oriented data analysis.

In the rest of this chapter, I will share the design process for sense.us: how we selected and processed the data, developed a suite of visualizations, and designed collaboration features to enable social data analysis. I conclude by looking at the ways people worked together through the system to construct insight from the data.

Data

Martin, Fernanda, and I came to this project in the mindset of researchers: we wanted to understand how best to support social interaction in the visual analysis process. Our choice of data set was not predetermined, though it was clear that a good data domain would satisfy some specific properties: we wanted a large, real-world data set, relevant to a general audience, and rich enough to warrant many different analyses. According to these criteria, census data seemed ideal. I had also long been interested in making census data more publicly accessible: I believe it is an important lens through which we might better understand ourselves and our history.

I started by rummaging through the U.S. census bureau's website (*http://www.census.gov*). This proved only mildly productive. The census bureau provides a number of data sets at various levels of aggregation (e.g., by zip code, metro area, region), but this rich data is only available for recent census decades. I also realized that I was in a bit over my head. I had much to learn about the ins and outs of how census data has been collected and modeled over the decades. For example, the questions and categories used by the census bureau have evolved over the decades, meaning that even if one has data for every year, it does not guarantee that the data can be easily compared.

In general, one should not dive into visualization design before gaining at least a basic familiarity with the data domain. So my next step was to meet with domain experts: my colleagues in the Sociology and Demography departments at UC Berkeley, where I was a graduate student at the time. Through these discussions I gained a deeper appreciation of how the census works and which data sources demographers use to study the population. In the process, I was introduced to a valuable resource: the Integrated Public Use Microdata Series (IPUMS) databases maintained by the University of Minnesota Population Center (*http://www.ipums.org*).

The IPUMS-USA database consists of United States census data from 1850 to 2000. Data from each decade in this period is included, with the exception of 1890, the records for which were destroyed by a fire in the Commerce Building in 1921. For each decade, the IPUMS data consists of representative sample data, either a 1% or 5% sample of that decade's census records.

Each record represents a characteristic person sampled from the population. In some cases, persons and households with certain characteristics are over-represented, and so different weights are associated with the records.

What makes this database particularly attractive is that the IPUMS project has developed uniform codes and documentation for all demographic variables, facilitating analysis of change over time. This "harmonization" is a monumental service, enabling comparative analyses and, by extension, new insights. However, the process of fitting disparate data into a shared schema inevitably introduces artifacts, an issue that will surface again later.

All told, the IPUMS-USA database contains 413 demographic variables, ranging over common categories such as gender, age, race, marital status, and occupation, down to estimates of how many households have washers, dryers, flush toilets, and televisions (Figure 12-2). In many cases, variables are recorded only in a subset of decades; in other years, the variables simply were not measured.

Demographic Variables (Person) top

Detailed Version	General Version	Variable	Label	Case Selection	Attach Variables	1850	1860	1870	1880	1900	1910	1920	1930	1940	1950	1960	1970	1980	1990	2000
☐	☐	RELATE	Relationship to household head	☐	☐	x	x	x	x	x	x	x	x	x	x	x	x	x	x	x
☐		IMPREL	Imputed relationship to household head	☐	☐	x	x	x	x	x	x	x	x	x						
☐		AGE	Age	☐	☐	x	x	x	x	x	x	x	x	x	x	x	x	x	x	x
☐		SEX	Sex	☐	☐	x	x	x	x	x	x	x	x	x	x	x	x	x	x	x
☐		MARST	Marital status	☐	☐				x	x	x	x	x	x	x	x	x	x	x	x
☐		AGEMONTH	Age in months	☐	☐	x	x	x	x	x	x	x	x	x						
☐		BIRTHMO	Month of birth		☐					x	x	x				x				
☐		BIRTHQTR	Quarter of birth	☐	☐					x	x					x	x	x	x	
☐		BIRTHYR	Year of birth		☐						x	x								
☐		AGEMARR	Age at first marriage	☐	☐								x	SL		x	f1	x		
☐		DURMARR	Duration of current marital status	☐	☐						x	x			SL					
☐		MARRNO	Times married		☐							x		SL	SL	x	f1	x		
☐		MARRINYR	Married within the past year	☐	☐	x	x	x	x					SL	SL	x	f1	x		
☐		MARMONTH	Month married	☐	☐				x											
☐		MARRQTR	Quarter of first marriage	☐	☐											x	f1	x		
☐		WIDOW	Marriage ended by death	☐	☐												f1			
☐		CHBORN	Children ever born	☐	☐						x	x		SL	SL	x	x	x	x	
☐		CHSURV	Children surviving	☐	☐						x	x								
☐		All Demographic Variables																		

FIGURE 12-2. An excerpt of the available demographic variables in the IPUMS-USA database.

The motto of the IPUMS project is *"use it for good, never for evil."* Fortunately, the enforcement of this maxim extends beyond the obligatory checkbox one must click when downloading a data extract. To protect individual privacy, the availability of some data has been restricted. For example, religious affiliation is not included, and the availability of detailed geographic data is highly limited, particularly for low-population areas.

We decided to use IPUMS-USA as the primary data source for sense.us. Using the IPUMS web interface, we first selected samples for the years 1850–2000 (excluding 1890) and then selected a set of variables to extract. The vast majority of variables are only available for a subset of census decades. To enable visual exploration of long-term change, we selected the variables that were available for at least a century. This set consisted of 22 variables, including age, sex, marital status, birthplace (either a U.S. state/territory or a foreign country), occupation, race, school attendance, and geographic region. Due to privacy constraints, geographic data was limited to coarse-grained regions such as New England and the west coast. The resulting data extract was a 520-megabyte GZIP file that decompressed into a 3.3-gigabyte text file.

I will largely spare you the details of what happened next. A straightforward yet tedious process of data processing, cleaning, and import ensued, ultimately resulting in a MySQL database containing the census data extract in queryable form. To facilitate analysis, we organized the data using a star schema (*http://en.wikipedia.org/wiki/Star_schema*): we stored the census measures in a large fact table containing a column for each demographic variable, with compact keys used to indicate categorical variable values. A collection of dimension tables then stored the text labels and descriptions for the values taken by each demographic variable.

This setup provided a base for conducting exploratory analysis. We generated data summaries by issuing queries that "rolled up" the data along chosen dimensions. For example, we could isolate the relationships between age, gender, and marital status by summing the number of people across all the other variables. In short, we had a foundation from which we could explore the data and prototype visualizations.

Visualization

Given the size and scope of the census data, we realized early on that trying to fit all the data within a single visualization design would be a recipe for disaster. Where we could, we wanted to boil down the data into the simplest forms that could support a range of analyses. As we were designing for a general audience, we settled on the approach of creating a collection of visualizations that present selected slices of the data. In essence, we wanted to make our visualizations as simple as possible while remaining useful, but no simpler.

Our design philosophy thus required that we figure out which data dimensions would be of greatest interest and which visualization designs and interaction techniques would best support active exploration of those dimensions. To do this, we began simultaneously exploring the data itself and the space of visualization designs.

Before crafting an interface to help others explore data, I wanted to ensure that the data was interesting enough for others to even bother. I used a number of methods to conduct my exploration, including SQL queries, Excel, and visualization systems. The most useful tool was Tableau, a database visualization system. Using Tableau, one can map database fields to visual encodings in a drag-and-drop fashion; the application then queries the database and visualizes the result. (Full disclosure: I have worked as a consultant for Tableau Software.) We were thus able to prototype a number of different approaches (for example, Figure 12-3). We generated a large collection of visualizations and shared them with our colleagues to collect feedback. The ability to quickly evaluate visualization approaches using the actual data saved us countless hours of experimentation and allowed us to conserve our development efforts for our final system design.

As I explored the data, I kept track of the interesting trends, patterns, and outliers I discovered. In some cases, interesting stories were found nested within a combination of dimensions. For example, stratifying marital status by both age and gender over time revealed

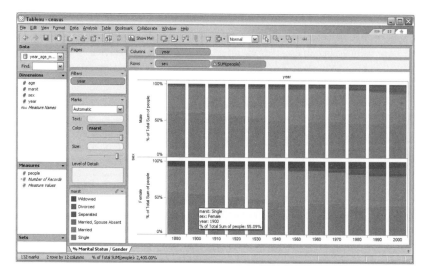

FIGURE 12-3. A prototype visualization built using Tableau showing the distribution of marital status over multiple decades. (See Color Plate 36.)

that the average age at which females (but not males) first get married has increased by about five years over the last century. In other cases, a single type of data plotted over time revealed a number of interesting stories, such as the wax and wane of farmers in the labor force and different waves of immigration from around the globe. I often found it useful to transform the data, alternately viewing the data as absolute population numbers or as percentages within a census decade.

Design Considerations

Prototypes in hand, Martin, Fernanda, and I then collaboratively designed the interactive visualizations for sense.us. To do so, we first outlined a set of design considerations.

Foster personal relevance

If no one cares about the data, no one will explore it. We hypothesized that familiar dimensions such as geography and time enable users to quickly look for themselves (or people like them) in the data and form narratives. Given that the geographic data available to us was limited, we focused on the presentation of data over time. We also tried to use interaction techniques that let users quickly search for data records of interest to them, such as particular occupations or countries of origin.

Provide effective visual encodings

Naturally, we wanted to use visual encodings that would facilitate comprehension of the data. In some cases, this task is straightforward: if I want to examine the correlation between two numerical values, I would be hard pressed to find a better representation than a scatterplot. In this case, we had to balance a number of trade-offs.

A common way to visualize change over time is to use a line graph. However, displaying over 200 occupations in a line graph results in a cluttered mess of occluding lines. We instead chose stacked graphs, which visually sum multiple time series by stacking them on top of one another (see Figures 12-4 and 12-5, later in this chapter). Our choice was influenced Martin's Baby Name Voyager visualization, a stacked graph of baby name popularity that became surprisingly popular online (Wattenberg and Kriss 2006). Stacked graphs show aggregate patterns clearly and comfortably support interactive filtering, but do so at the cost of obscuring individual trends—perception of a trend is biased by the contour of the series stacked beneath it. In response, we ensured that clicking a series would filter the display so that the trend could easily be viewed in isolation.

Furthermore, we followed established cultural conventions to encode data in a fashion familiar to many viewers (e.g., blue for boys, pink for girls). When considering how to visualize the interaction between a number of demographic variables, rather than try to invent something completely novel, we instead augmented a chart type already in common use by demographers: the population pyramid.

Make each display distinct

In some instances we used the same visualization type to show different data types. For example, we used stacked graphs for both occupation and birthplace data. However, we wanted to make each display visually distinct, so that users could recognize them at a glance. Consequently, we constructed a unique color palette for each visualization.

Support intuitive exploration

To foster interactive exploration, we wanted to make manipulating the interface as simple as possible. For stacked graphs, we let users type keyword searches to query for items of interest. In other cases, we provided a collection of drop-down menus to select or filter dimensions. We also included controls for selecting between absolute people counts and normalized percentages. Although more advanced manipulations are possible, we found that providing this level of control enabled a range of exploration with an uncluttered, easy-to-learn interface.

Be engaging and playful

In addition to fostering personal relevance, we wanted interaction with our system to be engaging and enjoyable. We thus strove for an aesthetic as well as effective presentation of data. We designed interaction techniques and animated transitions to promote a feeling of responsiveness and dynamism, but we did not want to take such stylistic features too far. We wanted to enhance, not disrupt, data exploration. We varied animation styles and timing until our designs "felt right." An animation duration of ~1 second provided transitions that viewers could follow without slowing down the analysis process.

Visualization Designs

By first engaging in data exploration of our own, we were able to determine the data dimensions we found most interesting. We applied these observations in conjunction with our design considerations to design a suite of visualizations of the census data.

Job Voyager

The Job Voyager is a stacked graph showing the composition of the U.S. labor force over the last 150 years (Figure 12-4). Each series represents an occupation, subdivided by sex: blue indicates male, pink indicates female. Users can explore the data by clicking on a series to show only the corresponding occupation, or by typing keyword queries to filter out jobs that do not match the query. We also included drop-down menus to filter by sex and to switch between views of absolute people count and percentage of the labor force. These operations support exploration of both aggregate trends (e.g., the influx of women into the labor force after World War II) and individual patterns (e.g., the rise and fall of locomotive engineers).

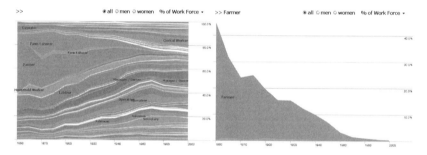

FIGURE 12-4.Job Voyager visualization: (left) an overview showing the constitution of the labor force over 150 years, and (right) a filtered view showing the percentage of farmers. (See Color Plate 37.)

We quickly realized that coloring the series solely on gender was not enough. When we filtered the view to show only males or only females, it became difficult to differentiate individual series. One solution is to enable perceptual discrimination by varying color saturation in an arbitrary fashion. Martin then suggested a clever variation on this approach: rather than vary colors arbitrarily, do so in a meaningful, data-driven way. We subsequently varied color saturation according to socio-economic index scores for each occupation. Thus a series with a higher median income was drawn darker. In practice, this encoding worked well to improve identification of different occupations without adding misleading or meaningless visual features to the display.

Birthplace Voyager

The Birthplace Voyager is similar in design to the Job Voyager, but instead shows the birthplace of U.S. residents in each census year (Figure 12-5). The recorded birthplaces are either U.S. states and territories or foreign countries. The interactive controls enable filtering by keyword query or by continent and the display of both absolute counts and percentages.

The visualization supports investigation of immigration trends across the world (e.g., past waves of immigration from Europe and current waves of immigration from Latin America) and within the U.S. (e.g., the changing proportion of residents in each state).

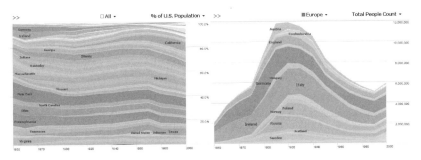

FIGURE 12-5. Birthplace Voyager visualization: (left) an overview showing the distribution of birthplaces over 150 years, and (right) a filtered view showing the total number of European immigrants. (See Color Plate 38.)

With the Birthplace Voyager, we encountered similar coloring issues as before. In this case, we assigned color hues according to continent, plus an extra dedicated hue for U.S. states. We then experimented with different means of varying color saturation until we settled on using the total number of people born in the state or country across all time slices as the backing data.

U.S. census state map and scatterplot

While the timelines of the Job and Birthplace Voyagers were designed to engage viewers in historical narrative, we wanted to include more conventional views as well. We provided a colored state map for viewing the distribution of demographic variables for each state. In an annotated map of population change for states between 2000 and 2005 (Figure 12-6, left), one can see substantial growth in the southwest while the population of North Dakota has decreased. We also provided a scatterplot display to examine potential correlations between variables. Users can map demographic variables to the x position, y position, and size of circles representing the U.S. states. For example, one may note a correlation between household income and retail sales across states (Figure 12-6, right). The backing data for these views includes additional statistics we downloaded from the U.S. census bureau website.

Population pyramid

Our most sophisticated visualization was an interactive population pyramid, designed to facilitate exploration of multiple demographic variables at once (Figure 12-7). Population pyramids (sometimes called "age-sex" pyramids) are a chart type introduced to us by our colleagues in demography. The pyramid is divided by a vertical axis into two halves: one for males, one for females. The y-axis represents age, often grouped into 5- or 10-year bins, and the x-axis represents the total number of people in that age group, with values

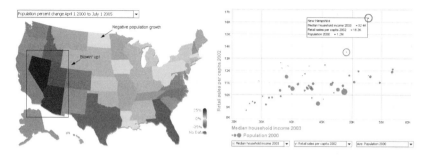

FIGURE 12-6. (Left) Interactive state map showing changes in each state's population from 2000 to 2005, and (right) scatterplot of U.S. states showing median household income (x-axis) versus retail sales (y-axis); New Hampshire and Delaware have the highest retail sales. (See Color Plate 39.)

for males increasing in one direction and values for females increasing in the opposite direction (Figure 12-7, left). The pyramid's shape communicates population dynamics: a steeply tapering pyramid indicates higher mortality rates than a more cylindrical shape.

We created an interactive pyramid incorporating demographic variables in addition to age and sex: geographic region, race, marital status, school attendance, and income level. By default, the two sides of the pyramids split the data by sex. We relaxed this restriction and added drop-down menus with which users could select a demographic variable and map two values to the sides of the pyramid. For example, users looked at geographic region, placing the west coast on one side of the pyramid and New England on the other.

We also introduced a color-encoding menu: selecting a demographic variable turns the pyramid sides into stacked graphs depicting the prevalence of values. For example, users can stratify the pyramid by school attendance to see what segments of the population were in school (Figure 12-7, right). We chose a distinct color palette for each variable, relying on existing cultural conventions where possible (e.g., blue=male, pink=female) and using ColorBrewer (*http://colorbrewer.org*) to determine color choices for the other cases. We used a gray color for bands representing missing or unknown values.

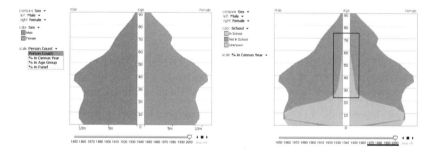

FIGURE 12-7. Population pyramid visualization: (left) a comparison of the total number of males and females in each age group in 2000, and (right) the distribution of school attendees in 2000 (an annotation highlights the prevalence of adult education). (See Color Plate 40.)

A timeline beneath the pyramid enables temporal exploration across census decades, and a playback feature animates changes to the pyramid over time. For example, animating population change over time dramatically shows the baby boom rippling through society in the post-war period. The mixture of layered colors and bubbling animation led users to endearingly rename our population pyramid "Georgia O'Keefe's lava lamp."

Finally, we included support for four data measures: total people count, percentage within decade, percentage within panel (useful when the two sides of the pyramid are dispropor-tionate), and percentage within age group (to explore proportional differences across ages). Our own explorations found that each measure helps reveal specific stories. For example, viewing percentage within age group shows that elderly men are more likely to be married than elderly women, presumably because on average women live longer and become widows.

Implementation details

We implemented each visualization as a Java applet so we could embed it on a web page. We chose Java over Flash partially for performance reasons, but mostly due to the avail-ability of visualization frameworks in Java at the time. The stacked graphs and population pyramid were built using the open source prefuse toolkit (*http://prefuse.org*). Backing each visualization is a flat text file extracted from our census database. In the case of the popu-lation pyramid, we created one file for every possible combination of demographic vari-ables, precomputing all the relevant projections of the data. This approach eliminated the need for data processing on the server, and resulted in a very manageable storage foot-print: though we started with a database of over 3 gigabytes, the final deployed data was reduced to little more than 3 megabytes! Of course, this approach does have limitations: it impedes users from exploring novel combinations of demographic variables and compli-cates the introduction of future visualizations requiring server-side data processing.

Collaboration

We then created the *sense.us* website, which couples the visualizations with collaborative analysis mechanisms (see Figure 12-8). In the left panel is the visualization applet (Figure 12-8a) and annotation tools (Figure 12-8b). The right panel provides a graphical book-mark trail (Figure 12-8c), providing access to views saved by the user, and a discussion area (Figure 12-8d and e), displaying commentary associated with the current view. We augmented the visualizations with a set of collaboration features, described in detail later: view sharing, doubly linked discussions, graphical annotations, bookmark trails, and social navigation via comment listings and user activity profiles.

View Sharing

When collaborating around visualizations, we reasoned that participants must be able to see the same visual environment in order to ground one another's actions and comments. To this aim, sense.us provides a mechanism for bookmarking views. We tried to make

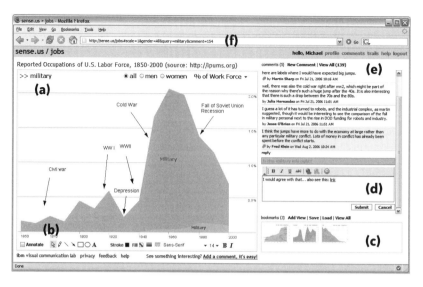

FIGURE 12-8. The sense.us collaborative visualization system: (a) An interactive visualization applet, with a graphical annotation for the currently selected comment. The visualization is a stacked time-series visualization of the U.S. labor force, broken down by gender. Here, the percentage of the workforce in military jobs is shown. (b) A set of graphical annotation tools. (c) A bookmark trail of saved views. (d) Text-entry field for adding comments. Bookmarks can be dragged onto the text field to add a link to that view in the comment. (e) Threaded comments attached to the current view. (f) URL for the current state of the application. The URL is updated automatically as the visualization state changes. (See Color Plate 41.)

application bookmarking transparent by tying it to conventional web bookmarking. The browser's location bar always displays a URL that links to the current state of the visualization, defined by the settings of filtering, navigation, and visual encoding parameters. As the visualization view changes, the URL updates to reflect the current state (Figure 12-8f), simplifying the process of sharing a view through email, blogs, or instant messaging by enabling users to cut-and-paste a link to the current view at any time. To conform to user expectations, the browser's back and forward buttons are tied to the visualization state, allowing easy navigation to previously seen views.

Doubly Linked Discussion

To situate conversation around the visualization, we created a technique we call *doubly linked discussion*. The method begins with an independent discussion interface in which users can attach comments to particular states (or views) of a visualization. Comments are shown on the right side of the web page and grouped into linear discussion threads (Figure 12-8e). Each comment shows the thread topic, comment text, the author's full name, and the time at which the comment was authored. Clicking on a comment takes the visualization to a bookmarked state representing the view seen by the comment's author.

Users can add comments either by starting a new thread or posting a reply to an existing thread. When a "New Comment" or "Reply" link is clicked, a text editor appears at the site where the comment will be inserted (Figure 12-8d) and the graphical annotation tools

(discussed next) become active. Upon submission, the comment text and any annotations are sent to the server and the comment listing is updated.

The interface just described is based on links from the commentary into the visualization. Our system also provides links in the other direction: from the visualization into the discussion. As users change parameters and views in the visualization, they may serendipitously happen upon a view that another person has already commented on. When this occurs, the relevant comments will automatically appear in the righthand pane. Our intuition was that this "doubly linked" discussion interface, which combines aspects of independent and embedded discussion, would facilitate grounding and enable the visualization itself to become a social place.

We quickly realized that our bookmarking mechanism was not sufficient to support doubly linked discussions. To see the challenge in linking from a view state back to all comments on that view, consider the visualization in Figure 12-8. When a user types "military" into the top search box (Figure 12-8f), he sees all jobs whose titles begin with the string "military." On the other hand, if he types only "mili," he sees all titles beginning with "mili"—but this turns out to be the identical set of jobs. These different parameter settings result in different URLs, and yet provide exactly the same visualization view. More generally, parameter settings may not have a one-to-one mapping to visualization states. To attach discussions to views, we therefore need an indexing mechanism that identifies visualization states that are equivalent despite having different parametric representations.

We solve this indexing problem by distinguishing between two types of parameters: filter parameters and view parameters. Filter parameters determine which data elements are visible in the display. Rather than index filter parameters directly, we instead index the filtered state of the application by noting which items are currently visible, thereby capturing the case when different filter parameters give rise to the same filtered state. View parameters, on the other hand, adjust visual mappings, such as selecting a normalized or absolute axis scale. Our current system indexes the view parameters directly. The bookmarking mechanism implements this two-part index by computing a probabilistically unique SHA-1 hash value based on both the filtered state and view parameters. These hash values are used as keys for retrieving the comments for the current visualization state.

Pointing via Graphical Annotation

In physical collaborations, people commonly use both speech and gesture, particularly pointing, to refer to objects and direct conversation. In the distributed, asynchronous context of the Web, graphical annotations can play a similar communicative role. We hypothesized that graphical annotations would be important for both pointing behavior and playful commentary. To add a pictorial element to a comment or point to a feature of interest, authors can use drawing tools (Figure 12-8b) to annotate the commented view.

These tools allow free-form ink, lines, arrows, shapes, and text to be drawn over the visualization view. The tools are similar to presentation tools such as Microsoft PowerPoint and are intended to leverage users' familiarity with such systems.

Comments with annotations are indicated by the presence of a small icon to the left of the author's name in the comment listing (see Figure 12-8e). When the mouse hovers over an annotated comment, the comment region highlights in yellow and a hand cursor appears. Subsequently clicking the region causes the annotation to be shown and the highlighting to darken and become permanent. Clicking the comment again (or clicking a different comment) will remove the current annotation and highlighting.

The graphical annotations take the form of vector graphics drawn above the visualization. When a new comment is submitted, the browser requests the current annotation (if any) from the visualization applet. The annotation is saved to an XML format, which is then compressed using gzip and encoded in a base-64 string representation before being passed to the browser. When comments are later retrieved from the server, the encoded annotations are stored in the browser as JavaScript variables. When the user requests that an annotation be displayed, the encoded annotations are passed to the applet, decoded, and drawn.

We refer to this approach as *geometric annotation*, which operates like an "acetate layer" over the visualization, in contrast to *data-aware* annotations directly associated with the underlying data. We chose to implement a free-form annotation mechanism so that we could first study pointing behaviors in an unconstrained medium. Aside from the freedom of expression it affords, geometric annotation also has a technical advantage: it allows reuse of the identical annotation system across visualizations, easing implementation and preserving a consistent user experience.

Collecting and Linking Views

In data analysis it is common to make comparisons between different ways of looking at data. Furthermore, storytelling has been suggested to play an important role in social usage of visualizations. Drawing comparisons and telling stories both require the ability to embed multiple view bookmarks into a single comment.

To support such multiview comments and narratives, we created a "bookmark trail" widget. The bookmark trail functions something like a shopping cart: as a user navigates through the site, she can click a special "Add View" link to add the current view to a graphical list of bookmarks (Figure 12-8c). Bookmarks from any number of visualizations can be added to a trail. A trail may be named and saved, making it accessible to others.

The bookmark trail widget also functions as a short-term storage mechanism when making a comment that includes links to multiple views. Dragging a thumbnail from the bookmark trail and dropping it onto the text area creates a hyperlink to the bookmarked view; users can then directly edit or delete the link text within the text editor. When the mouse hovers over the link text, a tool-tip thumbnail of the linked view is shown.

Awareness and Social Navigation

The term *social navigation* refers to our tendency to navigate in the world based on the actions or advice of others. On the Web, such navigation can be achieved by surfacing others' usage history to provide additional navigation options. We designed sense.us to support social navigation through comment listings and user profile pages that display recent activity. Comment listings provide a searchable collection of all comments made within the system, and can be filtered to focus on a single visualization (Figure 12-9). Comment listing pages include the text and a thumbnail image of the visualization state for each comment. Hovering over the thumbnail yields a tool tip with a larger image. Clicking a comment link takes the user to the state of the visualization where the comment was made, displaying any annotations included with the comment. The author's name links to the author's profile page, which includes his five most recent comment threads and five most recently saved bookmark trails. The view also notes the number of comments made on a thread since the user's last comment, allowing users to monitor the activity of discussions to which they contribute.

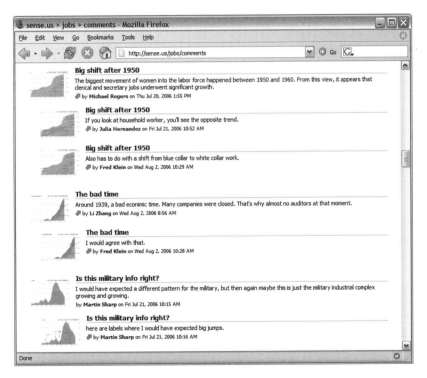

FIGURE 12-9. The sense.us comment listing page; comment listings display all commentary on visualizations and provide links to the commented visualization views. (See Color Plate 42.)

Although more elaborate social navigation mechanisms are possible, we wanted to observe system usage with just these basic options. We were particularly interested in observing the potential interplay between data-driven exploration and social navigation.

By allowing discussions to be retrieved unobtrusively while a user explores the data, potentially relevant conversation can be introduced into the exploration process. Meanwhile, comment listings and indications of recent posts may help users find views of interest, making social activity a catalyst for data exploration.

Unobtrusive Collaboration

We also followed a common design guideline from the field of computer-supported cooperative work: collaborative features should not impede individual usage. As a result, we do not litter views with annotations by default. Rather, comments for a visualization are displayed unobtrusively on the right side of the screen, and graphical annotations are displayed "on demand" by the user.

Voyagers and Voyeurs

After these steps of data acquisition, design, and system implementation, we now had a running website and were ready to do "field tests" with users. We deployed the system in a set of user studies to observe how people would react to our system, what insights they might produce, and how we might improve the site.

We invited 30 people into our lab to observe how they explored data with sense.us. Each person could view what the previous participants had contributed to the site. We also ran a live deployment on the IBM corporate intranet that all employees in the company could access. From these studies, we investigated how people engaged with the visualizations and how the collaboration features impacted their explorations. Next, I summarize some of the more interesting usage patterns we observed.

Hunting for Patterns

Most users' first instinct was to engage in "scavenger hunts" for interesting and amusing observations, often driven by personal context. For example, users would search for jobs they or their friends or family members have held, or look at birthplace data for the countries of their ancestors. Along the way, people often left comments documenting the trends they found most interesting.

For example, participants noticed that the number of bartenders dropped to zero around the 1930s and posted comments attributing the drop to alcohol prohibition. One person found a peak and then steady decline in Canadian immigration as a percentage of the population in 1800, and posted a question pondering what may have contributed to the trend. Yet another user noticed a drop in stockbrokers in the Great Depression, leading to the visual commentary in Figure 12-10.

Users also found interesting trends via the population pyramid. For example, users explored changes in marital status over time (see Figure 12-11). The green and purple bands indicate the prevalence of separation and divorce, which increases dramatically after 1960. One user investigated school attendance and commented that adult schooling noticeably rises from 1960 onward (the right panel of Figure 12-7, shown previously).

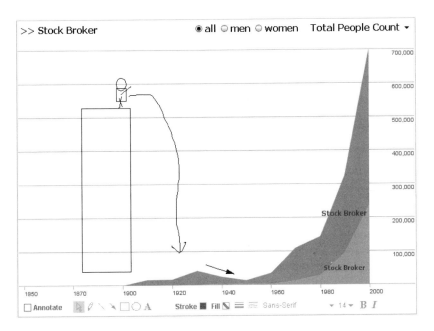

FIGURE 12-10. Annotated view of stockbrokers; the attached comment reads "Great depression 'killed' a lot of brokers." (See Color Plate 43.)

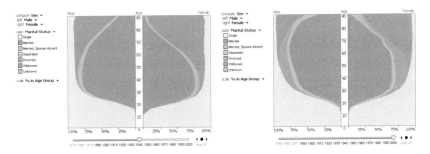

FIGURE 12-11. Population pyramid showing the distribution of marital status for each age group in (left) 1940, and (right) 2000. (See Color Plate 44.)

In another instance, a user mapped the two sides of the pyramid to the populations of the mid-Atlantic (i.e., New York, Pennsylvania, and New Jersey) and the west coast (see Figure 12-12). In 1850, the population of the Gold Rush–era west coast is decidedly different from the east, being dominated by young and middle-age males. Seen 90 years later, the demographics are more closely aligned, though a user noted that the west coast skewed about 10 years older.

Some users were less interested in specific views than in recurring patterns. One user was interested in exploring careers that were historically male-dominated, but have seen increasing numbers of females in the last half-century. The user systematically explored the data, saving views in a bookmark trail later shared in a comment named "Women's Rise."

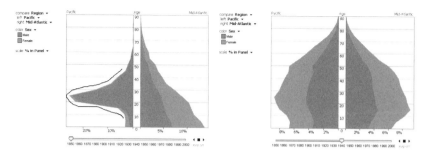

FIGURE 12-12. Population pyramid comparing the populations of the west coast and mid-Atlantic regions in (left) 1850, and (right) 1940. (See Color Plate 45.)

Similarly, a more mathematically minded participant was interested in patterns of job fluctuations, creating a trail showcasing recurring distributions. Another searched for jobs that had been usurped by technology, such as bank tellers and telephone operators. In each of these cases, the result was a tour or story winding through multiple views.

Making Sense of It All

As users made observations of the data, they commonly sought out explanations by posting questions or hypotheses that might make sense of a trend. Many of these questions and hypotheses attracted responses from other users, initiating a cyclic process of social interpretation.

In our live deployment, one user commented on a scatterplot view, asking why New Hampshire has such a high level of retail sales per capita (Figure 12-6). Another user noted that New Hampshire does not have sales tax, and neither does Delaware, the second highest in retail sales. In this fashion, discussion regularly involved the introduction of contextual information not present in the visualization. For instance, users iteratively constructed a timeline of events to annotate military build-ups (Figure 12-8), while another user annotated a graph of teachers with the introduction of compulsory education.

One instance of social data analysis occurred around a rise, fall, and slight resurgence in the percentage of dentists in the labor force (Figure 12-13). The first comment noted the trends and asked what was happening. One subject responded in a separate thread, *"Maybe this has to do with fluoridation? But there's a bump…but kids got spoiled and had a lot of candy??"* To this another subject responded, *"As preventative dentistry has become more effective, dentists have continued to look for ways to continue working (e.g., most people see the dentist twice a year now v. once a year just a few decades ago)."* Perhaps the most telling comment, however, included a link to a different view, showing both dentists and dental technicians. As dentists had declined in percentage, technicians had grown substantially, indicating specialization within the field. To this, another user asked, *"I wonder if school has become too expensive for people to think about dentistry, or at least their own practice when they can go to technical school for less?"* Visual data analysis, historical knowledge, and personal anecdote all played a role in the sensemaking process, explicating various factors shaping the data.

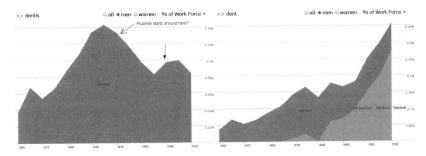

FIGURE 12-13. Annotated job voyager views highlighting (left) a decline in dentists after 1930, and (right) an overall increase in dentistry due to the rising ranks of dental technicians. (See Color Plate 46.)

Another role of comments was to aid data interpretation, especially in cases of unclear meaning or anomalies in data collection. Despite the hard work of the IPUMS project, missing data and obscure labels still occur. To enable comparison across census decades, a shared classification scheme has to be formed. In the case of the job data, a 1950s schema is used. The schema does not include modern jobs such as computer programmer, and some labels are vague.

One prominent occupation was labeled "Operative," a general category consisting largely of skilled labor. This term had little meaning to users, one of whom asked, *"What the hell is an operative?"* Others responded to reinforce the question or to suggest an explanation, e.g., *"I bet they mean factory worker."* Another subject agreed, noting that the large number of workers and the years of the rise and fall of operatives seemed consistent with machine-operators in factories.

In this fashion, users collectively engaged in data validation and disambiguation, often planting "signposts" in the data to help aid interpretation by others. Overall, about 16% of the comments referenced data naming, categorization, or collection issues.

Crowd Surfing

We observed that most users initially explored the data driven by their own interests or by items of interest found in the overview (e.g., *"Wow, look how the poor farmers died out"*). Eventually, users would run out of ideas or tire of exploration. At this point, every user we observed then left the visualizations to explore the comment listings. Some felt that by doing so they would find interesting views more quickly. Remarks to this effect included, *"I bet others have found even more interesting things"* and *"You get to stand on the shoulders of others."* Other subjects were interested in specific people they knew or discovering what other people had investigated. One user said, *"I feel like a data voyeur. I really like seeing what other people were searching for."*

Switching between data-driven exploration and social navigation was common: views discovered via comment listings often sparked new interests and catalyzed more data analysis

in the visualizations. After some exploration, participants routinely returned to the listings for more inspiration. Thus we observed a positive feedback loop between data-driven exploration and social navigation: surfacing social activity helped catalyze exploration of new analysis questions. In other words, users fluidly switched between the roles of voyager and voyeur.

Conclusion

Based on the results of the sense.us project, we observed that the combination of interactive visualization and social interpretation can help an audience more richly explore a data set. However, as a research prototype, the sense.us site was never publicly released. Instead, my colleagues at IBM succeeded sense.us with the launch of Many-Eyes.com: a public website where users can upload their own data sets, visualize data using a variety of interactive visualization components, and engage in discussion on-site or embed visualization views in external blogs and wikis.

In a similar spirit, web services such as Swivel.com and Data360.org, and commercial products such as Spotfire Decision Site Posters and Tableau Server, now enable users to post visualizations to the Web and engage others in the process of social data analysis. In parallel with the larger movement toward web-scale social computing, there remains much to learn about how to catalyze and support social forms of data exploration. Many exciting research questions regarding how to integrate data analysis and social activity remain to be addressed. Open problems include the design of better social navigation cues, richer annotation techniques, and new methods for combining users' observations, questions, and hypotheses into a reasoned analysis story.

Though the forms of analysis we observed in sense.us were exploratory in nature, the system had a clear educational benefit and users reported that using sense.us was both enjoyable and informative. Furthermore, many of the observations, questions, and hypotheses generated by users invite follow-up by trained analysts. Accessible presentations of data, coupled with social interaction, helped a population turn data into a richer understanding of society. I find that rather beautiful.

References

Anscombe, Francis J. (1973). "Graphs in Statistical Analysis." *American Statistician*, 27, 17–21.

Bertin, Jacques. (1967). *Sémiologie Graphique*, Gauthier-Villars. English translation by W. J. Berg as *Semiology of Graphics*, University of Wisconsin Press, 1983.

Card, Stuart K., Ben Shneiderman, and Jock D. Mackinlay. (1999). *Readings in Information Visualization: Using Vision To Think*, Morgan-Kaufmann.

Cleveland, William S. and Robert McGill. (1985). "Graphical Perception and Graphical Methods for Analyzing Scientific Data." *Science*, 229(4716), 828–833.

Croes, Marnix. (2006). "The Holocaust in the Netherlands and the Rate of Jewish Survival." *Holocaust and Genocide Studies*, 20(3), 474–499.

Robison, Wade, Roger Boisjoly, David Hoeker, and Stefan Young. (2002). "Representation and Misrepresentation: Tufte and the Morton Thiokol Engineers on the Challenger." *Science and Engineering Ethics*, 8, 59–81.

Tufte, Edward R. (1997). *Visual Explanations: Images and Quantities, Evidence and Narrative*, Graphics Press.

Ware, Colin. (2004). *Information Visualization: Perception for Design*, Second Edition, Morgan-Kaufmann.

Wattenberg, Martin and Jesse Kriss. (2006). "Designing for Social Data Analysis." *IEEE Transactions on Visualization and Computer Graphics*, 12(4), 549–557.

CHAPTER THIRTEEN

What Data Doesn't Do

Coco Krumme

DATA DOES A GREAT MANY THINGS: IT ALLOWS US TO SEPARATE SCIENCE FROM SUPERSTITION AND THE repeatable from the random. Over the past several decades, scientists have scaled tremendously the processes for collecting, collating, and storing data. From medical decision-making to soft drink marketing to supply chain management, we're relying more on fact and less on hunch. We're letting data drive.

But data doesn't drive everything. Over the past century, psychologists have poked holes in the theory that people interpret data with anything close to rational equanimity. In truth, we're biased in our interpretation of information. Moreover, the real world does not manifest itself with the easy probabilism of a game of dice. Rather, individuals must extract likelihoods from perceived patterns in experience.

This chapter is a discussion of the approximations and biases that stand between data and analysis. It describes a set of new experiments and tools to help people use data more effectively, and draws examples from the growing literature in medical, consumer, and financial decision-making.

Suppose I ask you to identify the odd one out from Figure 13-1.

FIGURE 13-1. The human visual system is adept at identifying the odd one out.

The answer is immediate and trivial: the human eye can pick out the ugly duckling from the swans. For a computer, however, the solution is not so simple: image recognition software lags far behind the human visual system for most tasks.

Our brains are wired to quickly place new items into old bins. We're adept at drawing analogies and extensions: mittens and sweaters and skies go together; a cartoon mouse is similar to a cartoon bear; a cartoon bear is similar to a real bear; these two classes of similarity are themselves very different.

Even when you remove context, our visual system is remarkably skilled at picking up on patterns. Take Figure 13-2: how would you divide the data into two sets?

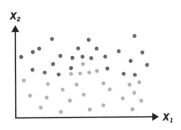

FIGURE 13-2. We can build models to discriminate between two sets of data. (See Color Plate 47.)

Start adding dimensionality and data points, and the task becomes too complex for a person; a computer, however, can parse it with some ease. You might be able to draw an approximate curve between the two sets of dots, but a computer will be able to construct a model to most precisely divide the data.

Now, look at the pattern in the charts in Figure 13-3, which shows the stock prices of three major manufacturers over a 10-month interval ending in October 2005. Consider the charts and decide on an answer before reading the next paragraph: based on the given pattern, which one of the three stocks do you expect to increase in value over the subsequent year?

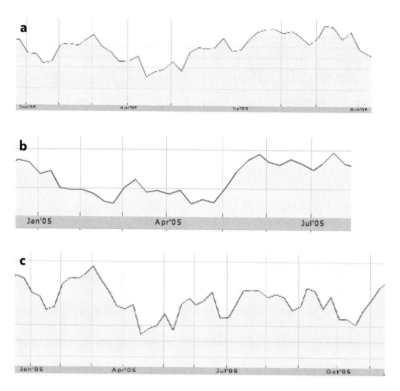

FIGURE 13-3. Performance of three securities (a, b, and c) in 2005. (See Color Plate 48.)

Did you pick the third chart? It looks as if it is headed up at the end. Well, you're wrong. In fact, if you picked the first or second chart, you're also, equally, wrong. Not one of the stocks is upward bound, and none is trending down. Actually, the charts don't even represent stock prices. They were randomly generated: data gibberish, one might say. But the implanted belief that they belong to a specific company (in this case, in the manufacturing sector) can generate all kinds of speculation. Even with real charts, unless you had specific knowledge about a company or industry, it would be difficult to predict the future direction of a stock based on 10 months of past performance.

The tendency to create a story out of noise is sometimes dubbed the narrative fallacy. Even if you were suspicious of the question—or read ahead too quickly—when we asked top MBA students—some of them applying for jobs in finance—the same question, they expressed a good deal of certainty about the direction in which such "stocks" were headed. Some said up, some said down. When the charts were supplemented with "news clips" randomly generated and placed in random order along the length of the chart, students claimed a still greater certainty about their predictions—showing, perhaps, the power of telling oneself a good story about data (Krumme [to appear]). (Consider, also, the loose causal quips thrown around by financial journalists: "the Dow dropped 100 points on fear of rising unemployment.")

If human beings are adept at spotting patterns, we're masters at making up stories about statistics. This is less problematic when we know where data comes from and what it means; it can be disastrous when we're faced with a lot of evidence from different sources and high-stakes outcomes.

As a final example, before looking at the question, consider your expectations. The tendency to apply a past conclusion to present analysis is called the "confirmation bias" (Lord et al. 1979). (Think of the people you know who read only to pick out statements that confirm a held worldview.) It's a very real phenomenon in dealing with data. Scientists have been observed to adhere preferentially to past hypotheses, sometimes in the face of overwhelming evidence to the contrary (Jeng 2006). Similarly, stock traders whose bets pay off experience a soothing release of dopamine, helping them keep their minds made up about the behavior of the market (Lo and Repin 2002).

For the moment, let's say you're neither a scientist nor a stock trader, but a petty investor: you're given a choice between two investment options:

- Option A: win $7,400 with 100% certainty
- Option B: win $10,000 with 75% certainty, $0 with 25% certainty

There is no trick here: you can see the expected utility of each outcome. Which would you choose?

Now, given the following two options, which would you choose?

- Option C: pay $7,400 with 100% certainty
- Option D: pay $10,000 with 75% certainty, $0 with 25% certainty

Most people choose options A and D. There's an asymmetry here: we tend to be risk-seeking on the downside and risk-averse on the upside. That is, the prospect of a sure win is more appealing than a bigger win with the possibility of getting nothing, but we'd rather bet on losing more than pony up a set amount. In addition, this combination of choices does not maximize payoff: if we thought purely opportunistically about gains and losses, we'd pick B and C, for a total expected utility of $1,000 instead of –$1,000 (that is, we'd be up $2,000 compared with A+D).

This experiment, first conducted by Daniel Kahneman and Amos Tversky in the 1970s, reveals that we don't always think probabilistically: instead, we imagine the emotional outcomes associated with each single outcome.

In fact, in a number of important ways, we don't treat data as we assume we do.

When Doesn't Data Drive?

The first section pointed out a couple of cognitive biases in the analysis of data. The remainder of the essay is a discussion of what data doesn't do: that is, of the various ways in which measurement and interpretation themselves can transform data. This is not a

treatise on "lies, damn lies, and statistics": we know that data can be used to purposefully confound; here, the focus is on how it can accidentally confuse. In particular:

- Our tools for using data are inexact.
- We process data with known biases.

Although the examples that follow focus on biomedical and financial data, they are more or less extensible. "Data" is used to mean any set of raw facts amassed from experience, observation, or experiment.

1. More Data Isn't Always Better

Statistics is a science of representation and approximation. The more of a system we capture or observe, the closer we can come to representing it honestly. An introductory statistics text will emphasize: as you increase sample size, you decrease confidence interval without any loss in confidence. In other words, more data helps rein in your margin of error (see Figure 13-4).

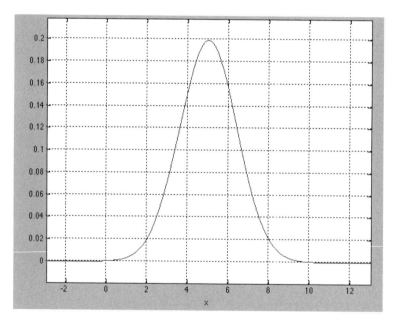

FIGURE 13-4. The normal distribution. (See Color Plate 49.)

A fine truth for the textbooks. Outside of that gossamer world, several assumptions must be examined. First, how is your data distributed? Is it necessarily normal? In much of finance, for example, distributions eschew normality. Biomedical data (the expression of a trait, for example) is more frequently Gaussian, but evolution needn't always conform to the central limit theorem.

If the data is not normal, more data will not reduce your margin of error in the expected manner. Karl Popper described an asymmetry in how we use data to answer questions:

while no number of results in support of a hypothesis will ever confirm it, a single contradictory result will disprove it. More data adds only marginal certainty, whereas one instance can dissolve a century of belief.

Second, is the cost of a false positive the same as that of a false negative? Even if your data is (or looks) normal, your interest in different outcomes might not be symmetrical. The cost of failing to detect a life-threatening illness may be greater, for example, than the cost of incorrect diagnosis. In such a case, data that improves the precision of diagnosis (by cutting out false negatives) will be more useful than reams of data to winnow down false positives.

2. More Data Isn't Always Easy

Data doesn't necessarily scale. One of the trite maxims of our information age is that it's just as easy to process 10 bits as it is 10 terabytes, whereas 10 billion widgets are much more expensive to make than 10.

In some cases, the costs of cleaning and processing data are not trivial. This is particularly true when verification requires a human eye, such as reading meaning into X-rays or transcribing data coded in a questionnaire. In Red Queen fashion,* better computers and the ability to collect more and more data has driven (and been driven by) the development of new tools to parse it and new ways to use it.

There are also cognitive costs that accompany more information. Whether we're choosing between jams at the supermarket or 401(k) plans, research has shown that as the number of options increases, it takes us longer to decide, we become more likely to give up without choosing anything, and we are less satisfied with any choice we make (Iyenger and Lepper 2000).

Finally, a subtle cost: more data can begin to blind us to other possibilities, especially if we're responsible for its collection and collation. It's hard not to imagine that seeing more data means a hypothesis is better supported—a corollary of the confirmation bias and sampling issues discussed earlier.

3. Data Alone Doesn't Explain

People explain. Correlation and causality, you may have heard, make strange bedfellows. Given two variables correlated in a statistically significant way, causality can work forward, backward, in both directions, or not at all. Statisticians have made a hobby (not to mention a number of blogs) of chronicling the abuses of correlation, like old ladies clucking at the downfall of traditional values in the modern world.

Journalists are the preferred targets of such statistical "tsks." A recent article in the *Wall Street Journal* (Shellenbarger 2008), for example, suggested that because premarital cohabitation is

---

* Lewis Carroll's Red Queen, from *Alice in Wonderland*, proclaims, "It takes all the running you can do, to keep in the same place." This idea has been used to describe a system that, due to an arms race of external pressures, must continue to co-evolve.

correlated with higher rates of divorce, unwed couples could avoid living together in order to improve their chances of staying together after marriage. The research described never suggested a causal link, but the journalist offered her own advice to couples based on the "data."

The substitution of correlation with causality need not be so explicit. When a scientific research project is undertaken, there exists the assumption that correlation, if discovered, would imply causation, albeit unknown. Else, why seek to answer a research question at all: large-scale search for correlation without causation is aleatory computation, not science. Even with so-called big data, science remains an intensely hypothesis-driven process.

The limits of empirical research is not grounds to throw up our hands, only to be careful to push discovery forward without getting rosy-eyed about causality. Creating stories about data is only human: it's the ability to revise consistently that makes a story sound.

4. Data Isn't Good for a Single Answer

Descriptive statistics can hide detail. The charts in Figure 13-5, for example, show four distributions that look dramatically different, yet share the same mean and variance. These two pillars of descriptive statistics—mean and variance—tell you very little about distribution (Anscombe 1973).

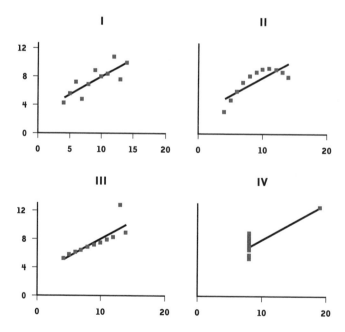

FIGURE 13-5. Anscombe's quartet: each data set has the same mean and variance.

When using data for decision-making, we tend to treat distributions as if they're good for one answer. We may need to base a binary decision—should the U.S. declare war? should the FDA approve this drug? who is predicted to win the election?—or a summary statement— how well-off are Americans? what will the Earth's climate look like in five years?—on data that's indeterminate. Even if variance is reported, the decision is what matters.

People think in terms of outcomes, not distributions. Consider a personal financial decision: how much should I invest in stocks, bonds, and cash? Even if past financial performance properly predicted future returns (which, as even the financial advisors are legally required to admit, it doesn't)—that is, even if we knew the shape of the distribution—we'd still have a number of risk and reward pairs from which to elect, and a number of possible outcomes within those distributions. With a given risk level, one's retirement could be characterized by abundance or by poverty, and it's difficult to imagine these several futures concurrently (one tends to suppose the average, or sometimes the best-case scenario—the so-called "planning fallacy").

A team of decision scientists has created an interesting tool to help investors understand the range of possibilities inherent in a distribution of outcomes (see Figure 13-6). Participants can adjust 100 "probability units" to form a distribution curve. For example, they might place all of their units at 75% of salary, or distribute it evenly among a variety of percentage levels. Then, they press go and watch as the units, one by one, disappear at random. The last one standing is the "outcome" (Goldstein et al. 2008). Thus, a level of risk is not an ambiguous distribution curve but a set of (here, 100) equally probable possibilities.

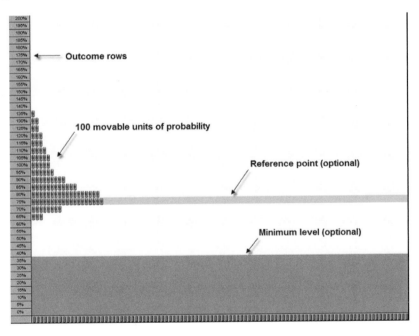

FIGURE 13-6. A tool by Goldstein et al. helps people understand a distribution as a set of outcomes. (See Color Plate 50.)

Biologist Stephen Jay Gould further illuminates the problem with equating descriptive statistics with outcomes. "The Median is not the Message" is Gould's reaction to a diagnosis of cancer and the warning that he had "eight months to live." Literature on the cancer revealed a right-skewed distribution based on a "prescribed set of circumstances"—that is, a long tail of long-lived survivors, under the assumption of past treatment conditions.

To claim "eight months" was to miss the bulk of the picture. As Gould elegantly characterizes the brutishness of statistics:

> [E]volutionary biologists know that variation itself is nature's only irreducible essence. Variation is the hard reality, not a set of imperfect measures for a central tendency. Means and medians are the abstractions.

5. Data Doesn't Predict

Building models (to forecast tomorrow's weather, the outcome of the 2012 Super Bowl, or the fate of the Fortune 500) is a seductive art. Indeed, an important extension of science's prime venture—to explain the world around us—is to try to understand the world as it will be.

In certain domains, namely in controlled -cosms of the physical world, it is possible to predict an outcome with near certainty. Future results will track past events with high fidelity: water will turn to gas when heated; a falling object will accelerate at 9.8 meters per second squared in a vacuum; if a creature's heart stops, it's dead. Epistomologically, Popper's notion of falsifiability is never moot, but it's possible to lead a sound and social life taking the previous three assumptions to be axiomatic.

In domains with less certainty, such as human or physical behavior, modeling is an important tool to help explain patterns. In our eagerness to make data say something, however, it's possible to overfit a model.

Consider the problem of finding exoplanets with Doppler radial velocity (a process I don't pretend to understand more than superficially: basically, bright stars make it hard to see planets, so astronomers identify combinations of Doppler shifts that would only occur due to the presence of a planet orbiting the star). It's difficult to test the sensitivity of a model, but with a mere 15 observations, it's possible to fit the very sexy sinusoidal curve in Figure 13-7 to the data (Ge et al. 2004)!

When we overfit a model, it loses predictive power. Also, if we're willing to accept any model that most optimally fits existing data, without a care for its complexity or sensitivity, we make several mistakes. First, we forget causality and do data a disservice; an overtuned model explains nothing.

Second, we forget that data (or data collection) may be limited, and that the world itself can change. Take the problem of trying to predict the world's climate 200 years from now. There are a few key pieces of evidence at high resolution over a long course of time—namely, global temperature data from the fossil record and ice cores. Climatologists can also infer local temperature and precipitation from diaries and tree rings, but with very different levels of precision: 18th-century storm glasses are not the same as 20th-century weather balloons with GPS. And, who knows if the same sets of interactions will drive climatic events in the 21st century as did in the 20th.

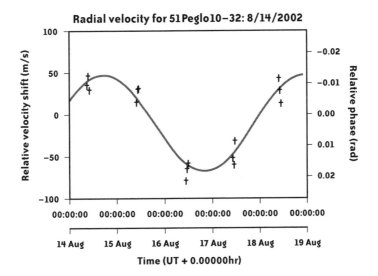

FIGURE 13-7. A model for extra-solar planet identification.

Similarly, Ford Motor Company in 1914 is not the same as Ford in 1975 nor as Ford today, yet many financial models assume the dynamics of the market's last cycle will also explain its future performance (and models make very different assumptions about the relevant time period to consider). As a result, risk analysis models may be only a little bit (acceptably) off on most days, but can break down entirely when the "unexpected" occurs (for example, when the housing market collapses).

Good scientists are aware of the dangers of a bad model, but it's not hard to be seduced by a fit that's too good to be true. Take, for example, this 2005 report from Moody's (Dwyer) discussing one unit's experience with overfit models (which it proceeded to correct, but—in hindsight—in a not nearly big enough way):

> A certain amount of skepticism is appropriate when a new modeling methodology yields a large increase in power. [It] will often be the result of fitting the data collection mechanism rather than an actual underlying behavioral relationship. In addition, these issues are clear afterward, but were not turned up in the ordinary pre-modeling data-cleansing process that we had in place at the time…

> At best, overfitting will introduce unneeded complexity into the model or discredit it with users. At worst, it can lead to systematic error in the risk assessment of a portfolio.

Oops.

There are many compelling reasons to build models beyond prediction, including to explore scenarios and illuminate assumptions; for an excellent enumeration, see Joshua Epstein's 2008 essay "Why Model?"

6. Probability Isn't Intuitive

This is another favorite flogging horse of the statistical establishment, and for good cause. Statisticians tirelessly devise cute games to demonstrate that a seemingly common-sense answer can fail to be probabilistically correct, and that conditional and joint probabilities are not intuitive. They are especially delighted when mathematicians and medical doctors are fooled by these games.

In a given U.S. city, about 1,000 out of 1 million (or 0.1% of) inhabitants are HIV-positive.

A new test to diagnose HIV has a 1% failure rate: one out of a hundred times, it will incorrectly diagnose an HIV-negative individual as having HIV, and 1% of the time it will incorrectly diagnose someone with HIV as HIV-negative.

Suppose an individual takes the test and is diagnosed as HIV-positive. What are the chances that he has the virus?

Many people will answer that there's a 99% chance he has the virus, because the test has a 1% failure rate. In fact, because the proportion of the population that has the disease is so small, any individual's chance of having it, even if diagnosed, is low: only 9.9%. (Of the 999,000 HIV-negative residents, 9,990 will be told they have the virus, while 990 of the HIV-positive residents will get a true positive. Given a positive diagnosis, the chances that you are in fact HIV-positive are 990/9,990, or 9.9%.)

Doctors, at least apocryphally, fail in droves.

In many situations, priors don't disappear. When using data to answer a question, we don't know what evidence to exclude and how to weight what we include. Daniel Kahneman—an indefatigable namer-of-concepts—names this one the "base rate fallacy."

7. Probabilities Aren't Intuitive

Not only is probability theory difficult to grasp, individual probabilities are fleeting. In the absence of a causal explanation to tie an event to a set of outcomes, individuals rely on past observations to estimate probabilities. And observations are often collected in a biased way (especially if they're garnered through experience, but often also when collected via experimentation), and are very difficult to document, reconcile, weight, preserve, and query.

8. The Real World Doesn't Create Random Variables

In the beginning, the earth was without form and void. Then Fisher said, "Let there be z-scores and ANOVA" and there were z-scores. And Fisher saw that regression was good, and he separated the significant from the nonsignificant.

The innovations of statistics seem so momentous that it can be difficult to keep in mind that they're not laws of nature. One can imagine an alternate universe in which the de facto

threshold for statistical significance had been set (arbitrarily, as it was in our universe) at p=0.01 or p=0.06, rather than at the current p=0.05. Think of the drugs that would have been approved or rejected, the misplaced correlations between environmental variables and health effects, the piles of cash you'd be saving on auto insurance!

In our non-Fisherian world, there are no such things as independent random variables. In fact, many things are highly connected. Good experimentation controls for interdependencies insofar as is possible, but dependencies can be hard to spot. As we've learned recently, it can be a mistake to assume discrete events (a homeowner defaulting on his mortgage, for example) are independent, and to build large edifices upon such assumptions (tradeable financial products sliced into tranches, for example) when they are not necessarily so.

Prediction markets and group decision-making processes can work exceptionally well—in some cases, better than the estimates of a set of experts. They've been shown to break down, however, when information cascades and interdependencies enter the system (Bikhchandani et al. 1998).

9. Data Doesn't Stand Alone

In real-world decision-making, data comes in many forms. Rarely is information cleaned and packaged in a well-labeled spreadsheet or matrix file; instead, we often need to make conclusions based on subjective as well as quantitative information.

Take, for example, the decision of whether to lend money to someone online (for a profit, as part of an established lending marketplace). An analysis that colleagues and I conducted of loan funding and repayment using a data set of 350,000 loans from the peer-to-peer platform Prosper.com reveals that any number of models (mixture models, neural nets, decision trees, regression) can predict who will get a loan and who will repay it on time with only about 75% accuracy. A huge amount of data—including over 100 personal financial health indicators for each member of the network—can be fed into the algorithms, but there remains uncertainty about which applicants will fare well and which will fail to be funded.

Our models can be refined in part by attempting to quantify subjective features. When an individual decides whether to lend money to a member of the network, the lender (unlike a bank) takes into account a number of "softer" factors: the borrower's statement of purpose, the accompanying image, spelling, grammar, and other profile information. To incorporate some of these features into our models, I used human workers (from Amazon's Mechanical Turk) to code images from Prosper.com members, first for content—whether the image depicts a person, a family, a vehicle, etc.—and then for a "trustworthiness" score: that is, for the answer to the question, "Would you lend money to this person?"

But the models still fell short: social factors play into loan dynamics in unexpected ways. Contrary to our assumptions, lending decisions aren't made independently. Rather, there's some evidence of herding behavior in bids: lenders follow other lenders, and bids-per-unit-time accelerate as more bids accumulate on a loan.

Even with these and other social factors taken into account, many lenders make suboptimal decisions. Prosper is, in theory, a market with near-perfect information: almost anyone can access the site's API and repeat our analysis. Yet lenders continually accept a low level of return for very risky investments: a surprising number make very bad bets given statistical expected payoffs. Even with good information (and modest proxies for subjective data), decisions aren't always made directly from data, and data, in turn, can only explain human decisions in part.

10. Data Isn't Free from the Eye of the Beholder

Finally, even in realms where solid causal explanation is possible, when data is collected honestly and modeled carefully by a judicious student of Fisher and (if our pupil is so inclined) Bayes, who accounts for variation and validates his model (and still remains skeptical of its results), a couple of cognitive biases cloud our thinking. In the real world, we operate pseudoprobabilistically at best.

Just as the statisticians tend to their tsk-tsk blogs, the behavioral economists have made a field from their own chronicles of infamy. The narrative fallacy, confirmation bias, paradox of choice, asymmetry of risk-taking, base rate fallacy, and hyperbolic discounting were mentioned earlier. Psychologists have indexed many others, ranging from anchoring (overreliance on a single recent data point in making a decision) to the Lake Wobegon effect (the phenomenon of more than half of individuals in a population believing they are above average).

As these effects become better documented, we can develop tools and intuitions to help take data at face value (part of my work is focused on developing tools for financial decision-making). In some sense, the solution is simple: data doesn't do much if you don't understand its limits.

Conclusion

It's no news that we live in an age of abundant data. Bits are cheap and loose. Evolutionary processes have equipped us to note jarring changes in the environment—the proverbial tiger or tsunami—to recognize faces and create narratives to aid memory. But we lack infrastructure to collect and sort massive and heterogeneous sets of data. What infrastructure we have must be carefully employed: we can begin to better use data by understanding both probabilities and the limits of probability, and by remaining careful of the cognitive biases that cloud interpretation.

Data in the eye of the beholder can be beautiful indeed.

References

Anscombe, F. J. "Graphs in Statistical Analysis." *The American Statistician*, vol. 27, no. 1 (February 1973), pp. 17–21.

Bikhchandani, S. et al. (1998). "Learning from the Behavior of Others: Conformity, Fads, and Informational Cascades," *Journal of Economic Perspectives*, vol. 12, issue 3, pp. 151–170.

Dwyer, D. W. 2005. "Examples of overfitting encountered when building private firm default prediction models" (*www.moodyskmv.com/research/files/wp/Overfitting_Private_Firm_Models.pdf*).

Epstein, Joshua M. (2008). "Why Model?". *Journal of Artificial Societies and Social Simulation* 11(4)12.

Ge, J. et al., 2004, "All Sky Extrasolar Planet Searches with Multi-Object Dispersed Fixed-delay Interferometer in Optical and near-IR." *Proc. SPIE*, 5492, 711.

Goldstein, Daniel G. et al. (2008). "Choosing Outcomes Versus Choosing Products: Consumer-Focused Retirement Investment Advice." *Journal of Consumer Research*, 35 (October), 440–456.

Gould, S. J. "The Median is not the Message." *Discover Magazine*, 1985.

Iyengar, S. S. and M. R. Lepper. "When choice is demotivating: can one desire too much of a good thing?" *Journal of Personality and Social Psychology*, 2000, vol. 79, no. 6, 995–1006.

Jeng, M. "A selected history of expectation bias in physics." *American Journal of Physics*, 2006.

Kahneman, Daniel and Amos Tversky (1979). "Prospect Theory: An Analysis of Decision under Risk," *Econometrica*, XLVII (1979), 263–291.

Krumme, C. "Telling tales: the effects of narrative creation on decision-making with data," working paper.

Lo, A. W. and D. V. Repin. "The Psychophysiology of Real-Time Financial Risk Processing" *Journal of Cognitive Neuroscience*, April 1, 2002, vol. 14, no. 3, 323–339.

Lord, C. G. et al. (1979). "Biased assimilation and attitude polarization: The effects of prior theories on subsequently considered evidence." *Journal of Personality and Social Psychology*, 37, 2098–2109.

Shellenbarger, Sue. *Wall Street Journal* "Work and Family" column, March 22, 2008.

CHAPTER FOURTEEN

Natural Language Corpus Data

Peter Norvig

MOST OF THIS BOOK DEALS WITH DATA THAT IS BEAUTIFUL IN THE SENSE OF BAUDELAIRE: "ALL WHICH IS beautiful and noble is the result of reason and calculation." This chapter's data is beautiful in Thoreau's sense: "All men are really most attracted by the beauty of plain speech." The data we will examine is the plainest of speech: a trillion words of English, taken from publicly available web pages. All the banality of the Web—the spelling and grammatical errors, the LOL cats, the Rickrolling—but also the collected works of Twain, Dickens, Austen, and millions of other authors.

The trillion-word data set was published by Thorsten Brants and Alex Franz of Google in 2006 and is available through the Linguistic Data Consortium (*http://tinyurl.com/ngrams*). The data set summarizes the original texts by *counting* the number of appearances of each word, and of each two-, three-, four-, and five-word sequence. For example, "the" appears 23 billion times (2.2% of the trillion words), making it the most common word. The word "rebating" appears 12,750 times (a millionth of a percent), as does "fnuny" (apparently a misspelling of "funny"). In three-word sequences, "Find all posts" appears 13 million times (.001%), about as often as "each of the," but well below the 100 million of "All Rights Reserved" (.01%). Here's an excerpt from the three-word sequences:

```
outraged many African      63
outraged many Americans   203
outraged many Christians   56
outraged many Iraqis       58
outraged many Muslims      74
outraged many Pakistanis  124
outraged many Republicans  50
outraged many Turks       390
outraged many by           86
outraged many in          685
outraged many liberal      67
outraged many local        44
outraged many members      61
outraged many of          489
outraged many people      444
outraged many scientists   90
```

We see, for example, that Turks are the most outraged group (on the Web, at the time the data was collected), and that Republicans and liberals are outraged occasionally, but Democrats and conservatives don't make the list.

Why would I say this data is beautiful, and not merely mundane? Each individual count *is* mundane. But the *aggregation* of the counts—billions of counts—is beautiful, because it says so much, not just about the English language, but about the world that speakers inhabit. The data is beautiful because it represents much of what is worth saying.

Before seeing what we can do with the data, we need to talk the talk—learn a little bit of jargon. A collection of text is called a *corpus*. We treat the corpus as a sequence of *tokens*— words and punctuation. Each distinct token is called a *type*, so the text "Run, Lola Run" has four tokens (the comma counts as one) but only three types. The set of all types is called the *vocabulary*. The Google Corpus has a trillion tokens and 13 million types. English has only about a million dictionary words, but the corpus includes types such as "www. njstatelib.org". "+170.002", "1.5GHz/512MB/60GB", and "Abrahamovich". Most of the types are rare, however; the 10 most common types cover almost 1/3 of the tokens, the top 1,000 cover just over 2/3, and the top 100,000 cover 98%.

A 1-token sequence is a *unigram*, a 2-token sequence is a *bigram*, and an *n*-token sequence is an *n-gram*. P stands for *probability*, as in P(*the*) = .022, which means that the probability of the token "the" is .022, or 2.2%. If W is a sequence of tokens, then W_3 is the third token, and $W_{1:3}$ is the sequence of the first through third tokens. $P(W_i =the \mid W_{i-1}=of)$ is the *conditional probability* of "the", given that "of" is the previous token.

Some details of the Google Corpus: words appearing fewer than 200 times are considered unknown and appear as the symbol <UNK>. *N*-grams that occur fewer than 40 times are discarded. This policy lessens the effect of typos and helps keep the data set to a mere 24 gigabytes (compressed). Finally, each sentence in the corpora is taken to start with the special symbol <S> and end with </S>.

We will now look at some tasks that can be accomplished using the data.

Word Segmentation

Consider the Chinese text 浮法像蝴蝶. This is the translation of the phrase "float like a butterfly." It consists of five characters, but there are no spaces between them, so a Chinese reader must perform the task of *word segmentation*: deciding where the word boundaries are. Readers of English don't normally perform this task, because we have spaces between words. However, some texts, such as URLs, don't have spaces, and sometimes writers make mistakes and leave a space out; how could a search engine or word processing program correct such a mistake?

Consider the English text "choosespain.com." This is a website hoping to convince you to choose Spain as a travel destination, but if you segment the name wrong, you get the less appealing name "chooses pain." Human readers are able to make the right choice by drawing upon years of experience; surely it would be an insurmountable task to encode that experience into a computer algorithm. Yet we can take a shortcut that works surprisingly well: look up each phrase in the bigram table. We see that "choose Spain" has a count of 3,210, whereas "chooses pain" does not appear in the table at all (which means it occurs fewer than 40 times in the trillion-word corpus). Thus "choose Spain" is at least 80 times more likely, and can be safely considered the right segmentation.

Suppose we were faced with the task of interpreting the phrase "insufficientnumbers." If we add together capitalized and lowercase versions of the words, the counts are:

```
insufficient numbers  20751
in sufficient numbers 32378
```

"In sufficient numbers" is 50% more frequent than "insufficient numbers" but that's hardly compelling evidence. We are left in a frustrating position: we can guess, but we can't be confident. In uncertain problems like this, we don't have any way of calculating a definitive correct answer, we don't have a complete model of what makes one answer right, and in fact human experts don't have a complete model, either, and can disagree on the answer. Still, there is an established methodology for solving uncertain problems:

1. **Define a probabilistic model.** We can't define all the factors (semantic, syntactic, lexical, and social) that make "choose Spain" a better candidate for a domain name, but we can define a simplified model that gives approximate probabilities. For short candidates like "choose Spain" we could just look up the *n*-gram in the corpus data and use that as the probability. For longer candidates we will need some way of composing an answer from smaller parts. For words we haven't seen before, we'll have to estimate the probability of an unknown word. The point is that we define a *language model*—a probability distribution over all the strings in the language—and learn the parameters of the model from our corpus data, then use the model to define the probability of each candidate.

2. **Enumerate candidates.** We may not be sure whether "insufficient numbers" or "in sufficient numbers" is more likely to be the intended phrase, but we can agree that they are both candidate segmentations, as is "in suffi cient numb ers," but that "hello

world" is not a valid candidate. In this step we withhold judgment and just enumerate possibilities—all the possibilities if we can, or else a carefully selected sample.

3. **Choose the most probable candidate.** Apply the language model to each candidate to get its probability, and choose the one with the highest probability.

If you prefer mathematical equations, the methodology is:

$$best = \mathrm{argmax}_{c \in \text{ candidates}} P(c)$$

Or, if you prefer computer code (we'll use Python), it would be:

```
best = max(c in candidates, key=P)
```

Let's apply the methodology to segmentation. We want to define a function, segment, which takes as input a string with no spaces and returns a list of words that is the best segmentation:

```
>>> segment('choosespain')
['choose', 'spain']
```

Let's start with step 1, the probabilistic language model. The probability of a sequence of words is the product of the probabilities of each word, given the word's context: all the preceding words. For those who like equations:

$$P(W_{1:n}) = \Pi_{k=1:n}P(W_k \mid W_{1:k-1})$$

We don't have the data to compute this exactly, so we can approximate the equation by using a smaller context. Since we have data for sequences up to 5-grams, it would be tempting to use the 5-grams, so that the probability of an n-word sequence would be the product of each word given the four previous words (not all previous words).

There are three difficulties with the 5-gram model. First, the 5-gram data is about 30 gigabytes, so it can't all fit in RAM. Second, many 5-gram counts will be 0, and we'd need some strategy for *backing off*, using shorter sequences to estimate the 5-gram probabilities. Third, the search space of candidates will be large because dependencies extend up to four words away. All three of these difficulties can be managed, with some effort. But instead, let's first consider a much simpler language model that solves all three difficulties at once: a unigram model, in which the probability of a sequence is just the product of the probability of each word by itself. In this model, the probability of each word is independent of the other words:

$$P(W_{1:n}) = \Pi_{k=1:n}P(W_k)$$

To segment 'wheninrome', we consider candidates such as when in rome, and compute $P(when) \times P(in) \times P(rome)$. If the product is higher than any other candidate's product, then that's the best answer.

An n-character string has 2^{n-1} different segmentations (there are $n-1$ positions between characters, each of which can either be or not be a word boundary). Thus the string

'wheninthecourseofhumaneventsitbecomesnecessary' has 35 trillion segmentations. But I'm sure you were able to find the right segmentation in just a few seconds; clearly, you couldn't have enumerated all the candidates. You probably scanned "w", "wh", and "whe" and rejected them as improbable words, but accepted "when" as probable. Then you moved on to the remainder and found its best segmentation. Once we make the simplifying assumption that each word is independent of the others, it means that we don't have to consider all combinations of words.

That gives us a sketch of the segment function: consider every possible way to split the text into a first word and a remaining text (we can arbitrarily limit the longest possible word to, say, L=20 letters). For each possible split, find the best way to segment the remainder. Out of all the possible candidates, the one with the highest product of P(*first*)×P(*remaining*) is the best.

Here we show a table of choices for the first word, probability of the word, probability of the best segmentation of the remaining words, and probability of the whole (which is the product of the probabilities of the first and the remainder). We see that the segmentation starting with "when" is 50,000 times better than the second-best candidate.

first	*P(first)*	*P(remaining)*	*P(first)* × *P(remaining)*
w	$2 \cdot 10^{-4}$	$2 \cdot 10^{-33}$	$6 \cdot 10^{-37}$
wh	$5 \cdot 10^{-6}$	$6 \cdot 10^{-33}$	$3 \cdot 10^{-38}$
whe	$3 \cdot 10^{-7}$	$3 \cdot 10^{-32}$	$7 \cdot 10^{-39}$
when	$6 \cdot 10^{-4}$	$7 \cdot 10^{-29}$	$4 \cdot 10^{-32}$
wheni	$1 \cdot 10^{-16}$	$3 \cdot 10^{-30}$	$3 \cdot 10^{-46}$
whenin	$1 \cdot 10^{-17}$	$8 \cdot 10^{-27}$	$8 \cdot 10^{-44}$

We can implement segment in a few lines of Python:

```
@memo
def segment(text):
    "Return a list of words that is the best segmentation of text."
    if not text: return []
    candidates = ([first]+segment(rem) for first,rem in splits(text))
    return max(candidates, key=Pwords)

def splits(text, L=20):
    "Return a list of all possible (first, rem) pairs, len(first)<=L."
    return [(text[:i+1], text[i+1:])
            for i in range(min(len(text), L))]

def Pwords(words):
    "The Naive Bayes probability of a sequence of words."
    return product(Pw(w) for w in words)
```

This is the entire program—with three minor omissions: product is a utility function that multiplies together a list of numbers, memo is a decorator that caches the results of previous calls to a function so that they don't have to be recomputed, and Pw estimates the probability of a word by consulting the unigram count data.

Without memo, a call to segment for an n-character text makes 2^n recursive calls to segment; with memo it makes only n calls—memo makes this a fairly efficient dynamic programming algorithm. Each of the n calls considers $O(L)$ splits, and evaluates each split by multiplying $O(n)$ probabilities, so the whole algorithm is $O(n^2 L)$.

As for Pw, we read in the unigram counts from a datafile. If a word appears in the corpus, its estimated probability is $Count(word)/N$, where N is the corpus size. Actually, instead of using the full 13-million-type unigram datafile, I created vocab_common, which (a) is case-insensitive, so that the counts for "the", "The", and "THE" are added together under a single entry for "the"; (b) only has entries for words made out of letters, not numbers or punctuation (so "+170.002" is out, as is "can't"); and (c) lists only the most common 1/3 of a million words.

The only tricky part of Pw is when a word has not been seen in the corpus. This happens sometimes even with a trillion-word corpus, so it would be a mistake to return 0 for the probability. But what should it be? The number of tokens in the corpus, N, is about a trillion, and the least common word in vocab_common has a count of 12,711. So a previously unseen word should have a probability of somewhere between 0 and $12,710/N$. Not all unseen words are equally unlikely: a random sequence of 20 letters is less likely to be a word than a random sequence of 6 letters. We will define a class for probability distributions, Pdist, which loads a datafile of (key, count) pairs. By default, the probability of an unknown word is $1/N$, but each instance of a Pdist can supply a custom function to override the default. We want to avoid having too high a probability for very long words, so we (rather arbitrarily) start at a probability of $10/N$, and decrease by a factor of 10 for every letter in the candidate word. We then define Pw as a Pdist:

```
class Pdist(dict):
    "A probability distribution estimated from counts in datafile."
    def __init__(self, data, N=None, missingfn=None):
        for key,count in data:
            self[key] = self.get(key, 0) + int(count)
        self.N = float(N or sum(self.itervalues()))
        self.missingfn = missingfn or (lambda k, N: 1./N)
    def __call__(self, key):
        if key in self: return self[key]/self.N
        else: return self.missingfn(key, self.N)

def datafile(name, sep='\t'):
    "Read key,value pairs from file."
    for line in file(name):
        yield line.split(sep)

def avoid_long_words(word, N):
    "Estimate the probability of an unknown word."
    return 10./(N * 10**len(word))

N = 1024908267229 ## Number of tokens in corpus

Pw = Pdist(datafile('vocab_common'), N, avoid_long_words))
```

Note that Pw[w] is the raw count for word w, while Pw(w) is the probability. All the programs described in this article are available at *http://norvig.com/ngrams*.

So how well does this model do at segmentation? Here are some examples:

```
>>> segment('choosespain')
['choose', 'spain']
>>> segment('thisisatest')
['this', 'is', 'a', 'test']
>>> segment('wheninthecourseofhumaneventsitbecomesnecessary')
['when', 'in', 'the', 'course', 'of', 'human', 'events', 'it', 'becomes', 'necessary']
>>> segment('whorepresents')
['who', 'represents']
>>> segment('expertsexchange')
['experts', 'exchange']
>>> segment('speedofart')
['speed', 'of', 'art']
>>> segment('nowisthetimeforallgood')
['now', 'is', 'the', 'time', 'for', 'all', 'good']
>>> segment('itisatruthuniversallyacknowledged')
['it', 'is', 'a', 'truth', 'universally', 'acknowledged']
>>> segment('itwasabrightcolddayinaprilandtheclockswerestrikingthirteen')
['it', 'was', 'a', 'bright', 'cold', 'day', 'in', 'april', 'and', 'the', 'clocks',
'were', 'striking', 'thirteen']
>>> segment('itwasthebestoftimesitwastheworstoftimesitwastheageofwisdomitwastheage
offoolishness')
['it', 'was', 'the', 'best', 'of', 'times', 'it', 'was', 'the', 'worst', 'of', 'times',
'it', 'was', 'the', 'age', 'of', 'wisdom', 'it', 'was', 'the', 'age', 'of',
'foolishness']
>>> segment('asgregorsamsaawokeonemorningfromuneasydreamsshefoundhimselftransformed
inhisbedintoagiganticinsect')
['as', 'gregor', 'samsa', 'awoke', 'one', 'morning', 'from', 'uneasy', 'dreams', 'he',
'found', 'himself', 'transformed', 'in', 'his', 'bed', 'into', 'a', 'gigantic',
'insect']
>>> segment('inaholeinthegroundtherelivedahobbitnotanastydirtywetholefilledwiththe
endsofwormsandanoozysmellnoryetadrybaresandyholewithnothinginittositdownonortoeat
itwasahobbitholeandthatmeanscomfort')
['in', 'a', 'hole', 'in', 'the', 'ground', 'there', 'lived', 'a', 'hobbit', 'not', 'a',
'nasty', 'dirty', 'wet', 'hole', 'filled', 'with', 'the', 'ends', 'of', 'worms', 'and',
'an', 'oozy', 'smell', 'nor', 'yet', 'a', 'dry', 'bare', 'sandy', 'hole', 'with',
'nothing', 'in', 'it', 'to', 'sitdown', 'on', 'or', 'to', 'eat', 'it', 'was', 'a',
'hobbit', 'hole', 'and', 'that', 'means', 'comfort']
>>> segment('faroutintheunchartedbackwatersoftheunfashionableendofthewesternspiral
armofthegalaxyliesasmallunregardedyellowsun')
['far', 'out', 'in', 'the', 'uncharted', 'backwaters', 'of', 'the', 'unfashionable',
'end', 'of', 'the', 'western', 'spiral', 'arm', 'of', 'the', 'galaxy', 'lies', 'a',
'small', 'un', 'regarded', 'yellow', 'sun']
```

The reader might be pleased to see the program correctly segmented such unusual words as "Samsa" and "oozy". You shouldn't be surprised: "Samsa" appears 42,000 times and "oozy" 13,000 times in the trillion-word corpus. Overall the results look good, but there are two errors: 'un','regarded' should be one word, and 'sitdown' should be two. Still, that's a word precision rate of 157/159 = 98.7%; not too bad.

The first error is in part because "unregarded" does not appear in our 1/3-million-word vocabulary. (It *is* in the full 1/3-million-word vocabulary at position 1,005,493, with count 7,557.) If we put it in the vocabulary, we see that the segmentation is correct:

```
>>> Pw['unregarded'] = 7557
>>> segment('faroutintheunchartedbackwatersoftheunfashionableendofthewesternspiral
armofthegalaxyliesasmallunregardedyellowsun')
['far', 'out', 'in', 'the', 'uncharted', 'backwaters', 'of', 'the', 'unfashionable',
'end', 'of', 'the', 'western', 'spiral', 'arm', 'of', 'the', 'galaxy', 'lies', 'a',
'small', 'unregarded', 'yellow', 'sun']
```

That doesn't prove we've solved the problem: we would have to put back all the other intervening words, not just the one we wanted, and we would have to then rerun all the test cases to make sure that adding the other words did not mess up any other result.

The second error happens because, although "sit" and "down" are common words (with probability .003% and .04%, respectively), the product of their two probabilities is just slightly less than the probability of "sitdown" by itself. However, the probability of the two-word sequence "sit down," according to the bigram counts, is about 100 times greater. We can try to fix this problem by modeling bigrams; that is, considering the probability of each word, given the previous word:

$$P(W_{1:n}) = \Pi_{k=1:n}P(W_k \mid W_{k-1})$$

Of course the complete bigram table won't fit into memory. If we keep only bigrams that appear 100,000 or more times, that works out to a little over 250,000 entries, which does fit. We can then estimate P(*down* | *sit*) as Count(*sit down*)/Count(*sit*). If a bigram does not appear in the table, then we just fall back on the unigram value. We can define cPw, the conditional probability of a word given the previous word, as:

```
def cPw(word, prev):
    "The conditional probability P(word | previous-word)."
    try:
        return P2w[prev + ' ' + word]/float(Pw[prev])
    except KeyError:
        return Pw(word)

P2w = Pdist(datafile('count2w'), N)
```

(Purists will note cPw is not a probability distribution, because the sum over all words for a given previous word can be greater than 1. This approach has the technical name *stupid backoff*, but it works well in practice, so we won't worry about it.) We can now compare "sitdown" to "sit down" with a preceding "to":

```
>>> cPw('sit', 'to')*cPw('down', 'sit') / cPw('sitdown', 'to')
1698.0002330199263
```

We see that "sit down" is 1,698 times more likely than "sitdown", because "sit down" is a popular bigram, and because "to sit" is popular but "to sitdown" is not.

This looks promising; let's implement a new version of segment using a bigram model. While we're at it, we'll fix two other issues:

1. When segment added one new word to a sequence of *n* words segmented in the remainder, it called Pwords to multiply together all *n*+1 probabilities. But segment had already multiplied all the probabilities in the remainder. It would be more efficient to remember the probability of the remainder and then just do one more multiplication.

2. There is a potential problem with arithmetic underflow. If we apply Pwords to a sequence consisting of the word "blah" repeated 61 times, we get $5.2 \cdot 10^{-321}$, but if we add one more "blah," we get 0.0. The smallest positive floating-point number that can be represented is about $4.9 \cdot 10^{-324}$; anything smaller than that rounds to 0.0. To avoid underflow, the simplest solution is to add logarithms of numbers rather than multiplying the numbers themselves.

We will define segment2, which differs from segment in three ways: first, it uses a conditional bigram language model, cPw, rather than the unigram model Pw. Second, the function signature is different. Instead of being passed a single argument (the text), segment2 is also passed the previous word. At the start of the sentence, the previous word is the special beginning-of-sentence marker, <S>. The return value is not just a list of words, but rather a pair of values: the probability of the segmentation, followed by the list of words. We return the probability so that it can be stored (by memo) and need not be recomputed; this fixes problem (1), the inefficiency. The function combine takes four inputs—the first word and the remaining words, plus their probabilities—and combines them by appending the first word to the remaining words, and by multiplying the probabilities—except that in order to solve problem (2), we introduce the third difference: we add logarithms of probabilities instead of multiplying the raw probabilities.

Here is the code for segment2:

```
from math import log10

@memo
def segment2(text, prev='<S>'):
    "Return (log P(words), words), where words is the best segmentation."
    if not text: return 0.0, []
    candidates = [combine(log10(cPw(first, prev)), first, segment2(rem, first))
                  for first,rem in splits(text)]
    return max(candidates)

def combine(Pfirst, first, (Prem, rem)):
    "Combine first and rem results into one (probability, words) pair."
    return Pfirst+Prem, [first]+rem
```

segment2 makes O(*nL*) recursive calls, and each one considers O(*L*) splits, so the whole algorithm is O(nL^2). In effect this is the *Viterbi* algorithm, with memo implicitly creating the Viterbi tables.

segment2 correctly segments the "sit down" example, and gets right all the examples that the first version got right. Neither version gets the "unregarded" example right.

Could we improve on this performance? Probably. We could create a more accurate model of unknown words. We could incorporate more data, and either keep more entries from the unigram or bigram data, or perhaps add trigram data.

Secret Codes

Our second challenge is to decode a message written in a secret code. We'll look at *substitution ciphers*, in which each letter is replaced by another. The description of what replaces what is called the *key*, which we can represent as a string of 26 letters; the first letter replaces "a", the second replaces "b", and so on. Here is the function to encode a message with a substitution cipher key (the Python library functions maketrans and translate do most of the work):

```
def encode(msg, key):
    "Encode a message with a substitution cipher."
    return msg.translate(string.maketrans(ul(alphabet), ul(key)))

def ul(text): return text.upper() + text.lower()

alphabet = 'abcdefghijklmnopqrstuvwxyz'
```

Perhaps the simplest of all codes is the *shift cipher*, a substitution cipher in which each letter in the message is replaced by the letter n letters later in the alphabet. If $n = 1$, then "a" is replaced by "b" and "b" is replaced by "c", up to "z", which is replaced by "a". Shift ciphers are also called *Caesar ciphers*; they were state-of-the-art in 50 BC. The function shift encodes with a shift cipher:

```
def shift(msg, n=13):
    "Encode a message with a shift (Caesar) cipher."
    return encode(msg, alphabet[n:]+alphabet[:n])
```

We use the function like this:

```
>>> shift('Listen, do you want to know a secret?')
'Yvfgra, qb lbh jnag gb xabj n frperg?'

>>> shift('HAL 9000 xyz', 1)
'IBM 9000 yza'
```

To decode a message without knowing the key, we follow the same methodology we did with segmentations: define a model (we'll stick with unigram word probabilities), enumerate candidates, and choose the most probable. There are only 26 candidate shifts to consider, so we can try them all.

To implement this we define logPwords, which is like Pwords, but returns the log of the probability, and accepts the input as either a long string of words or a list of words:

```
def logPwords(words):
    "The Naive Bayes probability of a string or sequence of words."
    if isinstance(words, str): words = allwords(words)
    return sum(log10(Pw(w)) for w in words)

def allwords(text):
    "Return a list of alphabetic words in text, lowercase."
    return re.findall('[a-z]+', text.lower())
```

Now we can decode by enumerating all candidates and picking the most probable:

```
def decode_shift(msg):
    "Find the best decoding of a message encoded with a shift cipher."
    candidates = [shift(msg, n) for n in range(len(alphabet))]
    return max(candidates, key=logPwords)
```

We can test to see that this works:

```
>>> decode_shift('Yvfgra, qb lbh jnag gb xabj n frperg?')
'Listen, do you want to know a secret?'
```

This is all too easy. To see why, look at the 26 candidates, with their log-probabilities:

```
Yvfgra, qb lbh jnag gb xabj n frperg? -84
Zwghsb, rc mci kobh hc ybck o gsqfsh? -83
Axhitc, sd ndj lpci id zcdl p htrgti? -83
Byijud, te oek mqdj je adem q iushuj? -77
Czjkve, uf pfl nrek kf befn r jvtivk? -85
Daklwf, vg qgm osfl lg cfgo s kwujwl? -91
Eblmxg, wh rhn ptgm mh dghp t lxvkxm? -84
Fcmnyh, xi sio quhn ni ehiq u mywlyn? -84
Gdnozi, yj tjp rvio oj fijr v nzxmzo? -86
Heopaj, zk ukq swjp pk gjks w oaynap? -93
Ifpqbk, al vlr txkq ql hklt x pbzobq? -84
Jgqrcl, bm wms uylr rm ilmu y qcapcr? -76
Khrsdm, cn xnt vzms sn jmnv z rdbqds? -92
Listen, do you want to know a secret? -25
Mjtufo, ep zpv xbou up lopx b tfdsfu? -89
Nkuvgp, fq aqw ycpv vq mpqy c ugetgv? -87
Olvwhq, gr brx zdqw wr nqrz d vhfuhw? -85
Pmwxir, hs csy aerx xs orsa e wigvix? -77
Qnxyjs, it dtz bfsy yt pstb f xjhwjy? -83
Royzkt, ju eua cgtz zu qtuc g ykixkz? -85
Spzalu, kv fvb dhua av ruvd h zljyla? -85
Tqabmv, lw gwc eivb bw svwe i amkzmb? -84
Urbcnw, mx hxd fjwc cx twxf j bnlanc? -92
Vscdox, ny iye gkxd dy uxyg k combod? -84
Wtdepy, oz jzf hlye ez vyzh l dpncpe? -91
Xuefqz, pa kag imzf fa wzai m eqodqf? -83
```

As you scan the list, exactly one line stands out as English-like, and Pwords agrees with our intuition, giving that line a log-probability of −25 (that is, 10^{-25}), which is 10^{50} times more probable than any other candidate.

The code maker can make the code breaker's job harder by eliminating punctuation, spaces between words, and uppercase distinctions. That way the code breaker doesn't get clues from short words like "I," "a," and "the," nor from guessing that the character after an apostrophe should be "s" or "t". Here's an encryption scheme, shift2, that removes nonletters, converts everything to lowercase, and then applies a shift cipher:

```
def shift2(msg, n=13):
    "Encode with a shift (Caesar) cipher, yielding only letters [a-z]."
    return shift(just_letters(msg), n)

def just_letters(text):
    "Lowercase text and remove all characters except [a-z]."
    return re.sub('[^a-z]', '', text.lower())
```

And here's a way to break this code by enumerating each candidate, segmenting each one, and choosing the one with the highest probability:

```python
def decode_shift2(msg):
    "Decode a message encoded with a shift cipher, with no spaces."
    candidates = [segment2(shift(msg, n)) for n in range(len(alphabet))]
    p, words = max(candidates)
    return ' '.join(words)
```

Let's see how well it works:

```
>>> shift2('Listen, do you want to know a secret?')
'yvfgraqblbhjnaggbxabjnfrperg'

>>> decode_shift2('yvfgraqblbhjnaggbxabjnfrperg')
'listen do you want to know a secret'

>>> decode_shift2(shift2('Rosebud'))
'rosebud'

>>> decode_shift2(shift2("Is it safe?"))
'is it safe'

>>> decode_shift2(shift2("What's the frequency, Kenneth?"))
'whats the frequency kenneth'

>>> msg = 'General Kenobi: Years ago, you served my father in the Clone
Wars; now he begs you to help him in his struggle against the Empire.'

>>> decode_shift2(shift2(msg))
'general kenobi years ago you served my father in the clone wars now he
begs you to help him in his struggle against the empire'
```

Still way too easy. Let's move on to a general substitution cipher, in which any letter can be substituted for any other. Now we can no longer enumerate the possibilities, because there are 26! keys (about 4×10^{26}), rather than just 26. *The Code Book* by Simon Singh (Anchor) offers five strategies (and we'll mention a sixth) for breaking ciphers:

1. Letter unigram frequencies. Match common letters in the message to common letters in English (like "e") and uncommon to uncommon (like "z").

2. Double letter analysis. A double in the coded message is still double in the decoded message. Consider the least and most common double letters.

3. Look for common words like "the," "and," and "of." One-letter words are most often "a" or "I."

4. If possible, get a frequency table made up of the type of messages you are dealing with. Military messages use military jargon, etc.

5. Guess a word or phrase. For example, if you can guess that the message will contain "your faithful servant," try it.

6. Use word patterns. For example, the coded word "abbccddedf" is very likely "bookkeeper," because there are no other words in the corpus with that pattern.

For messages that do not contain spaces between words, strategies 3 and 6 do not apply. Strategies 1 and 2 contain only 26 probabilities each, and seem targeted for a human analyst with limited memory and computing power, not for a computer program. Strategies 4 and 5 are for special-purpose, not general-purpose, decoders. It looks like we're on our own in coming up with a strategy. But we know the methodology.

I. Define a probabilistic model: We could evaluate candidates the same way we did for shift ciphers: segment the text and calculate the probability of the words. But considering step II of the methodology, our first few candidates (or few thousand) will likely be very poor ones. At the start of our exploration, we won't have anything resembling words, so it won't do much good to try to segment. However, we may (just by accident) have decoded a few letters in a row that make sense. So let's use *letter n-grams* rather than words for our language model. Should we look at letter bigrams? 3-grams? 5-grams? I chose 3-grams because they are the shortest that can represent common short words (strategy 3). I created the datafile count_3l by counting the letter 3-grams (with spaces and punctuation removed) within the word bigram datafiles (I couldn't just look at the vocabulary file, because I need to consider letter trigrams that cross word boundaries). All of the $26^3 =$ 17,576 trigrams appear. Here are the top and bottom 10:

the	2.763%	fzq	0.0000004%
ing	1.471%	jvq	0.0000004%
and	1.462%	jnq	0.0000004%
ion	1.343%	zqh	0.0000004%
tio	1.101%	jqx	0.0000003%
ent	1.074%	jwq	0.0000003%
for	0.884%	jqy	0.0000003%
ati	0.852%	zqy	0.0000003%
ter	0.728%	jzq	0.0000002%
ate	0.672%	zgq	0.0000002%

The letter trigram probability is computed like this:

```
def logP3letters(text):
    "The log-probability of text using a letter 3-gram model."
    return sum(log10(P3l(g)) for g in ngrams(text, 3))

P3l = Pdist(datafile('count_3l'))
P2l = Pdist(datafile('count_2l')) ## We'll need it later
```

II. Enumerate candidates: We can't consider all 4×10^{26} possible keys, and there does not appear to be a way to systematically eliminate nonoptimal candidates, as there was in segmentation. That suggests a *local search* strategy, such as *hill climbing*. Suppose you wanted to reach maximum elevation, but had no map. With the hill-climbing strategy, you would start at a random location, *x*, and take a step to a neighboring location. If that location is higher, continue to hill-climb from there. If not, consider another neighbor of *x*. Of course, if you start at a random location on Earth and start walking uphill, you probably won't end up on top of Mt. Everest. More likely you'll end up on top of a small local hill, or get stuck wandering around a flat plain. Therefore we add *random restarts* to our hill-climbing algorithm: after we've taken a certain number of steps, we start all over again in a new random location.

Here is the general `hillclimb` algorithm. It takes a starting location, *x*, a function f that we are trying to optimize, a function `neighbors` that generates the neighbors of a location, and a maximum number of steps to take. (If the variable `debugging` is true, it prints the best *x* and its score.)

```python
def hillclimb(x, f, neighbors, steps=10000):
    "Search for an x that miximizes f(x), considering neighbors(x)."
    fx = f(x)
    neighborhood = iter(neighbors(x))
    for i in range(steps):
        x2 = neighborhood.next()
        fx2 = f(x2)
        if fx2 >= fx:
            x, fx = x2, fx2
            neighborhood = iter(neighbors(x))
    if debugging: print 'hillclimb:', x, int(fx)
    return x

debugging = False
```

To use `hillclimb` for decoding, we need to specify the parameters. The locations we will be searching through will be plain-text (decoded) messages. We will attempt to maximize their letter trigram frequency, so f will be `logP3letters`. We'll start with *x* being the message decrypted with a random key. We'll do random restarts, but when we gather the candidates from each restart, we will choose the one best according to `segment2`, rather than by `logP3letters`:

```python
def decode_subst(msg, steps=4000, restarts=20):
    "Decode a substitution cipher with random restart hillclimbing."
    msg = cat(allwords(msg))
    candidates = [hillclimb(encode(msg, key=cat(shuffled(alphabet))),
                            logP3letters, neighboring_msgs, steps)
                  for _ in range(restarts)]
    p, words = max(segment2(c) for c in candidates)
    return ' '.join(words)

def shuffled(seq):
    "Return a randomly shuffled copy of the input sequence."
    seq = list(seq)
    random.shuffle(seq)
    return seq

cat = ''.join
```

Now we need to define `neighboring_msgs`, which generates decryptions of the message to try next. We first try to repair improbable letter bigrams. For example, the least frequent bigram, "jq", has probability 0.0001%, which is 50,000 times less than the most probable bigrams, "in" and "th". So if we see a "jq" in msg, we try swapping the "j" with each of the other letters, and also try swapping the "q". If a swap yields a more frequent bigram, then we generate the message that results from making the swap. After exhausting repairs of the 20 most improbable bigrams, we consider random swaps:

```
def neighboring_msgs(msg):
    "Generate nearby keys, hopefully better ones."
    def swap(a,b): return msg.translate(string.maketrans(a+b, b+a))
    for bigram in heapq.nsmallest(20, set(ngrams(msg, 2)), P2l):
        b1,b2 = bigram
        for c in alphabet:
            if b1==b2:
                if P2l(c+c) > P2l(bigram): yield swap(c,b1)
            else:
                if P2l(c+b2) > P2l(bigram): yield swap(c,b1)
                if P2l(b1+c) > P2l(bigram): yield swap(c,b2)
    while True:
        yield swap(random.choice(alphabet), random.choice(alphabet))
```

Let's see how well this performs. We'll try it on some ciphers from Robert Raynard's book *Secret Code Breaker* (Smith and Daniel; see *http://secretcodebreaker.com*). First a warm-up message:

```
>>> msg = 'DSDRO XFIJV DIYSB ANQAL TAIMX VBDMB GASSA QRTRT CGGXJ MMTQC IPJSB AQPDR
SDIMS DUAMB CQCMS AQDRS DMRJN SBAGC IYTCY ASBCS MQXKS CICGX RSRCQ ACOGA SJPAS
AQHDI ASBAK GCDIS AWSJN CMDKB AQHAR RCYAE'
```

```
>>> decode_subst(msg)
'it is by knowing the frequency which letters usually occur and other distinctive
characteristics of the language that crypt analysts are able to determine the
plain text of a cipher message j'
```

This is correct except that "crypt analysts" should be one word. (It isn't in Pw, but it is in the 13-million-word vocabulary.) Note the last character ("E" in the cipher text) was added to make the blocks of five letters come out even.

Now an actual message from Baron August Schluga, a German spy in World War I:

```
>>> msg = 'NKDIF SERLJ MIBFK FKDLV NQIBR HLCJU KFTFL KSTEN YQNDQ NTTEB TTENM QLJFS
NOSUM MLQTL CTENC QNKRE BTTBR HKLQT ELCBQ QBSFS KLTML SSFAI NLKBR RLUKT LCJUK
FTFLK FKSUC CFRFN KRYXB'
```

```
>>> decode_subst(msg)
'english complaining over lack of munitions they regret that the promised support of
the french attack north of arras is not possible on account of munition insufficiency
wa'
```

Here's a 1992 message from the KGB to former CIA officer Aldrich Ames, who was convicted of spying in 1994:

```
>>> msg = 'CNLGV QVELH WTTAI LEHOT WEQVP CEBTQ FJNPP EDMFM LFCYF SQFSP NDHQF OEUTN
PPTPP CTDQN IFSQD TWHTN HHLFJ OLFSD HQFED HEGNQ TWVNQ HTNHH LFJWE BBITS PTHDT
XQQFO EUTYF SLFJE DEFDN IFSQG NLNGN PCTTQ EDOED FGQFI TLXNI'
```

```
>>> decode_subst(msg)
'march third week bridge with smile to pass info from you to us and to give assessment
about new dead drop ground to indicate what dead drop will be used next to give your
opinion about caracas meeting in october xab'
```

This 1943 message from German U-Boat command was intercepted and decoded, saving a convoy of Allied ships:

```
msg = 'WLJIU JYBRK PWFPF IJQSK PWRSS WEPTM MJRBS BJIRA BASPP IHBGP RWMWQ SOPSV PPIMJ
BISUF WIFOT HWBIS WBIQW FBJRB GPILP PXLPM SAJQQ PMJQS RJASW LSBLW GBHMJ
QSWIL PXWOL'

>>> decode_subst(msg)
'a cony ov is headed northeast take up positions fifteen miles apart between point yd
and bu maintain radio silence except for reports of tactical importance x abc'
```

This answer confuses the "y" and "v." A human analyst would realize "cony ov" should be "convoy" and that therefore "point yd" should be "point vd." Our program never considered that possibility, because the letter trigram probability of the correct text is less than the one shown here. We could perhaps fix the problem by inventing a better scoring function that does not get trapped in a local maximum. Or we could add a second level of hill-climbing search: take the candidates generated by the first search and do a brief search with segment2 as the scoring function. We'll leave that exercise to the reader.

Spelling Correction

Our final task is spelling correction: given a typed word, w, determine what word c was most likely intended. For example, if w is "acomodation", c should be "accommodation". (If w is "the", then c too should be "the".)

Following the standard methodology, we want to choose the c that maximizes P(c | w). But defining this probability is not straightforward. Consider w = "thew". One candidate c is "the"—it's the most common word, and we can imagine the typist's finger slipping off the "e" key and hitting the "w". Another candidate is "thaw"—a fairly common word (although 30,000 times less frequent than "the"), and it is common to substitute one vowel for another. Other candidates include "thew" itself (an obscure term for muscle or sinew), "threw", and "Thwe", a family name. Which should we choose? It seems that we are conflating two factors: how probable is c on its own, and how likely is it that w could be a typo for c, or a mispronunciation, or some other kind of misspelling. One might think we will have to combine these factors in some ad hoc fashion, but it turns out that there is a mathematical formula, Bayes's theorem, that tells us precisely how to combine them to find the best candidate:

$$\text{argmax}_c \, P(c \mid w) = \text{argmax}_c \, P(w \mid c) \, P(c)$$

Here P(c), the probability that c is the intended word, is called the *language model*, and P(w | c), the probability that an author would type w when c is intended, is called the *error model* or *noisy channel model*. (The idea is that the ideal author intended to type c, but some noise or static on the line altered c to w.) Unfortunately, we don't have an easy way to estimate this model from the corpus data we have—the corpus says nothing about what words are misspellings of others.

We can solve this problem with more data: a list of misspellings. Roger Mitton has a list of about 40,000 *c,w* pairs at *http://www.dcs.bbk.ac.uk/~ROGER/corpora.html*. But we can't hope to just look up P(*w*=thew | *c*=thaw) from this data; with only 40,000 examples, chances are slim that we will have seen this exact pair before. When data is sparse, we need to generalize. We can do that by ignoring the letters that are the same, the "th" and "w", leaving us with P(*w*=e | *c*=a), the probability that an "e" was typed when the correct letter was "a". This is one of the most common errors in the misspelling data, due to confusions like "consistent/consistant" and "inseparable/inseperable."

In the following table we consider five candidates for *c* when *w*=thew. One is thew itself, and the other four represent the four types of single edits that we will consider: (1) We can *delete* the letter "w" in "thew", yielding "the". (2) We can *insert* an "r" to get "threw". For both these edits, we condition on the previous letter. (3) We can replace "e" with "a" as mentioned earlier. (4) We can transpose two adjacent letters, swapping "ew" with "we". We say that these single edits are at *edit distance* 1; a candidate that requires two single edits is at edit distance 2. The table shows the words *w* and *c*, the edit *w* | *c*, the probability P(*w* | *c*), the probability P(*c*), and the product of the probabilities (scaled for readability).

w	*c*	*w* | *c*	P(*w* | *c*)	P(*c*)	10^9 P(*w* | *c*) P(*c*)
thew	the	ew | e	0.000007	0.02	144.
thew	thew		0.95	0.00000009	90.
thew	thaw	e | a	0.001	0.0000007	0.7
thew	threw	h | hr	0.000008	0.000004	0.03
thew	thwe	ew | we	0.000003	0.00000004	0.0001

We see from the table that "the" is the most likely correction. P(*c*) can be computed with Pw. For P(*w* | *c*) we need to create a new function, Pedit, which gives the probability of an edit, estimated from the misspelling corpus. For example, Pedit('ew|e') is 0.000007. More complicated edits are defined as a concatenation of single edits. For example, to get from "hallow" to "hello" we concatenate a|e with ow|o, so the whole edit is called a|e+ow|o (or ow|o+a|e, which in this case—but not always—is the same thing). The probability of a complex edit is taken to be the product of its components.

A problem: what the probability of the empty edit, Pedit('')? That is, given that the intended word is *c*, how likely is it that the author would actually type *c*, rather than one of the possible edits that yields an error? That depends on the skill of the typist and on whether any proofreading has been done. Rather arbitrarily, I assumed that a spelling error occurs once every 20 words. Note that if I had assumed errors occur only once in 50 words, then P(*w* | *c*) for *w*="thew" would be 0.98, not 0.95, and "thew" would become the most probable answer.

Finally, we're ready to show the code. There are two top-level functions, correct, which returns the best correction for a single word, and corrections, which applies correct to

every word in a text, leaving the surrounding characters intact. The candidates are all the possible edits, and the best is the one with the highest P(w | c) P(c) score:

```
def corrections(text):
    "Spell-correct all words in text."
    return re.sub('[a-zA-Z]+', lambda m: correct(m.group(0)), text)

def correct(w):
    "Return the word that is the most likely spell correction of w."
    candidates = edits(w).items()
    c, edit = max(candidates, key=lambda (c,e): Pedit(e) * Pw(c))
    return c
```

P(w | c) is computed by Pedit:

```
def Pedit(edit):
    "The probability of an edit; can be '' or 'a|b' or 'a|b+c|d'."
    if edit == '': return (1. - p_spell_error)
    return p_spell_error*product(P1edit(e) for e in edit.split('+'))
```

p_spell_error = 1./20.

P1edit = Pdist(datafile('count1edit')) ## Probabilities of single edits

The candidates are generated by edits, which is passed a word, and returns a dict of {word: edit} pairs indicating the possible corrections. In general there will be several edits that arrive at a correction. (For example, we can get from "tel" to "tell" by inserting an "l" after the "e" or after the "l".) We choose the edit with the highest probability. edits is the most complex function we've seen so far. In part this is inherent; it *is* complicated to generate four kinds of edits. But in part it is because we took some efforts to make edits efficient. (A slower but easier-to-read version is at *http://norvig.com/spell-correct.html*.) If we considered *all* edits, a word like "acommodations" would yield 233,166 candidates. But only 11 of these are in the vocabulary. So edits works by precomputing the set of all prefixes of all the words in the vocabulary. It then calls editsR recursively, splitting the word into a head and a tail (hd and tl in the code) and assuring that the head is always in the list of prefixes. The results are collected by adding to the dict results:

```
def edits(word, d=2):
    "Return a dict of {correct: edit} pairs within d edits of word."
    results = {}
    def editsR(hd, tl, d, edits):
        def ed(L,R): return edits+[R+'|'+L]
        C = hd+tl
        if C in Pw:
            e = '+'.join(edits)
            if C not in results: results[C] = e
            else: results[C] = max(results[C], e, key=Pedit)
        if d <= 0: return
        extensions = [hd+c for c in alphabet if hd+c in PREFIXES]
        p = (hd[-1] if hd else '<') ## previous character
        ## Insertion
        for h in extensions:
            editsR(h, tl, d-1, ed(p+h[-1], p))
```

```
            if not tl: return
            ## Deletion
            editsR(hd, tl[1:], d-1, ed(p, p+tl[0]))
            for h in extensions:
                if h[-1] == tl[0]: ## Match
                    editsR(h, tl[1:], d, edits)
                else: ## Replacement
                    editsR(h, tl[1:], d-1, ed(h[-1], tl[0]))
            ## Transpose
            if len(tl)>=2 and tl[0]!=tl[1] and hd+tl[1] in PREFIXES:
                editsR(hd+tl[1], tl[0]+tl[2:], d-1,
                    ed(tl[1]+tl[0], tl[0:2]))
    ## Body of edits:
    editsR('', word, d, [])
    return results

PREFIXES = set(w[:i] for w in Pw for i in range(len(w) + 1))
```

Here's an example of edits:

```
>>> edits('adiabatic', 2)
{'adiabatic': '', 'diabetic': '<a|<+a|e', 'diabatic': '<a|<'}
```

And here is the spell corrector at work:

```
>>> correct('vokabulary')
'vocabulary'

>>> correct('embracable')
'embraceable'

>>> corrections('thiss is a teyst of acommodations for korrections
of mispellings of particuler wurds.')
'this is a test of acommodations for corrections of mispellings
of particular words.'
```

Thirteen of the 15 words were handled correctly, but not "acommodations" and "mispellings". Why not? The unfortunate answer is that the Internet is full of lousy spelling. The incorrect "mispellings" appears 18,543 times in the corpus. Yes, the correct word, "misspellings", appears half a million times, but that was not enough to overcome the bias for no edit over a single edit. I suspect that most of the 96,759 occurrences of "thew" are also spelling errors.

There are many ways we could improve this spelling program. First, we could correct words in the context of the surrounding words, so that "they're" would be correct when it stands alone, but would be corrected to "their" when it appears in "in they're words." A word bigram or trigram model would do the trick.

We really should clean up the lousy spelling in the corpus. Look at these misspellings:

```
misspellings    432354
mispellings     18543
misspelings     10148
mispelings      3937
```

The corpus uses the wrong word 7% of the time. I can think of three ways to fix this. First, we could acquire a list of dictionary words and only make a correction to a word in the dictionary. But a dictionary does not list all the newly coined words and proper names. (A compromise might be to force lowercase words into the dictionary vocabulary, but allow capitalized words that are not in the dictionary.) Second, we could acquire a corpus that has been carefully proofread, perhaps one restricted to books and periodicals from high-quality publishers. Third, we could spell-correct the corpus we have. It may seem like circular reasoning to require spell-correction of the corpus before we can use it for spell-correction, but it can be done. For this application we would start by grouping together words that are a small edit distance from each other. For each pair of close words, we would then check to see if one is much more common than the other. If it is, we would then check the bigram (or trigram) counts to see if the two words had similar distributions of neighboring words. For example, here are four bigram counts for "mispellings" and "misspellings":

mispellings allowed	99	misspellings allowed	2410
mispellings as	50	misspellings as	749
mispellings for	122	misspellings for	11600
mispellings of	7360	misspellings of	16943

The two words share many bigram neighbors, always with "misspellings" being more common, so that is good evidence that "mispellings" is a misspelling. Preliminary tests show that this approach works well—but there is a problem: it would require hundreds of CPU hours of computation. It is appropriate for a cluster of machines, not a single computer.

How does the data-driven approach compare to a more traditional software development process wherein the programmer codes explicit rules? To address that, we'll peek at the spelling correction code from the ht://Dig project, an excellent open source intranet search engine. Given a word, ht://Dig's metaphone routine produces a *key* representing the sound of the word. For example, both "tough" and "tuff" map to the key "TF", and thus would be candidates for misspellings of each other. Here is part of the metaphone code for the letter "G":

```
case 'G':
      /*
       * F if in -GH and not B--GH, D--GH,
       * -H--GH, -H---GH else dropped if
       * -GNED, -GN, -DGE-, -DGI-, -DGY-
       * else J if in -GE-, -GI-, -GY- and
       * not GG else K
       */
      if ((*(n + 1) != 'G' || vowel(*(n + 2))) &&
          (*(n + 1) != 'N' || (*(n + 1) &&
                              (*(n + 2) != 'E' ||
                               *(n + 3) != 'D'))) &&
          (*(n - 1) != 'D' || !frontv(*(n + 1))))
        if (frontv(*(n + 1)) && *(n + 2) != 'G')
          key << 'J';
        else
          key << 'K';
      else if (*(n + 1) == 'H' && !noghf(*(n - 3)) &&
              *(n - 4) != 'H')
                key << 'F';
      break;
```

This code correctly maps "GH" to "F" in "TOUGH" and not in "BOUGH". But have the rules correctly captured all the cases? What about "OUGHT"? Or "COUGH" versus "HIC-COUGH"? We can write test cases to verify each branch of the code, but even then we won't know what words were *not* covered. What happens when a new word like "iPhone" is introduced? Clearly, the handwritten rules are difficult to develop and maintain. The big advantage of the data-driven method is that so much knowledge is encoded in the data, and new knowledge can be added just by collecting more data. But another advantage is that, while the data can be massive, the code is succinct—about 50 lines for correct, compared to over 1,500 for ht://Dig's spelling code. As the great ex-programmer Bill Gates once said, "Measuring programming progress by lines of code is like measuring aircraft building progress by weight." Gates knew that lines of code are more a liability than an asset. The probabilistic data-driven methodology is the ultimate in agile programming.

Another issue is portability. If we wanted a Latvian spelling-corrector, the English metaphone rules would be of little use. To port the data-driven correct algorithm to another language, all we need is a large corpus of Latvian; the code remains unchanged.

Other Tasks

Here are some more tasks that have been handled with probabilistic language models.

Language Identification

There are web protocols for declaring what human language a page is written in. In fact there are at least two protocols, one in HTML and one in HTTP, but sometimes the protocols disagree, and sometimes they both lie, so search engines usually classify pages based on the actual content, after collecting some samples for each known language. Your task is to write such a classifier. State of the art is over 99% accuracy.

Spam Detection and Other Classification Tasks

It is estimated that 100 billion spam email messages are sent every day. Given two corpora of spam and nonspam messages, your task is to classify incoming messages. The best spam classifiers have models for word n-grams (a message with "10,000,000.00 will be released" and "our country Nigeria" is probably spam) and character n-grams ("v1agra" is probably spam), among other features. State of the art on this task is also over 99%, which keeps the spam blockers slightly ahead of the spammers. Once you can classify documents as spam/nonspam, it is a short step to do other types of classification, such as urgent/nonurgent email messages, or politics/business/sports/etc. for news articles, or favorable/neutral/unfavorable for product reviews.

Author Identification (Stylometry)

Language models have been used to try to identify the disputed authors of the Federalist Papers, Shakespeare's poems, and Biblical verses. Similar techniques are used in tracking terrorist groups and in criminal law, to identify and link perpetrators. This field is less mature; we don't yet know for sure what the best practices are, nor what accuracy rate to

expect, although the winner of a 2004 competition had 71% accuracy. The best performers in the competition were linguistically simple but statistically sophisticated.

Document Unshredding and DNA Sequencing

In Vernor Vinge's science fiction novel *Rainbows End* (Tor Books), the Libreareome project digitizes an entire library by tossing the books into a tree shredder, photographing the pieces, and using computer algorithms to reassemble the images. In real life, the German government's E-Puzzler project is reconstructing 45 million pages of documents shredded by the former East German secret police, the Stasi. Both these projects rely on sophisticated computer vision techniques. But once the images have been converted to characters, language models and hill-climbing search can be used to reassemble the pieces. Similar techniques can be used to read the language of life: the Human Genome Project used a technique called shotgun sequencing to reassemble shreds of DNA. So-called "next generation sequencing" shifts even more of the burden away from the wet lab to large-scale parallel reassembly algorithms.

Machine Translation

The Google *n*-gram corpus was created by researchers in the machine translation group. Translating from a foreign language (*f*) into English (*e*) is similar to correcting misspelled words. The best English translation is modeled as:

$$best = \text{argmax}_e \, \text{P}(e \mid f) = \text{argmax}_e \, \text{P}(f \mid e) \, \text{P}(e)$$

where $\text{P}(e)$ is the language model for English, which is estimated by the word *n*-gram data, and $\text{P}(f \mid e)$ is the translation model, which is learned from a bilingual corpus: a corpus where pairs of documents are marked as translations of each other. Although the top systems make use of many linguistic features, including parts of speech and syntactic parses of the sentences, it appears that the majority of the knowledge necessary for translation resides in the *n*-gram data.

Discussion and Conclusion

We have shown the power of a software development methodology that uses large amounts of data to solve ill-posed problems in uncertain environments. In this chapter it was language data, but many of the same lessons apply to other data.

In the examples we have explored, the programs are simple and succinct because the probabilistic models are simple. These simple models ignore so much of what humans know—clearly, to segment "choosespain.com", we draw on much specific knowledge of how the travel business works and other factors, but the surprising result is that a program does not have to explicitly represent all that knowledge; it gets much of the knowledge implicitly from the *n*-grams, which reflect what other humans have chosen to talk about. In the past, probabilistic models were more complex because they relied on less data.

There was an emphasis on statistically sophisticated forms of *smoothing* when data is missing. Now that very large corpora are available, we use approaches like stupid backoff and no longer worry as much about the smoothing model.

Most of the complexity in the programs we studied in this chapter was due to the search strategy. We saw three classes of search strategy:

Exhaustive

For shift ciphers, there are only 26 candidates; we can test them all.

Guaranteed

For segmentation, there are 2^n candidates, but most can be proved nonoptimal (given the independence assumption) without examining them.

Heuristic

For full substitution ciphers, we can't guarantee we've found the best candidate, but we can search a representative subset that gives us a good chance of finding the maxima. For many problems, the majority of the work will be in picking the right function to maximize, understanding the topology of the search space, and discovering a good order to enumerate the neighbors.

If we are to base our models on large amounts of data, we'll need data that is readily available "in the wild." *N*-gram counts have this property: we can easily harvest a trillion words of naturally occurring text from the Web. On the other hand, labeled spelling corrections do not occur naturally, and thus we found only 40,000 of them. It is not a coincidence that the two most successful applications of natural language—machine translation and speech recognition—enjoy large corpora of examples available in the wild. In contrast, the task of syntactic parsing of sentences remains largely unrealized, in part because there is no large corpus of naturally occurring parsed sentences.

It should be mentioned that our probabilistic data-driven methodology—maximize the probability over all candidates—is a special case of the *rational* data-driven methodology—maximize expected utility over all candidates. The *expected utility* of an action is its average value to the user over all possible outcomes. For example, a rational spelling correction program should know that there are some taboo naughty words, and that suggesting them when they were not intended causes embarrassment for the user, a negative effect that is much worse than just spelling a word wrong. The rational program takes into account both the probability that a word is correct or wrong, and the positive or negative value of suggesting each word.

Uncertain problems require good discipline in validation and testing. To evaluate a solution to an uncertain problem, one should divide the data into three sets: (1) A *training* set used to build the probabilistic model. (2) A *validation* set that the developer uses to evaluate several different approaches, seeing which ones score better, and getting ideas for new algorithms. (3) A *test* set, which is used at the end of development to accurately judge how

well the algorithm will do on new, unseen data. After the test set has been used once it ideally should be discarded, just as a teacher cannot give the same test twice to a class of students. But in practice, data is expensive, and there is a trade-off between paying to acquire new data and reusing old data in a way that does not cause your model to *overfit* to the data. Note that the need for an independent test set is inherent to uncertain problems themselves, not to the type of solution chosen—you should use proper test methodology even if you decide to solve the problem with ad hoc rules rather than a probabilistic model.

In conclusion, as more data is available online, and as computing capacity increases, I believe that the probabilistic data-driven methodology will become a major approach for solving complex problems in uncertain domains.

Acknowledgments

Thanks to Darius Bacon, Thorsten Brants, Andy Golding, Mark Paskin, Franco Salvetti, and Casey Whitelaw for comments, corrections, and code.

CHAPTER FIFTEEN

Life in Data: The Story of DNA

Matt Wood and Ben Blackburne

DNA IS A BIOLOGICAL BUILDING BLOCK, A CONCISE, SCHEMA-LESS, FAULT-TOLERANT DATABASE OF AN organism's chemical makeup, designed and implemented by a population over millions of years. Over the past 20 years, biologists have begun to move from the study of individual genes to whole genomes, with genomic approaches forming an increasingly large part of modern biomedical research. In recent years, however, biologists have been learning to handle DNA as both a data store and a data source.

There are two stories to tell about DNA pertinent to this book. DNA itself is a method of encoding data, a digital store of information that predates your hard drive by quite some time. But there is a second, interlinked story, that of the massive undertaking of producing this data and determining its meaning.

DNA As a Data Store

A genome is the database for an organism. It is written in the molecules of DNA, copies of which are stored in each cell of the human body (with a few exceptions). This pattern is repeated across nature, right down to the simplest forms of life. The information encoded within the genome contains the directions to build the proteins that make up the molecular machinery that runs the chemistry of the cell. Now that's what I call fault-tolerant and redundant storage.

Almost every cell in your body contains a central data center, which stores these genomic databases, called the nucleus. Within this are the chromosomes. Like all humans, you are diploid, with two copies of each chromosome, one from your father and one from your mother. Added to these are the sex chromosomes, two X chromosomes for a female, or an X and a Y chromosome for a male. The primary components of these genetic data stores are two strands of DNA, intertwined in the charismatic double helix, as seen in Figure 15-1.

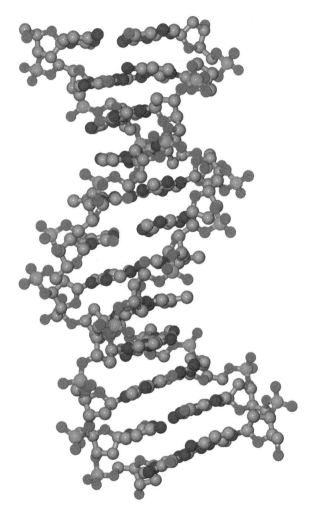

FIGURE 15-1. A short section of DNA, rendered in POV-Ray from PDB file 1BNA, doi: 10.2210/pdb1bna/pdb. (See Color Plate 51.)

Each strand of DNA is made up of a chain of bases. There are four bases in DNA—Adenine, Guanine, Cytosine, Thymine (or A, G, C, and T)—and it is in this quaternary system that the database is encoded. In humans, there are 3 gigabases of DNA present in two slightly different copies.

DNA Makes RNA Makes Proteins

What is DNA for, exactly? The majority of the human genome is apparently of little to no direct use (although it may have subtle roles). Two percent of your genome comprises the genes, the sequences that are responsible for building proteins. Just as DNA is a large molecule written in a 4-letter alphabet, proteins are smaller molecules written in a 20-letter alphabet. The sequence that makes up a protein encodes for its shape, and the shape and chemical structure of a protein determines its function as a cog in the molecular machinery of the cell.

Much like any file format, reading and displaying the encoded information of a DNA sequence requires a special set of reading apparatus. Unlike any other kind of file, however, this apparatus operates at the nano-scale inside living cells, aligning individual molecules in a specific sequence, based on the order of bases in the genome. RNA is DNA's shorter-lived cousin. It has an analogous four-letter code, and when a gene is activated, the protein machinery produces copies of that gene in RNA. These copies are transferred to the protein-based machinery for translation into protein molecules; each molecule of RNA can form the template for many protein molecules.

In this way, DNA and protein form a partnership, with proteins providing the machinery that builds new proteins, as directed by the sequences in the genome. Although DNA is held to be the "blueprint for life," it makes sense only in the context of the pre-existing molecules in the cell, especially the proteins.

By controlling the production of the proteins responsible for activating a gene, the cell can control the production of a protein in response to stimulus or another need. Through these mechanisms, other cells can control a cell by sending signal-molecules—for instance, hormones. Many drugs also work through these mechanisms.

Each gene is "tagged" by surrounding sequences that control the production of the protein (see Figure 15-2). There are proteins encoded within the genome that specifically target these tags. Some proteins will increase production, whereas others will block it.

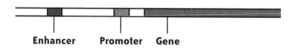

FIGURE 15-2. A stretch of DNA containing a gene also contains nearby regions that interact with the cellular machinery to regulate its expression; here, a gene is preceded by a promoter element and an enhancer element, which "tag" the gene so the cell knows when it should be expressed. (See Color Plate 52.)

Hacking Your DNA Data Store with Drugs

Imagine if O'Reilly were to produce a book in its "Hacks" series called *DNA Hacks*, containing 100 ways to modify, refactor, or otherwise "enhance" your genetic database. Half of these hacks would likely be ways of blocking or promoting the action of a set of proteins called "G-protein coupled receptors" (GPCR), as it is estimated that half of all drugs target these proteins. For instance, gastric acid secretion is stimulated by signals in the body that act on a particular GPCR. When the signal molecule hits the GPCR, a series of interactions take place

that turn on and off genes in your DNA. Zantac, used to treat ulcers and heartburn, acts by getting in between it and the GPCR and blocking this signal. Just as people have long used clever hacks in their email clients to prevent spam email getting through (e.g., preventing signals containing "V1Agr4"), Zantac is a clever hack that prevents the signal "more acid" from getting past the cell wall.

There is a form of DNA "metadata" worth mentioning here. Although the genome is generally best regarded as a read-only database, DNA can be chemically modified as a response to environmental factors, resulting in the suppression of some genes. These chemical changes don't alter the code itself; rather, they provide an additional "annotation" that makes the cellular machinery less likely to transcribe the gene. The study of these modifications, known as epigenetics, and the discovery of their role in our makeup is still in its infancy. It is known that some epigenetic changes switch off genes that won't be needed in a particular cell (a cell directed to be muscle will need a different complement of genes than a liver cell). What is exciting, and would doubtless feature in future editions of *DNA Hacks*, is that genes may be switched off in response to the environment. For instance, growth-promoting hormones can be switched off as a response to starvation. This is of great interest because these changes may be passed on to children, meaning that changes acquired in response to how we live our lives affect our descendants' genes in ways previously thought impossible.

Cancer

Cancer is a disease where a group of cells grows uncontrollably. A cell's growth and location are controlled by its genes, meaning it will only divide in a controlled fashion. Furthermore, the human genome contains many genes known as tumor-supressor genes, which are responsible for shutting a cell down when it displays uncontrolled growth. So how does cancer happen? The answer lies in database corruption. Chemical carcinogens (e.g., those in tobacco), radiation, and viruses can all make modifications to your DNA.

When a computer hard drive suffers a small number of changes, you might not even notice the difference. But enough damage, and programs will start crashing, and files won't open. The same is true of the genome. Do enough damage, and the regulation of genes will go haywire, causing uncontrolled expression. If you hit the right gene, then the cell could start sending itself signals to grow and divide. Other genes (such as tumor-supressors) could be deactivated entirely, and you are on the road to cancer.

Of course, hard drives are mostly quite reliable. Most include systems that detect and remap bad sectors. They also contain systems that detect when a disk has been damaged and alert the user (e.g., SMART monitoring). For additional reliability, you might mirror one hard drive on another in a RAID1 array. With two hard drives that should be identical, if one goes wrong it can be replaced with another and the data put back. The cell contains its own machinery to detect and repair DNA damage. Recall that the DNA molecule exists as a double helix, with each base on one strand complementary to the matching base on the other. If damage is done to one strand, it can be repaired by using the other as a template (the RAID1 approach). Other mechanisms exist to repair more extensive damage.

If the damage cannot be repaired, then the tumor suppressor genes kick in, preventing cell division, and ultimately initiating programmed cell death, and hopefully the cell can be replaced (the SMART approach).

Consider that the human body is estimated to have 100 trillion cells. Anyone involved in the running of a compute cluster with (say) 5,000 hard disks will know how often they fail, and may wonder why it is that we don't get cancer a lot more than we do!

Replication

As mentioned earlier, DNA is structured as two intertwined strands. They are complementary: each of the four bases of DNA has a complement (A complements G, and C complements T) that appears opposite it on the other strand. Watson and Crick noticed this in the now famous understatement in their paper revealing this structure of DNA: "It has not escaped our notice that the specific pairing we have postulated immediately suggests a possible copying mechanism for the genetic material."

Each DNA strand is a template for the other, so to make copies of a double helix, the cell can separate the two and build up a new strand on each template using each base's complement. When a cell divides to make two new cells, this is exactly what happens (see Figure 15-3).

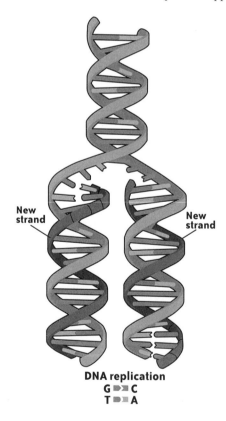

FIGURE 15-3. DNA replication proceeds by using the original two strands (white) as templates for two new strands (black), resulting in two new double-stranded molecules (image from http://genome.gov/glossary.cfm).

Cracking the Code

Imagine a future civilization unearthing a 21st-century disk drive. Even if the civilization were able to understand the filesystem (as detailed earlier), a text file on the disk is ultimately stored in binary. Without knowledge of the 7-bit ASCII table that converts each stretch of 7 bits into a letter, the message is unintelligible.

The equivalent code in the genome began to be reverse-engineered in 1961 by Francis Crick and Sydney Brenner. ASCII was designed to take a two-letter alphabet and convert it to around 90 characters, necessitating the use of 7 bits per character as $2^7=128$ (in practice, an extra bit was originally used for parity). In DNA, a four-letter alphabet must encode for 21 characters (20 amino acids and a STOP signal). Thus three bases are needed ($4^3=64$) per character (see Table 15-1).

TABLE 15-1. The universal genetic code; each possible three-letter combination corresponds either to the "stop" code or to one of 20 amino acids represented by their three-letter abbreviation

First base		T	C	A	G	Third base
T		Phe	Ser	Tyr	Cys	T
		Phe	Ser	Tyr	Cys	C
		Leu	Ser	STOP	STOP	A
		Leu	Ser	STOP	Trp	G
C		Leu	Pro	His	Arg	T
		Leu	Pro	His	Arg	C
		Leu	Pro	Gln	Arg	A
		Leu	Pro	Gln	Arg	G
A		Ile	Thr	Asn	Ser	T
		Ile	Thr	Asn	Ser	C
		Ile	Thr	Lys	Arg	A
		Met	Thr	Lys	Arg	G
G		Val	Ala	Asp	Gly	T
		Val	Ala	Asp	Gly	C
		Val	Ala	Glu	Gly	A
		Val	Ala	Glu	Gly	G

For instance, the three bases ACT encode for the amino acid threonine. Whenever the ACT triplet is encountered within a gene by the translation machinery, a threonine is inserted into the growing protein molecule. Notice that there are many more codes (64) than signals (20 amino acids + the stop signal). This means the triplet code can have built-in redundancy—most amino acids are encoded by more than one codon.

In practice, for many codons, the last base either doesn't matter or is the least significant. The result of this is to maximize the probability that a mutation (a change of base, e.g., an A instead of a T) will have no effect on the protein, and so protect against the potentially damaging effect of changes in protein structure.

The human genome has grown over billions of years by the incorporation of chance mistakes. Accordingly, it is full of elements that have no functional purpose, and others whose functional purpose is only dimly understood. Although the term "Junk DNA" has now fallen out of fashion, there are certainly huge amounts of DNA that exist only because the selective pressure to remove them is too weak, or nonexistent.

Some elements are able to copy and paste themselves around the genome. For instance, the Alu element, a fragment of around 300 bases, contains the information required to copy itself into RNA (a shorter-lived molecule very similar to DNA), and then back into the genome in another position. The result of this is similar to the effect of asking Jack Torrance from Stanley Kubrick's *The Shining* to cowrite a book with you, inserting the phrase "All work and no play makes Jack a dull boy" thousands of times in between sentences. Alu elements make up 10% of the human genome. The presence of these elements makes human genomics more difficult than that of smaller organisms, whose constraints on genome size prevent these elements from proliferating.

DNA As Digital Storage

The forces of evolution shape the genome. But when Darwin first postulated the idea of evolution, he knew he had a problem. Common sense would tell you that should a taller and a shorter person breed, and their child happens to be of intermediate height, then the hereditary information for "tallness" and "shortness" have been blended together irreversibly. Sexual reproduction should be driving species to a state of averageness. In fact, genes do not mix together irreversibly, as was first discovered by Darwin's contemporary, Gregor Mendel.

The reason is the digital nature of DNA. The medium-size child will have exact copies of one set of genes from the father, and another from the mother. There is no mixing together of the genes: for instance, at no point does a sequence have a half-A-half-T state in it. So the information there is not lost, and can be passed on unmodified to the grandchildren. Complex life can evolve, and hence exist, because of the digital storage allowed by DNA.

Evolution As an Algorithm

We know the basic algorithm that created the DNA in your cells: evolution. The DNA sequence changes, due to mutations. So how does evolution shape DNA? Surprisingly, the majority of evolution (defined as change in the DNA sequence from one generation to the next) is selectively neutral, i.e., it involves changes that have no effect on the organism. Why is this? Clearly, when such a change occurs in a small population there is a chance that this change could, in the future, predominate in the population. For a larger population, such changes are less likely to predominate, but there is a corresponding increase in the number of such changes—so neutral evolution still dominates.

This is important for interpreting differences between individuals, and between species. Neutral evolution is the null model for any differences between two genomes. This means that to show that the differences on the same gene between two species are of interest, scientists frequently seek to show that the "algorithm" of neutral evolution could not have produced the two sequences. This means estimating the rate of change and determining if

it is either faster or slower than would be thought by the neutral theory. If there are more changes than would be expected, then perhaps this is because such changes have provided functional improvements to the organism, and the changes spread rapidly through the population. If changes are slower, then the gene is likely important enough that the majority of changes are not neutral and so have been rejected by evolution.

The huge number of variations within species means that the reference human genome, currently thought of as a linear string that represents an amalgam of several people, could be more reasonably represented as a graph that includes the variations within the population. An individual's genome could then be represented by a traversal of the reference graph.

DNA As a Data Source

To a programming language, DNA is simply a string:

```
char(3*10^6) human_genome;
```

The full genomic information for man consists of 3 billion characters and is easily handled in memory by even the most inefficient home-brewed language. However, the process of determining the exact order of these 3 billion bases requires a significant effort spanning chemistry, bioinformatics, laboratory procedures, and a lot of spinning disks.

The Human Genome Project aimed, for the first time, to sequence every one of these characters. A number of large, high-throughput institutes from around the world put academic competition aside and set about a task that would last 13 years and consume billions of dollars. Their aim was to produce a robust, accurate map of the human genome, available to all, for free. The consortium of scientists from the UK, America, and Japan succeeded, with the first draft human genome appearing in the scientific literature in February 2001. The genome, without any additional annotations or associated data, weighed in at 10 gigabits, a reasonably large size in an era without iPods or USB thumb drives. However, the overall weight of this data was much greater, thanks to the exponentially increasing storage requirements as this data was replicated across the globe. Scientists proceeded to analyze the data, scouring it for genetic markers and disease indicators, and comparing it to other available genomes from mice, yeast, and pathogens. These 10 gigabits have formed the foundation of modern biological research.

Skip forward to 2008. The human genome has been well annotated (*http://ensembl.org*), and over 40 other species have been sequenced, including the mouse, chimpanzee, and the duck-billed platypus. In a corner meeting room of the Morgan Building on the Genome Campus, a meeting is taking place at the Wellcome Trust Sanger Institute between IT professionals, informaticians, and scientists to discuss the next generation of DNA sequence production.

Numbers are presented from several competing sequencing technology platforms, all looking to exploit the nonredundant nature of genomic information. Instead of sequencing long reads of thousands of base pairs as had been done with the original human genome

sequence, these short reads would consist of only 30–50 bases, sufficient to place that read at a specific position on a specific chromosome with a high degree of certainty in the sea of 3 billion. The kilobase counts of capillary genome sequencing are quickly eclipsed by megabases as the details of the data requirements of short-read sequencing became apparent. Whiteboards fill quickly with hand-drawn diagrams of the process, which uses images of fluorescing bases to identify the correct sequence of these shorter fragments of DNA.

The throughput and number of new instruments required to support the scientific goals of the Institute were discussed. One number stood out on the whiteboard against all the rest. Within six months, the Institute would be producing 50 terabits of fresh data. Each week.

A hush fell on the meeting.

Even to facilities capable of supporting the large numbers of sequencing instruments (100+) for the human genome sequencing, and with dedicated on-site hardware for analyzing and annotating this data, no realm of biology had handled so much raw information at that date.

The new sequencing platform would eclipse the already large-scale data requirements of the Institute by orders of magnitude. To that point, data requirements had grown roughly exponentially within the Institute's 15-year history, culminating in around 17,000 online disks driving a multi-petabyte storage system. The new sequencing technologies would generate as much again over the next 12 to 18 months.

True to form, the new wave of sequencing instruments started to arrive at the Genome Campus, and six months later the hush of that initial meeting was drowned out by the furious construction of server farms, storage arrays, software, databases, and information management tools in the largest scale-up in an industry's history.

A Quantum Leap

The new technologies presented a quantum leap in genomic sequencing. Previous generations of instruments required very large-scale facilities to produce a megabase of usable sequence. Sequencing a single genome took many years and was expensive.

Sequencing a single genome is useful when looking to compare the genomes between species. Portions of DNA sequence with biological importance are conserved through evolutionary history, and identifying these conserved regions helps biologists identify novel genes, which may play a role in disease.

Since an individual kilobase sequencing run is rarely completely accurate, for statistical power there is real benefit in being able to sequence the same base on multiple, independent measurements, hence the need for such large-scale deployments of instruments. The new generation of short-read sequencing instruments, however, read a single base many millions of times per run, providing additional resolution to the resulting genome, which is essential in comparative genomics.

Because of this additional resolution, short-read sequencing allows the construction of a large number of individual human genomes for the first time, which can provide huge insight into the genomic database of a single person. The comparison of these genomes can help identify why one person might be more disposed to high blood pressure or breast cancer, for example, compared to others. Differences in a very small number of bases in the sequence of a genome can lead to these genetic predispositions; from a single base (called SNPs, single nucleotide polymorphisms), to collections of repeating units (CNV), these small changes amongst 3 billion bases can hold the key to many disease states. By comparing the bases sequenced at a particular location on the DNA string from the many millions of copies sequenced by the short-read technologies, one can decide with confidence whether a particular difference in a base between two individuals is a sequencing error or really the site of one of these small nucleotide changes. Additional annotation from patient records and other research can then reveal whether these are linked to disease.

"My God, It's Full of Bases..."

The technical implementation of such genomic sequencing platforms is worthy of discussion. It is essentially a linear assembly pipeline, in which an individual's DNA acts as a raw material, quantified and then prepared for a photochemical reaction in the sequencing instrument. After being sheared into millions of short fragments, those fragments are copied millions of times, and then adhered to a specially prepared glass slide. Specially tagged bases are washed over these prepared strands of short bases, binding to their complementary pair: As to Ts, Cs to Gs. When placed under a laser, these bases fluoresce with different wavelengths, and a photograph is taken that shows thousands of dots, each one a cluster of glowing DNA bases (see Figure 15-4). It is at this point that the huge requirements of the platform appear, in the form of a multiplier. While each image is only at a megapixel resolution, four images are taken for each base in the short reads (one per base, at each location). That's just 148 images.

However, each image covers only a fraction of the clusters of DNA, which are imaged in 330 individual tiles (48,840 images) and arranged into 8 lanes (390,720 images). Usually, the DNA strand is sequenced in both the forward and reverse directions, too (781,440 images). There is also additional metadata produced by the sequencing run in the form of laser intensity and fluidic measurements.

All in all, an instrument can produce 1 terabits of data a day.

This data is then passed through image analysis software, which aligns each set of images to determine the sequence of bases based on the intensity of the fluorescence. This in turn generates files containing the individual strings, quality scores, and intensity details, along with cluster position and other associated metadata. In practice, to aid with additional analysis downstream, this information is actually written in two file formats: fastq and SRF, a hierarchial data format reappropriated from colleagues in the astronomy world.

FIGURE 15-4. An Illumina GA2 sequencing image; each bright dot is a cluster of many thousands of DNA molecules, fluorescing under a laser.

Simple increases in image resolution or read length have huge implications for data handling and analysis. The first version of the new sequencing platform at Sanger was capable of working with short reads of 36 bases each. A read length of 100 base pairs (such as the prototype currently up and running in Sanger's R&D labs) would lead to a three-fold increase in images (2,334,320 images), across a platform of just under 40 instruments (maybe more by the time you read this), giving a grand total of 93 million images for each and every platform run, which lasts around a week. In total, that's around 75 terabits of data per week.

How is it handled?

Fighting the Data Deluge

Large deployments of sequencing instruments are necessary to support the construction of these genomic data sets, and to support large-scale, genome-wide associate studies such as the 1000 Genomes Project (*http://1000genomes.org*) and the International Cancer Genome Consortium (*http://www.icgc.org*), which hope to add tremendous value to biological research now and over the next 20 years. The large genome centers around the world have taken up this challenge admirably. Sanger, for example, has over 35 Illumina GA2 genome analyzers, which run in a high-throughput facility on the Genome Campus in Hinxton, about 10 miles south of Cambridge in the UK.

The Sanger Institute's Sequencing Platform

The sequencing platform operates as a core service within the Institute, available to all genomic research currently underway by the faculty and their collaborators. Demand for the facility is extremely high, and the Institute has developed a range of operational tools and processes to help handle this demand.

Project management

A friendly collection of project management tools called Sequencescape helps investigators plan their experiments, and sequencing facility administrators plan capacity and through-put. Sequencescape was developed and is maintained by a small core team located in-house. It's written in Rails, runs on a standard stack of blades, uses MySQL, and is delivered to users via the intranet (*http://www.sanger.ac.uk/*).

When a new project requires sequencing (which can be anywhere from a single run on a single sample of interest yielding around 1 gigabase to many thousands of runs across tens of thousands of samples), it is registered in Sequencescape, along with some associated metadata, such as scientific rationale, budget information, and contact details.

Each sample to be sequenced is then registered in the same way, and requests for sequencing runs are submitted to the facility. This request forms the basic unit of work for the sequencing platform, and the physical DNA samples are handed over to the laboratory teams for preparation and sequencing.

Preparing a sample for sequencing is a complex, manual process involving a continually refined laboratory pipeline. Physical samples of DNA are moved from one tube to another, between pieces of manual apparatus, robotic and computerized components, and even between physical laboratories. Recording the "life story" of a sample is crucial, since this provenance metadata can be important when reviewing sequence results or laboratory throughput or in identifying laboratory pipeline components that are miscalibrated or malfunctioning. Should the DNA in a sample be mishandled in any way, the instrument will fail to sequence it: an expensive and time-consuming problem. By evaluating and analyzing the provenance metadata, it is possible to view commonalities between failures, highlighting protocol deviations, malfunctioning equipment, or miscalibrations. Through continual monitoring and review, the laboratory procedures can continue to roll out quality DNA samples, ready to sequence.

Biological laboratory procedures are, if you'll excuse the pun, continually evolving. Refinements, updates, novel approaches, or complete overhauls are common as new methods are published in the scientific literature or discussed at conferences. New instruments and robotic automation is introduced. Maintaining robust provenance capture in a highly flexible domain such as laboratory workflows is extremely difficult. It soon becomes unworkable in high-throughput environments where even small inefficiencies or holdups can lead to long backlogs.

Nowhere is this truer than in genomic sequencing, where genomic material from individual patients may be of limited, short supply, with a short shelf life. DNA prepared for sequencing does not last forever, and for DNA that cannot be re-sourced, laboratory processing or sequencing delays can prove disastrous.

To balance the need for effective provenance collection with a time-sensitive, highly dynamic workflow, modern approaches to data capture are required: we never want software to be the rate-limiting step in a workflow.

Flexible Data Capture

Instead of classical database refactoring, typically involving adding, removing, or renaming fields on a database schema, the high-throughput production pipeline at Sanger uses a collection of data modeling tools that allow data descriptions to be changed at runtime. When a laboratory protocol is updated to include a new set of instruments or a faster approach to an existing step, the provenance information captured that relates to that task can be restructured on the fly by laboratory staff. This helps lead to the efficient running of the laboratory, frees up developer time, and keeps data collection bang up to date with the set of laboratory procedures currently in play.

For the most part, the databases that run the production systems are traditional, modeled around real-world objects such as Projects, Samples, and key protocol components, for example, Workflows and Tasks. However, in addition, metadata is also modeled as first-class objects, with representations for Descriptors, Values, and a class of object referred to as a Family. A Family can have many descriptors, each providing a definition of a data field, including the name, type, UI element, whether it is a required field, and more. Each workflow item then effectively inherits a family's fields, with individual values.

This allows the quick specification and revision of new types of projects, samples, and workflow tasks.

The user interfaces for all data entry pages are dynamically generated using this information, as are the various reporting tools used to monitor the sequencing platform and laboratory workflow throughput. Families are versioned, allowing older projects to continue to be accessible, and migration and curation tools provide easy routes for upgrading older objects to newer descriptions.

Computationally, this process is faster than you think. With sufficient indexing and data denormalization between tables, the web application remains responsive even under the heavy load of a high-throughput system. As certain properties begin to cement into the workflow (for example, everything has a name, a unique identifier, and creation and modification dates), they are easily refactored back into first class database fields for faster queries.

This attempt to streamline the data modeling of laboratory workflows has been largely successful. The benefits continue to be apparent, as this optimization for flexibility has allowed the same infrastructure to be used for other laboratory workflows within the Institute (genotyping followed quickly) with very little additional development overhead.

Sequencescape's project management and laboratory information management tools are open source, and available to download from *http://www.sanger.ac.uk*.

Instrument and Data Management

At Sanger, the entire short-read sequencing pipeline operates as a collection of hosted services, with interoperability built around defined interfaces to web services. Project management and laboratory information management eventually give way to instrument management tools, which monitor, control, and, where possible, automate the entire instrument platform.

Each sequencing instrument is attached to a PC, which controls the instrument and provides a temporary staging area for the image data streaming from the instrument. Unfortunately, especially for longer reads, disk space on this local machine quickly becomes insufficient to store an entire run's data, and the computational power of desktop-class machines is insufficient to run the image, sequence, and quality analysis of the data.

For this reason, the data is moved from the attached instrument PC through a 10-gigabit pipe to a larger storage array: 400 terabits of Lustre managed EVA storage. This is networked to a 1,000-node cluster, which performs the primary analysis and image alignment duties on the raw images. Managing storage on this scale is hugely problematic, requiring constant intervention, extension, and supervision from a crack team of system administrators, vendors, and in-house data managers. This array holds data for around four weeks; following analysis and eventual base calling, this raw data from the instrument and associated instrument-run details (laser intensity, fluidic data, etc.) is curated and archived as necessary, before being deleted.

The scale of the raw sequencing data is vast and expensive to handle; however, once the images have been aligned and the individual bases of sequence identified, each run produces around 30 gigabits of sequence and quality data. While the raw data is not backed up (restoring from tape would take three months), each raw image from the sequencing run is scaled down to low-quality JPEG files, and stored in a database. Although unsuitable for analysis, this data is useful should any run require a manual review to identify imaging problems or artifacts (oil, poor DNA clustering, and even fingerprints aren't uncommon).

Once the sequencing data is available, it is stored in two formats in a high-performance Oracle database. While production systems make good use of databases, bioinformatics tools tend to continue to work against flat files on a physical filesystem. To be sure that we cater to all tastes, the vast swaths of sequence information available in this sequence archive are also presented to Sanger's internal compute farms via a Fuse user-space filesystem. This approach scales surprisingly well.

The sequence data is then passed through a series of quality control steps, which again run on the sequencing analysis cluster, and check for low sequencing yield, high levels of unknown bases, or low complexity sequence, all of which are telltale signs for sequencing

errors. The QC results are passed back to Sequencescape, and the investigator and collaborators are alerted to their new data and its location in the Fuse filesystem. In the event that the sequencing results are not of sufficient quality, or if there has been a problem in the laboratory, Sequencescape automatically queues the sample for reprocessing.

For many of the projects undertaken at Sanger, and only when consent has been given, this data is made available to all: from the original project and sample metadata, to the laboratory provenance information and each and every single one of the millions of sequencing reads per sample. These are all available to download to anyone who might have interest, for free, including the latest draft genome data (*http://www.ensembl.org/index.html*), the individual sequencing traces (*http://trace.ensembl.org/*), and in the next few months, every single short-read sequence across all projects (keep an eye on *http://www.ebi.ac.uk*). This represents a fantastic resource for biomedical researchers, and continues the best traditions of free and open data access of the original human genome project.

The Future of DNA

These new sequencing technologies and the data generated as part of the projects using them are laying the foundation stones of the next era in modern biology. The data management, curation, and analysis tools using this data will continue to evolve, and so it's worth taking a slightly longer view on the future of DNA.

How to Become a Genetic Hacker

More than other data-intensive areas, genomics has a great history of providing open, online data repositories, from a variety of genome browsing and annotation tools (such as Enesembl and UCSC), to details of diseases linked to genes (HapMap, SNPedia) and personalized genomics services such as 23andMe and Navigenics. So much so that anyone can become a genetic hacker these days.

Next Next-Gen

At present, such companies provide only a high-level overview of certain points of interest along the genome. But innovation continues unabated with the development of the next generation of sequencing instrumentation and génome analyzers. Companies such as Pacific Biometrics and Oxford Nanopore are hard at work on driving the current megabase read counts into the gigabase region and beyond. With the advent of higher throughput, and the associated drop in costs, the goal of the $5,000 and even the $1,000 genome, and the point at which therapeutic genetic sequencing becomes cost-effective, draw ever closer.

The Era of Big Data

With any of these approaches, one thing is for sure: data requirements are only going to increase. The era of big data has arrived for genomics, and also for modern biological research, which is built upon it. Data will continue to provide extremely large constraints

on analysis and research, and it is clear that as more and more research and hospital teams perform genetic sequencing in-house, the role of the large genomic centers will look very different. Providing a flexible computational platform, along with efficient sequence search, alignment, and assembly tools, plus safe housing for the millions of genomes, will become vitally important. They will also bring with them questions of technical implementation, privacy, and efficacy, all of which are hotly discussed topics today in the biomedical arena.

While these impeding constraints may point to some clouds gathering on the horizon, the future of DNA is definitely bright.

Acknowledgments

The authors would like to thank the Wellcome Trust for their continual support of open access and open data in biomedical research.

CHAPTER SIXTEEN

Beautifying Data in the Real World

Jean-Claude Bradley, Rajarshi Guha, Andrew Lang, Pierre Lindenbaum, Cameron Neylon, Antony Williams, and Egon Willighagen

The Problem with Real Data

THERE ARE AT LEAST TWO PROBLEMS WITH COLLECTING "BEAUTIFUL DATA" IN THE REAL WORLD AND presenting it to the interested public. The first is that the universe is inherently noisy. In most cases collecting the same piece of data twice will not give the same answer. This is because the collection process can never be made completely error-free. Fluctuations of temperature, pressure, humidity, power sources, water or reagent quality, precision of weighing, or human error will all conspire to obscure the "correct" answer. The art in experimental measurement lies in designing the data collection process so as to minimize the degree to which random variation and operator error confuse the results. In the best cases this involves a careful process of refining the design of the experiment, monitoring size and source of errors. In the worst case it leads to people repeating experiments until they get the answer they are expecting.

The traditional experimental approach to dealing with the uncertainty created by errors is to repeat the experiment and subject the results to statistical analysis. Examples of repetition can be found in most issues of most scientific journals by looking for a figure panel that contains the text "typical results are shown." "Typical results" is generally taken to mean "the best data set we obtained." Detailed statistical analysis, although in principle a more rigorous approach, can also be controversial and misleading. Arguments often rage

in the comments pages of medical journals over the appropriate approaches to take to remove confounding correlations from the analysis. The links between skepticism about "typical" results and arguments over statistical approaches is a lack of access to the raw data. If the underlying data were available, then people could simply do the analysis and check it themselves. This would likely not reduce the number of arguments, but would at least mean they were better informed.

The second part of the problem is that, until recently, space limitations in print journals have limited the amount of data that can be presented, making it difficult or impossible to present the whole body of data and analysis that supports the argument of the paper. However, in a world where publishing has moved online, this is no longer a viable excuse. It is possible to present the entire data set on which an argument is based, at least in research where data volumes are in the kilobyte to gigabyte scale. There is therefore a strong argument for presenting the whole of the data. This, however, raises the problem of how to present data that may be inconsistent, that may include mistakes, but nonetheless presents the whole picture of how a conclusion was reached. In short, the question is how to show the beauty that lies under the surface of the data in a clear way, while at the same time not avoiding or hiding the blemishes that may lie on the surface.

We believe that the key to successfully reconciling these apparently conflicting needs is transparency. Providing the raw data in as comprehensive a fashion as possible and a full description of all the processing and filtering that has taken place means that any user can dig down to the level of detail he or she requires. The raw data will often be difficult or impossible to present in a form that is naturally machine-readable and processable, so the filtering and refinement process also involves making choices about categorization and simplification to provide clear and clean datafiles that can be repurposed. Here we describe the approach we have taken in "beautifying" a set of crowdsourced data by filtering and representing the data in an open form that allows anyone to use it for his own purposes. We show the way this has enabled multiple researchers to prepare a variety of tools for visualization and analysis, creating a collaborative network that has been effective in analyzing the results, suggesting further experiments, and presenting the results to a wider audience in a way that traditional research communication does not allow.

Providing the Raw Data Back to the Notebook

As part of a wider program of drug discovery research (Bradley 2007) led by Professor Jean-Claude Bradley, we wished to predict the solubility of a wide range of chemicals in nonaqueous solvents such as ethanol, methanol, etc. Of greatest interest was the solubility of aldehydes, carboxylic acids, isonitriles, and primary amines—components required for the Ugi reaction that the Bradley group use to synthesize potential antimalarial targets (Bradley et al. 2008). The solubility of a specific compound is the quantity of that compound that can be dissolved in a specific solvent. Building and validating a model that could predict solubility would require a large data set of such solubility values. Surprisingly, there was no readily available database of nonaqueous solubilities. We therefore elected to crowdsource the data, opening up the measurements to anyone who wanted to

be involved (*http://onchallenge.wikispaces.com/*). However, this poses a series of problems. As anyone can contribute measurements, we have no upfront way of checking the quality of those measurements.

The first stage in creating our data set therefore required the creation of a detailed record of how each and every measurement was made. The measurement techniques, precision, and accuracy of different contributions all vary, but all the background information is provided in human-readable form. This "radical sharing" approach of making the complete research record available as soon as the experiments are done, called Open Notebook Science (*http://en.wikipedia.org/wiki/Open_Notebook_Science*), is not common amongst professional researchers, but it is a good fit with our desire to make a complete and transparent data set available. We utilize a Wiki, hosted on Wikispaces (*http://onchallenge.wikispaces. com*) to hold these experimental records, and other services such as GoogleDocs (*http://docs. google.com*) and Flickr (*http://flickr.com*) to hold data (Figure 16-1).

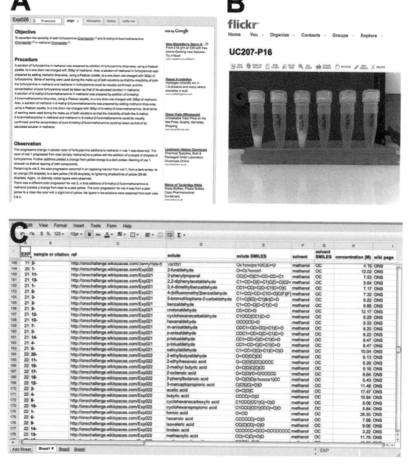

FIGURE 16-1. *Using free generic services to host the record of experimental work and processed data. (A) Part of the page of a single experimental measurement. (B) Images taken of the experiment hosted on Flickr. (C) A portion of the primary data store on a GoogleDocs spreadsheet. (See Color Plate 53.)*

The actual database of values extracted from the experimental descriptions is stored in a GoogleDocs spreadsheet to generate the primary aggregated record of the project. Each and every measurement is presented, along with a link back to the primary record. This link is crucial whether the data is being read by a machine or by a human, as it provides both the provenance of the measurement (i.e., who is making the assertion) and the record of evidence for that assertion. A human can click through to check how the measurement was made, and a machine reader can download or scrape the record if desired.

In a sense the spreadsheet is the first point at which the record from the lab notebooks is converted into data that can then be criticized and filtered. The choice of a GoogleDoc may appear an idiosyncratic choice from a technical perspective, but it is based on a number of requirements: functionality that enables us to present and share the data in its primary form; an interface that is familiar to experimental scientists and requires a minimum of additional work on their part; and free and hosted services, maintained by a large stable company, enabling anyone in the world to replicate this information-processing model with minimal effort. Finally, there is the ability to access the data via a powerful and flexible API. Very few other approaches both enable the average scientist to work with, add to, and download the primary data in a form that is familiar, and also provide powerful programmatic access to the underlying data.

Validating Crowdsourced Data

As data is collected by different researchers using different methods, incompatible values are likely to arise. These may appear as outliers or simply as a wide spread of results. Traditionally, with no additional information, researchers had little choice but to give equal weight to each measurement or apply statistical methods to exclude outliers. But, as we have adopted an Open Notebook approach requiring the full record of how each measurement was carried out, each measurement can be evaluated in the context of the information recorded. In several cases this allows a scientist familiar with the methods reported to exclude questionable data points on the basis of inappropriate conditions or a failure to report an important parameter.

In the case of solubility, mixing time and evaporation conditions proved to be important factors. A good example of this was the determination of the solubility of 4-nitrobenzaldehyde in methanol. Of the five measurements taken, three are significantly lower than the other two (Figure 16-2, shown later in this chapter; *http://oru.edu/cccda/sl/solubility/ugidata. php?solute=4-nitrobenzaldehyde&solvent=methanol*). This method was based on preparing a saturated solution of 4-nitrobenzaldehyde in methanol, evaporating the methanol, and then weighing the residue left behind. It is crucial that a fully saturated solution is prepared, and this was generally done by adding solute with mixing until visible solid remained in the tube. By examining the detailed record of the experiments, it is clear that the three lower values are from experiments where the solutions were mixed only briefly. The two higher measurements are from experiments where the mixing was carried out over several hours, showing that extended mixing is required (*http://usefulchem.blogspot. com/2008/12/mechanical-turk-does-solubility-on.html*).

The availability of the raw experimental record enables all researchers both to identify those measurements that are doubtful and to benefit from the experience of these "failed" experiments. This is the nature of scientific research. A balance has to be struck between recording the details of an experiment and being efficient. Often the purpose of initial experiments is for the researchers to identify what factors are important to pay attention to. Unfortunately, this information is generally not shared with the research community.

Rather than exclude results that are doubtful, we have opted to tag the measurements (with "DONOTUSE") and provide a reason for exclusion. This allows other researchers to click through to the original lab notebook pages and evaluate the raw data for themselves. Errors can occur everywhere—including during the validation process—and "incorrect" values may be useful for some purposes. Full transparency makes it possible for each user to decide what values she wishes to include in her analysis. It also reduces (but does not eliminate) the risk that errors remain hidden. An example of this type of markup is demonstrated in the reporting of the measurements for the solubility of vanillin in methanol (*http://usefulchem.blogspot.com/2008/11/what-is-solubility-of-vanillin-in.html*).

There is clearly a gray area here between those values we have marked as doubtful or untrustworthy and those that we have left unmarked despite potential issues or areas of disagreement. At the end of the day these are matters of scientific judgment, and there is much opportunity for disagreement. The primary record of the experiments remains available in every case and can be examined. In addition, the history of the spreadsheet is available and can also be examined. A balance needs to be struck between providing a useful data set and the degree to which every decision and mistake can be presented. This is a challenging balance to get right.

Representing the Data Online

Our aim is to make all of the experimental record and processed data available online. This raises a number of issues for how to represent the data in a useful form on the Web, including the choice of standardized identifiers, visualization tools, and approaches to data integration.

Unique Identifiers for Chemical Entities

To make our data useful, it is important that the chemical entities be described using a recognized standard. Without this, integration with other data sets will be difficult or impossible. In chemistry, some would argue that CAS Registry Numbers (*http://en.wikipedia.org/wiki/CAS_registry_number*) would be ideal for identifying chemical entities. However, CAS numbers are proprietary in nature, cannot be converted to the chemical structure, are a lookup only, and are dependent on an external organization to issue. We would prefer identifiers that are open in nature, freely available for exchange, and can be converted to and from a chemical connection table.

The IUPAC International Chemical Identifier (InChI, pronounced "INchee") provides a non-proprietary standard and algorithms along with supporting open source software (*http://en.wikipedia.org/wiki/Inchi*) that enable the generation of identity strings that can be converted

back to structures (see *http://www.qsarworld.com/INCHI1.php* for a recent review). InChI is gaining significant support as a standard across software vendors, publishers, and developers. The problems with the algorithm—which mean it is possible to generate multiple InChIs for a single structure—are being addressed by the development of the Standard InChI. For some purposes the InChIKey, a hash of the InChIString, is useful, but this cannot be converted to a structure and must be used via a lookup table to *resolve* the chemical structure.

SMILES (*http://en.wikipedia.org/wiki/SMILES*) is a common format for representing chemical compounds, providing strings that are quite compact and can be converted to and from chemical structures. However, there are multiple forms and implementations of the SMILES algorithm, leading to multiple SMILES for the same entity. We are currently using SMILES in this work due to their simplicity and ease of searching. As noted in "Enabling Data Integration via Unique Identifiers and Self-Describing Data Formats" on page 269, it is possible to convert our SMILES to InChIs, automatically enabling us to integrate our data into the growing web of data represented by this preferred identifier.

Open Data and Accessible Services Enable a Wide Range of Visualization and Analysis Options

Given a standardized, free, and accessible storage infrastructure for the primary solubility data, the next step is to analyze the data. Analysis could range from simply generating a summary of which measurements have been carried out to complex statistical representations of models derived from the data. In either case, it is necessary to access the data for processing by automated routines. It is also desirable to be able to use other sources of information to enrich the data. This in turn requires a recognized standard to be used in the primary representation of the data.

The spreadsheet contains a number of columns, with each row being the record of a single measurement. Both solvent and solute are represented in two different forms: a human-readable common name and a SMILES code. As with the choice of GoogleDocs as the primary representation of the data, the use of both human-readable and machine-readable representations is crucial to gaining the most benefit from the data set. The only piece of information that does not require two representations is the numerical representation of the solubility itself.

As has been noted earlier, we made the decision to not remove the most questionable values from the primary data record. This poses a problem for machine readability, as there is no accepted standard approach for saying "this number is a bit dodgy." For this work we have elected to mark records that are believed to be inaccurate after human curation and to give a reason for the marking. This enables any user to make choices about which records he wishes to include in any analysis, either manually or automatically. For any further analysis, the data, as represented in the spreadsheet, must be accessed. The simplest approach would be to simply export the data, for example, into a comma-separated text file, and analyze it using some external software. However, this would lose the immediate

link to the most up-to-date data. The GoogleDocs API makes it straightforward to generate web-accessible applications while maintaining the link to the "live" data.

As an example of such an application, we have created a web service that allows users to query the data stored in the spreadsheet and obtain a tabular summary (Figure 16-2). The form-based query interface provides a rapid and intuitive mode of access to the relevant data. The page is simple HTML along with JavaScript and does not require any software on the client side. The data is accessed asynchronously from the Google spreadsheet using the API provided by Google. Once the data is retrieved, one can perform a variety of calculations. In this case, we determine the mean and standard deviations of the solubility, which can then be used to dynamically highlight entries that appear to be anomalous.

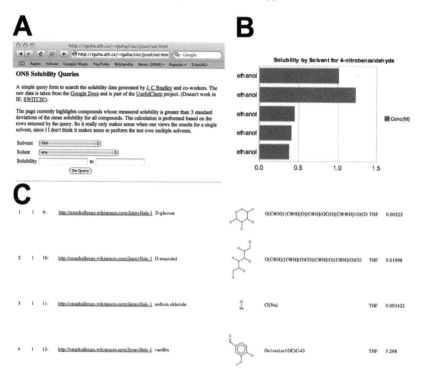

FIGURE 16-2. Visualization tools for examining the solubility data.(A) A simple form-based input uses JavaScript and the GoogleDocs API to generate (B) a graphical representation of the solubility values selected and (C) a tabular output of the data with rendered 2-D chemical structures. The service is available at http://toposome.chemistry.drexel.edu/~rguha/jcsol/sol.html. Note that these and other services described are dynamic and may not give the same results as those shown here for the same query. (See Color Plate 54.)

While the tabular display of subsets of the raw data is very useful, visualizations can be used to effectively summarize the results of queries. The query application employs the Google Visualization API to generate bar charts based on the data extracted from the spreadsheet. Given the ease with which the data can be extracted from the spreadsheet, one can easily generate a variety of visualizations. In our case, a simple bar chart displaying the solubility of a compound in various solvents provides a rapid summary of the results.

Another aspect of the application is that the table contains 2-D depictions of the chemical structures provided via a REST-based service at Indiana University. A SMILES code is appended to the service URL to insert the 2-D image of the structure into an arbitrary web page. Once again, these features require no special software on the client side. This makes distribution of this specific application extremely simple; one simply has to copy the HTML page to another web server.

Although this is a fairly simple application, it highlights the distributed nature of the solution, combining open data with free visualization methods from multiple sources. More importantly, the distributed nature of the system and free accessibility of the data allow experts in different domains—experimentalists generating data, software developers creating interfaces, and computational modelers creating statistical models—to easily couple their expertise. The true promise of open data, open services, and the ecosystem that supports them is that this coupling can occur without requiring any formal collaboration. Researchers will find and use the data in ways that the generators of that data never considered. By doing this they add value to the original data set and strengthen the ecosystem around it, whether they are performing complementary experiments, doing new analyses, or providing new services that process the data. And, all the time, the link back to the original record can be maintained.

Integrating Data with a Central Aggregation Service

A valid criticism of our approach is that if it is widely taken up, it will lead to the presence of many disparate and disconnected data resources. Although it is technically feasible to aggregate such resources together using search tools, it remains the case that the researchers usually use a small set of preferred services as their route into the data they are interested in. The gold standard of curated data sets of chemical information is the Chemical Abstracts Service (CAS) maintained by the American Chemical Society. The CAS Registry contains over 40 million substances (*http://www.cas.org/newsevents/connections/derivative. html*) comprised of data extracted from publications, patents, chemical catalogs, and, increasingly, online data sources such as ChemSpider (*http://www.chemspider.com/blog/cas-chemspider-connectivies-and-unintended-collaboration.html*).

ChemSpider is a web-based resource for chemists developed with the intention of "Building a Structure Centric Community for Chemists." Containing well over 20 million unique chemical entities, sourced from over 150 data sources, ChemSpider has become one of the primary Internet resources for chemists seeking information about chemical entities. For each individual chemical compound, various types of information are associated. This includes different types of identifiers (systematic names, trade names, registry numbers, multilingual names), predicted physicochemical properties, and links to a wide variety of experimental physical, chemical, and spectral data from a wide range of sources (*http://www. chemspider.com/DataSources.aspx*). ChemSpider can therefore be considered as a structure-based link farm to other resources. ChemSpider also provides an environment that allows users to both cleanse and expand the data online. Users can annotate and curate the data,

thereby removing erroneous associations with the chemical entities and adding their own information, including links to external resources and other annotations of the data. Users can also deposit new chemical structures to the database and associate spectral data, images, and even video files. A myriad of search capabilities exist, including searching predicted data and structure or substructure-based searches.

ChemSpider therefore provides an ideal environment for connecting to other sources of chemical information where the primary key to the data is the formal identity of the molecule. The combination of providing a central resource for searching for chemical data as well as the deposition of user data makes ChemSpider the logical place through which other researchers would find our data. Although some of the data associated with Chem-Spider has been gathered by scraping data from online resources, great care must be taken with such approaches (*http://www.chemspider.com/blog/care-in-nomenclature-handling-and-why-visual-inspection-will-remain.html*), and increasingly data is added only after some form of curation. At present the decision has been made to add specific measurements to ChemSpider on a case-by-case basis to ensure a further human curation step.

The nonaqueous solubility data measured as a part of the ONS-Solubility project is being added to ChemSpider. Currently a few values are available online as supplementary information, presented along with all other physicochemical data that might be available for a specific chemical compound. The solubility data is presented along with a link back to the experimental page, which is consistent both with the ChemSpider approach of acting as a link to the primary data source and our approach of providing a path to the data and then on to the original record. An example ChemSpider record is shown in Figure 16-3. As more nonaqueous solubility values are inserted into the record, either manually or robotically, this data will be exposed and its associated originating source information will be just one click away.

As more data, albeit with differing levels of quality and curation, is made available in the future, it can be expected that this data ingest process will be automated. Efforts are already underway to facilitate this process for the current project, but two major issues will need to be overcome before this process can become widespread. The primary issue is one of trust: which sources of data can be trusted sufficiently to be automatically ingested, and what level of curation should those data sources be expected to have? Is the current level of curation on the primary GoogleDocs spreadsheet adequate, or would a further level of filtering be required? In the current case it seems clear that our approach is not adequate for a service that aims to provide data that chemists can trust without requiring further investigation. As researchers expose more primary data and the interest in automatically ingesting it grows, there will need to be a detailed discussion about when and how data is presented, and what markup is required prior to being placed on a white list. Certification processes can be expected to grow up around the exposure of data, providing a mark of both quality and functionality for exposed data sets.

The second major issue is that of functionality. The number of exposed data sets that are relevant to ChemSpider is currently small, and in most cases reasonably stable, and so

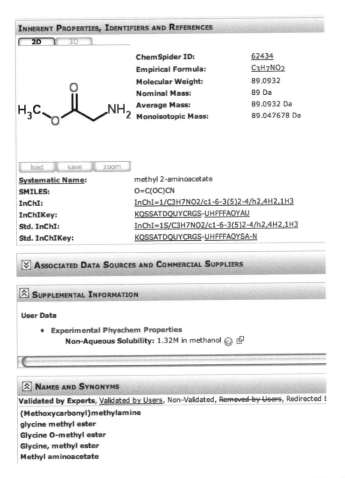

INHERENT PROPERTIES, IDENTIFIERS AND REFERENCES

| 2D | 3D |

ChemSpider ID:	62434
Empirical Formula:	$C_3H_7NO_2$
Molecular Weight:	89.0932
Nominal Mass:	89 Da
Average Mass:	89.0932 Da
Monoisotopic Mass:	89.047678 Da

load   save   zoom

Systematic Name:	methyl 2-aminoacetate
SMILES:	O=C(OC)CN
InChI:	InChI=1/C3H7NO2/c1-6-3(5)2-4/h2,4H2,1H3
InChIKey:	KQSSATDQUYCRGS-UHFFFAOYAU
Std. InChI:	InChI=1S/C3H7NO2/c1-6-3(5)2-4/h2,4H2,1H3
Std. InChIKey:	KQSSATDQUYCRGS-UHFFFAOYSA-N

⊻ ASSOCIATED DATA SOURCES AND COMMERCIAL SUPPLIERS

⊼ SUPPLEMENTAL INFORMATION

User Data

• **Experimental Physchem Properties**
    Non-Aqueous Solubility: 1.32M in methanol 🔵 🔗

⊼ NAMES AND SYNONYMS

Validated by Experts, Validated by Users, Non-Validated, ~~Removed by Users~~, Redirected l

(Methoxycarbonyl)methylamine
glycine methyl ester
Glycine O-methyl ester
Glycine, methyl ester
Methyl aminoacetate

FIGURE 16-3. This example ChemSpider entry shows the solubility value and link to the original data. (See Color Plate 55.)

manual ingest is practical though labor-intensive. As the numbers rise, such manual processes will become impossible. The presentation of the data as an online spreadsheet is convenient for the research group, but it does not necessarily directly map onto the *schema* of ChemSpider, or of any other centralized aggregation service. ChemSpider is based on a relational database running on Microsoft SQL Server. Physicochemical data, represented in the standard web page view, is held in tables within the database. In a world with tens of thousands of data providers creating heterogeneous data sets, a common language is required to enable widespread aggregation and reuse of the data. There are many competing standards for describing chemical information. The most reliable approach will be to develop a way of presenting the data that is as general as possible. Then, services can be developed to translate between different descriptive standards.

Enabling Data Integration via Unique Identifiers and Self-Describing Data Formats

Although the GoogleDoc API provides an easy route toward developing analysis tools and visualization methods that are designed specifically for this data set, it remains the case, even with a unique identifier, that the presentation of the data is not in a standard format. These tools are written against the data set as it is presented in the GoogleDoc spreadsheet. In short, they require a human to understand what descriptors and values are in which column of the spreadsheet. Although it is technically feasible to recognize that a given column contains a SMILES code, it will not be clear to a machine whether this is a solvent or solute, or indeed that the data is about solubility at all. To realize the full promise of connected data (e.g., by supporting automated ingest into ChemSpider and other services), and to provide the data in the most general possible way to other researchers, it is necessary to provide a representation that adheres to a recognized standard in syntax as well as in descriptors.

The Resource Description Framework, or RDF, provides a route toward exposing the data set in a recognized, machine-readable format. With this format, any information is transformed into statements made up of a "subject," a "predicate," and a "value." For example, the fragment shown in the following code states that the object found in the spreadsheet called solute#59 is defined as the resource at the given URL. RDF uses "namespaces," or sets of recognized concepts, to define relationships between "resources," where a resource is any object that can be pointed at by a unique identifier. There are four main namespaces used here. The first is the RDF namespace itself, which defines that the file is in RDF and provides other top-level concepts such as "is defined by" or "is a resource." The second namespace is the spreadsheet containing the data, which is a resource, defined here by the namespace ons, which contains specific resources within it, one in each cell of the spreadsheet. The third namespace is Dublin Core (dc), which deals with concepts such as name, author, and version. A fourth namespace (chem), hosted at *http://rdf.openmolecules.net* (RON), is used to specify that the molecules identified in a specific cell are defined by a specific resource.

As noted earlier, the spreadsheet has its own data *schema*, essentially relying on the fact that each row refers to a single measurement. The GoogleDocs API makes it straightforward to reference a cell using a simple URL. To make this into a declaration in RDF, we need to describe a relationship between the contents of that cell, e.g., "2-octenoic acid" and some other resource. One simple relationship is to identify "2-octenoic acid" as being defined by a specific resource at RON, which again is referenced by a simple HTTP URL. As the contents of the cell are now defined, it is possible to use the external resource to find more information related to that molecule. Resolving the URL will lead to more RDF statements about the same molecule, defined by the service at RON. Similarly, it gives the SMILES and a title to the molecule, all derived from the spreadsheet. For each and every entry representing a molecule in our data set, it is possible to define a standard description and to connect that with other standard definitions, including systematic name, InChI, and SMILES.

```
<ons:Solute rdf:about="http://spreadsheet.google.com/.../onto#solute59">
  <rdfs:isDefinedBy rdf:resource="http://rdf.openmolecules.net/?InChI=
1/C8H14O2/c1-2-3-4-5-6-7-8(9)10/h6-7H,2-5H2,1H3,(H,9,10)"/>
  <chem:inchi>InChI=1/C8H14O2/c1-2-3-4-5-6-7-8(9)10/h6-7H,2-5H2,1H3,
(H,9,10)</chem:inchi>
  <chem:smiles>CCCCCC=CC(=O)O</chem:smiles>
  <dc:title>2-octenoic acid</dc:title>
</ons:Solute>
```

Having defined each of the chemical entities found in the spreadsheet, we can now represent each measurement using a piece of RDF similar to that just shown. The RDF defines a new measurement, and gives the solvent, solute, solubility, and the experiment to which this measurement belongs. Again, because we have already defined the identity of each solvent and solute in chemical terms, this measurement information can be linked in and used with any other RDF file that describes data about the same molecule. The fragment shown next uses the XML entity ons with the value `http://spreadsheet.google.com/plwwufp3OhfqOudnEmRD1aQ/onto#` essentially as an alias to make the XML more readable (`&ons;measurement179` is expanded to the full URL with "measurement179" appended):

```
<ons:Measurement RDF:about="&ons;measurement179">
  <ons:solubility>0.44244235315106</ons:solubility>
  <ons:solvent RDF:resource="&ons;solvent8"/>
  <ons:solute RDF:resource="&ons;solute26"/>
  <ons:experiment RDF:resource="&ons;experiment2"/>
</ons:Measurement>
```

These statements, or triples, can then be read or analyzed by any RDF engine and query systems such as SPARQL. By using appropriate namespaces, especially where they are agreed and shared, it is possible to generate datafiles that are essentially self-describing. A parser has been developed (*http://github.com/egonw/onssolubility/tree/*) to generate the full RDF document, available at *http://github.com/egonw/onssolubility/tree/master/ons.solubility.RDF/ons.RDF*. The Chemistry Development Kit (CDK; see *http://cdk.sourceforge.net/*) is used to derive molecular properties from the SMILES, including the InChI. This is a key step: the conversion of experiment-specific information into a datafile that can be read by any system or service that understands RDF. Such services may not necessarily know what to do with specific concepts from new namespaces but will understand how to deal with the categories these concepts fall into, and will be able to parse the data against other resources that use the same namespace.

The real power of RDF arises when multiple resources are linked together via links (see Figure 16-4). It is possible, for instance, to link our experimental data with information in DBPedia, an online resource of information represented in RDF (*http://dbpedia.org/*). DBPedia uses a namespace called the Simple Knowledge Organization System (SKOS; see *http://www.w3.org/TR/skos-primer/*) to introduce concepts such as "category." Within DBPedia different solvents have been described as belonging to various categories, such as hydrocarbons or ethers. By combining the RDF statements from our data with that from DBPedia, it is possible to query our experimental data for examples of measurements done in different solvent categories. This is possible because the resource at RON links specific concepts (the identity of a molecule) to resources in both our data and DBPedia. This works

despite the fact that DBPedia might contain incorrect chemical names (as long as the resource links to the object with the correct InChI), that our data contains no concept of solvent category, and that DBPedia understands nothing about the ONS namespace.

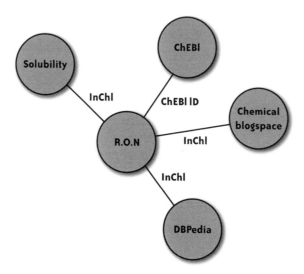

FIGURE 16-4. Connecting solubility measurements with the wider data web via RDF. RON is http://rdf.openmolecules. net, the resource that connects records from DBPedia, Chemical Blogspace, and ChEBI (a European Bioinformatics Institute Chemistry resource).

Taking this one step further, we can link our experimental data into a wider discussion on the Web by using RDF from RON to identify, for instance, which blogs have been discussing a particular chemical compound. This RDF contains links to Chemical blogspace (*http://cb. openmolecules.net/*) and shares the use of unique identifiers (in this case, the InChI is used in URI form). The rdf.openmolecules.net resource links to a range of data sources, again providing a way for data and analysis from multiple sources to be combined together. The value of the RDF approach is that additional data sources can be added at any point on the graph, without having to worry about how that information relates to that from other data sources. Work can always go into making the integration better by choosing to share more common vocabulary elements, but as long as a new data source has at least one common identifier, then data integration can begin.

Closing the Loop: Visualizations to Suggest New Experiments

As noted earlier, data from experiments can be utilized in a variety of ways, ranging from visualization to modeling. These activities are useful and can provide insight into the physical problem at hand. However, our main aim is to use the modeling and analysis to inform the design of new experiments. As the crowdsourcing effort expands, it is important to consider possible experiments and prioritize these, particularly if the ultimate aim is to enable interested, but not necessarily experienced, researchers to take part. Such computational prioritization is very useful in many scenarios, where resources (financial,

material, time) are limited and all possible experiments cannot be carried out. In the case of solubility, an experimentalist might ask, "Given the compounds tested so far, which ones should we do next?" Visualization of the data can be both compelling and provide a good guide to the best choice of the next experiment given the resources available. This enables a cyclical relationship between experiment and computation, making optimal use of both the experimentalist's and analyst's skills.

To identify which compounds we, or anyone else, should test next, we need a way of understanding where in a "chemical space" each of the compounds we have already tested lie. Then it will be possible to identify empty parts of that space in our data set, correlate that with specific molecules that lie in those spaces, and carry out those experiments. This requires the integration of information that is not found in our data. We have the identity of compounds and solvent as well as the solubility, but we do not know the characteristics of the molecules, i.e., their position in our chemical space. To obtain this information, we need to create a "mashup" of chemical data using a variety of services. We have provided a simple REST-based interface to CDK (Steinbeck 2006) descriptors. A URL of the form *http://www.chembiogrid.org/cheminfo/rest/desc/descriptors/c1ccccc1COCC* retrieves an XML document that contains multiple URLs, each one pointing to an XML document containing the value of the specific descriptor. The chemical space characteristics used in the visualizations shown here are the compound molecular weight (MW), predicted hydrophobicity (ALogP, a measure of the preference of the compound for water or oil solvents), and the calculated molecular surface area (TPSA). Many more descriptors are provided via the web service.

As all the services and data are provided on the open Web, it is possible for third parties to utilize these to prepare visualizations. Using the data in the GoogleDoc and the web services provided at Indiana, a visualization tool was independently developed that enables a multidimensional visualization of the solubilities of all compounds in a specific solvent (*http://oru.edu/cccda/sl/descriptorspace/ds.php*). In Figure 16-5, the X and Y axes display a specific molecular descriptor, the color identifies the type of compound, and the size or shape of each point shows the solubility. In addition, hovering over each point activates a tooltip giving further details, including structure and solubility. The figure shows clear areas of the chemical space that are not occupied by currently available data points (the bottom left of panel A, for instance). In principle, further services could be configured to suggest compounds that lie in those areas by querying data sources such as ChemSpider.

To expand the ability to display multiple dimensions, further visualizations were prepared in the 3-D environment of Second Life (*http://www.secondlife.com*; Figure 16-6). As with GoogleDocs, Second Life may seem an odd choice for a scientific visualization environment. However, once again it satisfies many of the criteria that we have applied to other parts of our project. It provides a (relatively) simple environment for the user in a generic package that is available free of charge. It therefore reduces barriers compared to other specially developed and often complex and expensive visualization environments. From the perspective of the visualization experience, Second Life also offers many advantages. It is possible to move around the graph, to zoom in and out, and even to walk inside and

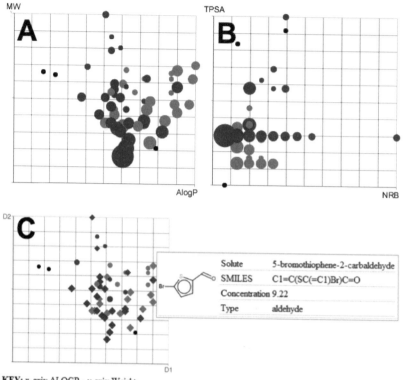

KEY: x-axis: ALOGP - y-axis: Weight
Pointsize is proportional to solubility value - Hover mouse over point to view data [Firefox].

FIGURE 16-5. Graphical representation of solubility data in chemical space. Panels A and B show two visualizations of the same data plotted onto axes representing different chemical characteristics. The color of the spots represents the chemical type (red for aldehyde, blue for carboxylic acid, yellow for amine, and black for other) and the size the solubility. Panel C illustrates the clickable interface showing the chemical structure and value of the solubility for one data point. (See Color Plate 56.)

examine the graph from that perspective. Multiple users can also simultaneously view and manipulate the same graph. From the developer's perspective, Second Life provides the ability to bring in data from the outside Web, enabling the use of the web services described earlier, and provides a clickable interface for the user to manipulate the graph or to follow links from the data points to data source and experiments. In a theoretical sense it might be preferable to use an open source rendering system that worked entirely within a web browser, but open source systems are limited and no other system offers the combination of technical ability, simplicity of interface, and usability of Second Life. In a very real sense, these compelling visualizations speak for themselves.

It is clear that easy access to data allows computational scientists to perform a variety of analyses, but the close integration of experiment and computation allows the overall investigation to be much more efficient. Although many computational analyses require significant manual input and cannot be converted to an automated online service, many are simple enough to be converted to a service that can be incorporated into a variety of platforms. The result is that it is significantly easier to analyze and manipulate the data to

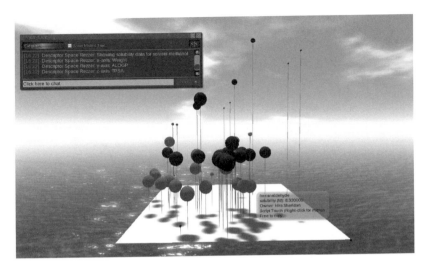

FIGURE 16-6. Representing multidimensional data using Second Life. Three chemical descriptors are represented on the three spatial axes. The color of the balls indicates the type of chemical entity (as defined in the previous figure), and the size shows the solubility in the current solvent. The visualization is available at http://slurl.com/secondlife/Drexel/165/178/24 on Drexel Island, Second Life. (See Color Plate 57.)

suggest new directions for experiments, as well as develop novel applications, by mashing together data and applications. These mashups demonstrate the power of using well-recognized and easily convertible, machine-readable identifiers. The SMILES code in this case is the key identifier that can be used to obtain further data from other web services, data sources, or data from experiments exposed by other researchers. In the future, the use of RDF to describe the results has immense promise in allowing automated integration. As RDF provides a self-describing framework based on agreed dictionaries, it is possible to search for data services that provide the desired information without any prior knowledge of where they are or what their internal data schema is. Most current mashups work by using a single common key (geographical location, search term, date) on known services with a known schema. The promise of an open data web where the links between objects are self-describing is that anyone will have the ability to create arbitrary mashups in which the search for data and information sources is an integral part of the process.

Building a Data Web from Open Data and Free Services

A large part of the art of performing and communicating science is in designing processes that remove inaccurate or misleading results, to provide a body of evidence that clearly supports a simplifying explanation that humans can understand. Science can be seen as the process of reducing pieces of the world into intelligible models. Part of the problem of this approach is the tendency to oversimplify to either strengthen an argument or, in the case of very complex systems, just to make it comprehensible.

Our approach is to embrace the complexity of real measurements by making all the detail available. We aim to balance the issues that this complexity creates with the need for clear and useful data sets by filtering the primary record in as transparent a way as possible to create the primary data set. The availability of storage space on the Web at near zero cost and the wide availability of high-quality, freely hosted services makes it possible to host the whole of the research record in the public view. There is simply no longer any excuse for writing "data not shown." But the desire to provide access to the full record creates new problems.

The first of these is simply volume. The research record itself tends to be a large body of largely unstructured text and images. Widespread standards do not exist to represent this type of information in a way that is easily parsed by either humans or machines. Summaries and filtering are required to make available the information contained in the record. We chose to use a GoogleDocs spreadsheet as the primary source of extracted data. The process of extracting data from the record remains subjective and manual for the moment. The spreadsheet provides a natural interface for humans, and in particular experimental scientists, while also providing a range of effective interface options for web services to reprocess and represent the data.

It is possible to imagine scraping data directly from the experimental report. With a small amount of informal formatting and regular expression analysis and conversion of a feed generated from the record, it would be possible to automatically populate the spreadsheet. We have not pursued this, because we wish to include a human filtering process at this stage. As the project increases in size, this will become untenable at some scale. The choices about what scale will depend on the project, the type of data, and the need or desire for precision and accuracy in the presented data set.

Once the data is made public it is open for use by any interested researcher, and the Google-Doc API makes it possible to exploit the data for a wide range of services. This can include visualization or analysis services. These services will be dependent on understanding how the data is structured within the spreadsheet. This means they will generally be written against the specific data set. However, even in this case it is straightforward to leverage a wide range of services, data sources, and visualization tools to create highly effective data displays, ranging from tables and simple graphs to clickable interfaces in five, seven, or more dimensions. Open standards and open systems provide the ability to move data and information to the places where it can be most effectively used. The promise of truly open and self-describing data formats is immense but unrealized, even in data-driven sciences such as chemistry, due to both technical and social difficulties in translating from records in the form that experimentalists understand to properly structured machine-readable forms as understood by computers and the people who code on them. Here we have shown the ability to convert data in the form of a spreadsheet (something that experimentalists are familiar and comfortable with) to RDF, but other formats could be served just as easily.

The provision of such general data formats makes it possible to create services that integrate data from multiple sources. A wide range of data sources containing information on solubility, or perhaps other information in our data set, could be integrated and analyzed together. This will make it possible for aggregation and link farm services, such as Chem-Spider and others, not just to automatically aggregate data, something that is already technically feasible, but to make educated decisions about the level of curation required by data from different sources, and to deploy human curation where it is most needed. This centralization, in turn, provides a valuable indexing service, providing a central location online where users can find sources for the data they are looking for.

One of the central themes of all the work described here is the use of free hosted systems that provide enough functionality without overburdening the user with complexity. For most of the recording, aggregating, analysis, visualization, and presentation steps, there are more advanced, more general, or more sophisticated tools available. To record the research, we could have used a commercial Electronic Laboratory Notebook or a specially designed online system; instead, we used a freely hosted wiki service. The presentation of the primary data could have used a database backend with a content management system to provide sophisticated visualizations; we used an online spreadsheet and its API with some JavaScript to present a range of visualizations. There are many highly functional and sophisticated 3-D viewing environments available; we used Second Life.

Part of the rationale for this is cost. All the services we used are free at point of access, allowing an essentially unmanaged development process to grow and attract new collaborators with low barriers to their entry. However, a significant part of the rationale is to use services that are fit for purpose without being overly sophisticated. Forging an effective link between experimentalists and analytical and theoretical scientists is always a challenge. The use of the spreadsheet as a source of data that can be automatically or manually converted to well-described formats (a formal relational database), or self-describing and extensible formats (RDF), or simply readily transformed directly into sophisticated visualizations, illustrates the use of the spreadsheet as a meeting point. Experimental scientists like and understand spreadsheets. Computational scientists may prefer either text files over which code can be run, databases, or formats such as XML and RDF. Key to bringing these communities together will be the ability to convert backward and forward into preferred formats in a fully automated fashion.

Finally, the key to the whole project is trust and transparency. As a record is converted into data, and data is converted into information, and finally as information is converted into a model or theory, context is lost at every stage. The details, which are often messy, get left behind so that the bigger picture can emerge. This is entirely appropriate. Science is the process of summarizing observations in a way that allows us to predict what will happen in the future. As with our choice of services, a scientific model or theory is useful if it is good enough to save us the time of doing the experiments most of the time. Traditionally, however, this summarizing process has come at the price of losing access to the detail. In the world of the Web, where storage is cheap, this no longer needs to be the

case. Now the choice lies in how to present the underlying detail, what filters to apply in the summarizing process, and how to retain the links between the summaries and the original records.

These are not easy decisions, and we would not claim to have got all of them right. Nonetheless, we believe this project can act as an exemplar of the approach. Over the course of four months, a project that started as a discussion between two people on a train has grown into a multinational data collection, visualization, and modeling effort where all participants have access to all of the data and analysis in real time. The collaboration can easily grow as new researchers become interested. Our open data and open services have enabled the creation of compelling new visualizations without requiring any direct involvement from the experimentalists themselves. These visualizations are both useful to the experimentalists and strikingly beautiful in their own right. Yet they represent only a small proportion of what could be done, by anyone, with the data we have exposed. At the same time they always provide a link back to the original record, with all its blemishes and weaknesses, allowing any user to assess the validity and strength of any specific data point at the resolution she chooses.

Beauty is often seen as being related to simplicity or symmetry, a sense that the whole can be described using a simple mathematical description. This is rarely the case with real experimental data. The beauty that lies, sometimes hidden, within experimental data may take extensive filtering to reveal. But, if the true beauty lies in understanding, as far as we can, what is really happening at the deepest possible level in the world around us, then we can uncover only a limited amount of that beauty through any given analysis. By providing access to as much of the record as we can, we make it possible for other researchers to discover and reveal more of the beauty that is hidden beneath the surface.

Acknowledgments

The authors would like to acknowledge the efforts of the researchers who collected the majority of the data, Khalid Mirza, Jennifer Hale, and Tim Bohinski; Bill Hooker for assisting with judging of the Open Notebook Science Challenge; and the financial and in-kind support of Submeta and Nature Publishing Group.

References

Bradley, Jean-Claude. 2007. "Open Notebook Science Using Blogs and Wikis." Available from *Nature Precedings, http://dx.doi.org/10.1038/npre.2007.39.1.*

Bradley, Jean-Claude et al. 2008. "Optimization of the Ugi reaction using parallel synthesis and automated liquid handling." *Journal of Visualized Experiments, http://dx.doi.org/10.3791/942.*

Steinbeck, C. et al. 2006. *Current Pharmaceutical Design*, 12, 2110–2120.

Superficial Data Analysis: Exploring Millions of Social Stereotypes

Brendan O'Connor and Lukas Biewald

Introduction

HOW DO WE PERCEIVE AGE, GENDER, INTELLIGENCE, AND ATTRACTIVENESS? WHAT INSIGHT CAN WE extract from millions of anonymous opinions?

Last year we, with Chris Van Pelt, built the website *FaceStat.com*, where users can upload their own photos, as well as look at and judge photos of other people (see Figure 17-1). The site became surprisingly popular. More than 100,000 brave users have uploaded pictures of themselves, friends, relatives, enemies, etc., and more than 10 million judgments have been collected for preselected questions such as:

- How old do I look?

- Do you think I look smart?

- Do you think I could win a fight with a medium-size dog?

- Describe me in one word.

We like to call it "multivariate Hot-or-Not."

FIGURE 17-1. The FaceStat judging interface. (See Color Plate 58.)

Researchers in psychology and sociology have extensively studied stereotypes and how our appearances influence the way we are perceived. But no one has had access to such a large pool of data from such a diverse group of people. This data is much messier than a typical lab experiment, but can volume make up for a lack of control? In fact, real-world data might be most revealing: someone who thinks she's playing a game could be more honest than a college sophomore taking a survey in his Psych 101 course.

We love exploring big data sets. Rather than confirm prebaked hypotheses, we'll search for interesting patterns and correlations. We won't try to hide or gloss over the messy outliers and missing values; instead, we'll show you explicitly the choices we're forced to make. We will refrain from drawing grand or controversial conclusions about stereotyping and let the data speak for itself.

Preprocessing the Data

We'll start from the beginning: like many websites, FaceStat runs on an SQL database. The judgment interface takes user judgments and saves them as a set of (face ID, attribute, judgment) triples. The first thing we do is extract those 10 million rows from the database. This gives us a file that looks like:

```
face_id    key          value
149777     describe     serious
18717      trustworthy  3
140467     attractive   2
149777     describe     five-head
...
```

We're interested in exploring the relationships between different types of perceived attributes. One interesting question is, "How old do I look?" The very first thing to do is to look at the responses that people have given. Unix command-line tools make it easy to quickly see a histogram of responses. The most common responses look like reasonable ages, but we also see a problem:

Look at	`$ cat data.tsv |`
age judgments'	`grep "age" |`
values	`cut -f3 |`
and count how many times	`sort |`
each value occurs,	`uniq -c |`
and order by this count.	`sort -nr`

Here's the output of this shell pipeline. For each line, the first number is the frequency count. The second string is the response value—exactly what the user typed in the web form in response to the question *How old do I look?* Most often, she typed in a number, but there are some issues:

```
70472 19
70021 22
69387 18
68423 17
...
27 24\r\n
27 17\r\n
23 01
21 16\r\n
...
1 old enough to know better
1 hopefully over 21
1 e
1 ??
...
```

FaceStat has existed for eight months and undergone many changes, so data has been collected under different circumstances. Some weird web browsers seem to add the white-space control codes \r\n. At some point there was a bug and users slipped in textual responses and other problematic data. Looking at rare values from the bottom of the sort | uniq -c | sort -nr histogram is an easy way to reveal data bugs, since they often manifest as outliers. We have to write some regular expressions that can clean out bad values like this.

It would be tedious to go into detail about all of the sanity checks and data cleanup, but they are a crucial first step for any data analysis. With any human-generated data set, there's bound to be messy outliers. For example, we found one person who figured out a way to circumvent the randomness in the selection of which face to judge, and labeled one face "mr. cool" hundreds of times.

Besides cleanup, some critical decisions to make for this particular data set are: (1) how to map from multiple-choice responses such as "very trustworthy" versus "not to be trusted" to a numerical value, and (2) how to aggregate results from multiple people into a single

description of a face. Every face has some 100 judgments among several different attributes. We'll simply average the numeric judgments. (Under this paradigm, we ignore textual judgments; we'll get to those later.) So each face has an average perceived age, perceived intelligence, etc. Using SQL and Python scripts, we eventually end up with a file with one row per face. It looks something like Table 17-1.

TABLE 17-1. Per-face data

male	age	intelligence	attractive	poli_affil
TRUE	24.26667	NA	2.800000	NA
TRUE	47.00000	3.400000	2.120000	3.2
TRUE	29.27273	2.700000	2.083333	1.8
FALSE	17.63636	3.111111	2.428571	NA
FALSE	19.58333	NA	2.750000	NA
TRUE	22.80953	NA	2.250000	NA
TRUE	29.77778	1.833333	1.900000	NA
FALSE	18.16667	NA	2.571429	NA
TRUE	46.60000	3.200000	2.120000	3.4
TRUE	52.06667	3.000000	2.080000	NA

In all, there are tens of thousands of faces with about 20 different attributes. There are many missing values: different questions were asked of different people. With those caveats in mind, we're ready to load the data into a package for more detailed analysis. If you want to follow along, we've made a subset of the data and useful code available at *http://data.doloreslabs.com*.

Exploring the Data

There are many great tools for data analysis. Some of the most commonly used are compared in Table 17-2.

TABLE 17-2. Comparison of data analysis packages

Name	Advantages	Disadvantages	Open source?	Typical users
R	Library support; visualization	Steep learning curve	Yes	Statistics
Matlab	Elegant matrix support; visualization	Expensive; incomplete statistics support	No	Engineering
SciPy/NumPy/Matplotlib	Python: flexible and general-purpose programming language	Components poorly integrated	Yes	Engineering
Excel	Easy; visual; flexible	Large data sets; weak numeric and programming support	No	Business
SAS	Very large data sets	Very baroque; hardest to learn	No	Business
SPSS, Stata	Easy statistical analysis	Inflexible	No	Science (bio and social)

We like to use R, which is an open source statistical and visualization programming environment with a vibrant and growing development community. It's emerged as a de facto standard among statisticians. For exploratory data analysis, we prefer it to the other options because of its graphing libraries, convenient indexing notation, and an amazing array of statistically sophisticated, community-maintained packages. You can read about it and download it at *http://www.r-project.org*; also look at the references at the end of this chapter.

R provides many excellent tools for looking at what's in the data. From its interactive interpreter:

Load the data   > data = read.delim("http://data.doloreslabs.com/face_scores.tsv", sep="\t")
and plot.   > plot(data)

Given a basic table of records, R's default plotting action is to give us a scatterplot matrix of every pair of variables. (See Figure 17-2.) One thing that jumps out is that the age correlations look funny—the rightmost column and bottommost row.

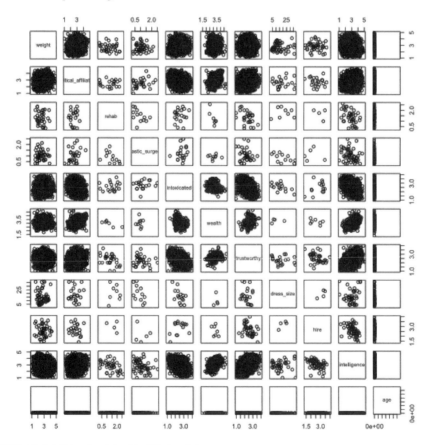

FIGURE 17-2. Initial scatterplot matrix of the face data.

We need to investigate. The first thing to do is look at the distribution of age values. (See Figure 17-3.)

```
> hist(data$age)
```

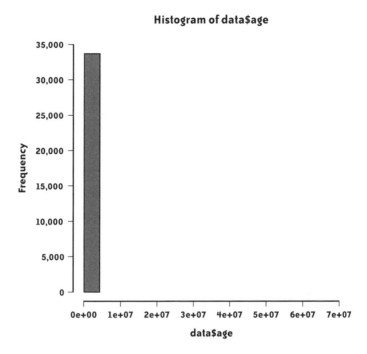

Histogram of data$age

FIGURE 17-3. Initial histogram of face age data.

This doesn't look right. The x-axis has been scaled all the way up to 70 million because of outliers. Let's look at the records with outlying age values:

Select records with age greater than 100.   > data[which(data$age > 100),]

id	num_judgments	age	male	attractive	intelligence
40623	150	402.3333	TRUE	2.416667	NA
57021	133	47882.3010	TRUE	NA	NA
66441	197	66666692.0000	TRUE	NA	NA

Earlier, we cleaned out the non-numeric age values, but we didn't check for absurdly high values. For now the easiest thing to do is just remove these outliers. If you haven't used a data analysis language before, notice how R's rich subscripting notation makes basic exploration and cleaning easy and fun:

Subselect rows with age less than 100.   > clean_data = data[which(data$age < 100),]

We check the histogram again—Figure 17-4—and find out that most of our users are (or appear to be) between 18 and 30, which seems reasonable.

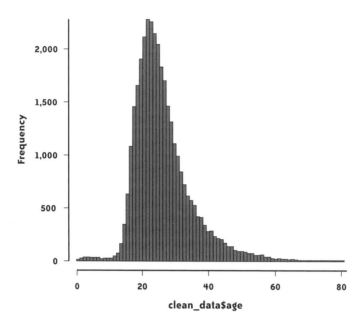

Histogram of clean_data$age

FIGURE 17-4. Histogram of cleaned face age data.

Age, Attractiveness, and Gender

We want to zoom in on interactions of some of the most interesting perceived attributes: age, gender, and attractiveness. Whenever we have a table with a few interesting columns, it's straightforward and often informative to throw it up as a scatterplot (see Figure 17-5):

Draw a scatterplot of age vs. attractiveness,
using gender to define the points' colors.

```
> plot(d$age, d$attractive,
    col = ifelse(d$male, 'blue', 'deeppink'))
```

This plot is suggestive; for example, women seem to be more attractive than men. But it's hard to tell anything for sure, since tens of thousands of points are being drawn over one another. When there is an overload of data, scatterplots can be misleading. One way to deal with this is to smooth the data, by plotting an estimated distribution rather than the points themselves (see Figure 17-6). We use a standard technique called kernel density estimation:

Lay out side-by-side plots.
For males and females,
draw smoothed plots,
with a color gradient,
and aligned axes.

```
> par(mfrow=c(1,2))
> dm = d[d$male,];  df = d[d$female,]
> smoothScatter(df$age, df$attractive,
    colramp = colorRampPalette(c("white", "deeppink")),
    ylim=c(0,4))
> smoothScatter(dm$age, dm$attractive,
    colramp = colorRampPalette(c("white", "blue")),
    ylim=c(0,4))
```

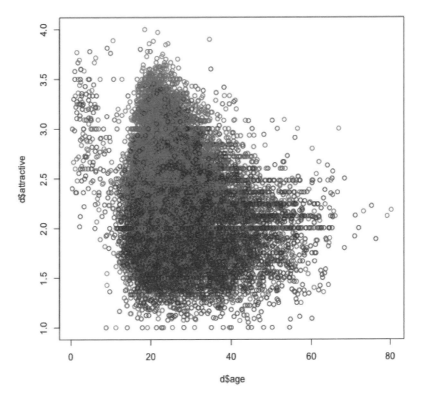

FIGURE 17-5. Scatterplot of attractiveness versus age, colored by gender. (See Color Plate 59.)

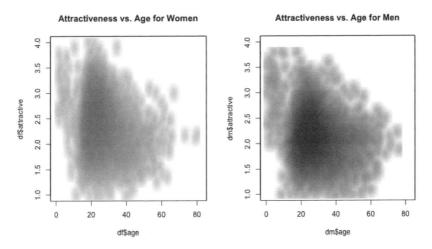

FIGURE 17-6. Smoothed scatterplots for attractiveness versus age, one plot per gender. (See Color Plate 60.)

We can even try putting them on the same plot (see Figure 17-7):

```
> smoothScatterMult(d$age, d$attractive, d$male, blendFun=bl_burn, colramps =
c(colorRampPalette(c("white", "red")), colorRampPalette(c("white", "blue")),
colorRampPalette(c("white", "green"))), pch="", nrpoints=10000)
```

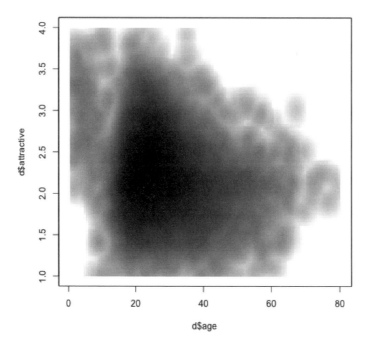

FIGURE 17-7. Smoothed scatterplots for attractiveness versus age, colored by gender and overlaid on one plot. (See Color Plate 61.)

These graphs show the full distribution of the data, but it's hard to see patterns. For example, how does age affect attractiveness? It's easier to see this by computing summary statistics and plotting them. (See Figure 17-8a.)

For males	`> dm = d[which(d$male),]`
and females,	`> df = d[which(d$female),]`
average across faces	`> male_avg_by_year = by(dm$attractive,`
within bins	`    cut(dm$age, breaks=0:80), mean)`
(one per year)	`> female_avg_by_year = by(df$attractive,`
then	`    cut(df$age, breaks=0:80), mean)`
plot them	`> plot(male_avg_by_year, col='blue')`
all together.	`> points(female_avg_by_year, col='deeppink')`

This graph starts to tell a story, but it's still a bit hard to read. Some of the points are averages from thousands of faces, whereas some of the more elderly points come from just a handful of observations. Therefore, there's more noise on the right since the samples are smaller.

We'll add two new features to the plot (see Figure 17-8b). First, we compute 95% confidence intervals to make sure we're not fooling ourselves into seeing patterns from noise. Confidence intervals are a way to estimate a range of possible means with the limited data we have. Second, we'll fit a loess curve to help visualize aggregate patterns in this noisy sequential data. Ordinarily, we might fit a linear regression to the data, but this data isn't linear, and doesn't look like any function we know of. A loess function ("locally weighted regression") is a way to fit an arbitrary curve to data. It's basically a fancier moving average.

This graph still isn't perfect. There are a number of points around the edges with just one or two samples where it's impossible to compute confidence intervals. This is not surprising if you look back at that age histogram in Figure 17-4—people who appear to be over 50 make up only 1.7% of the data set. Furthermore, many intervals are so big that the data points they represent aren't that meaningful. So, for the areas where we have fewer data points—the very young and the old—we use larger 5- and 10-year buckets. This graph looks far less noisy (see Figure 17-8c).

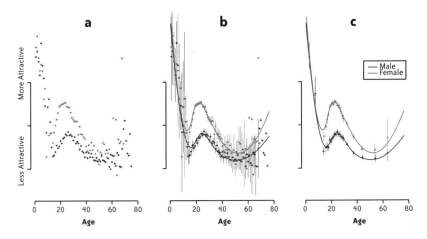

FIGURE 17-8. Three iterations of plotting attractiveness versus age versus gender: (a) ages averaged within buckets per age year, (b) 95% confidence interval for each bucket, plus loess curves, and (c) larger buckets where the data is sparser. (See Color Plate 62.)

Women are generally judged as more attractive than men across all ages except babies. Babies are found to be most attractive, but the attractiveness drops until around age 18 (perhaps users are uncomfortable judging adolescents as "attractive"?), after which it rises and peaks around age 27. After that, attractiveness drops until around age 50, at which point it seems to increase again. But it's hard to say for sure, since the data is very sparse among people perceived to be older than 50.

Of course, among the 20 or so nontextual attributes, there are many more relationships to explore. We could make many more plots similar to Figure 17-8, but could we view all interesting interactions at once? Let's stay with the approach of looking at pairwise interactions and make a variant of the pairs plot from earlier. Instead of trying to show a scatterplot in every panel, we instead show a single color indicating the overall correlation between the attributes. Blue is a positive correlation, and red is a negative one (see Figure 17-9).

First compute pairwise correlations, and order the attributes to try to put similar attributes next to each other. Plot the correlation matrix, with axis labels.

```
> cors = cor(d, use='pair')
> ord = order.hclust(cors)
> cors = cors[ord,ord]
> image(cors, col=col.corrgram(7))
> axis(1, at=seq(0,1, length=nrow(cors)),
      labels=row.names(cors))
```

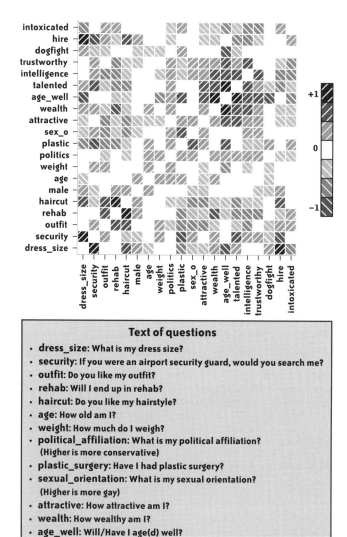

Text of questions

- **dress_size:** What is my dress size?
- **security:** If you were an airport security guard, would you search me?
- **outfit:** Do you like my outfit?
- **rehab:** Will I end up in rehab?
- **haircut:** Do you like my hairstyle?
- **age:** How old am I?
- **weight:** How much do I weigh?
- **political_affiliation:** What is my political affiliation? (Higher is more conservative)
- **plastic_surgery:** Have I had plastic surgery?
- **sexual_orientation:** What is my sexual orientation? (Higher is more gay)
- **attractive:** How attractive am I?
- **wealth:** How wealthy am I?
- **age_well:** Will/Have I age(d) well?
- **talented:** Am I talented?
- **intelligence:** How smart am I?
- **trustworthy:** How trustworthy am I?
- **dogfight:** Do you think I would win a fight with a medium sized dog?
- **hire:** Would you hire me?
- **intoxicated:** How intoxicated am I?

FIGURE 17-9. Pearson correlation matrix; attribute pairs with blue squares and upward sloped lines are positively correlated, while pairs with red squares and downward sloped lines are anticorrelated. (See Color Plate 63.)

This plot is rich with interesting correlations that could warrant further investigation:

- Women are judged as more intelligent than men.

- Women are judged more likely to win a dogfight.

- Dress size is only weakly correlated with weight.

- Women are more likely to be hired as security guards.

- People who look like they have had plastic surgery are less likely to be hired as security guards.

- Trustworthiness, intelligence, talent, aging well, wealth, and conservativeness all correlate with one another. An "axis of responsibility"?

Looking at Tags

In addition to all this ordinal and numeric data, we have a set of free-form tags that users are able enter about a person's picture. The tags range from descriptive ("freckles", "nosering") to crass ("takemetobed", "dirtypits") to friendly ("you.look.good.in.red") to advice ("cutyourhair", "avoidsun") to editorial ("awwdorable!!!!!", "EnoughUploadsNancy") to mean ("Thefatfriend") to nonsensical ("...", "plokmnjiuhbygvtfcrdxeszwaq"). In general, free-text data is more complicated to process.

The first thing to do is examine the distribution of the tags. What's the most common tag?

Load our tags	`> face_tags = read.delim("face_tags.tsv",sep="\t",as.is=T)`
then count	`> counts = table(face_tags$tag)`
and rank them.	`> sorted_counts = sort(counts, decreasing=T)`
Show the most common tags.	`> sorted_counts[1:20]`

The following table contains the output.

cute	pretty	happy	nice	fun	young
81333	40954	36263	33221	30622	27900
sweet	friendly	cool	weird	hot	gay
20362	14895	14709	12731	12662	12409
Cute	funny	scary	sexy	old	goofy
12132	11508	11445	11287	10958	10511
emo	shy				
10292	10207				

What are the least common tags?

Show the least common tags.	`> tail(sorted_count, 20)`

überdude	übersöt	ünsall
1	1	1
ýour.nose.is.sexymamama!!	我	浅
1	1	1
良	?	♥haiir!!
1	1	1
白人	賢母	— —;
1	1	1
шдд	オタク	ロンリー
1	1	1
ешкув	сшеет	херня
1	1	1
ダースベイダー	Красивая!	
1	1	1

Glancing at a few of the tags raises questions about normalization. Should "cute" and "Cute" be merged into the same tag? Should punctuation be dropped entirely? Should that funny-looking full-width question mark for Asian languages be considered the same as the standard ASCII question mark? Clearly, it depends on the application. Whenever possible, our instinct is to err on the side of caution and leave the original data intact. This preserves information; for example, the tags "hot" and "HOT!!!" certainly have different semantic content. It's always easier to carefully merge data when necessary for a specific visualization or analysis, rather than try to guess ahead of time what all the requirements are and be forced to undo earlier normalization decisions.

A basic plot of a tag distribution looks at frequency of a tag against its frequency rank. Typically, when counting words or other lexical items, we see a quick drop-off from the most frequent words to less frequent words. In our data, there are 290,000 unique tags out of 2.4 million total. The top 1,000 unique tags have 1.4 million occurrences—more than half the total mass of tags. And just among those, there's a sharp fall-off. From our table of common tags, we see that the most common tag, "cute", has 36,000 occurrences, but the second most common, "pretty", has just half of that. (See Figure 17-10.)

For the top 1,000 tags, draw a plot of their counts.

```
> s = sorted_counts[1:1000]
> barplot(s)
```

In 1935, the linguist George Zipf observed that word frequency distributions often follow a "power law," where the frequency of the nth word is proportional to $(1/ns)$, where s is a constant. Unlike a Gaussian distribution, this distribution has infinite variance, which can make it somewhat unwieldy for certain statistical algorithms. Popular books such as Nassim Nicholas Taleb's *The Black Swan* (Random House) and Chris Anderson's *The Long Tail* (Hyperion) have made these distributions famous as "fat tail" and "long tail" distributions, respectively. Indeed, our data has quite a long tail: 220,000 words, or 76% of the vocabulary, occur only once.

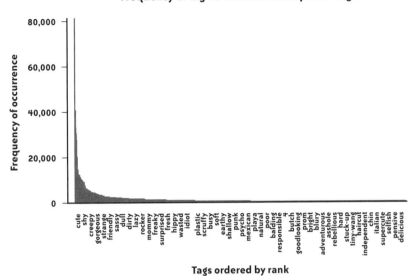

Frequency of tag vs. Rank for the top 1000 tags

FIGURE 17-10. Tag frequencies for top 1,000 tags.

We can check to see whether we have a power-law distribution by plotting our word frequencies in log space (see Figure 17-11):

Plot log ranks against log frequency.

```
> log_ranks = log(1:length(sorted_counts))
> plot(log_ranks, log(sorted_counts))
```

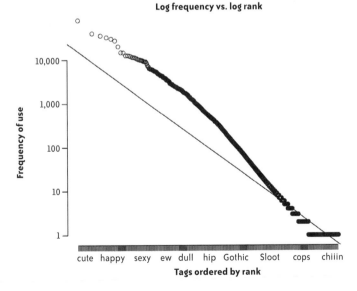

Log frequency vs. log rank

FIGURE 17-11. Tags' log frequencies by log rank, with fitted line from the power law model.

A power-law distribution should look linear in the log-log space:

Fit a model of log count against log rank and draw it on Figure 17-10.

```
> model = lm(log(sorted_counts) ~ log_ranks)
> abline(model)
```

We find our tags' frequencies are fairly close to a $(1/n^{.80})$ distribution. (If you don't think it looks like the best-fit line, keep in mind that 76% of all the points are on that last bottom-right ledge of the data.)

If you do this log-log frequency plot on any sort of text—newspapers, novels, web pages, etc.—it looks similar.[*] Perhaps unsurprisingly, when FaceStat users write description tags, they're engaging in a linguistic behavior that has some fundamental similarities to other types of human communication.

How do the tags fit in with the rest of our data? A first pass is to randomly sample from the tags and overlay them on plots that we've already generated. (See Figure 17-12.)

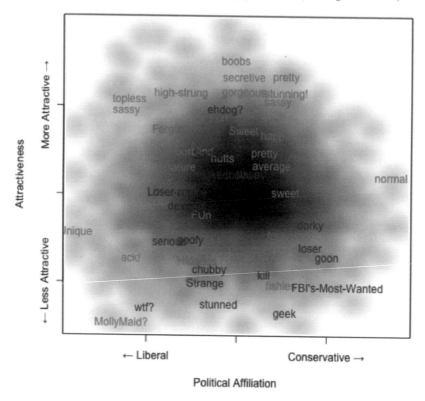

FIGURE 17-12. Tag sample plotted on a smoothed attractiveness versus age scatterplot. (See Color Plate 64.)

---

[*] Zipf, George. 1935. *The Psychobiology of Language* (MIT Press). See also *http://en.wikipedia.org/wiki/Zipf's_law.*

Here the darkness of the plot shows the density in the overall distribution of Political Affiliation versus Attractiveness. Words are randomly sampled from throughout the distribution. The blue words are tags for males, and the pink words indicate tags for females. This gives us a sense for whether or not the tags are corresponding to the variables in the plot. The data looks roughly reasonable: the tag "average" shows up in the middle of the graph, while someone tagged "topless" is in the liberal/attractive quadrant and someone tagged "dorky" is in the conservative/unattractive quadrant. The graph can be regenerated multiple times with different random number seeds to look at distributions of tags throughout the data.

Which Words Are Gendered?

Many social theorists have wondered to what extent gender is reflected in language. Our data set lets us explore this at the word level: we can find which description tags are most characteristic of male or female faces. We could just count the words that occur most often for men and the words that occur most often for women, but generally this just gets words that are frequent everywhere. A better approach is to score tags by their ratio of occurrences between genders. That is, to determine how characteristic a tag T is for gender G, look at:

$$\frac{\text{no. of occurrences of tag } T \text{ for a face with gender } G}{\text{no. of occurrences of tag } T \text{ overall}}$$

This has a flaw: rare tags introduce noise. For example, any tag that appears just once automatically gets a perfect score of 1 for whichever gender it appeared with. (This is another example of error due to small sample sizes that we saw for sparse age buckets.) A simple way around this is to use a frequency threshold. In this case, we'll only look at tags that occur more than 100 times.

Calculating these scores—in statistical terminology, they're maximum likelihood estimates of the conditional probabilities $Pr(G|T)$—we get the following tables.

Words most characteristic of men are shown in the following table.

	G	T	Ratio
daddy	122	122	1.0000000
fatherly	115	115	1.0000000
fratboy	177	177	1.0000000
father	172	173	0.9942197
dad	341	343	0.9941691
douche	229	231	0.9913420
Handsome	110	111	0.9909910
scruffy	149	151	0.9867550
bald	343	350	0.9800000
jock	395	404	0.9777228
handsome	510	524	0.9732824

	G	T	Ratio
thug	141	145	0.9724138
tool	255	264	0.9659091
player	522	542	0.9630996
Gay	307	319	0.9623824
jerk	131	137	0.9562044
gamer	103	108	0.9537037
fag	148	156	0.9487179
pimp	121	128	0.9453125

Words most characteristic of women are as follows.

	G	T	Ratio
Bubbly	118	118	1.0000000
Mom	161	161	1.0000000
busty	148	148	1.0000000
milf	267	267	1.0000000
mom	1,088	1,088	1.0000000
motherly	396	396	1.0000000
partygirl	221	221	1.0000000
mommy	307	308	0.9967532
mother	358	360	0.9944444
ditzy	144	145	0.9931034
fjortis	113	114	0.9912281
MILF	103	104	0.9903846
Pretty	926	935	0.9903743
cheerleader	159	161	0.9875776
boobs	153	155	0.9870968
makeup	143	145	0.9862069
bitchy	284	288	0.9861111
cougar	141	143	0.9860140
slutty	538	546	0.9853480
slut	509	517	0.9845261

It's perhaps surprising how extremely gendered words such as "handsome," "gamer," "Bubbly," and "slut" are. They appear with their gender almost *all* of the time.

Clustering

What are the typical types of people in our data? Clustering is a powerful statistical method to find this sort of pattern. A clustering algorithm splits data points into several characteristic classes by grouping together similar instances. There are many methods for clustering, but one of the most popular and simple methods is called *k-means*. In k-means, each cluster has a center point, a "centroid." Several different centroids are found in the

data and each data point is assigned to a centroid. The algorithm iteratively adjusts the clusters so that as many data points as possible are close to their assigned centroids.

In our data set, each face has about 20 numeric attributes. Thus, faces are points in a 20-dimensional space. K-means will place faces into several different clusters within that space, trying to select clusters where faces are as similar to their cluster's center as possible.

One unfortunate aspect about k-means clustering is that you have to pick a fixed number of clusters, "k", upfront. However, there isn't an obvious way to choose the number of clusters. The best thing to do is to try a few different numbers and see what patterns emerge. Here's one run of k-means we did that gave reasonable output:

Preprocess the data,
by changing missing values to the mean,
and unit-normalizing values,
which usually makes k-means work better.
Then run k-means for 5 clusters,
and plot attractiveness vs. age,
but color by
cluster assignment,
and have fun with unicode.

```
> norm_data = apply(d, 2, function(x) {
    x[is.na(x)] = mean(x, na.rm=TRUE)
    x = (x - mean(x)) / sd(x)
    x })
> clus = kmeans(norm_data, 5)
> plot(d$age, d$attractive,
    col = c("red", "purple", "blue", "orange",
    "green","darkturquoise")[clus$cluster],
    pch = ifelse(d$male, '\u2642', '\u2640'))
```

Points on the scatterplot represent faces, with colors corresponding to the clusters they were assigned to. We're showing faces within the attractiveness versus age space, like our earlier plots. A few clusters are already interpretable: the orange cluster corresponds to older people, purple seems to be attractive young people, and so on.

This plot shows only 2 or 3 dimensions of the data, so does not adequately summarize the clustering algorithm, which compares faces in the full 20-dimensional space. That's why some clusters overlap: for example, red and green seem to have fairly similar ranges of age and attractiveness. Those clusters must differ by other attributes.

Let's look at individual clusters in several ways. First we show a cluster's attribute weights. This is the position of the cluster's centroid point, which can be thought of as the typical attributes for a face in that cluster. So if you looked at the average points per cluster in Figure 17-13, that would give you the cluster weightings for age and attractiveness. (We'll show eight attributes; the rest are insignificant because of too many missing values.) Second, we show the top 10 characteristic tags for faces in that cluster, ranked by conditional probability like in the earlier gender analysis.

First off, here's the purple cluster in Figure 17-14. This is a heavily female, highly attractive cluster. The tags are interesting. They uncannily resemble the attributes; in fact, if you cover up the graph on the left, you probably could guess many of the attributes for the group. The tags paint a coherent and vivid picture—even though our k-means algorithm completely ignored this information! This illustrates that tags have intuitive correlations to social attributes. (Perhaps this is not surprising.)

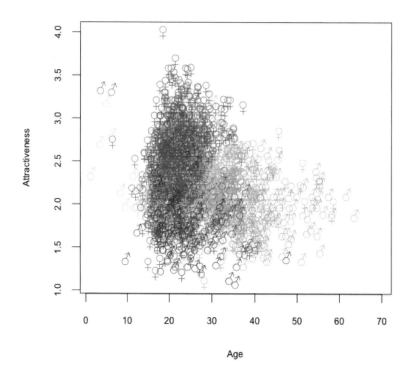

Attractiveness

Age

FIGURE 17-13. Attractiveness versus age, colored by cluster, showing a subsample of 2,000 points. (See Color Plate 65.)

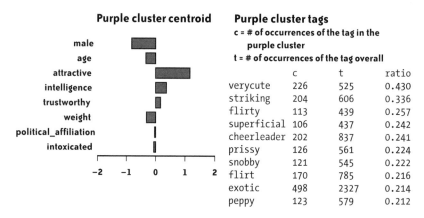

Purple cluster centroid

male
age
attractive
intelligence
trustworthy
weight
political_affiliation
intoxicated

Purple cluster tags

c = # of occurrences of the tag in the
   purple cluster
t = # of occurrences of the tag overall

	c	t	ratio
verycute	226	525	0.430
striking	204	606	0.336
flirty	113	439	0.257
superficial	106	437	0.242
cheerleader	202	837	0.241
prissy	126	561	0.224
snobby	121	545	0.222
flirt	170	785	0.216
exotic	498	2327	0.214
peppy	123	579	0.212

FIGURE 17-14. Cluster 2.

We've put all the clusters in Figures 17-15 and 17-16, along with the four most representative faces (meaning those closest to the centroid) per cluster.

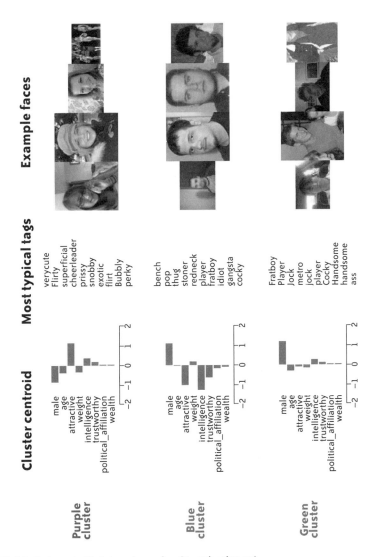

FIGURE 17-15. Cluster centroids, tags, and exemplars. (See Color Plate 66.)

Some of the clusters have straightforward interpretations, and some are less clear:

Purple cluster
Young, attractive women.

Blue cluster
Unattractive, unintelligent men. ("Losers"?)

Green cluster
Other, more generic young men. Many of its tags are also highly likely for the blue cluster.

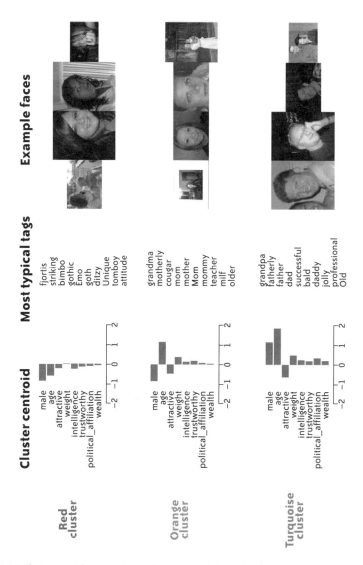

FIGURE 17-16. Cluster centroids, tags, and exemplars, continued. (See Color Plate 67.)

Red cluster
Other young women.

Orange cluster
Older women.

Turquoise cluster
Older men.

Clustering can be useful to find high-dimensional patterns or groups in data that are hard to visualize in two dimensions. On the other hand, it's hard to validate whether clustering is telling you anything "real." There are many clustering algorithms and many parameters to tweak (such as that *k*), which can give different results. Was this exercise useful?

Well, the clusters seem fairly coherent, and are quite suggestive of a number of patterns. It's interesting to see vivid sets of tags are associated with each. And k-means might provide an analogue to how our minds think of people. From the centroids and tag sets, we can imagine a prototypical person representing each cluster.

Conclusion

Our data indicates that people hold some familiar stereotypes. Women are considered more attractive than men. Age has a stronger attractiveness effect for women than men. The space of social attributes falls along lines that feel familiar to us: jocks, fathers, attractive young women. But there are also some potential surprises: babies are most attractive, conservatives look more intelligent, etc. We also found examples of gendered words.

We're tempted to go on and on with suggestive findings, but the point of this chapter is not to come to any particular conclusion. Instead, we wanted to show some examples of the rich set of significant patterns contained in a large, messy data set of human judgments. A more rigorous data collection process—such as carefully controlled lab experiments—would never produce such a volume of data, but could be useful as follow-up experiments.

Every day we reveal more and more about ourselves through the things we buy, the websites we use, the queries we search for, the messages we send, and the places we go. Whether we like it or not, for the first time in human history all this data is being carefully saved. Setting aside the important privacy concerns, the value to social science is enormous. Through this mess of repurposed information, we will learn about ourselves in completely new ways.

Acknowledgments

Many thanks to all the people who gave feedback for early drafts of this chapter: Joanna Gubman, Sasha Goodman, Jeff Hammerbacher, Mike Love, Will Moffat, and Toby Segaran. FaceStat owes its existence to the hard and brilliant work of our colleague Chris Van Pelt.

References

We have uploaded a subset of the data, as well as notes and code to help replicate our analyses, at *http://data.doloreslabs.com*.

If you're interested in learning R, we recommend two websites:

Quick-R (http://statmethods.net)
  High-level overviews and topic guides, by Robert Kabacoff.

RSeek (http://rseek.org)
  A search engine for R documentation, packages, and mailing lists, by Sasha Goodman.

R's official website is *http://www.r-project.org*. If you are interested in how it compares to other data analysis packages, see the many comments on an early draft of Table 17-2 at *http://anyall.org/blog/?p=421*.

The most commonly recommended book for learning R is Peter Dalgaard's *Introductory Statistics with R* (Springer; 2008).

Aside from R's core functionality, some of the add-on packages we used include corrgram, flowCore, gclus, geneplotter, plyr, and pixmap.

Good overviews of clustering, loess, and other machine learning techniques are in *The Elements of Statistical Learning* by Trevor Hastie, Robert Tibshirani, and Jerome Friedman (Springer; 2008).

The section on tags barely touches the surface of statistical language analysis. For more, see the chapters on corpus linguistics from *Foundations of Statistical Natural Language Processing* by Christopher Manning and Hinrich Schütze (MIT Press; 1999) and also *Speech and Language Processing* by Daniel Jurafsky and James H. Martin (Prentice Hall; 2008).

There are many better ways for estimating confidence intervals for the attractiveness versus age analysis. One method is partial pooling; see pp. 252–258 of Andrew Gelman and Jennifer Hill's *Data Analysis Using Regression and Multilevel/Hierarchical Models* (Cambridge University Press; 2006).

What we do in this chapter is called "exploratory data analysis" (EDA)—as opposed to the ploddingly careful hypothesis testing that is usually taught in statistical methodology courses. Exploratory data analysis was strongly advocated by statistician John Tukey in his 1977 book of the same name (Addison-Wesley).

Our startup, Dolores Labs, specializes in crowdsourcing: collecting human task data from large masses of people to solve practical problems in content moderation, information extraction, web search relevance, and other domains. We collect, look at, and automatically analyze lots of human judgment data. You can see follow-ups to this chapter, and analyses of other subjects such as sex, colors, and ethics, at our blog: *http://blog.doloreslabs.com*.

CHAPTER EIGHTEEN

Bay Area Blues: The Effect of the Housing Crisis

Hadley Wickham, Deborah F. Swayne, and David Poole

Introduction

THE HOUSING MARKET HAS RECEIVED A GREAT DEAL OF ATTENTION IN THE MEDIA FOR THE PAST SEVERAL years. From about 2000 until 2006, we watched with excitement and apprehension as prices soared; since then, we've watched them tumble as credit became scarce and fore-closures mounted. In this chapter, we take a closer look at this story by analyzing the sales of half a million homes in the San Francisco Bay Area from 2003 to 2008. What can we learn about the way prices rose and fell throughout a single region and across a wide range of prices?

We begin by describing the data, how we obtained it, and how we prepared it for analysis by restructuring, transforming, cleaning, and augmenting the raw data. As our analysis proceeds, we communicate most of our observations using graphical displays. Along the way, we will also describe some of the tools we use, most of which are freely available. Our main tool is R, a statistical programming and data analysis environment, and we used it at all stages: fetching, cleaning, analysis, diagnostics, and presentation.

How Did We Get the Data?

Once we decided that we were interested in real estate sales, the search for data began. Data searches are not always successful, so we felt particularly lucky when we found weekly sales of residential real estate (houses, apartments, condominiums, etc.) for the Bay Area produced by the *San Francisco Chronicle* at *http://www.sfgate.com/homesales/*. We felt even luckier when we figured out that we didn't have to extract the data by parsing web pages, but that the data is already available in a machine-readable format.

Each human-readable (HTML web page) weekly summary is built from a text file that looks like this:

```
rowid: 1
county: Alameda County
city: Alameda
newcity: 1
zip: 94501
street: 1220 Broadway
price: $509,000
br: 4
lsqft: 4420
bsqft: 1834
year: 1910
```

The data for each week is available at a URL of the form *http://www.sfgate.com/c/a/<year>/<month>/<day>/REHS.tbl*. This is pretty convenient and only requires generating a list of all Sundays from the first on record, 2003/04/27 (which we found on the archive page), to the most recent (at the time of analysis), 2008/11/16. With this list of dates in hand, we generated a list of URLs in the correct format and downloaded them with the Unix command-line tool wget. We used wget because it can easily resume where it left off if interrupted.

With all the data on a local computer, the next step was to convert the data into a standard format. We often use the *csv* (comma-separated values) format; it is easy to generate *csv* files, and every statistical package (and Excel!) can read them. We generated a *csv* file of the form:

```
county,city,zip,street,price,br,lsqft,bsqft,year,date,datesold
Alameda County,Alameda,94501,1220 Broadway,509000,4,4420,1834,1910,2003-04-27,NA
Alameda County,Alameda,94501,429 Fair Haven Road,504000,4,6300,1411,1964,2003-04
-27,NA
Alameda County,Alameda,94501,2804 Fernside Boulevard,526000,2,4000,1272,1941,200
3-04-27,NA
Alameda County,Alameda,94501,1316 Grove Street,637000,3,2700,1168,1910,2003-04-2
7,NA
```

The original format may have been easier for a human to read, but this is easier for computers. It is both more standard and more compact (45 megabytes instead of 90). If you look closely at the sample data you might notice something that needs some explanation: the NAs. NA stands for "not applicable," and is the sentinel value that R uses to represent missing values. We must take care to account for the missing values in our analysis.

It takes only a few minutes to parse the files for all 293 weeks and create *house-sales.csv*, a *csv* file with 521,726 observations and 11 variables. It took much more time to tweak the parser to get all the edge cases right: we needed to convert prices to regular numbers (by removing $ and ,), parse the dates into a consistent format, and fill in missing values for fields that didn't occur in all of the tables.

Geocoding

When we first looked at the data, we thought it would be really important to geocode all 436,106 unique addresses. That is, we wanted to associate a latitude and longitude with each address so that it would be easy to explore fine-grained spatial effects. This is an interesting challenge: how can you geocode nearly half a million addresses?

We started by looking at the well-known web services provided by Google and Yahoo!. These were unsuitable for two reasons: they impose strict daily limits on the number of requests, and there are cumbersome restrictions on the use of the resulting data. The request limit alone meant that it would take well over a month to geocode all the addresses, and then the licensing would have affected publication of the results! After further investigation we found a very useful open service, the USC WebGIS, provided by the GIS research laboratory at the University of Southern California (Goldberg and Wilson 2008). This service is free for noncommercial use and makes no restrictions on the uses of the resulting data. There was no daily usage cap when we began using the service, but there is an implicit cap caused by the speed: we could only geocode about 80,000 addresses per day, so it took us around five days to do all 400,000. The disadvantage of this free service is that the quality of the geocoding is not quite as good (it uses only publicly available address data), but the creators were very helpful and have published an excellent free introduction to the topic in (Goldberg 2008).

As well as latitude and longitude, the USC results also include a categorical variable indicating their degree of accuracy: exact address, zip code, county, etc.

Data Checking

It is generally worth spending a significant amount of time at every stage of an analysis to make sure that the data is accurate, and geocoding was no different. Errors in geocoding came from a number of sources: there are typographical errors in the addresses, new buildings are often not listed in public databases, and zip codes may be reassigned over time. We further suspect that the USC software included a bug during the period we used it, because large numbers of addresses were falsely assigned to the Los Angeles area and elsewhere around the state; we remapped these addresses using another free online service at *http://gpsvisualizer.com*. Our debugging process included using R to draw simple maps of latitude versus longitude for each county and most towns to identify the addresses that had been located far outside the Bay Area.

The addresses in San Jose posed an interesting geocoding challenge. Sales are listed for several "towns" that are not recognized by any mapping sites we could find, so we assume they are informal names for neighborhoods: North, South, East and West San Jose, Berryessa, Cambrian, and a few others.

Where possible we tried to correct any errors. When that was not possible, we used R's missing values to indicate that we do not know the exact latitude and longitude. This is a better approach than throwing out bad matches, because we need varying levels of accuracy for different purposes: when we map the data at the level of county or city, we can be satisfied with an approximate location. The use of missing values for latitude and longitude ensures that any location with a suspicious geocoding will be dropped from analyses that use latitude and longitude, but included in all others.

Analysis

For a broad overview of the changes in the housing market, we'll start with the evolution of the average sale price and number of sales. Since the data is reported weekly, that's a natural time unit to use.

Figure 18-1 shows weekly average sale price and number of sales for the 293 weeks in the data. There are some very interesting patterns. The behavior of the average price is striking, with an increasing trend until June 2007 and then a precipitous drop to the present day—a clear illustration of the boom and bust in housing prices.

Sales look quite different. Most years (especially 2004 and 2005) show a marked seasonal effect, with a peak in mid- to late summer and fewer sales in the winter months. (This may be a good place to note that the data only rarely includes the true closing date, so we're using the date when the sale was reported in the newspaper, which may be four to six weeks later than the closing.) Once we look past the seasonal effect, we see something else. From the middle of 2006 until early 2008, sales volume decreases, surely an indicator of the housing bust. However, the sharpness of the drop in early 2008 may also reflect the winter slowdown in sales. And what about the increase starting in early 2008? One possibility is that by this point house prices had dropped enough that buyers were shopping for bargains with the arrival of spring. Another possibility is that some of this increase is due to foreclosure sales. Perhaps the explanation will be clearer in a few more months.

These simple plots suggest some directions for further exploration. Are these patterns the same for homes in all price ranges? What about different cities, or within neighborhoods of a single city? To investigate these questions, we'll follow roughly the same procedure: we'll partition the data in different ways and compare the patterns for each partition. We will create partitions based on house price (from most expensive to least) and physical location, both between cities and within a single city (San Francisco).

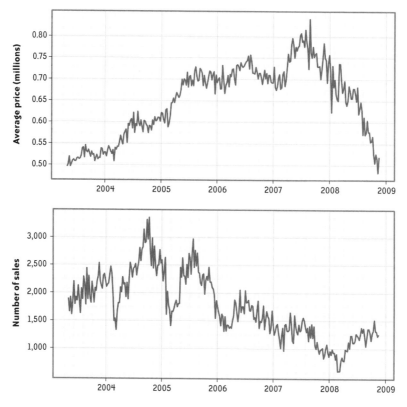

FIGURE 18-1. Weekly average prices (top) and sales (bottom), showing clear evidence of the housing boom and bust. Note, however, the uptick in sales in 2008.

The Influence of Inflation

Before proceeding with the analysis, though, we pause to consider inflation. The data was collected over a relatively short period of time (almost six years), but we wonder if we should adjust for inflation to ensure that the prices paid in 2003 are comparable to the prices paid in 2008. A commonly used reference for calculating inflation is the consumer price index (CPI) produced by the Bureau of Labor Statistics at *http://www.bls.gov/CPI*. The CPI calculates the price of a weighted "basket" of frequently purchased consumer goods and services. This price is calculated monthly, and we will use the west coast series, series CUUR0400SA0, to adjust for inflation as follows. We want to adjust all values to 2003 dollars, so we divide each CPI value by its value in March 2003. This operation is also known as indexing. It gives the relative worth of a 2003 dollar at each point in time and makes it easy to read the effect of inflation from the graph: a value of 1.1 represents a cumulative inflation of 10% from the start of the data. Figure 18-2 shows the CPI-based inflation measurement and the effect of adjusting prices for inflation. Inflation has been steadily climbing over the last five years, and we can see that the inflation-adjusted rise in house prices is slightly less pronounced than the unadjusted trend.

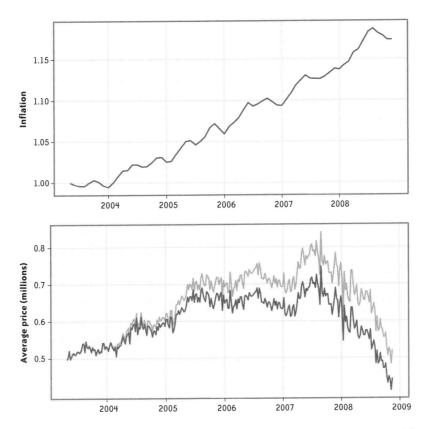

FIGURE 18-2. (Top) Inflation, indexed at 1 at start of series. (Bottom) Inflation-adjusted house prices in 2003 dollars (black), and unadjusted prices (gray). Failing to adjust for inflation makes the rise look a bit steeper, but has little effect on the decline. Monterey, San Benito, San Joaquin, and Santa Cruz counties are excluded because we only have data for 2008.

Finally, though, we decided not to adjust the sale prices for inflation. Housing prices have an influence on the CPI because one of its subindices is a housing index, a measure of rent and "owner's equivalent rent." It could probably be argued that housing prices had a significant effect on the CPI throughout the period under study.

With this basic overview in hand, we now drill down into the details. In the following sections we break the house sales into smaller groups, first by price and then by location. We are interested in finding out whether the housing crisis has affected some groups of homeowners more than others.

The Rich Get Richer and the Poor Get Poorer

Has the housing crisis equally affected the rich and the poor? Has the effect of the crisis been to improve or worsen the relative equality of these two groups? In this section, we will explore how the crisis has affected the distribution of housing prices. A big caveat is that we are looking at the Bay Area, so homes will be more expensive than in many other

places in the country, but we still expect to see some relative inequalities. (NB. In the following, we will frequently use the word "houses" to refer to all categories of residential real estate: houses, townhouses, apartments, etc.)

As a first step, we calculate price deciles for each month. The deciles are the nine prices for which 10%, 20%, 30%, 40%, 50%, 60%, 70%, 80%, and 90% of houses cost less. This is a succinct summary of the *distribution* of the prices for each month: instead of just looking at the average price, as we did earlier, we have nine numbers that summarize the complete distribution of the prices. (We don't display the curves for the minimum or maximum price, because they would be too choppy.)

Figure 18-3 shows how these deciles have changed over time. The top line is the ninth decile, the price that 90% of houses are less than, and the bottom line is the first decile, the price that only 10% of houses are cheaper than. The line in the middle is the median, the price that divides the houses into halves, half cheaper and half more expensive. The lines are colored from dark to light, from most to least expensive. Each line follows a similar pattern, and we can see the effect of the housing bubble in mid-2007, particularly in the most expensive houses.

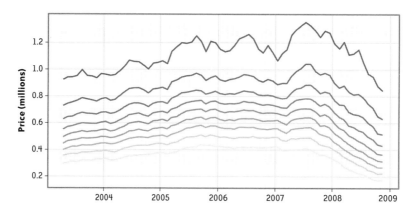

FIGURE 18-3. Monthly average house price within each decile. Lower deciles have lighter colors. This plot clearly shows the nature of the bubble for the more expensive residences, but it is unrevealing about its effects at the lowest price ranges.

This plot lets us compare the absolute values of each decile, but maybe it is more appropriate to look at the relative prices: how have the prices changed proportionately? One way to look at the relative price is to compare each decile to its initial value. To do this we index each decile, dividing each series by its initial price, just as we did for the CPI. Figure 18-4 shows these indices. Each decile starts at 1.0, and we can see the relative change in price over time. The interesting aspect of this plot is that the cheaper houses (the lighter lines) seem to peak higher and earlier (mid-2005), and then drop more rapidly thereafter. (Note the way the dark and light lines switch places in early 2007.) The cheapest houses, in the lowest decile, lost 43% of their 2003 value compared to only 9% for the

most expensive houses. Comparing Figures 18-3 and 18-4, we see that although the biggest absolute decline in actual prices occurred at the expensive end, it was the cheapest houses that proportionately lost the most value.

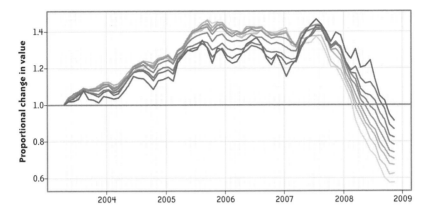

FIGURE 18-4. Indexed house price within each decile. (The lighter the color, the lower the price.) The bust began earlier at the low end: the average price of less expensive houses peaked higher and earlier, and fell more steeply.

Another way to look at this inequality is Figure 18-5. Here we have divided all the prices by the median price. The values now represent a proportion of the median house price: a value of 1.2 represents a price 20% higher than the median, and 0.8 is 20% lower. Since the beginning of 2007, while the boom was still in full force at the high end, relative inequality has been growing. Does this suggest that a widening of the price gap between expensive and cheap homes is a precursor to a subsequent crisis? Has this preceded other crises? These questions could be investigated further, but we don't have the data to pursue them here.

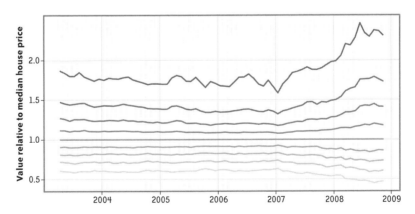

FIGURE 18-5. House prices relative to the price of the median-priced home. The disparity in home prices has been increasing since early 2007.

Geographic Differences

In this section we explore the changes in home prices in different cities in the Bay Area. Because we are looking at average prices, we must take care not to include cities with only a few sales. We decided to focus on all cities with an average of at least 10 sales per week. This gave us 58 cities (24% of the 245 cities in the data) with 428,415 sales (82% of the sales).

We then calculated the average weekly house price. Figure 18-6 shows these prices, with each city drawn with a different line. Statisticians have an evocative name for this type of display: the spaghetti plot. It's very hard to see anything in the big jumble of lines. One method of improvement is to smooth each line, removing short-term variation and allowing us to focus on the long-term trends we are looking for.

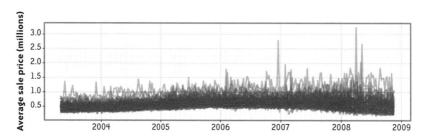

FIGURE 18-6. Average sale price for each week for each city. This type of plot is often called a spaghetti plot. It suggests the need for smoothing, because the week-to-week variation in the curves makes it impossible to detect trends.

To create smooth curves, we used generalized additive models (GAM), a generalization of linear models (Wood 2006). This method fits smooth curves by optimizing the trade-off between being close to the data and being very smooth, in effect removing noisy short-term effects and emphasizing the long-term trend. This is exactly what we need: we are not interested in daily or weekly changes, only the long-term changes related to the housing crisis.

The top part of Figure 18-7 shows the result of this smoothing. This is a big improvement. Now we can actually see some patterns! Note the big difference in scales between this plot and the first: smoothing the data has removed the large spikes that represent the sales of a few very expensive houses. We will also index each city in the same way we indexed each decile: dividing by the starting price puts each city onto a common scale and allows us to focus on the changes. This is shown at the bottom of Figure 18-7.

There is a still a lot of variation, but we can start to see a pattern of increasing values until mid-2007, and then decreasing values afterward. To get any further, we need to look at the cities individually, as in Figure 18-8. This plot takes up a lot of space but is worthwhile for the extra information it affords. We can pick out some interesting patterns: Berkeley and San Francisco show less of a peak and less of a drop, and Mountain View is unique in that it has seen no drop at all in housing prices. Other cities, such as Oakley, Vallejo, and San Pablo, show both big peaks and big drops.

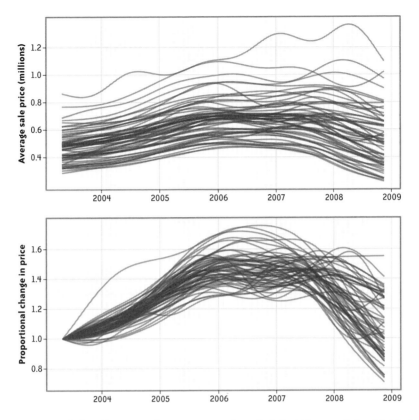

F I G U R E 1 8 - 7 . *Smoothed weekly average sale prices, one curve for each city (top). The curves in the plot at the bottom have been indexed to show proportional changes in price. Patterns are beginning to emerge.*

Recall that in our earlier discussion of San Jose, we noted that the raw data describes many neighborhoods of San Jose as cities in their own right. Because of this, it sometimes happens that the same address is assigned to more than one neighborhood, but this data suggests that the neighborhoods have distinct characters. Berryessa, East San Jose, North San Jose, and South San Jose have similar curves, showing a sharp peak and an equally sharp drop; Cambrian, San Jose, and West San Jose, on the other hand, don't show much of a decline.

After further investigation, we concluded that there was one main feature that seemed to distinguish the different cities: the difference between prices at the peak of the boom and the depth of their most recent plummet. We created a new variable called *price drop*, which is the relative decrease in average price between February 2006 (at the height of the boom) and November 2008 (the doldrums at the time of writing). Figure 18-9 groups the cities by this new variable. The divisions are arbitrary, but one can see how the cities in each group follow a similar pattern: the bigger the boom, the bigger the collapse. This suggests that this single number does a good job of summarizing the boom-and-bust aspect of the housing crisis.

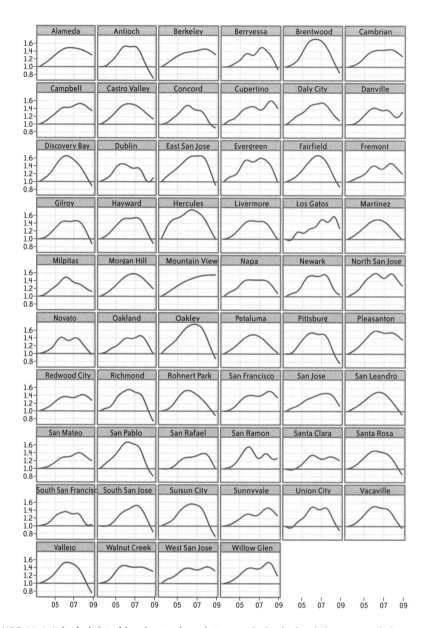

FIGURE 18-8. Individual plots of the sales price for each city, smoothed and indexed. These are exactly the curves that were plotted on top of one another in the previous figure (bottom). San Pablo's curve shows the boom and bust of the housing market; Berkeley's curve shows less variation; Mountain View seems to be the only city where prices continue to rise.

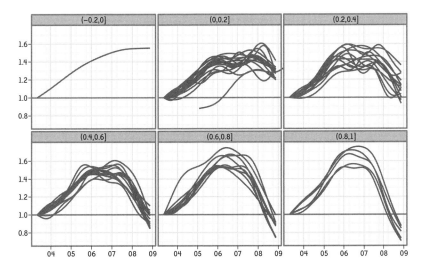

FIGURE 18-9. Plots grouping the curves for towns by their value of price drop. The towns in the upper-left plot had the largest price declines (between 0.8 and 1, or 80% and 100%); the town at the lower right (Mountain View) is the only one that shows no decline. The patterns within each group are similar, suggesting that this single number provides a useful way to divide the cities into groups.

We have determined that cities have different patterns, but we don't yet know why that might be so. The geographic pattern, as in Figure 18-10, does not reveal anything particularly striking except that the worst-hit towns tend to be to the north and east of San Francisco. This does not offer much in the way of explanatory power, so we looked for additional data that might help us gain a deeper understanding.

Census Information

The U.S. Census Bureau provides demographic data from recent surveys at both the county and city levels. The quickfacts website (e.g., *http://quickfacts.census.gov/qfd/states/06/ 0649670.html*) displays a number of interesting demographic variables for each city. Unfortunately, city-level data is not available in an easily downloadable format, but we were able to use scripting methods (like those we used for the sales data) to collect the demographic information and convert it into *csv* format. In addition, the definition of a city differed slightly between the census data and the sales data, so we could match only 46 out of the full 58 cities. The census data didn't cover some of cities we chose, because their population was below some cutoff, and some of what the housing data calls "cities" are actually neighborhoods within larger cities, as we noted earlier with respect to San Jose.

A glance at the demographic variables revealed that the most affected cities have a high percentage of babies and children, bigger households, fewer bachelor's degrees, and longer commutes. Most significantly, these cities also have lower average incomes, which is probably the factor that drives many of the other relationships. Figure 18-11 includes three scatterplots that illustrate the relationship between the drop in home prices and income,

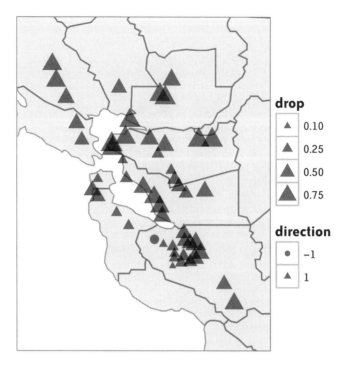

FIGURE 18-10. The geographic distribution of price drop. The worst-hit towns tend to be to the north and the east. The single circle represents the location of Mountain View, the only city where the sale price has continued to increase.

percentage of college graduates, and commute time. The correlation between price drop and commute time is weak, but note that all of the cities with the longest commute times (more than 35 minutes) have particularly large drops in price. It appears that the housing crisis has been relatively more damaging in poorer areas.

The county-level census data contains more variables than the data for cities, so we analyzed the county data for further explanation of the housing crisis. The plot at the top of Figure 18-12 shows, for each county in which we had sales data, the percentage change in the number of housing units (from 2000 to 2006) plotted against the median sale price in 2008. There is a strong negative relationship between recent home values and the amount of new construction. In other words, most of the building boom in recent years occurred in poorer neighborhoods, and as we noted earlier, these are also the areas where the subsequent slump has been the most severe. San Joaquin county in particular, which has consistently low prices across towns, experienced by far the most new construction in recent years. We should note that we do not have many sales in a few of these counties (e.g., San Benito and Santa Cruz), but the overall nature of this relationship is still very clear. The effect is further illustrated by the bottom plot in Figure 18-12, which again shows the percentage change in housing units from 2000 to 2006, but this time plotted against the 2005 per-capita income at the county level, obtained from the census data. We notice the similarity to the previous plot, and it illustrates again that the intensity of new construction was higher in less affluent areas, even when aggregated across cities to the county level.

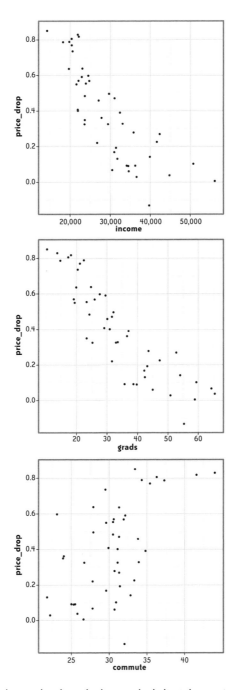

FIGURE 18-11. From top to bottom, the relationship between the decline in house prices (price drop) and average income, percentage of college graduates, and average commute time.

It is clear too that prices and income are strongly positively correlated, which we observed at the city level in Figure 18-11.

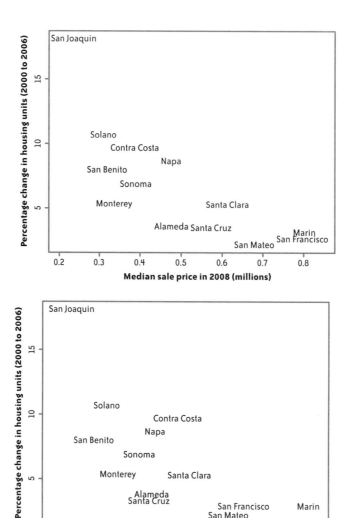

FIGURE 18-12. Relationship between new construction and recent prices (top) and personal income (bottom); data is aggregated by county. The relative increase in the number of housing units was greatest in towns with lower-cost housing (top) and lower per-capita income (bottom).

According to an article in the *New York Times* (McKinley 2007), the city of Stockton, one of the larger cities in San Joaquin county, already had the highest rate of foreclosures in the U.S. by the summer of 2007.

Unfortunately, we do not have any sales for Stockton prior to 2008, but it appears it was a leading indicator of the slump in the region that would continue into 2008. The population of Stockton grew rapidly in the last decade as commuters moved farther out to escape the overheated housing market in the immediate Bay Area. This helps to explain the new construction noted earlier, and also ties into our observation regarding commute times.

The article also lists Modesto and Merced, two other towns in the Central Valley, in the top 10 nationwide for foreclosures at that time.

Exploring San Francisco

Having explored the differences between cities, we turned to look at a single city in more detail. San Francisco is the obvious choice: it is the largest city in the data, it is the city with which we are most familiar, and it has some iconic features that should be easy for others to identify, too. We started our exploration by extracting all addresses within San Francisco that were geocoded with a fairly high degree of accuracy, giving us a total of 25,377 addresses. We created a simple scatterplot of the latitudes and longitudes, shown in Figure 18-13.

FIGURE 18-13. (Top) A small point is drawn for every residential sale in the data. It gives us a pretty good feel for the layout of San Francisco. (Bottom) For comparison, a street map of San Francisco from http://openstreetmap.com. (See Color Plate 68.)

For the residential parts of the city, this gives an amazingly detailed picture. We can see the orientation of the streets, the waterfront boundaries, and parks. Our view of some areas, like downtown, is patchier because there are fewer residential homes there. (In this section, we will avoid using the shorthand term "house" since it is obvious that so many of the home sales represent apartments.)

One problem with this plot is we cannot see the number of sales at each specific location. Figure 18-14 shows two attempts to recapture the information. At the top, we have a bubbleplot with the size of the location proportional to the number of sales. We now get quite a different view of the downtown: there are many sales there. Looking more closely at the data reveals that these are apartment buildings with hundreds of apartments. At the bottom, we have divided San Francisco into squares of 0.005 latitude and longitude and counted the number of homes in each bin. This gives us a higher-level view showing where the majority of homes are located.

Using that same binning, we calculated the mean and coefficient of variation of the home prices. The coefficient of variation is the standard deviation divided by the mean. We use it here because a variation of $100,000 is relatively much more important when houses are cheap compared to when they are expensive.

Figure 18-15 shows the geographic distribution of these two summary statistics. We can see the most expensive homes border the Presidio and coast to the north of the city. There also seems to be a peak in the southwest: this is the affluent St. Francis Wood area, near San Francisco State University. There is an interesting geographic trend in the coefficient of variation: it appears to increase toward the northwest.

Conclusion

We have looked at the data from multiple angles, and we have seen the same thing: the housing crisis has been relatively more damaging in poorer areas. The boom and the bust hit lower-priced homes both earlier and harder; cities with lower average incomes peaked higher and dropped lower. A great deal of the boom was associated with new construction, most of which was aimed at the lower end of the market.

Many of these new residences were built farther from San Francisco, in less developed areas where residents had lower average incomes, more children, and longer commutes. Although the biggest absolute decline in prices occurred at the high end, it was the less expensive houses that lost a greater proportion of their value.

All of this is consistent with what we have learned about subprime mortgages since the housing bust hit the headlines. Many people with poor credit were granted mortgages with initially low monthly payments. When those payments grew, they were unable to meet them, and the rates of mortgage defaults and foreclosures began to rise. We speculated earlier that the increase in sales in 2008 may be associated with foreclosures, and an interesting next step would be to locate data on foreclosures and align it with our sales data.

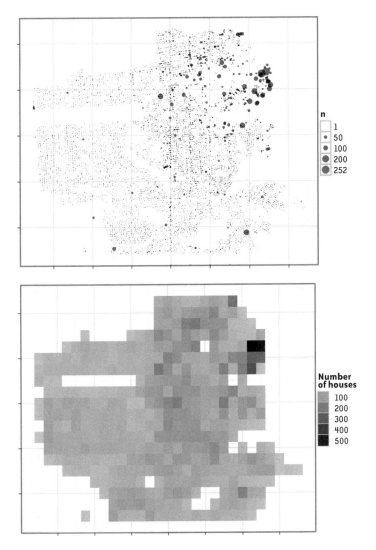

FIGURE 18-14. *The geographic distribution of numbers of residential sales. (Top) This plot is similar to the previous plot, but the size of the dot is now proportional to the number of sales at each unique location. This changes the picture significantly, as the large apartment complexes in the city now pop out. (Bottom) A display of sales at a higher level of aggregation: latitude and longitude are divided into a small number of bins, and the number of sales in each bin is counted and displayed as the color of the bin.*

We have used relatively simple statistical methods such as indexing, computing quantiles, smoothing, and binning to explore this large and complex data set. We began with broad summaries and then dug deeper to explore the details, but we have only scratched the surface. If the data has caught your interest and you'd like to follow our work in more detail, or try out some of your own ideas, you can find all data and code in a git repository

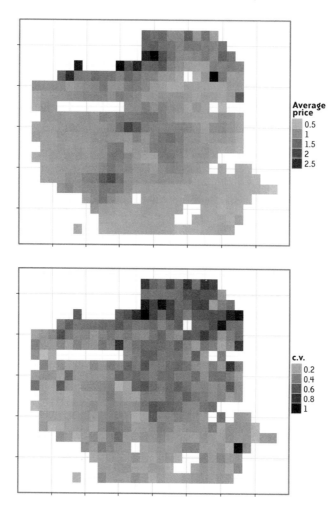

FIGURE 18-15. Using the same binning of latitude and longitude as in the previous figure, the mean (top) and coefficient of variation (bottom) are computed and displayed using shades of gray.

at *https://github.com/hadley/sfhousing*. All the code we wrote (R, Perl, and shell scripts) runs on open source software, so anyone can replicate our work without buying expensive software. The principle of reproducibility (Gentleman and Temple Lang 2007), so critical in the laboratory sciences, is also important here: if we made a mistake, you can discover it, fix it, and observe the effects on our conclusions.

Throughout this exercise, we have enjoyed the challenge of extracting, exploring, analyzing, and ultimately gaining useful insights from this housing data. Further, we hope that the general description of our strategies, methods, and techniques will prove useful to others who share our interest in working with—and learning from—real data.

References

Gentleman, Robert and Duncan Temple Lang. 2007. "Statistical analyses and reproducible research." *Journal of Computational and Graphical Statistics*, 16(1): 1–23.

Goldberg, Daniel W. 2008. "A geocoding best practices guide." Technical report, GIS Research Laboratory, University of Southern California. *http://www.naaccr.org/filesystem/pdf/Geocoding_Best_Practices.pdf*.

Goldberg, D. W., and J. P. Wilson. 2008. USC WebGIS Services. *https://webgis.usc.edu*. Last accessed December 2008.

McKinley, Jesse. "From housing to haven to foreclosure leader." *New York Times*. August 13, 2007.

Wood, Simon. 2006. *Generalized Additive Models: An Introduction with R*. Boca Raton, FL: Chapman & Hall/CRC.

CHAPTER NINETEEN

Beautiful Political Data

Andrew Gelman, Jonathan P. Kastellec, and Yair Ghitza

SOME OF THE EARLIEST HISTORICAL EXAMPLES OF DATA ANALYSIS INVOLVE POLITICS AND GOVERNMENT; even the word "statistics" reveals the connection of data collection for and about the state. Statistical pioneers, including Playfair, Laplace, and Galton, devoted much of their effort to designing and analyzing public data, and, in the 20th century, statistics was associated with Gallup polls, economic and military organization (Five Year Plans and all that), and even Svengali-like political consultants (as in *The 480*, a novel from 1964 by the coauthor of *The Ugly American*, *Fail-Safe*, and other Cold War–era bestsellers). More recently, TV viewers have become accustomed to colored maps and charts of the latest polls and election results broken down by locality and demographic slices. And at the next level of sophistication are *USA Today*, the *New York Times*, and blogs such as FiveThirtyEight.com.

This chapter gives some examples where data visualization has increased our understanding of politics, along with a discussion of the factors involved in making each choice. Here we are focusing on the uses of graphics for research as well as presentation.

We try to apply the following template:

- "Figure X shows…"
- "Each point (or line) in the graph represents…"
- "The separate graphs indicate…"

- "Before making this graph, we did…which didn't work, because…"
- "A natural extension would be…"

We do not have a full theory of statistical graphics—our closest attempt is to link exploratory graphical displays to checking the fit of statistical models (Gelman 2003)—but we hope that this small bit of structure can help readers in their own efforts. We think of our graphs not as beautiful standalone artifacts but rather as tools to help us understand beautiful reality.

We illustrate using examples from our own work, not because our graphs are particularly beautiful, but because in these cases we know the story behind each plot.

Example 1: Redistricting and Partisan Bias

Figure 19-1 shows the estimated effect on partisan bias from redistricting (redrawing of the lines dividing the districts from which legislators get elected). Each point in the graph represents a state legislative election year (such as Missouri in 1972), with the vertical and horizontal axes displaying an estimate of partisan bias in that election and in the previous election, two years earlier.

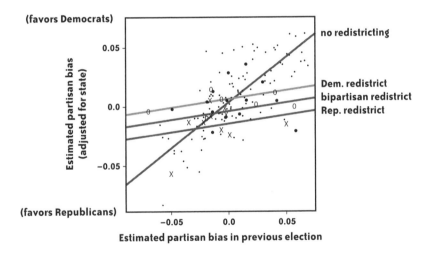

FIGURE 19-1. Effect of redistricting on partisan bias. Each symbol represents a state election year, with dots indicating controls (years with no redistricting) and the other symbols corresponding to different types of redistricting. As indicated by the fitted lines, the "before" value is much more predictive of the "after" value for the control cases than for the treated (redistricting) cases. The dominant effect of the treatment is to bring the expected value of partisan bias toward 0, and this effect would not be discovered with the usual approach, which is to fit a model assuming parallel regression lines for treated and control cases. This graph is just beautiful enough to reveal the key pattern in the data.

"Partisan bias," as defined here, is a measure of how much the electoral system favors the Democrats or Republicans, after accounting for their vote share. Roughly speaking, the partisan bias is the expected Democratic share of the seats won in the legislature, if they were to average 50% of the vote. Biases are typically between –5% and 5%, implying that a party that wins half the vote for a state legislature will win between 45% and 55% of the seats.

The small dots in the graph represent "control" cases in which there was no redistricting, and the larger symbols correspond to different kinds of redistrictings, which here we lump together as "treated" cases. Elections come every two years, and redistricting typically happens every 10 years, so most of the data points are controls. The correlation between before and after measurements is much larger for controls than treated cases. The difference in slopes for the two groups should be no surprise at all. In the control cases with no redistricting, the state legislature changes very little, and so the partisan bias will probably change very little from the previous election. In contrast, when the legislative districts are redrawn, larger and more unpredictable changes occur. It was crucial to model the variation in the treatment to see this effect.

The simplest way to get partisan bias from redistricting is for Democrats, say, to draw the district lines so that they are winning with 60% of the vote in each of their districts, with Republicans packed together so that they are winning their seats with close to 100% of the vote. However, such manipulation ("gerrymandering") may not be possible in practice, given constraints including equal population and contiguity of districts, as well as the potential for egregious gerrymanders to be overturned in court challenges.

The graph in Figure 19-1 is beautiful because, until we made it (in Gelman and King 1994), the discussion of partisan redistricting had focused on whether or not parties could make large gains and whether districting reduced the competitiveness of the electoral system (because legislators who are drawing the district lines can try to preserve "safe seats" for themselves and their colleagues).

In our first attempt to use this data to model the consequences of redistricting, we fit a linear regression model with no interaction—thus completely missing the most important part of the story. It was only after plotting the data and the fitted regression line that we noticed the elephant in the room and fit a more appropriate model.

Our graph showed that the main consequence of redistricting was to reduce the magnitude of partisan bias (and also to make the electoral system more responsive to voters, but that is the subject of a different graph, not shown here).

Example 2: Time Series of Estimates

Figure 19-2 illustrates a problem with classical logistic regression (a standard statistical tool for predicting yes/no outcomes) and how it can be resolved using a so-called weakly informative Bayesian approach. Using polling data in each presidential election from 1952 through 2000, we fit a separate logistic regression model to each year's data, predicting Republican vote choice given race, income, and several other variables.

Within each of the little graphs, each dot displays a logistic regression coefficient with a vertical line indicating the uncertainty in the estimate. The series of dots shows separate estimates for each election, and the two rows of graphs show the time series of estimated coefficients for race and income. (For simplicity, we do not display the other coefficients here.) The left column of the display shows classical estimates, and the two right columns show different Bayesian estimates (which in this case give essentially identical answers).

The estimates in Figure 19-2 look fine except in 1964, where there is complete separation, with all black respondents supporting the Democrats. As a result, the coefficient for race is estimated at negative infinity—that is, an inference that being black results in a 0% chance of voting Republican that year. 1964 was indeed a year in which Republicans did not do well among black voters (the Republican candidate that year was Barry Goldwater, who had opposed the Civil Rights Act), but they certainly received more than 0% of the black vote. The purpose of this regression, as in nearly all survey analysis, is to draw conclusions about the general population, not merely the small sample surveyed, and, as such, we cannot be satisfied with the classical estimate of negative infinity. (The estimate displayed in the left column of Figure 19-2 is not actually infinite, but that is because the software used to fit the model is iterative and stopped at some point before diverging.)

The Bayesian approach, as shown in the rightmost two columns of Figure 19-2, stabilizes the coefficient for black voters in 1964 at a reasonable value—lower than in any other year from 1952–2000 and with a larger uncertainty bound but not infinite. While fixing this problem, the Bayesian procedures did not mess up the coefficient estimates for other years or for other variables in the model (as illustrated by the coefficients for income in the second row of plots).

This graph is hardly beautiful, but it illustrates an important and general principle, which is that graphing isn't just for raw data. The usual practice in the statistical literature is to display this sort of result in a table, but a well-made graph can show more information in less space (Gelman et al. 2002).

From our own perspective, the graph of parameter estimates was useful both for conveying to others the effectiveness of our method and to reassure ourselves that our series of estimates was reasonable, in a way that a table of coefficient estimates (or, more typically, a long series of computer output) would not.

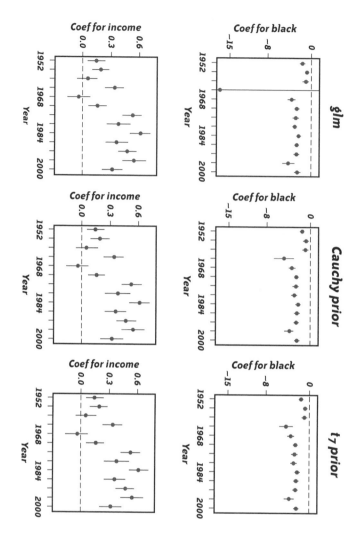

FIGURE 19-2. The left column shows the estimated coefficients (±1 standard error) for two predictors in a logistic regression predicting probability of Republican vote for President given demographics, as fit separately to data from the National Election Study for each election 1952 through 2000. The numerical variable income (originally on a 1–5 scale) has been centered and then rescaled by dividing by two standard deviations. There is complete separation in 1964 (with none of the African-American respondents supporting the Republican candidate, Barry Goldwater), leading to a coefficient estimate of –1 that year. (The particular finite values of the estimate and standard error are determined by the number of iterations used by glm function in R before stopping.) The other two columns show Bayesian estimates for the same model using different "weakly informative" prior distributions. The Bayesian inferences fix the problem with 1964 without doing much to the estimates in the other years.

The beauty of this graph, and others like it, is that its strict parallelism (the "small multiples" idea discussed by Tufte, 1990, and Bertin, 1967) allows the reader—and also the creator of the graph—to make many comparisons at once.

Example 3: Age and Voting

Immediately after Barack Obama's historic election, there was speculation about the role of young voters in the winning coalition. Exit poll data showed that Obama did particularly well among the young, but was this really newsworthy? For example, political consultant Mark Penn wrote on the *New York Times* website, "Sure, young people voted heavily for Mr. Obama, but they voted heavily for John Kerry." Was Penn right?

As always, the clearest way to make a comparison is using a graph. Figure 19-3 shows the results, with four versions: first the basic graph that we made on election night (pulling exit poll data off the CNN website), then an improved version posted by a student who had noticed our graph on the Web, then to more time series plots of our own. In each of these graphs, points are connected with lines, with points representing the Republican candidate's share of the two-party vote among each of four different age groups in several recent elections. 2008 clearly was different, and so Mark Penn was wrong—another case of a pundit looking at numbers and not seeing the big picture. This is what graphics is all about: showing the details and the patterns all at once.

To get to the even larger picture, there is a huge amount of research in this area, and we do not mean to imply that these graphs, which reveal some simple patterns, are in any sense a replacement for more serious study of patterns of age cohorts and voting over time.

Example 4: Public Opinion and Senate Voting on Supreme Court Nominees

Few decisions made by U.S. senators are as visible to the public as votes to confirm or reject a Supreme Court nominee. Whereas the outcomes of many Senate votes, such as spending bills or the modification of a statute, are ambiguous or obscured in procedural detail, the result of a vote on a Supreme Court nomination is stark: either the nominee is confirmed, allowing her to serve on the nation's highest court, or she is rejected, forcing the president to name another candidate (Kastellec et al. 2008). Do senators follow state-level public opinion when casting such votes?

Figure 19-4 presents a preliminary answer to this question by graphing the relationship between state-level public opinion on nine recent Supreme Court nominees and senators' votes on whether to confirm those nominees. On each graph, the curve shows the probability that a senator votes to confirm the nominee as a function of public opinion in the senator's state. The solid black line displays the estimated curve from a fitted logistic regression, and the clusters of light-gray lines depict uncertainty in this estimation. The hash marks (or "rugs") indicate votes of approval ("1") and rejection ("0") of nominees, while the numbers in the lower-right corner of each plot denote the overall vote tally by the Senate. The bottom plot pools all nominees together. We order the plots across and down by increasing mean support for each nominee.

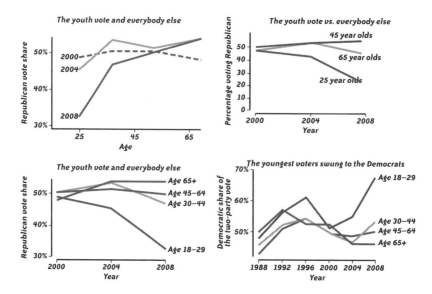

FIGURE 19-3. Some graphs showing recent patterns of voting by age. The top-left graph shows my first attempt, created on election night based on immediate exit poll data. The top-right graph was created by Hober Short, a student who saw my graph on the Web and made his own, displaying time on the x-axis. The lower-left graph is my cleaned-up version of Short's graph, labeling all four age categories directly on the lines of the graph. All these graphs show the dramatic difference between 2008 and the two previous elections. Finally, the lower-right graph extends the data back to 1988, showing that Bill Clinton in 1996 also did well among young voters—like Barack Obama, he was a young Democrat facing older Republican opponents—but not so well as Obama in 2008.

These graphs show the choices involved in making even the simplest possible graphs. As in many political settings, the largest gains come from incorporating additional data—in this case, the comparison of 2008 with earlier years, the comparison of young voters with those of other ages, and the comparison of the three other age groups with one another (with the lack of variation in this last comparison being a motivation to focus on trends among young voters in particular).

In addition, we improved our final graph by focusing on Democratic rather than Republican vote (more appropriate given the focus on Obama's strength among young voters) and by giving the graph a more descriptive title.

The graph shows that the relationship between public opinion and confirmation is generally positive, though it varies across nominees. Not surprisingly, there is greater uncertainty for nominees with lopsided confirmation votes. At the same time, the plot for "All Nominees" shows that, in general, as state public support for a nominee increases, a senator is more likely to vote yes. (This relationship holds even if one controls for other predictors of roll call voting, such as nominee quality and ideological distance between the senator and the nominee.)

The beauty of this graph is that it combines raw data with a simple inferential model in a single plot. Typically, bivariate relationships are presented in tabular form; in this example, doing so would require either nine correlation coefficients or regression coefficients and standard errors from nine regression models, which would be ungainly, make it difficult to visualize the relationship between opinion and voting for each nominee, and create difficulties in making comparisons across nominees. The only actual numbers we include

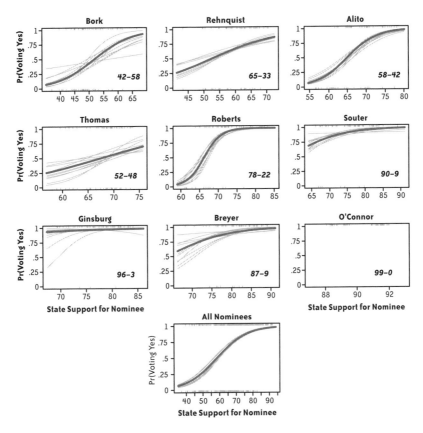

FIGURE 19-4. Correlation between state opinion and Senate roll call voting on Supreme Court nominees. For each nominee, the black line depicts the estimated logit curve from regressing senators' votes on state public opinion. Light-gray lines depict uncertainty in the estimates. Hash marks indicate votes of approval ("1") and rejection ("0") of nominees, while the numbers in the lower-right corner of each plot denote the overall vote tally by the Senate. The bottom plot pools all nominees together. The beauty of this graph is that it combines raw data with a simple inferential model in a single graph.

in the plot (which we do in an unobtrusive manner that does not distract from the plots themselves) are the roll call margins, which are both easily interpretable and give the reader a sense of how contentious each nomination was. Finally, as with Figure 19-2, the use of small multiples in the display allows the reader to make several comparisons at once, and prevents the information overload that can occur with a single plot.

Example 5: Localized Partisanship in Pennsylvania

In 1986, political strategist James Carville, who later ran Bill Clinton's first presidential campaign, described Pennsylvania as Paoli and Penn Hills with Alabama in between. Paoli is a suburb of Philadelphia, and Penn Hills is a suburb of Pittsburgh, and so Carville was referring to the two urban centers of this long-standing "swing state" as Democratic strongholds, with the remaining rural areas of the state as Republican territory.

Carville's words are indicative of the broader desire of both the public and the highest level of political punditry to divide the country into red and blue areas. For most Americans with an even passing familiarity with elections in the 21st century, one of the defining images of recent American politics has been the ubiquitous electoral map from 2000 and 2004, featuring slivers of blue states along the north and west coast, and a sea of red states in the south and the heartland. Despite President-elect Barack Obama's insistence that we are not a collection of red and blue states, this salient imagery is difficult to overcome.

Figure 19-5 presents a clarification of sorts for Carville's description of Pennsylvania and a different way of looking at geographic partisanship, based on a new and exciting type of data and a rich visualization technique. The bottom layer of the map shows Pennsylvania counties shaded by their 2004 presidential election returns, with blue indicating higher support for the Democratic candidate John Kerry, red indicating higher support for the Republican candidate George W. Bush, and shades of purple in between. By using the continuous red-purple-blue scale instead of the more common solid red or solid blue indicating each county's winner, we can better visualize the varying degrees of partisanship across the state.

FIGURE 19-5. *Geographic partisanship in Pennsylvania. The base layer shows Pennsylvania counties shaded by their 2004 presidential election returns, with blue indicating higher support for the Democratic candidate John Kerry, red indicating higher support for the Republican candidate George W. Bush, and shades of purple in between. The scattered cylinders represent localized partisanship for 4,000 random registered voters in the state, defined as the percentage of people living within a 1-mile radius who are registered Democrats. Each cylinder is located on the voter's household and has a radius of 1 mile, thus replicating the region for the partisanship measure. Again, blue cylinders indicate highly Democratic regions—this time with regard to individual-level registration—red cylinders indicate highly Republican regions, and shades of purple indicate regions in the middle. The beauty of this graph is that it reveals complexity in the idea of red and blue regions of the country, of individual states, and even of individual counties. (See Color Plate 69.)*

The top layer of the map—the scattered cylinders—displays *localized partisanship* for a random sample of 4,000 registered voters in the state. Localized partisanship is a measure of the concentration of Democrats or Republicans in each neighborhood. Specifically, it is

defined as the percentage of people living within a 1-mile radius who are registered Democrats. Each cylinder is located on the voter's household and has a radius of 1 mile, thus replicating the region for the partisanship measure. Again, blue cylinders indicate a highly Democratic region—this time with regards to individual-level registration—red cylinders indicate a highly Republican region, and shades of purple indicate regions in the middle.

The beauty of this graph is that it reveals complexity in the idea of red and blue regions of the country, of individual states, and even of individual counties. Although it is sometimes convenient to think of red and blue states, this graph reveals that there are shades of purple going down to the neighborhood (and even the individual) level. Just outside Philadelphia, the biggest city in the state, you can easily find pockets of red neighborhoods. Conversely, even in the reddest counties in the middle of the state, there are areas of purple and blue.

The graph is also beautiful because it demonstrates how our commonly held beliefs can be challenged and our understanding can be deepened through the careful analysis and visualization of data. This particular graph uses data provided by Catalist, a company that maintains a national database of all voting-age individuals in the United States. As detailed and large-scale data sources become increasingly accessible, multilayered visualization techniques will be instrumental in our abilities to use data to understand the world around us.

Conclusion

Political data is increasingly accessible and is increasingly being plotted and shared in the media and on the Web. At the research level, articles in political science journals are starting to make use of graphical techniques for discovery and presentation of results. And online tools ranging from NationMaster.com to the Name Voyager (*http://www. babynamewizard.com/voyager*) are becoming increasingly accessible, with data dumps such as Hans Rosling's TED talk (*http://www.ted.com/index.php/talks/hans_rosling_shows_the_best_ stats_you_ve_ever_seen.html*) becoming cult favorites. We expect statistical visualization to become more important and more widespread in political analysis.

References

Bertin, J. (1967). *Semiology of Graphics*. Translated by W. J. Berg (1983). Madison: University of Wisconsin Press.

Gelman, A. (2003). "A Bayesian formulation of exploratory data analysis and goodness-of-fit testing." *International Statistical Review* 71, 369–382.

Gelman, A., A. Jakulin, M. G. Pittau, and Y. S. Su (2008). "A weakly informative default prior distribution for logistic and other regression models." *Annals of Applied Statistics*, to appear.

Gelman, A. and G. King (1994). "Enhancing democracy through legislative redistricting." *American Political Science Review* 88, 541–559.

Gelman, A., C. Pasarica, and R. Dodhia (2002). "Let's practice what we preach: turning tables into graphs." *American Statistician* 56, 121–130.

Kastellec, J., J. Lax, and J. Phillips (2008). "Public opinion and Senate confirmation of Supreme Court nominees." Technical report, Department of Political Science, Columbia University.

Tufte, E. R. (1990). *Envisioning Information*. Cheshire, CT: Graphics Press.

CHAPTER TWENTY

Connecting Data

Toby Segaran

EVERY YEAR, PEOPLE INVENT DOZENS OF NEW OR REFINED STATISTICAL AND MACHINE-LEARNING TECHNIQUES for combing through data sets. What almost all of these have in common is that they presuppose the existence of a clean data set containing all the information that will be needed for the task at hand, which is often lacking in real-world situations. As Andreas Weigend, former chief scientist at Amazon, put it, "People are always asking 'what great technique can I use on this data set?' when they should be asking 'what's the best data set I can get?'"

Meanwhile, scientists are generating terabytes of data every day through their research and experiments and putting it online; governments all over the world are allowing downloads of data they have collected in operations; and the proliferation of user-generated content has created massive databases of restaurants, science fiction novels, and geolocations of streets where there was simply no comprehensive data before. So much of this is available and sits unused except by a few specialists for whom it is sufficient on its own—for everyone else it remains upsettingly free of the one or two pieces of context that would make it 10 times more valuable.

I believe some of the biggest challenges and opportunities for the current generation of data wranglers lie in connecting disparate data sets to create new sets for analysis, and in taking advantage of the proliferation of data, new techniques that have been developed, and the incredible hardware resources available. Data integration has been a problem

since databases have existed, but the amount of potentially relevant data available to a researcher or curious individual is now thousands of times larger—the problem has moved from enterprise to mainstream.

To me, this is a big, hairy, important problem, and one that's touched almost every aspect of my career. So rather than talk about a single project, I'm going to break with most of the essays in this book and talk about a series of lessons I learned from projects spanning several years.

What Public Data Is There, Really?

In my work on Freebase (*http://www.freebase.com*), I've looked at hundreds of data sets that were interesting on their own, but even more interesting as augmentation and context for other data sets. These come from nonprofits, governments, companies, and grassroots efforts. Lest I be accused of glossing over details, here's a pretty big list (but a very small sample) of what's out there:

- The **Center for Responsible Politics** (*http://opensecrets.org*) publishes contributions by individuals to political candidates in the United States.

- Many countries have data from their **Census** available online. In the United States, you can download census data from *http://www.census.gov*.

- The **Geonames** (*http://www.geonames.org*) database has the longitude, latitude, containment, and class of named places all over the world.

- The **Securities and Exchange Commission** (*http://sec.gov*) has downloadable financial data for all companies listed on U.S. stock exchanges.

- Agencies like the **Environmental Protection Agency** (*http://epa.gov*) have downloadable information about environmental pollution in certain places and the facilities that produce the most pollution.

- A surprisingly useful resource is the **Trademark database** (*http://uspto.gov*), which can be used to find which companies own rights to brand names, what the brand names are used to sell, and, often amusingly, all the art associated with different brands.

- Many **social networks** allow downloads of subsets of information, including relationships and other fields such as location.

- Nutritional information (calories, grams of fat, etc.) about almost every consumable product is available from the **U.S. Department of Agriculture** (*http://usda.gov*).

- The National Center for Biotechnology Information (**NCBI**; *http://ncbi.nlm.nih.gov*) publishes many databases related to genetic and medical informatics, including Genbank, Pubmed, Gene, and dbSNP.

- Many city or state **health departments** publish data about restaurant inspections, which is a good source of free data about which restaurants are in a city and also how clean they are.

- Agencies such as Medicare (*http://medicare.gov*) and the **Food and Drug Administration** (*http://www.fda.gov*) have huge downloadable data sets of drug availability, costs, and usage.

- Online **message boards** often contain mentions of companies, products, and places, along with text that can be mined for sentiment and relationships.

You'll notice that although a lot of these sources come from totally different places, they often talk about very similar things. This is the essence of the problem I'm exploring—how do we know when two databases are talking about the same thing? As you'll see in the rest of this chapter, this is a difficult problem, but one whose solution brings about many exciting possibilities.

The Possibilities of Connected Data

Back in the 1980s, I watched a movie called *Wall Street*, and one scene always stuck with me: a young stockbroker played by Charlie Sheen gives a very prescient stock tip to his future mentor, played by Michael Douglas. After the tip proves to be accurate, we see Douglas telling Sheen that he knows that the head of the union at the company is Sheen's father. The implication is that he has researchers who can find connections between people and companies, but at the time it got me thinking about what connected data could do.

Of course, in this context it sounds a little creepy, but this is exactly the sort of research that agencies like the Securities and Exchange Commission (SEC) have to do manually in order to detect fraud and insider trading. Setting privacy concerns and personal data like family connections aside for a moment, consider what would happen if public data from hundreds of sources could be combined and we could search for connections between things. What would we find?

Here are a few off-the-cuff ideas to inspire you. Chances are, you'll have no interest in implementing these exactly, but hopefully they'll lead you to your own connected-data ideas.

Using trademark data, we can determine which companies are responsible for different brands, which we might combine with nutritional data from the USDA to determine which companies make the most sugary beverages. We could also take the classification of the logos from the trademark data to see whether cartoons are more often used to sell high-calorie products. Introducing still more data, we could use EPA data to figure out how much pollution companies produce in different places and how well this correlates with the types of products they sell.

By combining a geographical database such as Geonames with a social network, we could determine how much people's locations and the distances between them affect their likelihood of being friends. Linking this up with census data could tell us if this is affected by the size or demographics of their locations (do people in small towns tend to be more tight-knit? Does a high unmarried population correlate with more social network use?).

On the politics side, we could combine data from the SEC about which companies are in which industries with data from Center for Responsible Politics (CRP) about political contributions. This would let us determine which industries donate the most to which political parties. Figure 20-1 shows a couple of pie charts I made demonstrating this particular data mashup.

FIGURE 20-1. Pie charts resulting from a data mashup of SEC industry data and Center for Responsible Politics political contribution data. (See Color Plate 70.)

I haven't even touched things like linking stock prices to sentiment analysis of message boards, trying to tie together genetics and drug data, or determining whether restaurants in low-income neighborhoods are dirtier (according to the health inspector), but this should give you just a small taste of what's possible when different data sources are connected. Unfortunately, the difficulty of automatically connecting sets ranges from nontrivial to nearly impossible. In the last example we took data from the CRP, which lists companies by name, but to find companies in the SEC database we need something called a Central Index Key (CIK). Further, companies like Exxon Mobile aren't always classified as "Energy" companies but more specifically as "Petroleum Mining" companies, so in order to find all the Energy companies, we need an established hierarchy of which industries are subsets of other industries.

Within Companies

We can think of integrating data across the Web as the big challenge, but microcosms of this challenge appear everywhere. It's especially striking (at least it was to me, when I first noticed it) how often large companies have several databases all referring to the same items and no way to query across them or even make employees aware that data about their area of interest exists in a database maintained by a coworker. This is often called the "information silo problem," referring to the fact that information is cleanly separated and largely inaccessible—like grain in a silo (yes, I always thought that metaphor was a bit of a stretch).

This problem was clearly noticeable when I worked in the biotech industry and spoke with people at many pharmaceutical companies about their data integration challenges. In many cases, the management structure of companies is divided into therapeutic areas (areas focused on a family of diseases). People in these groups might be working on a particular set of target proteins to hit with a drug or looking for genetic markers to predict whether a drug would work or not, all the time conducting expensive experiments and building up large sets of knowledge on these genes, proteins, and compounds.

At the same time, people in different parts of the company, or perhaps previous researchers on a long-since-finished project, were often studying or had studied the same or very similar genes, proteins, and compounds. Researchers on each project often had no way to take advantage of data that had been generated in different projects, so would miss important insights and wastefully replicate experiments.

Think for a moment about why this is the case: even assuming that everyone had agreed on a schema and a mechanism for querying, there's no guarantee that people would use the same nomenclature to describe their experiments. What are the correct fields to use? And how do you search for, say, a "lung cancer" experiment when another researcher might have described it as an "adenocarcinoma"? Many working groups have emerged to try to create a controlled vocabulary and fixed schema to make experiments easier to find, but so far none have completely cracked this problem.

Biotech is actually way ahead of the game, having at least identified the problem and made serious industry-wide attempts to solve it. At the other end of the spectrum, we've recently had spectacular failures of investment banks all over the world where no one had any idea what positions their traders held, and traders themselves had no way of knowing whether they held an opposing position to someone sitting across the room. And if too little data connection is a problem, connecting things that shouldn't be connected can be an even bigger problem. For example, governments have given us several high-profile cases of people being misidentified as terrorists or banned from flying simply because they had the same name as a known suspicious person.

This is, of course, not restricted to large companies or industry-specific information. Even small companies have problems keeping client and employee records consolidated.

Impediments to Connecting Data

Hopefully you're starting to be convinced that there are huge advantages to being able to easily integrate data from many different sources. But there are a few different reasons people aren't doing it already….

The Representation Problem

Perhaps the most basic problem with attempting to connect data sets is the fact that most data is stored in very inflexible structures. First of all, a surprising amount of important data in science and business is also kept in Excel spreadsheets, which are stored locally on people's computers, inaccessible to others and also not designed for integration anyway.

Even in companies where databases are made accessible, data is classically stored in relational databases, most of which have predefined schemas to fit the data that was initially believed to be important. Figure 20-2 shows a simple example of a relational schema for restaurant data. This is excellent for large, predictable data sets because relational databases have excellent performance when well configured, but presents problems when the application requires new kinds of data, new fields, or new relationships to be added frequently.

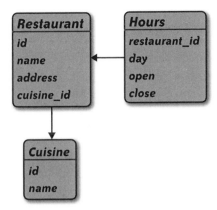

FIGURE 20-2. A relational schema for restaurant data.

I've seen people solve this problem in a number of ways, but two really stand out, mostly because they're opposite ends of a spectrum. The traditional approach is to continually refactor the database, adding new tables, new fields to existing tables, and new indices and connections between tables. This means constant migration of the data to the new schema, a process that can be expensive, disruptive, and slow (space considerations restrict me from going through examples here, but I get a lot of knowing nods whenever I give talks on this subject). It also leads to increasingly complex schemas that eventually become extremely difficult to visualize and interpret.

The other approach I've seen is to simply build a very basic schema that can support any type of data. The typical way to do this is to have a table of entities and a table of relationships, something like what's shown in Figure 20-3.

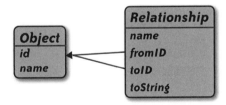

FIGURE 20-3. A basic schema.

This has the advantage of letting developers and data loaders add new kinds of relationships to the data on the fly. Essentially it represents data as a graph instead of a set of tables. Figure 20-4 shows a restaurant represented in a graph along with a lot of extra data that one could easily add later.

Unfortunately, relational databases are not designed to store data in that manner, and to do any useful queries on that schema will require a lot of self-joins and be very slow.

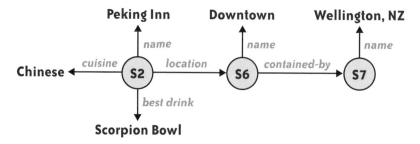

FIGURE 20-4. Graph database of restaurant data, leaving room for expansion.

Since this is such a common pattern, many commercial and open source "graph databases" have appeared in recent years, specifically designed to store data like this. A few examples are:

Sesame (http://openrdf.org)
  An open source graph database maintained by the Dutch software company Aduna

Jena (http://jena.sourceforge.net)
  Another open source graph database developed by Hewlett Packard

AllegroGraph (http://agraph.franz.com)
  A more feature-rich commercial graph database developed by Franz

Neo4J (http://neo4j.org)
  An open-source graph database with commercial licensing options

Although they represent a significant shift in data modeling and development practices, graph databases are much more flexible when it comes to connecting data from many sources. For this reason, they've been getting a lot more attention lately as people start to consider "scaling to complexity" in addition to scaling to size. Sadly, this is among the simplest of the problems we face when connecting data—it gets a lot worse from here.

Shared Nouns and Shared Verbs

Even assuming you have a nice graph or perfectly suitable relational schema in which to merge two databases, how do you know which items actually match each other? One database may list "Coca-Cola," which is the same as "The Coca-Cola Company" listed in another, or less trivially, "Coke" (but which, let it be noted, is not the same as "The Coca-Cola Bottling Company," which is separate and distinct).

To make matters even worse, there's nothing close to consistency in the way people name fields or object properties, either. In one database, the address of a restaurant might be in the *address* field and in another the *location* field. How can we tell that *location* when it's a property on a restaurant means the same thing as *address*, but *location* when used to describe a gene sequence means its position on a chromosome? In practice, this is usually

a manual process, but if we expect to build systems that can easily integrate hundreds or thousands of databases, we need to find ways to eliminate a lot of the manual work involved in such integrations.

Various efforts to resolve these naming problems have been attempted. In the Semantic Web community an effort called "Linked Open Data" has emerged, wherein people are encouraging one another to refer to specific objects (like a movie, a person, or a restaurant) by a standard Universal Resource Indicator (URI), so everyone knows when two people are talking about the same thing. There have also been several efforts to standardize on a set of *ontologies*, which describe what fields should be used to describe things like a restaurant or a movie in all cases.

So far, however, the number of groups that have agreed to use the same URIs to refer to things and the same ontologies to describe them is an exceedingly small fraction of all the free online databases out there, and covers almost none of companies' private databases. In many cases, even those trying to participate in the linked open data efforts aren't currently using the same URIs for things that clearly are the same thing.

Which means, for those of us trying to connect data sets, we're going to have to devise ways to automatically determine whether two things are the same.

The Same Thing with Different Names

Like many people, when I first started trying to connect data sets, I thought a nice first-order assumption was that the best way to determine if two items were the same thing was if they had the same name. I even thought I could cleverly get around problems like "Coca-cola" and "The coca-cola company" by using tricks like string distance or substring matching. This works much of the time, but often fails in the most interesting cases—the ones you care most about.

A simple example I came across when attempting to combine movie data from Wikipedia with movie data from Netflix was *Prêt-à-Porter*. This French name is the one used in Wikipedia (despite the fact that this is an American film), but the name in Netflix was the English *Ready to Wear*. Before you argue that we should translate every name to English before making a string comparison, note that there are many films with multiple titles in the same language, such as *B.U.S.T.E.D.* and *Everybody Loves Sunshine* or *Point of No Return* and *The Assassin*—these movies either came out with different names in different countries or had working titles that were different from their eventual release titles.

So, if we can't rely on searching for similar strings, how do we match movies? Well, the principle is simple and the details are fiendishly complex (and the subject of much personal and academic research). For example, we have two movies, both released in 1994, both directed by Robert Altman, and both starring Julia Roberts and Sophia Lauren: could these possibly be two different movies? As it happens, there is exactly one movie with those characteristics, so any movie with that set of properties—regardless of its name—must be the same movie. Later in this chapter I'll discuss how this is detected in practice.

As an aside, it turns out that string-distance is a particularly poor way to match movies. *Ghostbusters* and *Ghostbusters 2* are very similar strings but represent different movies, which you can easily tell by the fact that one was released in 1984 and the other was released in 1989. It's not even possible to assume that numbers following the title refer to a series of films—*The Madness of George III* and *The Madness of King George* in fact refer to the same film.

Different Things with the Same Name

Failing to recognize that two things are the same is often an irritation, producing duplicates that can be fixed later if necessary. Of far greater consequence is incorrectly deciding that two distinct items are the same thing because they share a name or some other attribute that's really insufficient for identity. The reason this is more dangerous is that once things in a database become improperly conflated, we start attaching facts about the separate items to the same thing, and when the error is finally noticed, we have no easy way to disentangle the facts without a lot of human effort.

There are seven towns in Wisconsin (U.S.) named "Franklin," only one of which contains a Wal-Mart. There are at least four books named *City of God*. And there are at least 50 people famous enough to appear in Wikipedia named "John Smith." Erroneous no-fly lists aside, it should be clear that having two items with the same name is very weak evidence that they're the same thing, especially when it comes to people. Although there are examples of unique keys for people, like Social Security numbers in the United States, these almost never appear in publicly accessible databases; unique identifiers for people almost always end up requiring some level of protection.

Except in very closed sets (names of countries, for example) or for exceedingly rare names ("Toby Segaran" comes to mind), it's strongly advisable not to conflate things based on name alone; algorithms should be designed to use additional evidence to determine whether two separate records really are the same thing.

I think it's important to point out here that there have been efforts to create canonical identifiers for certain things, but this has never been successfully applied to people for privacy reasons. In the United States we have Social Security numbers that many government and credit agencies use to track us, but we're taught that it's strongly inadvisable to share this with anyone, and we'd certainly never put it in a public database just so other people could link their data to us more easily. Thus we're permanently stuck with billions of people with similar names and no other way to identify them.

Possible Solutions

Although it's important to realize that this remains an unsolved problem in the general case, there are a number of ideas that people have tried that work in certain circumstances. Some of these approaches will be dead ends, but others, when further developed, seem to have the potential to work on a wide range of data sets.

Matching on Multiple Fields

In Chapter 7, "Data Finds Data," Jeff Jonas describes a hypothetical employee who could be discovered to also be a shoplifter through a combination of his name and his address. In that case, a combination of a name and an address is sufficient evidence to suggest that two different records in fact represent the same person. Jeff would also be quick to point out that he's come across cases where a "Patrick Smith" and a "Patricia Smith" shared an address and both went by "Pat Smith," so if you're not careful it's easy to get trapped in a maze of exceptions to otherwise obvious rules.

This does illustrate the basic and most common approach to matching items in data sets: choose a set of parameters and create a set of fixed rules that tell you whether things match or not. For example, "do two people have the same name and the same address?" or "do two films have the same name and were released the same year?"

This approach will work in many cases, but it has a few drawbacks. First of all, it requires the developer to identify the fields and rules by which things match. This can be incredibly tedious, since when they realize that *Prêt-à-Porter* doesn't match *Ready to Wear* according to the basic name/year rule, they have to go and invent another rule like "do two films that came out in the same year have a director and at least one actor in common?"

The second problem is that it requires a high level of consistency in the fields themselves. What if we didn't have the actor's full name? What if the year was missing for some movies in one of the databases? Finally, because we're choosing specific fields and creating flat records, this approach doesn't take advantage of the full network of data—which has the potential to give us far more information about identity.

Collective Reconciliation

I believe that taking advantage of the full network of data is the key to solving this matching problem. The idea is embodied in a series of techniques called *collective reconciliation* or *collective entity resolution*. For a very detailed discussion, I'd suggest reading Indrajit Bhattacharya's PhD dissertation, which you can find at *http://www.lib.umd.edu/drum/handle/1903/4241*.

In this section I'll take you through a very high-level overview of what collective reconciliation means. The details of how these algorithms are implemented varies greatly depending on the particular type of data you're working with, and is well beyond the scope of this chapter, but my hope is that a high-level overview will both help you experiment and make it easier for you to read other people's work on the subject.

First of all, consider that we have two movie data sets, each one containing slightly different information. Pieces of two of them, represented as graphs, are shown in Figure 20-5.

We've already decided it's unwise to match things based on name alone, so we can't just decide that any two of the objects are the same by just looking at the names. However, we can say we believe that *node10* in graph A *might* be the same as *node22* in graph B because they're both named "Julia Roberts," and that *node12* in graph A *might* be the same as *node27* in graph B because they're both named "Ready to Wear."

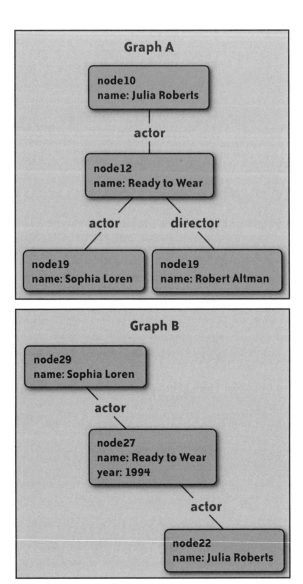

FIGURE 20-5. Pieces of two different movie databases.

The trick now is that we have potential matches between items in the two graphs, and these items *share a connection*—the potentially matched "Julia Roberts" nodes are connected to the potentially matched "Ready to Wear" nodes. This connection provides more evidence to both of these matches. Whether it's conclusive in the general case depends on a lot of probability assumptions about how likely it is that there are multiple actresses named Julia Roberts who starred in a movie called *Ready to Wear*, but in this case we can consider it to be the right answer.

The way this is implemented varies, but a popular technique is called *message-passing*. Essentially, *node12* in graph A, knowing that it might be the same as *node27* in graph B, looks at all the connections in graph B and sends messages to its own neighbors in graph A. The message to all the actors connected to it could say, "you might be the same as *node22* or *node25*," and *node10*, receiving this, realizes "in fact, I already thought I might be *node22*." At the same time, *node10* is doing the same thing, telling *node12* all the movies it could possibly be. Figure 20-6 shows what this might look like.

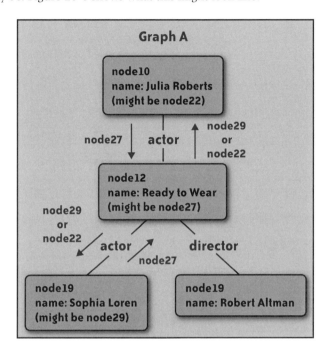

FIGURE 20-6. *Message-passing between nodes.*

You can probably see why this is called "collective reconciliation": rather than flattening records, we're actually trying to merge everything at once, and the nodes are helping one another decide whether to merge or not. This is a trivial example, of course, but consider the more difficult one shown in Figure 20-7.

Now the names of "Ready to Wear" don't match, and we don't even have a name for *node10*! How can we possibly know that it's Julia Roberts? However, we've extended the network out a little bit, with some other films in which Julia Roberts starred and, luckily, message-passing can be run over many iterations. Maybe you can figure out what a message-passing algorithm would do? Here's a rough idea:

1. *node11* decides it's a potential match for *node23* because they have the same name.

2. Likewise *node15* decides it's a potential match for *node9* (this would obviously go on if we had more Julia Roberts movies).

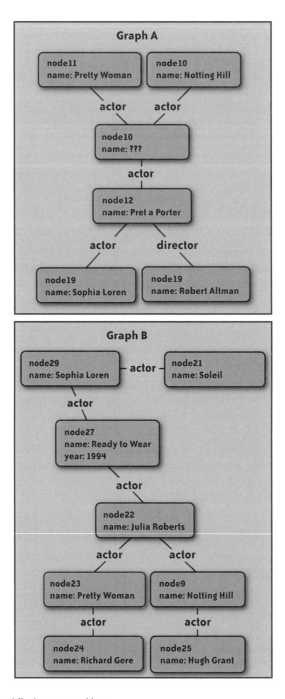

FIGURE 20-7. A more difficult merging problem.

3. *node11* sends a message to *node10* saying, "you might be *node22* or *node24*."

4. Similarly, *node15* sends a message to *node10* saying, "you might be *node22* or *node25*."

5. *node10*, upon receiving all these messages, concludes that it's probably *node22*, since that's what all its messages have in common.

6. Now that *node10* has identified itself, it can now send a message to *all* its connected nodes (including the ones it received messages from) saying what movies it thinks they could be.

7. *node12* now has messages from *node10* and *node19* saying, "you might be *node23*," so it can settle on that.

We've established that *Prêt-à-Porter* and *Ready to Wear* are the same film, despite the fact that we started with only one named actor in common.

Notice how we took advantage of the whole network of facts to determine identity? This is the essence of collective reconciliation, and what makes it so powerful. This notion can be extended even further: in some experiments, I've found that you can connect two data sets of films and actors using only the film release years. The fact that an actor appeared in films in 12 particular years and costarred with a different actor who appeared in films in a different set of 8 particular years is often enough to uniquely identify both people.

Of course, the implementation and mathematical details, which can get very tricky, are outside the scope of this chapter. Implementing custom versions of this technique is left as a very lucrative exercise for the reader.

Conclusion

By now, most people are aware that almost every field is becoming more reliant on data analysis for advancement. Where science used to rely primarily on theoretical models built from few observations, the future seems to be in the collection and mining of millions of measurements; where retail companies relied heavily on the insights of "trend spotters," many now believe that what they should be selling is buried somewhere in the piles of collected data.

Rather than independently building ever-larger data sets at great expense, I believe the future lies in taking advantage of the piles of data that have been generated by others, combining it and mixing it with our own data. Whether it comes from within our own organizations, nonprofit largesse, or the public domain, there is a lot of money to be saved and made by reusing and connecting data. Hopefully this essay has inspired you to find better ways to do just that.

Contributors

Ben Blackburne is a postdoctoral fellow in the sequence analysis and assembly team at the Wellcome Trust Sanger Institute.

Jean-Claude Bradley is an associate professor of chemistry and the E-Learning Coordinator for the College of Arts and Sciences at Drexel University. He leads the UsefulChem project, an initiative started in the summer of 2005 to make the scientific process as transparent as possible by publishing all research work in real time to a collection of public blogs, wikis, and other web pages. Jean-Claude coined the term Open Notebook Science to distinguish this approach from other more restricted forms of Open Science. He teaches undergraduate organic chemistry courses with most content freely available on public blogs, wikis, games, and audio and video podcasts. He has a PhD in organic chemistry and has published articles and obtained patents in the areas of synthetic and mechanistic chemistry, gene therapy, nanotechnology, and scientific knowledge management.

Lukas Biewald is founder and CEO of Dolores Labs, a company making crowdsourcing easy and reliable. Dolores Labs' blog (*http://blog.doloreslabs.com*) is full of fun crowdsourcing and data visualization experiments. Prior to Dolores Labs, he worked as a senior scientist at Powerset, and before that he built Yahoo! Japan's search engine ranking algorithm. He received a BS in math and an MS in computer science from Stanford University, where he

worked in the AI Lab and published two papers on machine learning applications. His personal website is *http://lukasbiewald.com/*. Lukas is an expert-level *Go* player.

Brian Cooper is a principal research scientist at Yahoo! Research. Before that, he was an assistant professor at Georgia Tech, and before that, he completed his PhD at Stanford. His interests are in building distributed systems and, in particular, distributed systems that do database-style management and processing of data. At Yahoo! he works on building very large distributed data storage and processing systems. In previous lives he has worked on self-adaptive peer-to-peer systems, distributed streaming event processing, reliable distributed archival data storage, and XML indexing.

Jason Dykes has been designing and developing interactive spatial interfaces for exploration since the early 1990s. He has used a range of flexible technologies for rapid development, including Tcl/Tk, SVG/JavaScript, and Processing to develop innovative software applications and novel views that reveal geographic structure. A senior lecturer in the giCentre at City University London (*http://gicentre.org*), he gained a BA in geography from Oxford University in 1990 and his PhD from the University of Leicester in 2000. Jason is co-chair of the International Cartographic Association Commission on Geovisualization and a National Teaching Fellow. He is currently engaged in helping his sons, Iko and Fred, learn to ride balance bikes.

Jonathan Follett, president and chief creative officer of Hot Knife Design, Inc., is an internationally published author on the topics of user experience, information design, and virtual teams. He contributes to *A List Apart*, *Digital Web*, and *UXmatters*, and speaks on web-related topics for Boston area technology groups. His articles have been translated into Chinese, Indonesian, Portuguese, Russian, and Spanish. Jon's visual design work has garnered several American Graphic Design Awards, a Horizon Interactive Award, and other industry recognition.

Andrew Gelman is a professor of statistics and political science at Columbia University. His most recent books are *Data Analysis Using Regression and Multilevel/Hierarchical Models* (Cambridge University Press); *Red State, Blue State, Rich State, Poor State: Why Americans Vote the Way They Do* (Princeton University Press); and *A Quantitative Tour of the Social Sciences* (Cambridge University Press).

Yair Ghitza is a PhD student in political science at Columbia University, specializing in American politics and quantitative methods. He previously worked for political analysis firms, including Catalist and Copernicus Analytics.

Rajarshi Guha is a research scientist at the NIH Chemical Genomics Center working on various aspects of high-throughput screening problems. Prior to this he was a visiting member of the faculty in the School of Informatics at Indiana University. Over the past few years he has worked in various areas of cheminformatics and computational drug discovery, ranging from QSAR modeling and algorithm development to software engineering of toolkits and web service infrastructure for the deployment of cheminformatics methods and models.

Alon Halevy heads the Structured Data Management Research group at Google Inc. Prior to that, he was a professor of computer science at the University of Washington in Seattle. In 1999, Dr. Halevy cofounded Nimble Technology, one of the first companies in the Enterprise Information Integration space, and in 2004, he founded Transformic Inc., a company that created search engines for the Deep Web, which was acquired by Google. Dr. Halevy is a Fellow of the Association for Computing Machinery, received the Presidential Early Career Award for Scientists and Engineers (PECASE) in 2000, and was a Sloan Fellow (1999–2000). He has published over 150 technical papers. He received his PhD in computer science from Stanford University in 1993.

Jeff Hammerbacher is the vice president of products and chief scientist at Cloudera. Jeff was an entrepreneur in residence at Accel Partners immediately prior to joining Cloudera. Before Accel, he conceived, built, and led the Data team at Facebook. The Data team was responsible for driving many of the statistics and machine learning applications at Facebook, as well as building out the infrastructure to support these tasks for massive data sets. The team produced several academic papers and two open source projects: Hive, a system for offline analysis built above Hadoop, and Cassandra, a structured storage system on a P2P network. Before joining Facebook, Jeff was a quantitative analyst on Wall Street. Jeff earned his bachelor's degree in mathematics from Harvard University.

Jeffrey Heer is an assistant professor of computer science at Stanford University, where his research focuses on human-computer interaction, interactive visualization, and social computing. His work has produced novel visualization techniques for exploring data, software tools that simplify visualization creation and customization, and collaborative analysis systems that leverage the insights of multiple analysts. He is the author of the prefuse and flare open source visualization toolkits, currently in use by the visualization research community and numerous corporations. Over the years, he has also worked at Xerox PARC, IBM Research, Microsoft Research, and Tableau Software. He holds BS, MS, and PhD degrees in computer science from the University of California, Berkeley.

Matthew Holm is the consulting creative director for Hot Knife Design, Inc., of Boston, where he contributes to corporate strategy and specializes in HTML/CSS development as well as CMS-driven websites. Matt is currently vice-chair of the Computer-Human Interaction Forum of Oregon (CHIFOO, the Oregon chapter of the Association of Computing Machinery's Special Interest Group on Computer-Human Interaction). In addition to his work in the online world, Matt is also a professional children's book author and illustrator; more than one million copies of his award-winning, critically acclaimed *Babymouse* graphic novels (published by Random House) are currently in print.

J. M. Hughes is an embedded systems and software engineer who is particularly fond of real-time control, data acquisition, and image processing. From 2003 to 2007 he was responsible for the design, implementation, and testing of the surface imaging software on the *Phoenix* Mars Lander. He is currently working on the electronics and control software for a multiwavelength laser interferometer system that will be used to verify the alignment of telescope mirror segments for a NASA project. He lives in Tucson, Arizona, with his wife and daughter.

Jeff Jonas is chief scientist, IBM Entity Analytics Group and an IBM Distinguished Engineer. The IBM Entity Analytics Group was formed based on technologies developed by Systems Research & Development (SRD), founded by Jonas in 1984 and acquired by IBM in January 2005. He blogs at *http://jeffjonas.typepad.com*.

Jonathan P. Kastellec is a professor of politics at Princeton University. His research has appeared in the *Journal of Law, Economics & Organization*; the *Journal of Empirical Legal Studies*; and *Perspective on Politics*.

Valdean Klump lives in San Francisco and is a writer at Google Creative Lab.

Aaron Koblin is an artist from San Francisco who is well known for such visual data projects as Flight Patterns, The Sheep Market, and Ten Thousand Cents. He was director of technology on the "House of Cards" video and is currently design technology lead at Google Creative Lab.

Coco Krumme is a graduate student at the MIT Media Lab. She also works for Metaweb Technologies in San Francisco.

Andrew Lang is a professor of mathematics at Oral Roberts University. His PhD training is in the area of quantum field theory in curved spacetime. While remaining active in this area, he has always enjoyed working collaboratively on interdisciplinary projects ranging from modeling basketball free throws to the stability of spinning spacecraft under thrust. His current interests include multidimensional data visualization, the relationship between science and science fiction, and the epistemological differences between teleology and metaphysical naturalism.

Pierre Lindenbaum obtained his PhD in virology in 2000, when he studied the virus-host interactions. He then switched his professional career to bioinformatics, and after one year at the French National Center of Genotyping (France) he joined the French startup Integragen in 2001. He now works as a bioinformatician at the Fondation Jean Dausset-CEPH, a genetic research center located in Paris.

Jayant Madhavan is a senior software engineer at Google Inc. and was the technical lead on its Deep Web crawling initiative. Prior to that, he was the chief architect at Tranformic Inc. (acquired by Google in 2005), a company that created search engines for the Deep Web. Dr. Madhavan received his PhD in computer science from the University of Washington in 2005.

Michal Migurski is a partner at Stamen Design, where he leads the technical and research aspects of the work. He has been building for the Web since 1995, specializing in big, exciting data sets and the means to communicate and disseminate them to broad audiences for a variety of clients. He speaks publicly on these and other topics to academic and industry audiences, participates actively in a variety of open source development efforts, maintains an active weblog at *http://mike.teczno.com*, and holds a degree in cognitive science from UC Berkeley.

Cameron Neylon is a biophysicist who has always worked in interdisciplinary areas and is a well-known advocate of open research practice and improved data management. He currently works as senior scientist in biomolecular sciences at the ISIS Neutron Scattering facility at the Science and Technology Facilities Council (STFC). He writes and speaks regularly on the interface of web technology with science and the successful (and unsuccessful) application of generic and specially designed tools in the academic research environment.

Peter Norvig is director of research at Google Inc. He is a Fellow of the AAAI and the ACM and coauthor of *Artificial Intelligence: A Modern Approach* (Prentice Hall), the leading textbook in the field. Previously he was head of computational sciences at NASA and a faculty member at USC and Berkeley.

Brendan O'Connor is a researcher in machine learning and natural language processing. He is a scientific consultant at Dolores Labs and worked previously as a relevance engineer at Powerset. He received a BS and MS in symbolic systems from Stanford University, and is back to academia this fall as a graduate student at Carnegie Mellon University. His blog, "Artificial Intelligence and Social Science," is at *http://anyall.org/blog*.

David Poole is a member of the Statistics Research Department at AT&T Labs and was recently the secretary/treasurer of the Section on Statistical Computing of the American Statistical Association. He has extensive experience with large-scale data mining, such as the analysis of customer calling data for traffic engineering and fraud detection.

Raghu Ramakrishnan is chief scientist for Audience and Cloud Computing at Yahoo!, and is a Research Fellow. His work in database systems—with a focus on data mining, query optimization, and web-scale data management—has influenced query optimization in commercial database systems and the design of window functions in SQL:1999. His paper on the Birch clustering algorithm received the SIGMOD 10-Year Test-of-Time award, and he has written the widely used text *Database Management Systems* (with Johannes Gehrke; McGraw-Hill). He is Chair of ACM SIGMOD, and a Fellow of the ACM and IEEE.

Toby Segaran is the author of two O'Reilly titles, the very popular *Programming Collective Intelligence* and the recently released *Programming the Semantic Web*. He currently works at Metaweb, where he develops large-scale reconciliation algorithms in an attempt to create a free database of shared keys for all other public databases. Prior to working at Metaweb, he started a biotech software company, which was acquired in 2003 by Genstruct, a systems biology company. Toby has a BS in computer science from MIT and lives in San Francisco with his wife, Brooke. You can read more of his writing and data experiments at *http://blog.kiwitobes.com*.

Lisa Sokol is currently a consultant within IBM's Global Business Services group, specializing in Entity Analytics. Her primary area of interest is helping the law enforcement and intelligence communities discover actionable information buried within their very large data collections. She has architected a large number of systems that detect and assess threat risk relative to fraud, terrorism, counterintelligence, and criminal activity.

She has helped pioneer the application of technologies such as data mining, text mining, and machine translation to exploit the information accessible to shared intelligence environments. Dr. Sokol has numerous papers published in these areas. She received her doctorate in Operations Research from the University of Massachusetts.

Utkarsh Srivastava is a senior research scientist at Yahoo! Research. His primary research interest is in building systems to solve large-scale data management problems. Prior to developing PNUTS, he played an active role in the development of Pig, a declarative query language over Hadoop. He obtained his PhD from Stanford University, where he worked on query processing over streaming data and several query optimization problems.

Deborah Swayne is a member of the Statistics Research Department at AT&T Labs, a Fellow of the American Statistical Association, and a past chair of the ASA Section on Statistical Graphics. She is a coauthor of the widely used ggobi high-dimensional data visualization software.

Jud Valeski is cofounder and CTO of Gnip, a data portability software initiative. From client-side consumer facing products to large-scale backend infrastructure projects, he has enjoyed working with technology for over 20 years. He's been a part of engineering, product, and M&A teams at IBM, Netscape, onebox.com, AOL, and me.dium. Jud has played a central role in the release of a wide range of products used by tens of millions of users worldwide.

Hadley Wickham is an assistant professor of statistics at Rice University and is interested in developing tools (both computational and cognitive) for making data preparation, visualization, and analysis easier. He has developed 15 R packages, and in 2006 won the John Chambers Award for Statistical Computing for his work on the ggplot and reshape R packages.

Antony Williams is the president of ChemZoo Inc. and the host of ChemSpider, an online free access service for chemists established with the intention of building a structure-centric community for chemists. He has spent over a decade in the commercial scientific software business as chief science officer for Advanced Chemistry Development (ACD/Labs), and during his tenure oversaw its product development, marketing, and sales teams. He is an accomplished NMR spectroscopist with over 100 peer-reviewed publications. During his career he was the NMR technology leader for the Eastman Kodak Company and has worked in both academia and national government research institutions. He has recently taken his passion for providing access to chemistry-related information and software services to the masses by hosting the ChemSpider service.

Egon Willighagen is a scientist at Uppsala University in Sweden working on data analysis in the field of pharmaceutical life sciences. His research involves the development of statistical methods and software for molecular chemometrics and proteochemometrics. He is release manager for the Chemistry Development Kit and Metware, and has contributed to other open source cheminformatics projects for more than 10 years, among which are Jmol and Bioclipse.

Jo Wood is a Reader in Geographic Information at the giCentre, City University London (*http://gicentre.org*). He has been involved in research in the analysis of landscape form since 1990 and is the author of the GIS *LandSerf* for the visual exploration of surfaces. As a geographer and programmer, he has been writing software in Java for the last decade or so to create geovisualization solutions for data analysis problems. He is the author of the textbook *Java Programming for Spatial Sciences* (CRC). When not analyzing landscapes with a computer, he can usually be found cycling over them.

Matt Wood heads up Production Software at the Wellcome Trust Sanger Institute, where he is responsible for the software that drives the Institute's world-class sequencing facility.

Nathan Yau is a statistics PhD candidate at the University of California, Los Angeles, and has a BS in electrical engineering and computer science from the University of California, Berkeley. His research focuses on data visualization, self-surveillance, and how our digital selves intertwine with the physical world. Largely inspired by a summer internship as a graphics editor at the *New York Times*, Yau also maintains the leading statistics and data visualization blog, FlowingData (*http://flowingdata.com/*), which revolves around how designers, statisticians, and computer scientists use data to help us make better decisions.

INDEX

collecting data (see data collection)

collective reconciliation, 344–348

color schemes in data visualization
    for customer survey project, 23
    for Geograph archive, 93, 95
    for PEIR system, 9, 10
    for sense.us website, 184, 191

conditional probability, definition of, 220

confirmation bias, 208

consistency of data after updates, 57–64

consumer price index (CPI), 307

contact information for this book, xiv

context-less directories, 113

Cooper, Brian F. (author), 55–71

corpus, definition of, 220
    (see also natural language corpus data)

correlation, not related to causality, 210

CPI (consumer price index), 307

Crimespotting project (see Oakland
        Crimespotting project)

CrimeWatch application (see Oakland
        CrimeWatch application)

crowdsourced data, 260, 262

CUBE operator, 76

customer survey project, 19
    data collection for, 19–30
    form design for, 21–30
    length of survey, 20, 24–27
    reporting results of, 30

D

data analysis
    biases in people's interpretation of
        data, 205, 217
    of corpus data (see natural language corpus
        data)
    correlation not related to causality, 210
    dependencies not controlled in, 215
    of free-form data, 290–294
    for housing market analysis, 306–319
    large data sets increasing cost of, 210
    large data sets not necessarily
        improving, 209
    limitations of data in, 208–217
    narrative fallacy in, 207
    patterns, people's skill at recognizing, 206
    predictions not made by, 213
    probabilities as not intuitive, 215
    single outcomes not answered by, 211
    for social stereotypes data, 282, 290–294
    stories created from data, 208, 211
    subjective and quantitative information
        required for, 216
    tools for, 282

data collection
    accessibility considerations for, 19, 23
    accuracy of data, 21, 29
    asynchronous, 4
    for customer survey project, 19–30
    for YFD system, 4
    history of, 1
    for housing market analysis, 304
    inherent problems with, 259
    motivation considerations for, 21, 30
    for music video, 150–154, 155–159, 164
    for Oakland Crimespotting project, 169–174
    of personal data, 3–5
    for PEIR system, 3, 4
    perception considerations for, 20–21
    for Phoenix Mars Lander system, 37
    for sense.us website, 186–188
    trust considerations for, 20, 28
    Twitter used for, 4, 13
    UX design practices for, 18
    for YFD system, 3

"data finds data" concept, 105
    benefits of, 106
    example of, 107–111
    requirements for, 115–117
    (see also discoverability of data; findability
        of data)

data integration, 335
    benefits of, 337
    collective reconciliation for, 344–348
    matching on multiple fields for, 344
    naming inconsistencies, problems
        with, 341–343
    representation problem of, 339
    sources of public data, 336
    within companies, 338

data management stack, by Microsoft, 82

data processing
    for music video, 160
    for PEIR system, 6
    for Phoenix Mars Lander system, 42,
        46–51, 53
    validating crowdsourced data, 262

data scientists, 83

data sharing
    for PEIR system, 12
    for sense.us website, 194–199, 201

data storage
    binary data, 41
    cloud system for, 56, 70
    DNA as a method of, 243–250
    for social data, 121
    geo-replication of data, 56, 58
    naming inconsistencies in, 341–343
    packing data for, 40

I

Image Compression Sub-System (ICS), 42
images (see Geograph archive; Phoenix Mars
     Lander system; Radiohead's "House
     of Cards" video)
Information Platforms, 74, 83
     (see also Facebook's Information Platform)
information visualization, 86
informative test for surfacing, 142
informativeness test for surfacing, 136
Inmon, Bill (Building the Data
     Warehouse), 76
Integrated Public Use Microdata Series
     (IPUMS) databases, 186
integrating data from separate sources (see
     data integration)
International Cancer Genome Consortium, 253
IPUMS (Integrated Public Use Microdata
     Series) databases, 186

J

Jonas, Jeff (author), 105–118

K

Kahneman, Daniel (experiment about prospect
     theory), 208, 215
Kastellec, Jonathan P. (author), 323–332
Kimball, Ralph (The Data Warehouse
     Toolkit), 76
Klump, Valdean (author), 149–165
Koblin, Aaron (author), 149–165
Krumme, Coco (author), 205–217

L

Lake Wobegon effect, 217
Lang, Andrew (author), 259–277
language identification of corpus data, 239
"Learning Organization" concept, 78
Lewin, Kurt ("action research" concept), 78
libraries, as Information Platforms, 73
Lidar scanner (see Velodyne Lidar scanner)
Lindenbaum, Pierre (author), 259–277
Lindsay, Jeff (Web Hooks concept), 127
Linguistic Data Consortium, 219
location information, representation of
     for Geograph archive, 95–98
     for Oakland Crimespotting project,
        174–181
     for PEIR system, 8–11
     for political data, 330
     for sense.us website, 188–194

Luhn, Hans Peter ("A Business Intelligence
     System"), 75
luxury product, survey for (see customer
     survey project)

M

machine translation of corpus data, 240
Madhaven, Jayant (author), 133–147
maps (see location information, representation
     of)
Mars Lander system (see Phoenix Mars Lander
     system)
mastership of records, 60, 61
materialized views, 66
Matlab (data analysis package), 282
Matplotlib (data analysis package), 282
Matsumoto, Yukihiro (Ruby programming
     language), 89, 98
MECA Optical Microscope (OM) camera, 38
mediator
     accessing Deep Web using, 135
     for social data (see Gnip)
Medicare website, 337
message boards, public data available
     from, 337
Microsoft Azure SDS, 70
Microsoft's data management stack, 82
Migurski, Michal (author), 167–182
MObStor system, 71
Modest Maps library, 8
Morville, Peter ("findability" concept)
motivation considerations for data
     collection, 21, 30
music video based on data (see Radiohead's
     "House of Cards" video)

N

narrative fallacy, 207
National Center for Biotechnology Information
     (NCBI) website, 336
natural language corpus data, 219, 240
     author identification of, 239
     DNA sequencing of, 240
     document unshredding of, 240
     language identification of, 239
     machine translation of, 240
     search strategies used for, 241
     secret codes in, analysis of, 228–234
     spam detection in, 239
     spelling correction of, 234–239
     word segmentation analysis of, 221–227
NCBI (National Center for Biotechnology
     Information) website, 336

Neylon, Cameron (author), 259–277
normalization of social data, 128–131
Norvig, Peter (author), 219–242
Num Py (data analysis package), 282

O

Oakland Crimespotting project, 167
    data collection from CrimeWatch, 169–174
    visualizing data online, 174–181
Oakland CrimeWatch application, 169–174
OAuth, 130
O'Connor, Brendan (author), 279–301
Open Notebook Science, 261
Optical Microscope (OM) camera, 38

P

P2P protocol, 121
partitioning data, 56
patterns, people's skill at recognizing, 206
PEIR (Personal Environmental Impact Report)
    system, 2
    data collection for, 3, 4
    data processing for, 6
    data visualization for, 8–12
    database design for, 5
    participating in, 15
    sharing data from, 12
perception considerations for data
    collection, 20–21
persistent context, 115
personal data
    collection of, 3–5
    visualization of, 7–14
Personal Environmental Impact Report (see
    PEIR system)
Phoenix Mars Lander system, 35–40
    cameras (imagers) for, 38, 53
    computer used for, 37
    data collection for, 37
    data packing for, 40
    data processing for, 42, 46–51, 53
    data storage for, 43–46
    data transfer for, 37, 52
    image compression for, 50
    websites about, 54
photographs (see Geograph archive; Phoenix
    Mars Lander system)
planning fallacy, 212
PNUTS system, 56
    comparison with Azure SDS, 70
    comparison with BigTable system, 68
    comparison with Cassandra system, 70
    comparison with Dynamo system, 69
    geo-replication of data in, 56, 58

partitioning data for scale-out, 56, 62
    querying data, 64–67
    updating data, 57–64
political data, 323
    age, effect on vote choice, 328
    graphics used for, 323
    mapping partisanship in Pennsylvania, 330
    predicting vote choice, 326
    redistricting, effect on partison bias, 324
    supreme court nominees, senate voting
        patterns on, 328
polling, 123
Poole, David (author), 303–321
Popper, Karl (statement about
        falsifiability), 209, 213
predictions, difficulty in making from
        data, 213
privacy, with "data finds data" systems, 118
probabilistic model, 221
probability, 215, 220
public data, sources of, 336
Purves, Ross (research using Geograph), 92
PyHive framework, 81

Q

Quants, as Data Scientists, 84

R

R (data analysis package), 282, 300
RAC (Robotic Arm Camera), 38
Radiohead's "House of Cards" video, 149
    data capture equipment for, 150–154
    data capturing process for, 155–159, 164
    data processing for, 160
    data sample for, 154
    launching, 161–164
Ramakrishnan, Raghu (author), 55–71
range-partitioned data, 62
rate limiting, used with polling, 123
raw data, providing to users
    application for querying live data, 265
    collecting crowdsourced data, 260
    further experiments suggested by, 271–274
    integrating data with other data
        resources, 266
    problems created by, 275–277
    reasons for, 259, 274, 276
    representing data online, 263–271
    self-describing data formats for, 269
    unique identifiers required for, 263, 269
    validating crowdsourced data, 262
Raynard, Robert (Secret Code Breaker), 233
RDF (Resource Description Framework), 269

real estate sales, analysis of (see housing market analysis)

record-level mastership, 61

relational model for data, 76

replication
    of DNA, 247
    geo-replication of data, 56, 58

reporting on data results (see data visualization)

REpresentational State Transfer (REST), 122

Resource Description Framework (RDF), 269

resources (see books and publications; website resources)

REST (REpresentational State Transfer), 122

Rice algorithm for compression, 51

Robotic Arm Camera (RAC), 38

roulette wheel example of "data finds data", 107–111

S

San Francisco housing market analysis (see housing market analysis)

Sanger Institute's sequencing platform for DNA data, 254–257

SAS (data analysis package), 282

scale-out feature for data storage, 56

Sci Py (data analysis package), 282

search engines, accessing Deep Web from (see surfacing)

search strategies for corpus data, 241

Secret Code Breaker (Raynard), 233

secret codes in corpus data, analyzing, 228–234

Securities and Exchange Commission website, 336

Segaran, Toby (author), 335–348

semantically reconciled and relationship-aware directories, 114

semantically reconciled directories, 114

Senge, Peter (The Fifth Discipline), 78

sense.us website, 184, 186
    Birthplace Voyager graph, 191
    census data used for, 186–188
    collaboration features of, 194–199, 201
    doubly linked discussions, 195
    field tests of, 199–203
    Job Voyager graph, 191
    pointing with graphical annotations, 196
    population pyramid, 192
    scatter plot display, 192
    social navigation, 198
    state map, 192
    views, collecting and linking, 197
    views, sharing, 194
    visualization of data, 188–194

Sequencescape tools, 254

sequencing platform for DNA data, 254–257

shift ciphers, 228

Singh, Simon (The Code Book), 230

social data, 119
    business value of, 129–131
    formats for, current, 121
    normalizing, 128–131
    public versus private data, 130
    sharing and collaborating on, 194–199, 201
    transporting, APIs for, 122–128
    transporting, current methods for, 120
    visualization and analysis of, 184, 199
    visualization of, 188–194

social networks, public data available on, 336

social stereotypes, researching, 279
    clustering types of people, 295–300
    data analysis, 282, 290–294
    gendered words, determining, 294
    preprocessing the data, 280
    presentation of data results, 285–290

Sokol, Lisa (author), 105–118

space missions (see Phoenix Mars Lander system)

spam detection in corpus data, 239

spelling correction of corpus data, 234–239

SPSS (data analysis package), 282

Srivastava, Utkarsh (author), 55–71

Stata (data analysis package), 282

Stereo Surface Imager (SSI), 38

stereotypes (see social stereotypes, researching)

storage cloud, 56, 70
    (see also PNUTS system)

stories created from data, 208, 211

stylometry of corpus data, 239

substitution ciphers in corpus data, analyzing, 228–234

surfacing, 135, 136
    challenges of, 136
    informative test for, 136, 142
    inputs for, selecting, 140, 144–146
    queries for, selecting, 138–144
    query templates for, 139, 141, 143

survey project (see customer survey project)

Swayne, Deborah F. (author), 303–321

The Syndicate (visual effects house), 160

T

timeline consistency of data, 59–61, 63, 71

tokens, definition of, 220

Trademark database, 336

transactions, with geo-replication, 57

translation by machine of corpus data, 240

COLOPHON

The cover image is a stock photo from Jupiter Images. The cover fonts are Akzidenz Grotesk and Orator. The text font is Adobe's Meridien; the heading font is ITC Bailey.